AJAX
HACKS™

Other resources from O'Reilly

Related titles

Ajax Design Patterns	Dynamic HTML: The
Google Maps Hacks™	Definitive Reference
Cascading Style Sheets:	Head Rush Ajax
The Definitive Guide	Head First HTML with
CSS Cookbook™	CSS and XHTML
Designing with JavaScript	JavaScript and DHTML
	Cookbook™

Hacks Series Home

hacks.oreilly.com is a community site for developers and power users of all stripes. Readers learn from each other as they share their favorite tips and tools for Mac OS X, Linux, Google, Windows XP, and more.

oreilly.com

oreilly.com is more than a complete catalog of O'Reilly books. You'll also find links to news, events, articles, weblogs, sample chapters, and code examples.

oreillynet.com is the essential portal for developers interested in open and emerging technologies, including new platforms, programming languages, and operating systems.

Conferences

O'Reilly brings diverse innovators together to nurture the ideas that spark revolutionary industries. We specialize in documenting the latest tools and systems, translating the innovator's knowledge into useful skills for those in the trenches. Visit *conferences.oreilly.com* for our upcoming events.

Safari Bookshelf (*safari.oreilly.com*) is the premier online reference library for programmers and IT professionals. Conduct searches across more than 1,000 books. Subscribers can zero in on answers to time-critical questions in a matter of seconds. Read the books on your Bookshelf from cover to cover or simply flip to the page you need. Try it today.

AJAX HACKS™

Bruce Perry

O'REILLY®

Beijing · Cambridge · Farnham · Köln · Paris · Sebastopol · Taipei · Tokyo

Ajax Hacks™
by Bruce Perry

Copyright © 2006 O'Reilly Media, Inc. All rights reserved.
Printed in the United States of America.

Published by O'Reilly Media, Inc., 1005 Gravenstein Highway North,
Sebastopol, CA 95472.

O'Reilly books may be purchased for educational, business, or sales promotional use. Online editions are also available for most titles (*safari.oreilly.com*). For more information, contact our corporate/institutional sales department: (800) 998-9938 or *corporate@oreilly.com*.

Editor: Simon St.Laurent
Production Editors: Mary Anne Weeks
   Mayo and Adam Witwer
Copyeditor: Rachel Wheeler
Indexer: John Bickelhaupt

Cover Designer: Linda Palo
Interior Designer: David Futato
Illustrators: Robert Romano, Jessamyn
   Read, and Lesley Borash

Printing History:

March 2006:   First Edition.

 This book uses RepKover™, a durable and flexible lay-flat binding.

ISBN: 0-596-10169-4
[M]

Contents

Foreword

The truth is, I've never built an Ajax application.

Sure, I've worked on Ajax projects. But when it comes to programming, my experience is pretty limited. I've done some JavaScripting here and there. I know a little Perl, but hardly enough to build a web application. As a programmer, I'm more of an occasional weekend hobbyist than anything else.

You can imagine how frustrating it is for people to learn this fact when they send me emails asking for help with their JavaScript. But you can hardly fault them for expecting me to be a technologist. After all, I wrote an article coining the term "Ajax," and Ajax is all about technology, right?

The funny thing is that I didn't see it that way when I was writing the essay. I didn't think I was writing for technologists at all. I'm a designer, and I thought I was writing for a design audience. If you look at some of the other things we've published on adaptivepath.com, you can see that we're much more likely to be talking about ways to analyze user behavior or make an experience connect with people than about the latest code libraries or data schemas.

That's one reason some people thought it was a little strange for me to be writing about Ajax at all. Designers, one way of thinking goes, should leave writing about technology to technologists.

But seeing Ajax as a purely technological phenomenon misses the point. If anything, Ajax is even more of a sea change for designers than it is for developers. Sure, there are a lot of ways in which developers need to change their thinking as they make the transition from building traditional web applications to building Ajax applications. But for those of us who design user experiences, the change brought about by Ajax is even more profound.

We've gotten pretty good at our jobs in the last 10 years or so. We've started to get a handle on what the Web does well and what the Web does poorly.

And we've developed an arsenal of conventions to rely on when we design applications: where the logo goes, how a link behaves when it is clicked, how to communicate that something even *can* be clicked...

All of that knowledge—well, most of it, anyway—goes out the window with Ajax. We have a wider palette to work with, but that also means we have more opportunities to make mistakes. And believe me, we'll make a lot of them. It takes time to get smart, and just as it took us a while to get a handle on the old static Web, it'll take us some time to get good at creating Ajax experiences as well.

And that's where you—and this book—come in.

One of the most inspiring things about the Web is that anyone can contribute to its development. Standards bodies and platform vendors are important, of course, but there is no master plan for the evolution of the Web. The Web goes where its users want it to go—but only when they're ready. Sometimes that means a great idea doesn't take hold right away, and sometimes that means it only takes one voice to bring that idea to an audience ready to hear it.

All of us, designers and developers together, are the architects of the Web. Through tools like this book, we can learn from each other, and we can use our creativity to spur on further innovation. The choices we make now lay the groundwork for what is to come. At this moment, Ajax is our manifest destiny, the obvious next chapter in the story of the Web. When this chapter is over, I'll be excited to see what the next one brings. But for now, let's see what we can do with what we've got.

Now get out there, and get hacking!

—*Jesse James Garrett*
San Francisco, CA
December 2005

Credits

About the Author

Bruce Perry is an independent software developer and writer, and the author of O'Reilly's *Java Servlet & JSP Cookbook*. Since 1996, he has developed web applications and databases for various nonprofits, design and marketing firms, as well as publishers. In his spare time, Perry is an active age-group triathlete and has cycled extensively in the Swiss Alps. He lives in the Newburyport, Massachusetts area with his wife Stacy LeBaron, daughter Rachel, and son Scott.

Contributors

- Micah Dubinko served as an editor and author of the XForms 1.0 W3C specification, and he began participating in the XForms effort in September 1999, nine months before the official Working Group was chartered. Micah received an InfoWorld Innovator award in 2004. He is the author of O'Reilly's *XForms Essentials*, available online at *http://www.xformsinstitute.com*. Currently, Micah works for Yahoo! in California as a senior research developer.

- Curt Hibbs is a senior software developer in St. Louis with more than 30 years' experience in platforms, languages, and technologies too numerous to list. With a keen (and always searching) eye for new methods and technologies to make his work easier and more productive, he has become very active in the Ruby development community.

- Brad Neuberg has done extensive work in the open source community, contributing code to Mozilla, JXTA, the Jakarta Feed Parser, and more. His experience includes developing on Wall Street with distributed systems, n-tier design, and J2EE. As senior software engineer at Rojo Networks, Brad focused on next-generation aggregators, the blogosphere,

MySQL, Ajax, and Lucene. Recent work includes consulting for the Internet Archive to create an Ajax book reader; focusing on Ajax/ DHTML open source frameworks, including the Really Simple History library recently adopted by Google; and working with the Ajax Massive Storage System (AMASS) and *dojo.storage*, which allow web applications to permanently and securely store megabytes of data.

- Premshree Pillai is a Technical Yahoo!. He hacks (maintains the Ruby APIs for Yahoo! Web Services, Flickr, Technorati, etc.), writes ("Ruby Corner," a column for *Linux For You*), and talks (at various conferences) about Ruby in his free time. He has previously contributed to O'Reilly's *Python Cookbook* and *Yahoo! Hacks*, and to the ACM's *Crossroads*.

- Mark Pruett is a programmer and writer living in Virginia, where he works for a Fortune 500 energy company. He's the author of two books and numerous articles on programming and technology. Mark received his master of science degree in computer science from Virginia Commonwealth University.

- Sean Snider is a senior web software engineer for Yahoo! and the Web User Interface Team manager for Yahoo! Music Unlimited. Sean has been building Ajax applications and rich web sites for over eight years within the music, video game, and e-commerce industries, for companies such as Electronic Arts (EA Sports, *http://www.easports.com*), Musicmatch (Musicmatch Jukebox, *http://www.musicmatch.com*), and iVillage.com.

Acknowledgments

My family members play the most important role in giving life to a book idea, nurturing its writing, and making its final publication possible. First, I thank my parents Anne and Robert Perry, who had the wisdom to settle in Concord, Massachusetts, where books are valued perhaps more than in any other town in the United States. They promoted reading during my childhood as an activity above most all others, perhaps second only to getting outside and appreciating the environment and Mother Nature.

Second, I would like to thank my wife Stacy and children Rachel and Scott, who exhibited great patience while dealing with the modest crises of publication deadlines, such as the temporary loss of their husband and father to the inner sanctorum of a home office, or the occasional over-cooking of the peas as I raced back to my lap top to complete some unfinished paragraph.

I'd like to thank my O'Reilly editor Simon St.Laurent, who tirelessly steered this book to publication from beginning to end, and offered cogent advice during the entire duration of writing, despite the challenging time line. This book greatly benefited from the technical reviews initiated by Micah Dubinko, Shelley Powers, Thinakorn Tabtieng, and Michael Buffington. They demonstrated impressive versatility in taking both a long view of the book's topic, as well as focusing on numerous fine-grained details that required corrections or greater exposition.

Preface

Ajax, a term coined in 2005 to describe the combination of a group of popular web technologies, has been an instant hit in the software world. Instant success can raise many doubts, but it would be a mistake to view this software model as simply the latest "next big thing" to make a big splash and then vanish into the ether of the Web.

Why? First of all, Ajax's interweaved technologies, including JavaScript, the Document Object Model (DOM), and Cascading Style Sheets (CSS), live in the world of the Web, where new information and technologies hit millions of people in milliseconds. If the technique represents an interesting idea with practical merit, a good probability exists that developers will at least dip their toes into the technology's waters, if not immediately add the new tool to their code arsenals. Second, the Ajax family of techniques are already well known and open source, or free of charge; therefore, few barriers exist to trying them out for at least a prototype version of new software. Third, a number of useful, well-known applications are based on Ajax, such as Flickr and Gmail. Fourth, web users are already accustomed to an Ajax application's desktop-like experience, where the application can make client/server connections without completely changing the browser page.

There are numerous other reasons why Ajax is here to stay, such as the excellent support for JavaScript, CSS, and DOM provided by modern browsers such as Firefox, as well as the pros and cons of using Macromedia Flash for Rich Internet Applications instead.

Building Single-Page Applications

The "single-page application" represented by Ajax, with client/server connections that do not interrupt the user's experience and dynamically change elements in different web page regions, is appropriate for numerous uses, such as blogs, learning tools, online newsletters, and small web portals or communities. Many of these types of sites are already built using Ajax techniques. Ajax can also improve the user experience in large web-based client/server applications that extend beyond the single-page model.

The time between the conception of this book and the writing of this preface has seen Ajax morph into a software platform that dominates headlines on the Web, not to mention the birth of new acronyms such as Ajaj (Asynchronous JavaScript and JSON) and lingo such as "Ajaxy" (as in an Ajaxy server connection). Software innovations and human language seem to share the same organic dynamic.

Explaining Ajax

Ajax Hacks was written by yours truly and seven different contributors, many of whom are among the innovators, bloggers, and early adopters who helped give Ajax and its open source tools the boost it enjoys today. They are senior web engineers and developers whose homes stretch from Bangalore to San Francisco, a scope reflecting the diverse and serendipitous nature by which the writers found this book and the book discovered its writers. (See the Credits for more details on these writers.)

Ajax Hacks collects not only dozens of easy-to-grasp, cutting-edge explorations of Ajax technology, such as Google/Yahoo! mapping mash-ups, drag-and-drop bookstores, and single-page web services apps, but a large number of hacks that represent practical advice for Ajax developers. *Ajax Hacks* also introduces JavaScript newbies and aficionados alike to useful code libraries, including Prototype, Rico, and *script.aculo.us*. Chapter 7 focuses on a practical and new web application framework with excellent Ajax tools including Ruby on Rails.

A number of the contributions are hacks in the original, clever sense of the term, exploring topics such as using algorithms and Flash objects to simulate a browser history list and store Ajax-related data offline, configuring Apache to fix the XMLHttpRequest cross-domain restrictions, running a search engine inside your browser, and mashing up Yahoo! Maps with a location-to-URL service called GeoURL.

Some of the contributed hacks illustrate cool web controls and embedded scripts, such as a hack that scripts an auto-complete field from scratch, a hack that creates JavaScript bookmarklets that do not have size limitations, and another that creates an RSS feed reader for an Ajax application. These are hacks that push the envelope, just as we approach the cusp of this web model's formulation. At the same time, web developers can adapt a number of this book's hacks, some of which are distributed as open source libraries, for their own applications.

How to Use This Book

You can read this book from cover to cover if you like, but for the most part, each hack stands on its own, so feel free to browse and jump to the different sections that interest you most. If there's a prerequisite you need to know about, a cross reference will guide you to the right hack. So, feel free to browse, flipping around to whatever sections interest you most.

How This Book Is Organized

The book is divided into several chapters, organized by subject:

Chapter 1, *Ajax Basics*
> What is Ajax? This chapter begins with a synopsis of the group of well-known technologies that make up Ajax. The chapter's hacks introduce the XMLHttpRequest JavaScript object and its properties and methods, then delve into the meat of the matter, such as sending GET and POST requests, as well as receiving data in plain text, XML, and JSON format. This chapter also illustrates the dynamic scripting of CSS styles in Ajax applications. Let the users change the colors and fonts inside the browser page!

Chapter 2, *Web Forms*
> Web forms have certainly changed in the Ajax world. As revealed in this chapter's hacks, it is typical now to submit form data and to build form widgets such as select lists and checkbox groups using server data fetched in the background with XMLHttpRequest. Because the page doesn't have to be completely rebuilt from a server response, the user experiences few application delays. These hacks show how to submit text from form fields and textareas and display server values in those fields, without making the user click a submit button. The hacks also generate various elements, such as select lists and unordered lists, using XMLHttpRequest and data that is dynamically accessed from a server.

Chapter 3, *Validation*
> Ajax applications can cut down on server hits by validating the format of email addresses, credit card numbers, zip codes, and other types of data that users enter into web forms before sending the data. A server component is obviously necessary for final credit card validation in a real-world application; however, the application may implement a "first layer of defense," as in these hacks, by validating the formats of text-field values with JavaScript regular expressions.

Chapter 4, *Power Hacks for Web Developers*
> Web developers have never had cooler, easier-to-work-with tools than the Yahoo! and Google web APIs. This chapter includes a mash-up of

Google Maps, Yahoo! Maps, and Yahoo! driving directions, as well as a software interaction involving Yahoo! Maps and a location-to-URL service called GeoURL. It also features more prosaic, pragmatic web hacks, such as sending an email with XMLHttpRequest; viewing, creating, and sending HTTP cookies with client-side script; fetching a postal code dynamically without altering the web page; as well as discovering and displaying the browser's locale information.

Chapter 5, *Direct Web Remoting (DWR) for Java Jocks*

DWR is a nifty toolkit that allows developers to make remote calls to Java server objects *from* JavaScript, without any Java applets or plug-ins. DWR uses Ajax requests behind the scenes; the toolkit's users, however, do not have to deal with XMLHttpRequest programming. These hacks populate select lists from Java arrays and Maps; call custom Java objects from their JavaScript proxies or counterparts; and use JavaScript objects to call built-in Java objects. This chapter is a treat for developers who are immersed in both Java and JavaScript.

Chapter 6, *Hack Ajax with the Prototype and Rico Libraries*

The hacks in this chapter use Prototype, a cool open source JavaScript library that includes its own Ajax tools. You'll see how to update DOM elements in a web page with server data using Prototype's Ajax.Updater object, and how to use the PeriodicalExecuter object to execute Ajax requests at timed intervals while another "observer" object monitors a text field for changes (imagine: a user enters data into text fields, and a JavaScript object automatically sends the data off to persistent server storage whenever the field value changes). Another hack in this chapter uses the open source library Rico in a Weather.com web services application. Finally, the chapter's last hack sets up a drag-and-drop bookstore, also using Rico.

Chapter 7, *Work with Ajax and Ruby on Rails*

Learn Ruby on Rails! Ruby on Rails (RoR) is an efficient and well-designed web application framework, based on the Model-View-Controller design pattern, that made its debut in 2005. This chapter begins with a simple hack that helps you get up and running with RoR, then moves on to several hacks that illustrate RoR's Ajax tools. Each hack is a web application task written in Ruby; for example, one of the hacks monitors a server connection and displays the status in the client. RoR bundles Prototype with the framework, then wraps the setup of the Ajax objects into its own easy-to-learn, embedded script language. Get ready to read a lot of Ruby code, a treat for those who may be new to this elegant and powerful tool!

Chapter 8, *Savor the script.aculo.us JavaScript Library*

script.aculo.us is another open source JavaScript library built on Prototype. It offers a broad menu of useful effects and controls for developers. These hacks create a Mac OS X–style login box that "shakes" in
response to invalid logins; an auto-complete field based on a *script.
aculo.us* object; a control that allows the user to edit textual content in
the browser and then save the changes on a server, without a web page
round trip; and, just for fun, a web form that disappears in a puff of
smoke when it's submitted.

Chapter 9, *Options and Efficiencies*

These hacks provide several tips for real-world Ajax developers. Ironi-
cally, several hacks illustrate how to *avoid* using XMLHttpRequest to hit
the server: you'll see how to run a search engine inside the browser,
cache data with JavaScript, and "fix" the browser back button in an
Ajax application by internally storing and accessing state. These hacks
also recommend ways to combine code libraries to increase download
speed, obfuscate or partially obscure JavaScript code to protect proprietary scripting, set a timer for aborting an Ajax request, as well as
dynamically request data in JavaScript Object Notation (JSON) format
using the HTML script tag.

Conventions Used in This Book

The following is a list of the typographical conventions used in this book:

Italics

Used to indicate URLs, filenames, filename extensions, and directory/
folder names, e.g., a path in the filesystem appears as */Developer/
Applications*

Constant width

Used to show code examples, the contents of files, console output, as
well as the names of variables, commands, and other code excerpts

Constant width bold

Used to highlight portions of code

Gray type

Used to indicate a cross reference within the text

You should pay special attention to notes set apart from the text with the
following icons:

This is a tip, suggestion, or general note. It contains useful supplementary information about the topic at hand.

 This is a warning or note of caution, often indicating that something might break if you're not careful, possibly quite badly.

The thermometer icons, found next to each hack, indicate the relative complexity of the hack:

 beginner   moderate   expert

Whenever possible, the hacks in this book are not *platform-specific*, which means you can use them on Linux, Macintosh, and Windows machines. However, some things are possible only on a particular platform.

Using Code Examples

This book is here to help you get your job done. In general, you may use the code in this book in your programs and documentation. You do not need to contact us for permission unless you're reproducing a significant portion of the code. For example, writing a program that uses several chunks of code from this book does not require permission. Selling or distributing a CD-ROM of examples from O'Reilly books *does* require permission. Answering a question by citing this book and quoting example code does not require permission. Incorporating a significant amount of example code from this book into your product's documentation *does* require permission.

We appreciate, but do not require, attribution. An attribution usually includes the title, author, publisher, and ISBN. For example: "*Ajax Hacks* by Bruce Perry. Copyright 2006 O'Reilly Media, Inc., 0-596-10169-4."

If you feel your use of code examples falls outside fair use or the permission given above, feel free to contact us at *permissions@oreilly.com*.

Safari® Enabled

 When you see a Safari® Enabled icon on the cover of your favorite technology book, it means the book is available online through the O'Reilly Network Safari Bookshelf.

Safari offers a solution that's better than e-books. It's a virtual library that lets you easily search thousands of top technology books, cut and paste code samples, download chapters, and find quick answers when you need the most accurate, current information. Try it for free at *http://safari.oreilly.com*.

How to Contact Us

We have tested and verified the information in this book to the best of our ability, but you may find that features have changed (or even that we have made mistakes!). As a reader of this book, you can help us to improve future editions by sending us your feedback. Please let us know about any errors, inaccuracies, bugs, misleading or confusing statements, and typos that you find anywhere in this book.

Please also let us know what we can do to make this book more useful to you. We take your comments seriously and will try to incorporate reasonable suggestions into future editions. You can write to us at:

O'Reilly Media, Inc.
1005 Gravenstein Highway North
Sebastopol, CA 95472
(800) 998-9938 (in the Unitd States or Canada)
(707) 829-0515 (international/local)
(707) 829-0104 (fax)

To ask technical questions or to comment on the book, send email to:

bookquestions@oreilly.com

The web site for *Ajax Hacks* lists examples, errata, and plans for future editions. You can find this page at:

http://www.oreilly.com/catalog/ajaxhks/

For more information about this book and others, see the O'Reilly web site:

http://www.oreilly.com

Got a Hack?

To explore Hacks books online or to contribute a hack for future titles, visit:

http://hacks.oreilly.com

Ajax Basics
Hacks 1–11

Remember when users called the Internet the "world wide wait?" Way back in the Neolithic era of the Web? With some applications, that aspect of the Web hasn't really changed that much: fill out form, click button, web page goes away, wait, page refreshes, correct mistake, click, wait, wait... You've been stuck in this limbo before.

A number of recent web sites, however, such as many of the cool mapping applications that have evolved of late, require much greater responsiveness in the way they interact with users. The old, conventional way of handling user interaction is to have the entire page "go away" with every click, with the new page reappearing in the browser view only when the server's response is finally complete. However, some new applications require small pieces of the web page to change instantaneously, without the entire page reloading.

For example, if you have ever used Google Maps, the way you can drag out-lying regions into your view conveys the impression that you have all of the maps stored locally on your computer, for your effortless manipulation. Imagine how unpopular this application would be if every time you tried to "drag" the map the page disappeared for a few (long) moments while the browser waited for another server response. The application would be so sluggish that no one would use it. So what's the magic that makes this work?

It's Not a Floor Wax

A blend of well-known technologies and a nifty JavaScript tool form the basis of a snappier and more powerful application model for the Web. If you're afraid of acronym overload, don't worry—this one's easy. It's called *Ajax*, which stands for Asynchronous JavaScript and XML.

Ajax is neither a floor wax nor a desert topping (nor, indeed, a lemon-scented cleaning product!). It's a blend of a number of standard technologies already familiar to developers and designers:

- JavaScript, a programming language that adds dynamic scripting to web pages. JavaScript code can be embedded in a web page to allow the page to implement cool new behaviors with a technique called *client-side scripting*. This technique is almost as old as the Web itself.

- XMLHttpRequest, a JavaScript object with an application programming interface (API) that can connect with a server using the HyperText Transfer Protocol (HTTP). A lot of the Ajax magic is propelled by this piece of code, which all the major browsers (such as Mozilla Firefox, Internet Explorer 6, Safari 1.3 and 2.0, and Opera 7.6) support. The asynchronous part of Ajax derives from this object's characteristics.*

- Extensible Markup Language (XML), a language designed to define other languages. The XMLHttpRequest object can handle the server response in standard XML format as well as plain text.

- HTML and Cascading Style Sheets (CSS), which control what the user sees on a web page. Web developers can use JavaScript to make dynamic changes to the visual interface by programming HTML elements and CSS styles.

- The Document Object Model (DOM), a model that represents an XML file or web page as a set of related objects that can be dynamically manipulated, even after the user has downloaded the page. The web page view is structured as a *tree* hierarchy made up of a root node, the parent, and its various *branches*, or children. Each HTML element is represented by a node or branch, which is accessible via JavaScript. We show a lot (a *lot*!) of DOM programming in these hacks.

- Extensible Stylesheet Language and Transformation (XSLT), a templating technology for transforming the display of XML information for a receiving client.

Ajax is far from new, as these are relatively old technologies. Microsoft issued the first implementation of a JavaScript object that makes HTTP requests, often referred to as the XMLHTTP object, with Version 5.0 of the Internet Explorer browser (as of this writing, IE is on Version 6, with v7 in a beta release).

---

* The XMLHttpRequest object can make an asynchronous request to a server, meaning that once the request has been initiated, the rest of the JavaScript code does not have to wait for a response to execute. XMLHttpRequest can also make synchronous requests.

The plethora of new web applications that use Ajax, however, suggests that this group of technologies has morphed into a new web model. "Web 2.0" is next-generation-speak encompassing Ajax, a form of *Rich Internet Application* (so called because much of the application's functionality can reside in the client browser). Examples of these applications are Google Maps, Gmail, a collaboration suite called Zimbra, an interesting personal search-engine tool called Rollyo (*http://www.rollyo.com*), and one of the first interactive web maps, this one of Switzerland (see *http://map.search.ch/index.en.html*). The number of Ajax applications is growing very rapidly. You can find a short list on Wikipedia, at *http://en.wikipedia.org/wiki/List_of_websites_using_Ajax*.

Handle with Care

Of course, Ajax is not for everyone (particularly those dessert topping fans!). Because Ajax technology can dynamically alter a web page that has already been downloaded, it may interfere with certain functions near and dear to many users, such as creating bookmarks for browser views. For example, in the absence of fancy scripting solutions, the dynamic changes you make with DOM in an existing web page cannot be linked to with a URL that you can send to your friends or save for later. (Both "Fix the Browser Back Button in Ajax Applications" **[Hack #68]** and "Handle Bookmarks and Back Buttons with RSH" **[Hack #69]** should help shed light on these issues and provide some hackable solutions.)

A number of the cool Ajax tips described in this book alter the behavior of many familiar web widgets, such as select lists, textareas, text fields, and radio buttons that submit their own data and talk to servers behind the scenes. However, bear in mind that Ajax-powered widgets should be first and foremost *usable*, and always avoid confusing and irritating web users.

XMLHttpRequest

At the center of many of the hacks in this book is the XMLHttpRequest object, which allows JavaScript to fetch bits of server data while the user is happily playing with the rest of your application. This object has its own API, which we will summarize in this introduction.

"Detect Browser Compatibility with the Request Object" **[Hack #1]** covers setting up the request object in JavaScript. Once the object is initialized, it has several methods and properties that you can use in your own hacks.

A common practice among programming types is to call the functions that are associated with particular JavaScript objects "methods." The XMLHttpRequest object's methods include open( ), send( ), and abort( ).

The following list shows the properties supported by the request objects defined by most of the major browsers, such as Internet Explorer 5.0 and later, Safari 1.3 and 2.0, Netscape 7, and Opera's latest releases (such as Opera 8.5). Mozilla Firefox's request object has additional properties and methods not shared by the request objects of other major browsers,* but it also supports all of the following:

onreadystatechange
> Callback function; the function assigned to this property is called whenever readyState changes.

readyState
> Number; 0 means *uninitialized*, open( ) has not yet been called; 1 means *loading*, send( ) has not been called; 2 means *loaded*, send( ) has been called, and headers/status are available; 3 means *interactive*, responseText holds partial data; 4 means *completed*.

responseText
> string; the plain text of the response.

responseXML
> DOM Document object; an XML return value.

status
> Response status code, such as 200 (Okay) or 404 (Not Found).

statusText
> string; the text associated with the HTTP response status.

The methods supported include:

abort( )
> void; cancels the HTTP request.

getAllResponseHeaders( )
> string; returns all of the response headers in a preformatted string (see "Dig into the HTTP Response" **[Hack #9]**).

---

* The Mozilla Firefox XMLHttpRequest object has onload, onprogress, and onerror properties that are event listener types. Firefox has also defined addEventListener( ), dispatchEvent( ), overrideMimeType( ), and removeEventListener( ) methods. See *http://www.xulplanet.com/ references/objref/XMLHttpRequest.html* for more details on these Firefox request object members.

`getResponseHeader(string header)`
> string; returns the value of the specified header.

`open(string url,string asynch)`
> void; prepares the HTTP request and specifies whether it is asynchronous or not.

`send(string)`
> void; sends the HTTP request.

`setHeader(string header,string value)`
> void; sets a request header, but you must call open( ) first!

Detect Browser Compatibility with the Request Object

Use JavaScript to set up Microsoft's and the Mozilla-based browsers' different request objects.

Browser compatibility is an important consideration. You have to make sure the "engine" behind Ajax's server handshake is properly constructed, but you can never predict which browsers your users will favor.

The programming tool that allows Ajax applications to make HTTP requests to a server is an object that you can use from within JavaScript code. In the world of Firefox and Netscape (as well as Safari and Opera), this object is named `XMLHttpRequest`. However, continuing with the tradition established by IE 5.0, recent vintages of Internet Explorer implement the software as an `ActiveX` object named `Microsoft.XMLHTTP` or `Msxml2.XMLHTTP`.

> `Microsoft.XMLHTTP` and `Msxml2.XMLHTTP` refer to different versions of software components that are a part of Microsoft XML Core Services (MSXML). Here's what our contributing IE expert says on this matter:
>
> "If you use `Microsoft.XMLHTTP`, the `ActiveXObject` wrapper will try to initialize the last known good version of the object that has this program (or "prog") ID. This object, in theory, could be MSXML 1.0, but almost no one these days has that version because it has been updated via Windows Update, IE 6, or another means. MSXML 1.0 was very short-lived. If you use `MSXML2.XMLHTTP`, that signifies to the wrapper to use at least MSXML 2.0 libraries. Most developers do not need to use a specific version of MSXML, such as `MSXML2.XMLHTTP.4.0` or `MSXML2.XMLHTTP.5.0`."

Although Microsoft and the engineers on the Mozilla project have chosen to implement this object differently, we will refer to the ActiveX and XMLHttpRequest objects simply as "request objects" throughout this book, because they have very similar functionality.

As a first step in using Ajax, you must check if the user's browser supports either one of the Mozilla-based or ActiveX-related request objects, and then properly initialize the object.

Using a Function for Checking Compatibility

Wrap the compatibility check inside a JavaScript function, then call this function before you make any HTTP requests using the object. For example, in Mozilla-based browsers such as Netscape 7.1 and Firefox 1.5 (as well as in Safari 2.0 and Opera 8.5), the request object is available as a property of the top-level window object. The reference to this object in JavaScript code is window.XMLHttpRequest. The compatibility check for these browser types looks like this:

```
if(window.XMLHttpRequest){
    request = new XMLHttpRequest();
    request.onreadystatechange=handleResponse;
    request.open("GET",theURL,true);
    request.send(null);
}
```

The JavaScript variable request is to a top-level variable that will refer to the request object.

> As an alternative model, the open-source library *Prototype* uses object-oriented JavaScript to wrap the request object into its own object, as in the object Ajax.Request (see Chapter 6).

If the browser supports XMLHttpRequest, then:

1. if(window.XMLHttpRequest) returns true because the XMLHttpRequest is not null or undefined.

2. The object will be instantiated with the new keyword.

3. Its onreadystatechange event listener (see the section "XMLHttpRequest" earlier in this chapter) will be defined as a function named handleResponse().

4. The code calls the request object's open() and send() methods.

What about Internet Explorer users?

Microsoft Internet Explorer–related blogs mentioned, at the time this book went to publication, that IE 7 would support a native XMLHttpRequest object.

In this case, the window.XMLHttpRequest object will not exist in the browser object model. Therefore, another branch of the if test is necessary in your code:

```
else if (window.ActiveXObject){
    request=new ActiveXObject("Microsoft.XMLHTTP");
    if (! request){
        request=new ActiveXObject("Msxml2.XMLHTTP");
    }
    if(request){
        request.onreadystatechange=handleResponse;
        request.open(reqType,url,true);
        request.send(null);
    }
}
```

This code fragment tests for the existence of the top-level window object ActiveXObject, thus signaling the use of Internet Explorer. The code then initializes the request using two of a number of possible ActiveX program IDs (here, Microsoft.XMLHTTP and Msxml2.XMLHTTP).

You can get even more fine-grained when testing for different versions of the IE request object, such as Msxml2.XMLHTTP.4.0. In the vast majority of cases, however, you will not be designing your application based on various versions of the MSXML libraries, so the prior code will suffice.

The code then makes one final check for whether the request object has been properly constructed (if(request){...}).

Given three chances, if the request variable is still null or undefined, your browser is really out of luck when it comes to using the request object for Ajax!

Here's an example of an entire compatibility check:

```
/* Wrapper function for constructing a request object.
 Parameters:
  reqType: The HTTP request type, such as GET or POST.
  url: The URL of the server program.
  asynch: Whether to send the request asynchronously or not. */

function httpRequest(reqType,url,asynch){
    //Mozilla-based browsers
    if(window.XMLHttpRequest){
```

```
        request = new XMLHttpRequest( );
    } else if (window.ActiveXObject){
        request=new ActiveXObject("Msxml2.XMLHTTP");
        if (! request){
            request=new ActiveXObject("Microsoft.XMLHTTP");
        }
    }
    //the request could still be null if neither ActiveXObject
    //initialization succeeded
    if(request){
        initReq(reqType,url,asynch);
    } else {
        alert("Your browser does not permit the use of all "+
            "of this application's features!");
    }
}
/* Initialize a request object that is already constructed */
function initReq(reqType,url,bool){
    /* Specify the function that will handle the HTTP response */
    request.onreadystatechange=handleResponse;
    request.open(reqType,url,bool);
    request.send(null);
}
```

"Use the Request Object to POST Data to the Server" [Hack #2] shows how to implement a POST request with XMLHttpRequest.

Use the Request Object to POST Data to the Server

#2

Step beyond the traditional mechanism of posting your user's form values.

This hack uses the POST HTTP request method to send data, communicating with the server without disrupting the user's interaction with the application. It then displays the server's response to the user. The difference between this hack's approach to posting data and the typical form-submission method is that with Ajax, the page is not altered or refreshed when the application connects with the server to POST it the data. Thus, the user can continue to interact with the application without waiting for the interface to be rebuilt in the browser.

Imagine that you have a web portal in which several regions of the page or view provide the user with a variety of services. If one of these regions involves posting data, the entire application might have a more responsive feel if the POST request happens in the background. This way, the entire page (or segments of it) does not have to be refreshed in the browser.

The example web page used in this hack is a simple one. It requests users to enter their first and last names, gender, and country of origin, and then click a button to POST the data. Figure 1-1 shows what the web page looks like in a browser window.

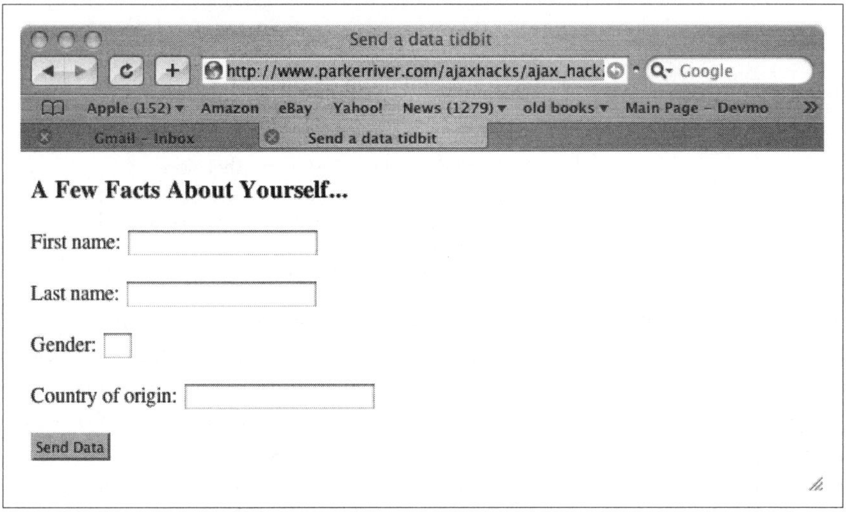

Figure 1-1. Please Mister POST man

Here's the code for the HTML page:

```html
<!DOCTYPE HTML PUBLIC "-//W3C//DTD HTML 4.01//EN"
        "http://www.w3.org/TR/1999/REC-html401-19991224/strict.dtd">
<html>
<head>
    <script type="text/javascript" src="/parkerriver/js/hack2.js"></script>
    <meta http-equiv="content-type" content="text/html; charset=utf-8" />
    <title>Send a data tidbit</title>
</head>
<body>
<h3>A Few Facts About Yourself...</h3>
<form action="javascript:void%200" onsubmit="sendData();return false">
    <p>First name: <input type="text" name="firstname" size="20"> </p>
    <p>Last name: <input type="text" name="lastname" size="20"> </p>
    <p>Gender: <input type="text" name="gender" size="2"> </p>
    <p>Country of origin: <input type="text" name="country" size="20"> </p>
    <p><button type="submit">Send Data</button></p>
</form>
</body>
</html>
```

You may be wondering about the weird-looking form action="javascript:void%200" part. Because we are calling JavaScript functions when the form is submitted, we do not want to give the action attribute anything but a JavaScript URL that has no return value, such as "javascript:void 0". We have to encode the space between void and 0, which is where the %20 comes in. If JavaScript is disabled in the user's browser, clicking the submit button on the form has no effect because the action attribute does not point to a valid URL. In addition, certain HTML validators will display warnings if you use action="". Another way of writing this code is to include the function calls as part of the window.onload event handler in the JavaScript .js file, which is the approach used by most hacks in this book.

The first code element of interest is the script tag, which imports the JavaScript code (in a file named *hack2.js*). The form tag's onsubmit attribute specifies a function called sendData( ), which in turn formats the data for a POST request (by calling another function, setQueryString( )) and sends the data to the server. For brevity's sake, we've saved the description of checking for blank fields for a later hack ("Validate a Text Field or textarea for Blank Fields" [Hack #22]), but web applications should take this step before they hit the server.

The *hack2.js* file defines the necessary JavaScript. Here is the setQueryString( ) function:

```
function setQueryString( ){
    queryString="";
    var frm = document.forms[0];
    var numberElements =  frm.elements.length;
    for(var i = 0; i < numberElements; i++) {
        if(i < numberElements-1) {
            queryString += frm.elements[i].name+"="+
                        encodeURIComponent(frm.elements[i].value)+"&";
        } else {
            queryString += frm.elements[i].name+"="+
                        encodeURIComponent(frm.elements[i].value);
        }

    }
}
```

This function formats a POST-style string out of all the form's input elements. All the name/value pairs are separated by an & character, except for the pair representing the last input element in the form. The entire string might look like:

```
firstname=Bruce&lastname=Perry&gender=M&country=USA
```

Now you have a string you can use in a POST HTTP request. Let's look at the JavaScript code that sends the request. Everything starts with the sendData( ) function. The code calls this function in the HTML form tag's onsubmit attribute:

```
var request;
var queryString;    //will hold the POSTed data
function sendData(){
    setQueryString();
    var url="http://www.parkerriver.com/s/sender";
    httpRequest("POST",url,true);
}

/* Initialize a request object that is already constructed.
 Parameters:
   reqType: The HTTP request type, such as GET or POST.
   url: The URL of the server program.
   isAsynch: Whether to send the request asynchronously or not. */
function initReq(reqType,url,isAsynch){
    /* Specify the function that will handle the HTTP response */
    request.onreadystatechange=handleResponse;
    request.open(reqType,url,isAsynch);
    /* Set the Content-Type header for a POST request */
    request.setRequestHeader("Content-Type",
            "application/x-www-form-urlencoded; charset=UTF-8");
    request.send(queryString);
}

/* Wrapper function for constructing a request object.
 Parameters:
   reqType: The HTTP request type, such as GET or POST.
   url: The URL of the server program.
   asynch: Whether to send the request asynchronously or not. */

function httpRequest(reqType,url,asynch){
    //Mozilla-based browsers
    if(window.XMLHttpRequest){
        request = new XMLHttpRequest();
    } else if (window.ActiveXObject){
        request=new ActiveXObject("Msxml2.XMLHTTP");
        if (! request){
            request=new ActiveXObject("Microsoft.XMLHTTP");
        }
    }
    //the request could still be null if neither ActiveXObject
    //initialization succeeded
    if(request){
        initReq(reqType,url,asynch);
    } else {
        alert("Your browser does not permit the use of all "+
            "of this application's features!");
    }
}
```

The purpose of the httpRequest( ) function is to check which request object the user's browser is associated with (see "Detect Browser Compatibility with the Request Object" [Hack #1]). Next, the code calls initReq( ), whose parameters are described in the comment just above the function definition.

The code request.onreadystatechange=handleResponse; specifies the event-handler function that deals with the response. We'll look at this function a little later. The code then calls the request object's open( ) method, which prepares the object to send the request.

Setting Headers

The code can set any request headers after calling open( ). In our case, we have to create a Content-Type header for a POST request.

Firefox required the additional Content-Type header; Safari 1.3 did not. (We were using Firefox 1.02 at the time of writing this hack.) It is a good idea to add the proper header because in most cases the server is expecting it from a POST request.

Here's the code for adding the header and sending the POST request:

```
request.setRequestHeader("Content-Type",
        "application/x-www-form-urlencoded; charset=UTF-8");
request.send(queryString);
```

If you enter the raw queryString value as a parameter, the method call looks like this:

```
send("firstname=Bruce&lastname=Perry&gender=M&country=USA");
```

Ogling the Result

Once your application POSTs data, you want to display the result to your users. This is the responsibility of the handleResponse( ) function. Remember the code in the initReq( ) function:

```
request.onreadystatechange=handleResponse;
```

When the request object's readyState property has a value of 4, signifying that the object's operations are complete, the code checks the HTTP response status for the value 200. This value indicates that the HTTP request has succeeded. The responseText is then displayed in an alert window. This is somewhat anticlimactic, but I thought I'd keep this hack's response handling simple, because so many other hacks do something more complex with it!

Here is the relevant code:

```
//event handler for XMLHttpRequest
function handleResponse( ){
    if(request.readyState == 4){
        if(request.status == 200){
            alert(request.responseText);
        } else {
            alert("A problem occurred with communicating between "+
                    "the XMLHttpRequest object and the server program.");
        }
    }//end outer if
}
```

Figure 1-2 shows what the alert window looks like after the response is received.

Figure 1-2. Alert! Server calling...

The server component returns an XML version of the POSTed data. Each parameter name becomes an element name, with the parameter value as the element content. This POSTed data is nested within params tags. The component is a Java servlet. The servlet is not the main focus of this hack, but here's some code anyway, for the benefit of readers who are curious about what is happening on the server end:

```
protected void doPost(HttpServletRequest httpServletRequest,
                HttpServletResponse httpServletResponse) throws
                ServletException, IOException {
    Map reqMap = httpServletRequest.getParameterMap( );
    String val=null;
    String tag = null;
    StringBuffer body = new StringBuffer("<params>\n");
    boolean wellFormed = true;
    Map.Entry me = null;
    for(Iterator iter= reqMap.entrySet().iterator( );iter.hasNext( );) {
        me=(Map.Entry) iter.next( );
        val= ((String[])me.getValue( ))[0];
```

```
        tag = (String) me.getKey( );
        if (! XMLUtils.isWellFormedXMLName(tag)){
            wellFormed=false; break;
        }
        body.append("<").append(tag).append(">").
        append(XMLUtils.escapeBodyValue(val)).
        append("</").append(tag).append(">\n");
    }
    if(wellFormed) {
        body.append("</params>");
        sendXML(httpServletResponse,body.toString( ));
    } else {
        sendXML(httpServletResponse,"<notWellFormedParams />");
    }
}
```

The code uses XMLUtils, a Java class from the Jakarta Commons Betwixt open source package, to check whether the parameter names are well formed, as well as whether the parameter values contain invalid XML content and thus have to be escaped. If for some reason the component is POSTed data that contains nonwell-formed parameter names (such as na< > me instead of name), the servlet returns an empty XML element reporting this condition.

H A C K #3 Use Your Own Library for XMLHttpRequest

Break out the code that initializes the request object and sends requests to its own JavaScript file.

To cleanly separate the concerns of big Ajax applications, create a separate file that manages the XMLHttpRequest object, then import that file into every web page that needs it. At the very least, this ensures that any necessary changes regarding how the code sets up the request object have to be made only in this file, as opposed to every JavaScript file that uses Ajax-style requests.

This hack stores all the request object–related code in a file called *http_request.js*. Any web page that uses XMLHttpRequest can then import this file in the following way:

```
<script type="text/javascript" src="js/http_request.js"></script>
```

Here's the code for the file, including all the comments:

```
var request = null;
/* Wrapper function for constructing a request object.
   Parameters:
     reqType: The HTTP request type, such as GET or POST.
     url: The URL of the server program.
```

asynch: Whether to send the request asynchronously or not.
respHandle: The name of the function that will handle the response.
Any fifth parameters, represented as arguments[4], are the data a
POST request is designed to send. */

```
function httpRequest(reqType,url,asynch,respHandle){
    //Mozilla-based browsers
    if(window.XMLHttpRequest){
        request = new XMLHttpRequest( );
    } else if (window.ActiveXObject){
        request=new ActiveXObject("Msxml2.XMLHTTP");
        if (! request){
            request=new ActiveXObject("Microsoft.XMLHTTP");
        }
    }
    //very unlikely, but we test for a null request
    //if neither ActiveXObject was initialized
    if(request) {
        //if the reqType parameter is POST, then the
        //5th argument to the function is the POSTed data
        if(reqType.toLowerCase( ) != "post") {
            initReq(reqType,url,asynch,respHandle);
        } else {
            //the POSTed data
            var args = arguments[4];
            if(args != null && args.length > 0){
                initReq(reqType,url,asynch,respHandle,args);
            }
        }
    } else {
        alert("Your browser does not permit the use of all "+
            "of this application's features!");
    }
}
/* Initialize a request object that is already constructed */
function initReq(reqType,url,bool,respHandle){
    try{
        /* Specify the function that will handle the HTTP response */
        request.onreadystatechange=respHandle;
        request.open(reqType,url,bool);
        //if the reqType parameter is POST, then the
        //5th argument to the function is the POSTed data
        if(reqType.toLowerCase( ) == "post") {
            request.setRequestHeader("Content-Type",
                "application/x-www-form-urlencoded; charset=UTF-8");
            request.send(arguments[4]);
        } else {
            request.send(null);
        }

    } catch (errv) {
        alert(
        "The application cannot contact "+
        "the server at the moment. "+
```

```
                      "Please try again in a few seconds.\n"+
                      "Error detail: "+errv.message);
            }
        }
}
```

The applications that use this code call the httpRequest( ) function with four or five (with POST requests) parameters. You see lots of examples of calling this function in the other hacks. Here's another:

```
var _url = "http://www.parkerriver.com/s/sender";
var _data="first=Bruce&last=Perry&middle=W";
httpRequest("POST",_url,true,handleResponse,_data);
```

The code comments describe the meaning of each of these parameters. The last parameter represents the data that accompanies a POST request.

> A POST HTTP request includes the POSTed data beneath the request-header information. A GET request, on the other hand, appends parameter names/values onto the URL.

If the code is not using POST, the client code uses only the first four parameters. The fourth parameter can be either the name of a function that is declared in the client code (i.e., a response-handling function that appears outside of the *http_request.js* file) or a function literal. The latter option involves defining a function inside a function call, which is often awkward and difficult to read. However, it is sensible in situations in which the HTTP response handling is short and simple, as in:

```
var _url = "http://www.parkerriver.com/s/sender";
//a debugging setup
httpRequest("POST",_url,true,function( ){alert(request.responseText);});
```

httpRequest( ) initiates the same browser detection and setup of XMLHttpRequest for Internet Explorer and non-Microsoft browsers as described in "Detect Browser Compatibility with the Request Object" [Hack #1]. initReq( ) handles the second step of setting up the request object: specifying the onreadystatechange event handler and calling the open( ) and send( ) methods to make an HTTP request. The code traps any errors or exceptions thrown by these request method calls using a try/catch statement. For example, if the code calls open( ) with a URL specifying a different host than that used to download the enclosing web page, the try/catch statement catches the error and pops up an alert window.

Finally, as long as the web page imports *http_request.js*, the request variable is available to code external to the imported file; request is, in effect, a global variable.

request is thus reserved as a variable name because local variables that use the var keyword will supercede (with unintentional consequences) the globally used request, as in the following example:

```
function handleResponse( ){
    //supercedes the imported request variable
    var request = null;
    try{
        if(request.readyState == 4){
            if(request.status == 200){...
```

Receive Data as XML

Ajax and server programs provide a DOM Document object that's ready to go.

Many technologies currently exchange data in Extensible Markup Language format, mostly because XML is a standardized and extensible format widely supported by the software world. Thus, different parties can use existing, well-known technologies to generate, send, and receive XML, without having to adapt to the software tools used by the parties with whom they are exchanging the XML data.

An example is a Global Positioning System (GPS) device that can share the data it has recorded about, say, a hike or a bike ride with a location-aware web application. You just stick the USB cable attached to the GPS device into a USB computer port, launch software that sends the device data to the Web, and that's it. The data format is usually an XML language that has been defined already for GPS software. The web application and the GPS device "speak the same language."

Although this book is not the place for an extensive introduction to XML, you have probably seen these text files in one form or another. XML is used as a "meta" language that describes and categorizes specific types of information. XML data starts with an optional XML declaration (e.g., <?xml version="1.0" encoding="UTF-8"?>), followed by a root element and zero or more child elements. An example is:

```
<?xml version="1.0" encoding="UTF-8"?>
<gps>
<gpsMaker>Garmin</gpsMaker>
<gpsDevice>
Forerunner 301
</gpsDevice>
</gps>
```

Here, gps is the root element, and gpsMaker and gpsDevice are child elements.

Ajax and the request object can receive data as XML, which is very useful for handling web-services responses that use XML. Once the HTTP request is complete, the request object has a property named responseXML. This object is a DOM Document object that your Ajax application can use. Here's an example:

```
function handleResponse( ){
    if(request.readyState == 4){
        if(request.status == 200){
            var doc = request.responseXML;
...
    }
```

In the previous code sample, the doc variable is a DOM Document object, offering a similar API to a browser's display page. This hack receives XML from a server, then initiates a little DOM programming with the Document object to pull some information out of the XML.

> If you just want to see the raw XML text, use the request. responseText property instead.

The HTML file for this hack is basically the same as the one used in "Use the Request Object to POST Data to the Server" [Hack #2], but a div element is added at the end, where the code displays information about the returned XML. Here's the code for the HTML page:

```
<!DOCTYPE HTML PUBLIC "-//W3C//DTD HTML 4.01//EN"
        "http://www.w3.org/TR/1999/REC-html401-19991224/strict.dtd">
<html>
<head>
    <script type="text/javascript" src="js/hack3.js"></script>
    <meta http-equiv="content-type" content="text/html; charset=utf-8" />
    <title>Receive XML response</title>
</head>
<body>
<h3>A Few Facts About Yourself...</h3>
<form action="javascript:void%200" onsubmit="sendData( );return false">
    <p>First name: <input type="text" name="firstname" size="20"> </p>
    <p>Last name: <input type="text" name="lastname" size="20"> </p>
    <p>Gender: <input type="text" name="gender" size="2"> </p>
    <p>Country of origin: <input type="text" name="country" size="20"> </p>
    <p><button type="submit">Send Data</button></p>
    <div id="docDisplay"></div>
</form>
</body>
</html>
```

Figure 1-3 shows what the page looks like before the user enters any information.

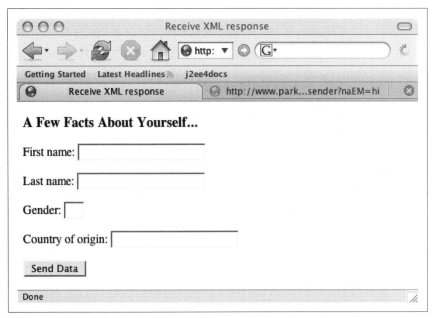

Figure 1-3. All set up to receive XML

The JavaScript code in the *hack3.js* file POSTs its data to a server application, which sends back a response in XML format. The field validation step [Hack #22] has been skipped for the sake of brevity, but web applications using forms should always implement this task.

Like other examples in this chapter, the server program echoes the parameter names and values back to the client, as in <params><firstname>Bruce</firstname></params>. "Use the Request Object to POST Data to the Server" [Hack #2] shows some of the code for the server component that puts together the return value. This technique suits our purpose for showing a simple example of programming XML in an Ajax application:

```
var request;
var queryString;    //will hold the POSTed data

function sendData(){
    setQueryString();
    var url="http://www.parkerriver.com/s/sender";
    httpRequest("POST",url,true);
}
//event handler for XMLHttpRequest
function handleResponse(){
    if(request.readyState == 4){
        if(request.status == 200){
            var doc = request.responseXML;
            var info = getDocInfo(doc);
```

```
            stylizeDiv(info,document.getElementById(""docDisplay""));
        } else {
            alert(""A problem occurred with communicating between ""+
                    ""the XMLHttpRequest object and the server program."");
        }
    }//end outer if
}


/* Initialize a request object that is already constructed */
function initReq(reqType,url,bool){
    /* Specify the function that will handle the HTTP response */
    request.onreadystatechange=handleResponse;
    request.open(reqType,url,bool);
    request.setRequestHeader(""Content-Type"",
            ""application/x-www-form-urlencoded; charset=UTF-8"");
    /* Only works in Mozilla-based browsers */
    //request.overrideMimeType(""text/xml"");
    request.send(queryString);
}


/* Wrapper function for constructing a request object.
 Parameters:
  reqType: The HTTP request type, such as GET or POST.
  url: The URL of the server program.
  asynch: Whether to send the request asynchronously or not. */
function httpRequest(reqType,url,asynch){
    //Snipped...See Hack #1
}
function setQueryString( ){
    queryString="";
    var frm = document.forms[0];
    var numberElements =  frm.elements.length;
    for(var i = 0; i < numberElements; i++) {
        if(i < numberElements-1) {
            queryString += frm.elements[i].name+"="+
                        encodeURIComponent(frm.elements[i].value)+"&";
        } else {
            queryString += frm.elements[i].name+"="+
                        encodeURIComponent(frm.elements[i].value);
        }
    }
}
/* Provide the div element's content dynamically. We can add
style information to this function if we want to jazz up the div */
function stylizeDiv(bdyTxt,div){
    //reset DIV content
    div.innerHTML="";
    div.style.backgroundColor="yellow";
    div.innerHTML=bdyTxt;
}


/* Get information about an XML document via a DOM Document object */
function getDocInfo(doc){
```

```
var root = doc.documentElement;
var info = "<h3>Document root element name: <h3 />"+ root.nodeName;
var nds;
if(root.hasChildNodes()) {
    nds=root.childNodes;
    info+= "<h4>Root node's child node names/values:<h4/>";
    for (var i = 0; i < nds.length; i++){
        info+=  nds[i].nodeName;
        if(nds[i].hasChildNodes()){
            info+=  " : \""+nds[i].firstChild.nodeValue+"\"<br />";
        } else {
            info+=  " : Empty<br />";
        }
    }
}
return info;
}
```

Mozilla Firefox can use the request.overrideMimeType()
function to force the interpretation of the response stream as
a certain mime type, as in request.overrideMimeType("text/
xml"). Internet Explorer's request object does not have this
function. This function call does not work with Safari 1.3,
either.

After the code POSTs its data and receives a response, it calls a method
named getDocInfo(), which builds a string that displays some information
about the XML document and its child or subelements:

```
var doc = request.responseXML;
var info = getDocInfo(doc);
```

The getDocInfo() function gets a reference to the root XML element (var
root = doc.documentElement;); it then builds a string specifying the name of
the root element and information about any of its child nodes or elements,
such as the child node name and value. The code then feeds this information to the stylizeDiv() method. The stylizeDiv() method uses the div
element at the end of the HTML page to dynamically display the gathered
information:

```
function stylizeDiv(bdyTxt,div){
    //reset div content
    div.innerHTML="";
    div.style.backgroundColor="yellow";
    div.innerHTML=bdyTxt;
}
```

Figure 1-4 shows what the web page looks like after the application receives
the XML response.

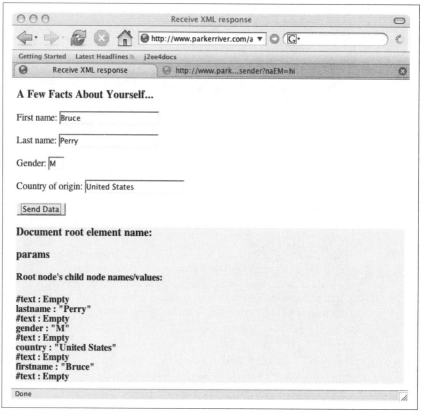

Figure 1-4. Delving into XML return values

The text nodes that the application shows are newline characters in the returned XML.

The core DOM API offered by the browser's JavaScript implementation provides developers with a powerful tool for programming complex XML return values.

 Get Plain Old Strings

H A C K
#5   Manage weather readings, stock quotes, web page scrapings, or similar non-XML data as plain old strings.

The request object has the perfect property for web applications that do not have to handle server return values as XML: `request.responseText`. This hack asks the user to choose a stock symbol, and the server returns the stock price for display. The code handles the return value as a `string`.

A variation to this program in the next hack requires the stock prices to be handled as numbers. These are old prices that a server component stores for certain stock symbols, not *live* quotes that you would obtain from a commercial web service or by HTML scraping. For an example of that mechanism, see "Use XMLHttpRequest to Scrape a Energy Price from a Web Page" **[Hack #39]**.

First, here is the HTML for the web page. It imports JavaScript code from a file named *hack9.js*:

```
<!DOCTYPE HTML PUBLIC "-//W3C//DTD HTML 4.01//EN"
        "http://www.w3.org/TR/1999/REC-html401-19991224/strict.dtd">
<html>
<head>
    <script type="text/javascript" src="js/hack9.js"></script>
    <meta http-equiv="content-type" content="text/html; charset=utf-8" />
    <title>Choose a stock</title>
</head>
<body>
<h3>Stock prices</h3>
<form action="javascript:void%200" onsubmit=
    "getStockPrice(this.stSymbol.value);return false">
    <p>Enter stock symbol: <input type="text" name=
        "stSymbol" size="4"><span id="stPrice"></span></p>
    <p><button type="submit">Get Stock Price</button></p>
</form>
</body>
</html>
```

Figure 1-5 shows the web page as displayed in Firefox. The user enters a symbol such as "GRMN" (case insensitive) and clicks the Get Stock Price button; the JavaScript then fetches the associated stock price and displays it within a span element to the right of the text field.

The function that sets the request process in motion is getStockPrice( ). This function takes the value of the text field named stSymbol and returns the associated stock price (it uses the request object to talk to a server component, which fetches the actual stock price). Here is the JavaScript code:

```
var request;
var symbol;    //will hold the stock symbol

function getStockPrice(sym){
    symbol=sym;
    if(sym){
        var url="http://localhost:8080/parkerriver/s/stocks?symbol="+sym;
        httpRequest("GET",url,true);
    }
}
```

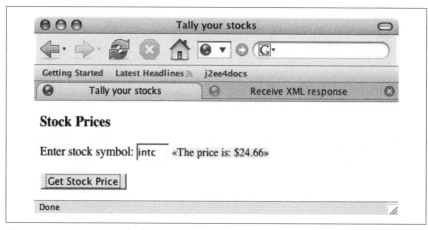

Figure 1-5. Instantaneously displaying a stock price

```
//event handler for XMLHttpRequest
function handleResponse( ){
    if(request.readyState == 4){
        if(request.status == 200){
            /* Grab the result as a string */
            var stockPrice = request.responseText;
            var info = "&#171;The  price is: $"+stockPrice+"&#187;";
            document.getElementById("stPrice").style.fontSize="0.9em";
            document.getElementById("stPrice").style.
            backgroundColor="yellow";
            document.getElementById("stPrice").innerHTML=info;

        } else {
            alert("A problem occurred with communicating between "+
                "the XMLHttpRequest object and the server program.");
        }
    }//end outer if
}

/* See Hack #1 for the httpRequest( ) code;
it is snipped here for the sake of brevity. */
```

The function getStockPrice( ) wraps a call to the function httpRequest( ),
which is responsible for setting up the request object. If you have already
read through some of this chapter's other hacks, you will recognize the
handleResponse( ) function as enclosing much of the interesting action.

"Detect Browser Compatibility with the Request Object"
[Hack #1] and "Use Your Own Library for XMLHttpRequest"
[Hack #3] explain the httpRequest( ) function in more detail.

If the request is complete (i.e., if request.readyState has a value of 4) and the HTTP response status is 200 (meaning that the request has succeeded), the code grabs the server response as the request.responseText property value. The code then uses DOM scripting to display the stock price with some CSS style-related attributes:

```
document.getElementById("stPrice").style.fontSize="0.9em";
document.getElementById("stPrice").style.backgroundColor="yellow";
document.getElementById("stPrice").innerHTML =info;
```

The style attributes make the font size a little bit smaller than the user's preferred browser font size and specify yellow as the background color of the text display. The innerHtml property of the span element is set to the stock price within double angle brackets.

HACK #6 Receive Data as a Number

Do numerical calculations that depend on the request object's return value as a number.

This hack receives a stock quote as a number, then dynamically displays the total value of a stock holding based on the number of shares a user enters. If the server does not send a valid number, the application displays an error message to the user.

The great advantage of Ajax technology is in receiving discrete values rather than entire web pages from a server. Sometimes, that discrete information has to be used as a number, rather than as a string (as discussed in the last hack) or some other object. JavaScript is usually pretty smart about converting values to number types without your intervention, but still, you don't want your application to multiply an innocent investor's share quantity by undefined or some other weird data the server returns!

This hack checks that the user has entered a proper number for a "number of shares" value. The code also checks the server return value to make sure it is numerically valid. It then dynamically displays the stock price and total value of the shares in the user's browser.

Figure 1-6 shows what the browser form looks like.

The following code shows the HTML for the web page:

```
<!DOCTYPE HTML PUBLIC "-//W3C//DTD HTML 4.01//EN"
     "http://www.w3.org/TR/1999/REC-html401-19991224/strict.dtd">
<html>
<head>
    <script type="text/javascript" src="/parkerriver/js/hack4.js">
    </script>
    <meta http-equiv="content-type" content="text/html; charset=utf-8" />
```

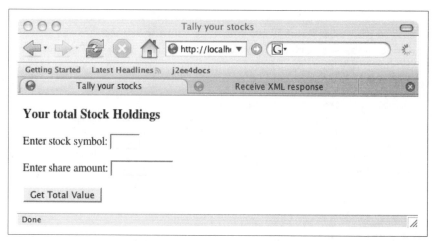

Figure 1-6. Discover a total share value

```
        <title>Tally your stocks</title>
    </head>
    <body>
    <h3>Your total Stock Holdings</h3>
    <form action="javascript:void%200" onsubmit=
        "getStockPrice(this.stSymbol.value,this.numShares.value);return
    false">
    <p>Enter stock symbol: <input type="text" name="stSymbol" size="4">
            <span id="stPrice"></span></p>
    <p>Enter share amount: <input type="text" name="numShares" size="10"></p>
    <p><button type="submit">Get Total Value</button></p>
    <div id="msgDisplay"></div>
    </form>
    </body>
    </html>
```

When the user clicks the Get Total Value button, this action triggers the
form element's onsubmit event. The event handler for this event is the
getStockPrice( ) function. This function takes the stock symbol and the
number of shares as its two parameters. The return false part of the event-
handling code *cancels* the browser's typical submission of the form values to
the URL specified by the form tag's action attribute.

Number Crunching

Now let's look at the JavaScript code, which the HTML file imports as part
of the *hack4.js* file:

```
var request;
var symbol;    //will hold the stock symbol
var numberOfShares;
```

```
function getStockPrice(sym,shs){
    if(sym && shs){
        symbol=sym;
        numberOfShares=shs;
        var url="http://localhost:8080/parkerriver/s/stocks?symbol="+sym;
        httpRequest("GET",url,true);
    }
}
//event handler for XMLHttpRequest
function handleResponse(){
    if(request.readyState == 4){
        alert(request.status);
        if(request.status == 200){
            /* Check if the return value is actually a number.
            If so, multiple by the number of shares and display the result
*/
            var stockPrice = request.responseText;
            try{
                if(isNaN(stockPrice)) { throw new Error(
                        "The returned price is an invalid number.");}
                if(isNaN(numberOfShares)) { throw new Error(
                        "The share amount is an invalid number.");}
                var info = "Total stock value: "+ calcTotal(stockPrice);
                displayMsg(document.
                getElementById("msgDisplay"),info,"black");
                document.getElementById("stPrice").style.fontSize="0.9em";
                document.getElementById("stPrice").innerHTML ="price:
                "+stockPrice;
            } catch (err) {
                displayMsg(document.getElementById("msgDisplay"),
                        "An error occurred: "+
                        err.message,"red");
            }
        } else {
            alert(
                    "A problem occurred with communicating between the "+
                    "XMLHttpRequest object and the server program.");
        }
    }//end outer if
}

/* See Hack #1 or #2 for the httpRequest() code sample and the associated
function
initReq(). They are snipped here for the sake of brevity. */

function calcTotal(price){
    return stripExtraNumbers(numberOfShares * price);
}
/* Strip any characters beyond a scale of four characters
past the decimal point, as in 12.3454678 */
function stripExtraNumbers(num){
    //check if the number's already okay
    //assume a whole number is valid
```

```
var n2 = num.toString( );
if(n2.indexOf(".") == -1)  { return num; }
//if it has numbers after the decimal point,
//limit the number of digits after the decimal point to 4
//we use parseFloat if strings are passed into the method
if(typeof num == "string"){
    num = parseFloat(num).toFixed(4);
} else {
    num = num.toFixed(4);
}
//strip any extra zeros
return parseFloat(num.toString( ).replace(/0*$/,""));
}

function displayMsg(div,bdyText,txtColor){
    //reset DIV content
    div.innerHTML="";
    div.style.backgroundColor="yellow";
    div.style.color=txtColor;
    div.innerHTML=bdyText;
}
```

All the number crunching starts in the call to handleResponse( ). First, the code receives the response as a string, in var stockPrice = request. responseText. The code then tests the validity of the stockPrice variable using a method that is part of JavaScript's core API: isNaN( ). This is the best way to test whether a string value in JavaScript can represent a valid number. For example, isNaN("goodbye") returns true because "goodbye" cannot be converted to a number. The code also tests the number of shares value with this function.

If either method returns true, indicating an invalid number value, the code throws an exception. This is another way of declaring, "We can't use these values; get them out of here!" The web page then displays an error message to the user.

Exception handling with Ajax is covered in "Handle Request Object Errors" [Hack #8].

However, we're not yet finished with our number crunching. The calcTotal( ) function then multiplies the share total by the stock price in order to display the total value to the user.

To make sure that the numerical display of the value is friendly enough to the eye (in terms of the U.S. stock exchange), the stripExtraNumbers( ) function keeps no more than four characters to the right of the decimal point.

Even though $10.9876 may look a little weird (stock prices are sometimes displayed with four or more characters to the right of the decimal point), I decided to allow this display for the total share value.

DOM-inating

The code uses Document Object Model programming to dynamically display new text and values on the page, all without having to make new server calls and refresh the entire page. The following bit of code, within the handleResponse( ) function, calls the displayMsg( ) function to show the user the total share value. The code also dynamically embeds the stock price just to the right of the text field where the user entered the stock symbol. All the code does here is get a reference to the div element with id stPrice, make its font-size style property a little smaller than the web user's font setting, and then set the div's innerHTML property:

```
displayMsg(document.getElementById("msgDisplay"),info,"black");
document.getElementById("stPrice").style.fontSize="0.9em";
document.getElementById("stPrice").innerHTML ="price: "+stockPrice;
```

The displayMsg( ) function is also simple. It has a parameter that represents the font color, which allows the code to set the font color "red" for error messages:

```
function displayMsg(div,bdyText,txtColor){
    //reset DIV content
    div.innerHTML="";
    div.style.backgroundColor="yellow";
    div.style.color=txtColor;
    div.innerHTML=bdyText;
}
```

Figure 1-7 shows what the page looks like when the user requests a stock value.

Figure 1-8 shows an example error message, in case the user enters values that cannot be used as numbers or the server returns invalid values.

Receive Data in JSON Format

#7

Ajax can receive data in efficient and powerful JavaScript Object Notation.

How would you like to use Ajax and receive data from the server as plain old JavaScript objects? Well, you can, using a format called JavaScript Object Notation (JSON). This hack takes information entered by a web user and initiates a server round trip, which returns the data in JSON syntax for the web page's use.

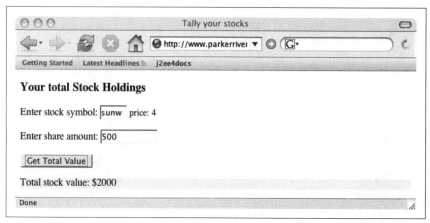

Figure 1-7. Tallying your investment

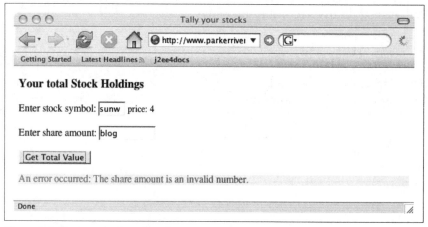

Figure 1-8. Having a bad number day

JSON is simple and straightforward, which is probably why a lot of developers like it. JSON-formatted data is appropriate for simple objects that are bundles of properties and values. An example is a server program that pulls product information from a database or cache and returns it to a retail web page in JSON format. Data in JSON format is represented by:

- An opening curly brace ({)
- One or more property names, separated from their values by colons, with property/value pairs separated by commas
- A closing curly brace (})

The values of each property in the object can be:

- Simple strings, such as "hello"
- Arrays, such as [1,2,3,4]
- Numbers
- The values true, false, or null
- Other objects, as in a composition, or an object containing one or more objects

 See *http://www.json.org* for further details.

This is exactly the format of an Object literal in JavaScript. As an example, here is what the information requested of the user in "Use the Request Object to POST Data to the Server" [Hack #2] looks like in JSON format:

```
{
firstname:"Bruce",
lastname:"Perry",
gender:"M",
country:"USA"
}
```

Magic JSON

In this section, we'll use a similar HTML page to the one used in "Use the Request Object to POST Data to the Server" [Hack #2], and we'll ask the user for the same information; however, this hack uses JavaScript code and Ajax to handle a JSON return value from the server. Two div elements at the bottom of the HTML page show the JSON return value from the server and then display the object's properties and values in a more friendly fashion.

Here's the code for the HTML page:

```
<!DOCTYPE HTML PUBLIC "-//W3C//DTD HTML 4.01//EN"
    "http://www.w3.org/TR/1999/REC-html401-19991224/strict.dtd">
<html>
<head>
    <script type="text/javascript" src="js/hack5.js"></script>
    <meta http-equiv="content-type" content="text/html; charset=utf-8" />
    <title>Receive JSON response</title>
</head>
<body>
<h3>A Few Facts About Yourself...</h3>
<form action="javascript:void%200" onsubmit="sendData();return false">
    <p>First name: <input type="text" name="firstname" size="20"> </p>
    <p>Last name: <input type="text" name="lastname" size="20"> </p>
```

```
    <p>Gender: <input type="text" name="gender" size="2"> </p>
    <p>Country of origin: <input type="text" name="country" size="20"> </p>
    <p><button type="submit">Send Data</button></p>
    <div id="json"></div>
    <div id="props"></div>
  </form>
  </body>
  </html>
```

Figure 1-9 shows what the web page looks like.

Figure 1-9. JSON is calling

The JavaScript code is imported by the script tag and specified by the file *hack5.js*. The JavaScript sends the user's entered values to the server; because this was discussed in "Use the Request Object to POST Data to the Server" [Hack #2] and other hacks, the code is reproduced here but doesn't go into great detail.

> Beware of cross-site scripting (XSS) attacks when evaluating any return values as JavaScript code in this manner. This is a potential threat for any use of eval( ) or the Function-related code discussed in this hack.
>
> As a countermeasure, the client-side JavaScript can filter and inspect the return value (e.g., by looking at the XMLHttpRequest responseText property) for the presence of the expected object property names before the code uses responseText in the eval( ) function (see *http://www.perl.com/pub/a/2002/02/20/css.html*).

Here's the code for this hack. Below, we'll go over the key parts that handle the return value as a JavaScript object.

```
var request;
var queryString;    //will hold the POSTed data

function sendData( ){
    setQueryString( );
    url="http://localhost:8080/parkerriver/s/json";
    httpRequest("POST",url,true);
}

//event handler for XMLHttpRequest
function handleJson( ){
    if(request.readyState == 4){
        if(request.status == 200){
            var resp =  request.responseText;
            var func = new Function("return "+resp);
            var objt = func( );
            var div = document.getElementById("json");
            stylizeDiv(resp,div);
            div = document.getElementById("props");
            div.innerHTML="<h4>In object form...</h4>"+
                          "<h5>Properties</h5>firstname= "+
                          objt.firstname +"<br />lastname="+
                          objt.lastname+ "<br />gender="+
                          objt.gender+ "<br />country="+
                          objt.country;
        } else {
            alert("A problem occurred with communicating between "+
                "the XMLHttpRequest object and the server program.");
        }
    }//end outer if
}

/* Initialize a request object that is already constructed */
function initReq(reqType,url,bool){
    /* Specify the function that will handle the HTTP response */
    request.onreadystatechange=handleJson;
    request.open(reqType,url,bool);
    request.setRequestHeader("Content-Type",
            "application/x-www-form-urlencoded; charset=UTF-8");
    request.send(queryString);
}

/* Wrapper function for constructing a request object.
 Parameters:
  reqType: The HTTP request type, such as GET or POST.
  url: The URL of the server program.
  asynch: Whether to send the request asynchronously or not. */

function httpRequest(reqType,url,asynch){
    //Snipped... See Hack #1 or #2
```

```
    }

    function setQueryString( ){
        queryString="";
        var frm = document.forms[0];
        var numberElements =  frm.elements.length;
        for(var i = 0; i < numberElements; i++){
            if(i < numberElements-1){
                queryString += frm.elements[i].name+"="+
                                encodeURIComponent(frm.elements[i].value)+"&";
            } else {
                queryString += frm.elements[i].name+"="+
                                encodeURIComponent(frm.elements[i].value);
            }
        }
    }

    function stylizeDiv(bdyTxt,div){
        //reset DIV content
        div.innerHTML=" ";
        div.style.fontSize="1.2em";
        div.style.backgroundColor="yellow";
        div.appendChild(document.createTextNode(bdyTxt));
    }
```

As in this chapter's previous hacks, the initReq( ) function initializes the
request object and sends an HTTP request to the server.

The event-handling function for when the response is ready is called
handleJson( ). The response is a JSON-formatted text string, as opposed to
XML or some other text type. As is, JavaScript interprets this returned text
as a string object. Therefore, the code initiates an opening step before the
server's return value is interpreted as a JavaScript object literal. (By the way,
in this hack, the server takes the request parameters and reformats the
parameter names and property values into JSON syntax, prior to sending
the reformatted data as its response.)

> Special error-handling code is not included here, because
> these elements require further explanation and are covered
> by "Handle Request Object Errors" **[Hack #8]**.

Within the handleJson( ) code (highlighted in the previous code sample), the
variable resp refers to the HTTP response text, which JavaScript interprets
as a string. The interesting stuff occurs in the Function constructor:

```
var func = new Function("return "+resp);
```

This code creates a new Function object on the fly and stores the Function in
a variable named func. JavaScript coders might note that most functions are
predefined and declared in code, or created as function literals. However, in

this case we need to define a function body dynamically using a string, and the Function constructor provides the perfect tool.

 Thanks to this site for guidance on this code usage: *http://www.jibbering.com/2002/4/httprequest.html*.

Another method for converting JSON strings that's making its way around the Web goes like this:

```
var resp = request.responseText;
var obj = eval( "(" + resp + ")" );
```

You do not have to use the parentheses characters when using eval( ) and an array, as in:

```
var resp = request.responseText;
//resp contains something like "[1,2,3,4]"
var arrObject = eval(resp);
```

The next line creates a function that returns an object literal, representing the server return value. You then call the function and use the returned object to dynamically display server values on the web page with DOM programming (all without complex object serialization or a page refresh!):

```
var objt = func( );
var div = document.getElementById("json");
stylizeDiv(resp,div);
div = document.getElementById("props");
div.innerHTML="<h4>In object form...</h4><h5>Properties</h5>firstname= "+
        objt.firstname +"<br />lastname="+
        objt.lastname+ "<br />gender="+
        objt.gender+ "<br />country="+
        objt.country;
```

A variable named objt stores the object literal. The values are pulled from the object with syntax such as objt.firstname. Figure 1-10 shows what the web page looks like after it has received a response.

On the Server Side

A Java servlet handles requests for this hack. For those interested in the server activity, here is the doPost( ) method for this code:

```
protected void doPost(HttpServletRequest httpServletRequest,
                HttpServletResponse httpServletResponse) throws
                ServletException, IOException {
    Map valMap = httpServletRequest.getParameterMap( );
    StringBuffer body = new StringBuffer("{\n");

    if(valMap != null) {
        String val=null;
        String key = null;
        Map.Entry me = null;
```

Figure 1-10. Visualizing JavaScript properties is sweet!

```
Set entries =  valMap.entrySet( );

int size = entries.size( );
int counter=0;
for(Iterator iter= entries.iterator( );iter.hasNext( );) {
    counter++;
    me=(Map.Entry) iter.next( );
    val= ((String[])me.getValue( ))[0];
    key = (String) me.getKey( );
    if(counter < size) {
        body.append(key).append(":\"").append(val).append("\",\n");
    } else {
        //remove comma for last entry
        body.append(key).append(":\"").append(val).append("\"\n");
    }
}

}
```

```
    body.append("}");
    AjaxUtil.sendText(httpServletResponse,body.toString( ));
}
```

The AjaxUtil class sends the HTTP response with a Content-Type of text/ plain; charset=UTF-8. Some web sites have discussed using a Content-Type of application/x-json for JSON, but as of this writing, developers and standards bodies have not yet settled on a standard relating to this matter.

The AjaxUtil class also sets the HTTP response header Cache-Control to no-cache, which tells the browser or user agent not to cache the responses:

```
    response.setHeader("Cache-Control", "no-cache");
```

H A C K Handle Request Object Errors

#8 Design your Ajax application to detect any server errors and provide a friendly user message.

Much of the oomph behind Ajax technology is that it allows JavaScript to connect with a server program without the user intervening. However, JavaScript developers often have no control over the server component itself (which could be a web service or other software designed outside their organizations). Even if your application involves your organization's server component, you cannot always be sure that the server is behaving normally or even that your users are online at the moment they trigger your request object. You have to make sure that your application recovers in the event that the backend program is unavailable.

This hack traps errors and displays a meaningful error message, in the event that the Ajax application loses server contact.

Problems, Problems...

This hack addresses the following exceptional events, and recommends ways for the application to recover from them:

- The web application or server component you are connecting with is temporarily unavailable.

- The server your application is connecting with is down, or its URL has changed unbeknownst to you.

- The server component you connect with has one or more bugs, and it crashes during your connection (yeech!).

- When you call the open( ) method with the request object, your code uses a different host address than the address from which the user downloaded the web page. The request object throws an exception in this case when you try to call its open( ) method.

You can use this hack's exception-handling code in any application. This hack uses the stock calculation code from "Receive Data as a Number" [Hack #6]. We'll take a look at the code that initializes the request object and the exception-handling mechanism in a moment, but first, here's the HTML file that imports the JavaScript code from *hack6.js*:

```
<!DOCTYPE HTML PUBLIC "-//W3C//DTD HTML 4.01//EN"
        "http://www.w3.org/TR/1999/REC-html401-19991224/strict.dtd">
<html>
<head>
    <script type="text/javascript" src="js/hack6.js"></script>
    <meta http-equiv="content-type" content="text/html; charset=utf-8" />
    <title>Tally your stocks</title>
</head>
<body>
<h3>Your total Stock Holdings</h3>
<form action="javascript:void%200" onsubmit=
        "getStockPrice(this.stSymbol.value,this.numShares.value);return
false">
    <p>Enter stock symbol: <input type="text" name="stSymbol" size="4">
            <span id="stPrice"></span></p>
    <p>Enter share amount: <input type="text" name="numShares" size="10"></
p>
    <p><button type="submit">Get Total Value</button></p>
    <div id="msgDisplay"></div>
</form>
</body>
</html>
```

When users load this file into their browsers, they see the screen shown in Figure 1-11.

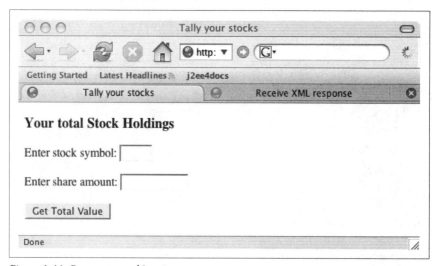

Figure 1-11. Request a stock's price

The code we are interested in can trap exceptions involving unavailable applications, backend servers that are down, backend server bugs, and erroneous URLs. The handleResponse( ) function is the event handler for managing the server response, as in request.onreadystatechange=handleResponse. The following code uses a nested try/catch/finally statement to deal with invalid numbers handled by the application, as discussed in "Receive Data as a Number" [Hack #6].

```
function handleResponse( ){
    var statusMsg="";
    try{
        if(request.readyState == 4){
            if(request.status == 200){
                /* Check if the return value is actually a number.
                If so, multiple by the number
                of shares and display the result */
                var stockPrice = request.responseText;

                try{
                    if(isNaN(stockPrice)) { throw new Error(
                            "The returned price is an invalid number.");}
                    if(isNaN(numberOfShares)) { throw new Error(
                            "The share amount is an invalid number.");}
                    var info = "Total stock value: $"+
                    calcTotal(stockPrice);
                    displayMsg(document.
                    getElementById("msgDisplay"),info,"black");
                    document.getElementById("stPrice").style.fontSize="0.
                    9em";
                    document.getElementById("stPrice").innerHTML ="price: "+
                            stockPrice;
                } catch (err) {
                    displayMsg(document.getElementById("msgDisplay"),
                            "An error occurred: "+
                            err.message,"red");
                }
            } else {
                //request.status is 503 if the application isn't available;
                //500 if the application has a bug
                alert(
                        "A problem occurred with communicating between the "
                        "XMLHttpRequest object and the server program. "+
                        "Please try again very soon");
            }
        }//end outer if
    } catch (err) {
        alert("It does not appear that the server "+
            "is available for this application. Please "+
            "try again very soon. \nError: "+err.message);

    }
}
```

Now, let's take a look at how this code handles the different types of exceptions previously enumerated.

Floored Server

A try block traps any exceptions thrown within its curly braces ({}). If the code throws an exception, this mechanism executes the code within the associated catch block. The inner try block, which is designed to manage exceptions thrown in the event of invalid numeric values, is explained in "Receive Data as a Number" [Hack #6].

So, what happens if the server host is completely down, even though the URL your application uses is otherwise correct? In this case, the code's attempt to access the request.status property throws an exception because the request object never receives the expected response header from the server and the status property is not associated with any data.

As a result, the code displays the alert window defined in the outer catch block. Figure 1-12 depicts what the alert window looks like after this type of error.

Figure 1-12. Uh-oh, server down

The code displays a user message, as well as the more techie error message associated with the exception. You can leave out that part of the message if you desire; it is mainly useful for debugging purposes.

> The err variable in the code is a reference to the JavaScript Error object. The message property of this object (as in err. message) is the actual error message, a string generated by the JavaScript engine.

If you do not include this try/catch/finally mechanism, the user sees just an alert window containing the indecipherable error message generated by JavaScript. After dismissing this window (or leaving the computer in frustration), the user has no way of knowing what state the application is in.

Backend Application Out to Lunch

Sometimes the application server or host is running okay, but the server component you want to connect with is out of service. In this case, the value of the request.status property is 503 ("Service Unavailable"). Because the status property holds a value other than 200, this hack's code executes the expression contained within the else statement block:

```
} else {
    //request.status is 503 if the application isn't available;
    // 500 if the application has a bug
    alert(
            "A problem occurred with communicating between the "
            "XMLHttpRequest object and the server program. "+
            "Please try again very soon");
}
```

In other words, the user sees an alert window explaining the application's status. This alert also appears if the server component has a bug and crashes. This event typically (such as with the Tomcat servlet container) results in a 500 response status code ("Internal Server Error"), so response. status evaluates to 500 instead of 200 ("Okay"). In addition, any 404 response codes involving a static or dynamic component that the server cannot find at the URL you provided are captured with this try statement.

> The try/catch/finally statement is available only with Java-Script engines of JS Version 1.4 or later. The optional finally statement block follows the catch block. The code enclosed by finally{...} executes regardless of whether or not an exception is thrown.

Whoops, Wrong URL

What if the URL that your Ajax application uses in the request.open( ) method is wrong or has changed? In this case, the request.open( ) call throws the exception, so this is where you have to position your try/catch/finally statement. The code at the top of the next example constructs a request object [Hack #1]. The following function definition, initReq( ), catches the exception just described:

```
function httpRequest(reqType,url,asynch){
    //Mozilla-based browsers
    if(window.XMLHttpRequest){
        request = new XMLHttpRequest( );
    } else if (window.ActiveXObject){
        request=new ActiveXObject("Msxml2.XMLHTTP");
        if (! request){
            request=new ActiveXObject("Microsoft.XMLHTTP");
        }
    }
```

```
    }
    //the request could still be null if neither ActiveXObject
    //initialization succeeded
    if(request){
        initReq(reqType,url,asynch);
    } else {
        alert("Your browser does not permit the use of all "+
            "of this application's features!");
    }
}
/* Initialize a request object that is already constructed */
function initReq(reqType,url,bool){
    try{
        /* Specify the function that will handle the HTTP response */
        request.onreadystatechange=handleResponse;
        request.open(reqType,url,bool);
        request.send(null);
    } catch (err) {

        alert(
            "The application cannot contact the server at the moment."+
            " Please try again in a few seconds.");
    }
}
```

Another variation of this error is when the URL you use with the request.
open( ) method includes a different host than the host from which the user
downloaded the web page. For example, say the user downloads the web
page from *http://www.myorg.com/app*, but the URL you use for open( ) is
http://www.yourorg.com. This type of error is also caught by the code's try/
catch/finally statement.

> You can also optionally abort or cancel the request in the
> catch block with request.abort( ). For more information,
> see "Set a Time Limit for the HTTP Request" **[Hack #70]** and
> its discussion of setting a timeout for the request and abort-
> ing it in the event that the request is not completed within a
> certain period.

H A C K   Dig into the HTTP Response
#9   Display the values of various HTTP response headers in addition to or in lieu
of a typical server return value.

An HTTP *response header* is descriptive information, laid out by the HTTP
1.1 protocol, that web servers send requestors along with the actual web
page or data. If you have already coded with the XMLHttpRequest object (discussed at the beginning of this chapter), you know that the request.status

property equates to an HTTP response status code sent from the server. This is an important value to check before your page does anything cool with the HTTP response.

Status values can include 200 (the request went through okay), 404 (the requested file or URL path was not found), or 500 (internal server error).

However, you might want to see some of the other response headers associated with the request, such as the type of web server software associated with the response (the Server response header) or the content type of the response (the Content-Type header). This hack requests the user to enter a URL in a text field. When the user tabs out of or clicks outside of the text field, the browser displays various HTTP response headers. As usual with Ajax, this happens without a page refresh.

This request object method returns only a subset of the available response headers, including Content-Type, Date, Server, and Content-Length.

Here is the HTML page code:

```
<!DOCTYPE HTML PUBLIC "-//W3C//DTD HTML 4.01//EN"
        "http://www.w3.org/TR/1999/REC-html401-19991224/strict.dtd">
<html>
<head>
    <script type="text/javascript" src="js/hack7.js"></script>
    <meta http-equiv="content-type" content="text/html; charset=utf-8" />
    <title>view response headers</title>
    <link rel="stylesheet" type="text/css" href="/parkerriver/css/hacks.css"
/>
</head>
<body onload="document.forms[0].url.value=urlFragment">
<h3>Find out the HTTP response headers when you "GET" a Web page</h3>

<form action="javascript:void%200">
    <p>Enter a URL:
        <input type="text" name="url" size="20" onblur="getAllHeaders(this.
value)">
        <span class="message">::press tab when finished editing the
                field::</span></p>
    <div id="msgDisplay"></div>
</form>
</body>
</html>
```

Figure 1-13 shows the page in the Safari browser.

Figure 1-13. Scoping the response

The application prefills the text field with a partial URL (e.g., *http:// localhost:8080/*) for the user to complete, because the request object cannot send a request to a different host from the host that uploaded the web page to the user. In other words, the partially completed URL provides a hint to the user that the application can only send a request to that specified host.

When the user completes the URL and then presses the Tab key or clicks outside the text field, the text field's onblur event handler is triggered. The event handler is defined as a function named getAllHeaders( ), which passes the URL the user has entered to the request object. The request object then sends a request to the URL and returns the available response headers to the web page.

The following code is from the *hack7.js* file that the page imports. After showing this code, I explain the parts that deal with displaying the server's response headers. "Detect Browser Compatibility with the Request Object" [Hack #1] explains how to initialize and open an HTTP connection with the request object, otherwise known as XMLHttpRequest. "Handle Request Object Errors" [Hack #8] explains trapping any errors with JavaScript's try/ catch/finally statement.

```
var request;
var urlFragment="http://localhost:8080/";

function getAllHeaders(url){
    httpRequest("GET",url,true);
}

//function for XMLHttpRequest onreadystatechange event handler
function handleResponse( ){
    try{
        if(request.readyState == 4){
            if(request.status == 200){
                /* All headers received as a single string */
```

```
                var headers = request.getAllResponseHeaders( );
                var div = document.getElementById("msgDisplay");
                div.className="header";
                div.innerHTML="<pre>"+headers+"</pre>";
            } else {
                //request.status is 503 if the application isn't available;
                //500 if the application has a bug
                alert(request.status);
                alert("A problem occurred with communicating between "+
                    "the XMLHttpRequest object and the server program.");
            }
        }//end outer if
    } catch (err)   {
        alert("It does not appear that the server is "+
            "available for this application. Please"+
            " try again very soon. \nError: "+err.message);


    }
}


/* Initialize a request object that is already constructed */
function initReq(reqType,url,bool){
    try{
        /* Specify the function that will handle the HTTP response */
        request.onreadystatechange=handleResponse;
        request.open(reqType,url,bool);
        request.send(null);
    } catch (errv) {
        alert(
                "The application cannot contact the server at the moment. "+
                "Please try again in a few seconds." );
    }
}


/* Wrapper function for constructing a request object.
 Parameters:
  reqType: The HTTP request type, such as GET or POST.
  url: The URL of the server program.
  asynch: Whether to send the request asynchronously or not. */
function httpRequest(reqType,url,asynch){
    //Mozilla-based browsers
    if(window.XMLHttpRequest){
        request = new XMLHttpRequest( );
    } else if (window.ActiveXObject){
        request=new ActiveXObject("Msxml2.XMLHTTP");
        if (! request){
            request=new ActiveXObject("Microsoft.XMLHTTP");
        }
    }
    //the request could still be null if neither ActiveXObject
    //initialization succeeded
    if(request){
        initReq(reqType,url,asynch);
```

```
        } else {
            alert("Your browser does not permit the use of all "+
                "of this application's features!");
        }
    }
```

The interesting stuff takes place in the handleResponse( ) function. This function calls the request object's getAllResponseHeaders( ) method, which returns (rather awkwardly) all the available response headers, preformatted into a string. A developer would probably prefer this value to be returned in JSON format as an associative array, rather than a monolithic string in which extra code is required to pull out individual header information.

 To get one header, you can also use request. getResponseHeader( ). An example would be request. getResponseHeader("Content-Type");.

The code then gets hold of the div element, where it will display the header values:

```
if(request.status == 200){
    /* All headers received as a single string */
    var headers = request.getAllResponseHeaders( );
    var div = document.getElementById("msgDisplay");
    div.className="header";
    div.innerHTML="<pre>"+headers+"</pre>";
}...
```

To provide a CSS style for the message display, the code sets the className property of the div to a class that is already defined in a stylesheet. Here's the stylesheet, which is linked to the web page:

```
div.header{ border: thin solid black; padding: 10%;
  font-size: 0.9em; background-color: yellow}
span.message { font-size: 0.8em; }
```

In this manner, the code dynamically connects a div to a certain CSS class, which is defined by a separate stylesheet. This strategy helps separate DOM programming from presentation decisions. Finally, the div's innerHTML property is set to the returned header values. You use the pre tag to conserve the existing formatting.

 You can, alternatively, manipulate the returned string and format the headers in a different way, using a custom function.

Figure 1-14 shows what the browser displays after the user submits a URL.

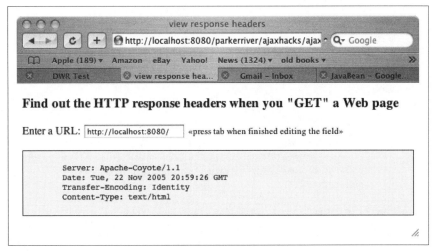

Figure 1-14. Separate the headers from the chaff

Generate a Styled Message with a CSS File

HACK #10

Let the users choose predesigned styles for the messages they see.

This hack sends a request to a server, which returns a text message. The user's choices determine the actual message content and appearance. The HTML for the page includes a select tag listing the styles the users can choose for the display of the results and a text field containing a partial URL they can complete and submit to a server.

The information returned relates to the response headers returned by the server [Hack #9]. However, what we are interested in here is this hack's dynamic message generation and style assignment. Here's the HTML code for the page:

```
<!DOCTYPE HTML PUBLIC "-//W3C//DTD HTML 4.01//EN"
        "http://www.w3.org/TR/1999/REC-html401-19991224/strict.dtd">
<html>
<head>
    <script type="text/javascript" src="js/hack8.js"></script>
    <script type="text/javascript">
    function setSpan(){
        document.getElementById("instr").onmouseover=function(){
            this.style.backgroundColor='yellow';};
        document.getElementById("instr").onmouseout=function(){
            this.style.backgroundColor='white';};
    }
    </script>
    <meta http-equiv="content-type" content="text/html; charset=utf-8" />
    <title>view response headers</title>
```

```
<link rel="stylesheet" type="text/css" href="/parkerriver/css/hacks.css"
/>
</head>
<body onload="document.forms[0].url.value=urlFragment;setSpan( )">
<h3>Find out the HTTP response headers when you "GET" a Web page</h3>
<h4>Choose the style for your message</h4>
<form action="javascript:void%200">
    <p>
        <select name="_style">
            <option label="Loud" value="loud" selected>Loud</option>
            <option label="Fancy" value="fancy">Fancy</option>
            <option label="Cosmopolitan" value="cosmo">Cosmopolitan</option>
            <option label="Plain" value="plain">Plain</option>
        </select>
    </p>
    <p>Enter a URL: <input type="text" name="url" size="20" onblur=
        "getAllHeaders(this.value,this.form._style.value)"> <span id=
        "instr" class="message">&#171;press tab or click outside the
field
            when finished editing&#187;</span></p>
    <div id="msgDisplay"></div>
</form>
</body>
</html>
```

The purpose of the setSpan( ) function defined within the web page's script tags is to give some instructions ("press tab or click outside the field when finished editing") a yellow background when the user passes the mouse pointer over them.

Before I describe some of the code elements, you may be interested in how the web page appears in a browser. Figure 1-15 shows this window.

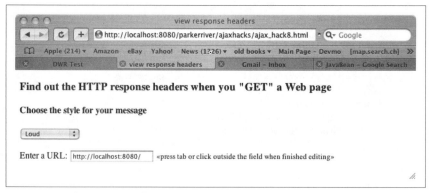

Figure 1-15. Choose your style

The CSS styles used by this web page derive from a stylesheet file named *hacks.css*. When the user chooses a style (say, "Cosmopolitan") from the select list, enters a value in the text field, and then tabs out of or clicks outside of the field, that user's chosen style is dynamically assigned to the container that will hold the message (a div element with id msgDisplay).

Here is the *hacks.css* stylesheet:

```
div.header{ border: thin solid black; padding: 10%;
 font-size: 0.9em; background-color: yellow; max-width: 80%}

span.message { font-size: 0.8em; }
div { max-width: 80% }

.plain { border: thin solid black; padding: 10%;
 font: Arial, serif font-size: 0.9em; background-color: yellow; }
.fancy { border: thin solid black; padding: 5%;
 font-family: Herculanum, Verdana, serif;
 font-size: 1.2em;  text-shadow: 0.2em 0.2em grey; font-style: oblique;
 color: rgb(21,49,110); background-color: rgb(234,197,49)}
.loud { border: thin solid black; padding: 5%; font-family: Impact, serif;
 font-size: 1.4em; text-shadow: 0 0 2.0em black; color: black;
background-color: rgb(181,77,79)}
.cosmo { border: thin solid black; padding: 1%;
 font-family: Papyrus, serif;
 font-size: 0.9em; text-shadow: 0 0 0.5em black; color: aqua;
 background-color: teal}
```

The stylesheet defines several classes (plain, fancy, loud, and cosmo). A *class* in a CSS stylesheet begins with a period (as in .fancy) and defines various style properties, such as the font family and background color. Using this technique, your CSS experts can define the actual styles in one place, for use in multiple web pages. Clearly, an experienced designer would have some, ah, differences with the style-attribute choices here, but please bear with me!

The Ajax-related JavaScript code can assign the predefined styles to page elements based on user choices. Therefore, the presentation tier of your web application is separated from the application logic or domain tier.

The onblur event handler for the text field submits the URL value and the style name to a function named getAllHeaders( ):

```
onblur="getAllHeaders(this.value,this.form._style.value)"
```

The reference this.form._style.value is JavaScript that represents the value of the option chosen from the select list (the style name). The reference this.value is the text entered by the user in the text field.

Here is the JavaScript code that the page imports from *hacks8.js*, with the code that dynamically assigns the style to the displayed message highlighted:

```
var request;
var urlFragment="http://localhost:8080/";
var st;

function getAllHeaders(url,styl){
    if(url){
        st=styl;
        httpRequest("GET",url,true);
    }
}

//event handler for XMLHttpRequest
function handleResponse( ){
    try{
        if(request.readyState == 4){
            if(request.status == 200){
                /* All headers received as a single string */
                var headers = request.getAllResponseHeaders( );
                var div = document.getElementById("msgDisplay");
                div.className= st == "" ? "header" : st;
                div.innerHTML="<pre>"+headers+"</pre>";
            } else {
                //request.status is 503 if the application isn't available;
                //500 if the application has a bug
                alert(request.status);
                alert("A problem occurred with communicating between "+
                    "the XMLHttpRequest object and the server program.");
            }
        }//end outer if
    } catch (err)   {
        alert("It does not appear that the server is available for "+
            "this application. Please"+
            " try again very soon. \nError: "+err.message);

    }
}

/* See Hacks #1, #2, and others for definitions of the httpRequest( )
   and initReq( ) functions; snipped here for the sake of brevity. */
```

Easy as Pie

The getAllHeaders( ) function sets a top-level st variable to the name of a CSS style class (plain, fancy, loud, or cosmo). The code then sets the className property of the div that holds the message in a shockingly simple way, which changes the style assigned to the message:

```
if(request.status == 200){
    /* All headers received as a single string */
    var headers = request.getAllResponseHeaders();
    var div = document.getElementById("msgDisplay");
    div.className= st == "" ? "header" : st;
    div.innerHTML="<pre>"+headers+"</pre>";
}
```

If for some reason the choice of class name derived from the web client is the
empty string (it cannot be here because the select tag only contains complete string values), the div element is assigned a default style class name of
header.

> This JavaScript could potentially be imported into *another*
> client web page, so you have to include some checks for
> invalid input values.

The *hacks.css* stylesheet also defines the header class.

The following figures are examples of the same message assigned different
styles by the user. Figure 1-16 shows the result if the user selects the "Cosmopolitan" style.

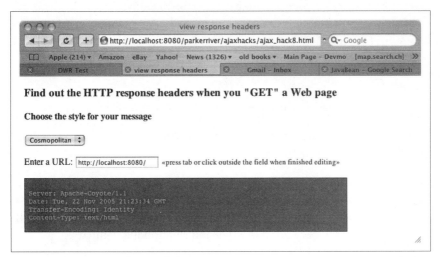

Figure 1-16. A Cosmopolitan-styled message

Figure 1-17 depicts an alternate style.

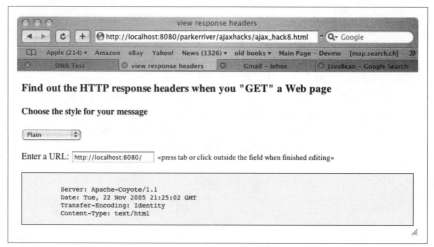

Figure 1-17. Alas, a Plain-styled message

HACK #11 Generate a Styled User Message on the Fly

Dynamically define and assign CSS styles to web page content.

JavaScript and DOM programming allow you to define CSS style attributes and apply them to page elements from scratch. An example of where you may want to implement these methods is a Wiki page that permits users to develop their own page designs and styles.

> In most cases, separating the style definitions from the JavaScript code is the way to go. Separating application concerns or tiers in this manner allows each element to evolve independently and makes web development less complex and more efficient.

This hack, like the one before it, dynamically displays server information based on the user's choice of style categories. *Unlike* the previous hack, this one formulates the styles in code, then applies the chosen style to an HTML element. Here is the code, with the style information highlighted:

```
var request;
var urlFragment="http://localhost:8080/";
var st;

function getAllHeaders(url,styl){
    if(url){
        st=styl;
        httpRequest("GET",url,true);
    }
}
```

```
/*  Set one or more CSS style attributes on a DOM element
CSS2Properties Object.
 Parameters:
  stType stands for a style name, as in 'plain,''fancy,''loud,' or 'cosmo'.
  stylObj is the HTML element's style property, as in div.style. */

function setStyle(stType,stylObj){
    switch(stType){
        case 'plain' :
            stylObj.maxWidth="80%";
            stylObj.border="thin solid black";
            stylObj.padding="5%";
            stylObj.textShadow="none";
            stylObj.fontFamily="Arial, serif";
            stylObj.fontSize="0.9em";
            stylObj.backgroundColor="yellow"; break;
        case 'loud' :
            stylObj.maxWidth="80%";
            stylObj.border="thin solid black";
            stylObj.padding="5%";
            stylObj.fontFamily="Impact, serif";
            stylObj.fontSize="1.4em";
            stylObj.textShadow="0 0 2.0em black";
            stylObj.backgroundColor="rgb(181,77,79)"; break;
        case 'fancy' :
            stylObj.maxWidth="80%";
            stylObj.border="thin solid black";
            stylObj.padding="5%";
            stylObj.fontFamily="Herculanum, Verdana, serif";
            stylObj.fontSize="1.2em";
            stylObj.fontStyle="oblique";
            stylObj.textShadow="0.2em 0.2em grey";
            stylObj.color="rgb(21,49,110)";
            stylObj.backgroundColor="rgb(234,197,49)"; break;
        case 'cosmo' :
            stylObj.maxWidth="80%";
            stylObj.border="thin solid black";
            stylObj.padding="1%";
            stylObj.fontFamily="Papyrus, serif";
            stylObj.fontSize="0.9em";
            stylObj.textShadow="0 0 0.5em black";
            stylObj.color="aqua";
            stylObj.backgroundColor="teal"; break;
        default :
            alert('default');

    }
}

//event handler for XMLHttpRequest
function handleResponse(){
    try{
        if(request.readyState == 4){
```

```
        if(request.status == 200){
            /* All headers received as a single string */
            var headers = request.getAllResponseHeaders( );
            var div = document.getElementById("msgDisplay");
            if(st){
                setStyle(st,div.style);
            } else {
                setStyle("plain",div.style);
            }
            div.innerHTML="<pre>"+headers+"</pre>";
        } else {
            //request.status is 503 if the application isn't available;
            //500 if the application has a bug
            alert(request.status);
            alert("A problem occurred with communicating between "+
                    "the XMLHttpRequest object and the server program.");
        }
    }//end outer if
} catch (err) {
    alert("It does not appear that the server is available for "
        "this application. Please"+
        " try again very soon. \nError: "+err.message);

}
}

/* Initialize a request object that is already constructed */
function initReq(reqType,url,bool){
    try{
        /* Specify the function that will handle the HTTP response */
        request.onreadystatechange=handleResponse;
        request.open(reqType,url,bool);
        request.send(null);
    } catch (errv) {

        alert(
                "The application cannot contact the server at the moment. "+
                "Please try again in a few seconds." );
    }
}

/* Wrapper function for constructing a request object.
 Parameters:
   reqType: The HTTP request type such as GET or POST.
   url: The URL of the server program.
   asynch: Whether to send the request asynchronously or not. */
function httpRequest(reqType,url,asynch){
    //Mozilla-based browsers
    if(window.XMLHttpRequest){
        request = new XMLHttpRequest( );
    } else if (window.ActiveXObject){
        request=new ActiveXObject("Msxml2.XMLHTTP");
        if (! request){
```

```
            request=new ActiveXObject("Microsoft.XMLHTTP");
        }
    }
    //the request could still be null if neither ActiveXObject
    //initialization succeeded
    if(request){
        initReq(reqType,url,asynch);
    } else {
        alert("Your browser does not permit the use of all "+
            "of this application's features!");
    }
}
```

Nudging Aside the Stylesheet

Each HTML element on a web page has a style property, if its host browser supports CSS stylesheets. For example, a div element has a property called div.style that allows a JavaScript writer to set inline style attributes for that div (as in div.style.fontFamily="Arial"). This is how the setStyle( ) function works in the prior code. The two function parameters are a style name such as "Fancy" (chosen from a predefined list) and the style property of a specific div element. The function then sets the appearance of the HTML div element on the web page.

The information that appears on the page (a bunch of response headers) is derived from the server using the request object. As in the previous hack, the user completes a URL, then clicks outside the text field or presses the Tab key, thus firing an onblur event handler that sets the request object and CSS styling in motion. The HTML for the page is not much different from that in "Generate a Styled Message with a CSS File" [Hack #10], but it omits the link to a stylesheet. All the styling for this hack is defined by the imported JavaScript file, *hack10.js*. Here's the code:

```
<!DOCTYPE HTML PUBLIC "-//W3C//DTD HTML 4.01//EN"
        "http://www.w3.org/TR/1999/REC-html401-19991224/strict.dtd">
<html>
<head>
    <script type="text/javascript" src="/parkerriver/js/hack10.js"></script>
    <script type="text/javascript">
    function setSpan( ){
        document.getElementById("instr").onmouseover=function( ){
            this.style.backgroundColor='yellow';};
        document.getElementById("instr").onmouseout=function( ){
            this.style.backgroundColor='white';};
    }
    </script>
    <meta http-equiv="content-type" content="text/html; charset=utf-8" />
    <title>view response headers</title>
</head>
```

```
<body onLoad="document.forms[0].url.value=urlFragment;setSpan( )">
<h3>Find out the HTTP response headers when you "GET" a Web page</h3>
<h4>Choose the style for your message</h4>
<form action="javascript:void%200">
    <p>
        <select name="_style">
            <option label="Loud" value="loud" selected>Loud</option>
            <option label="Fancy" value="fancy">Fancy</option>
            <option label="Cosmopolitan" value="cosmo">Cosmopolitan</option>
            <option label="Plain" value="plain">Plain</option>
        </select>
    </p>
    <p>Enter a URL: <input type="text" name="url" size="20" onblur=
        "getAllHeaders(this.value,this.form._style.value)">
        <span id="instr" class="message">&#171;press tab or
        click outside the field when finished editing&#187;
        </span></p>
    <div id="msgDisplay"></div>
</form>
</body>
</html>
```

The getAllHeaders( ) function, an event handler for onblur, passes in to the
application the name of the style the user has chosen from a select list (such
as "cosmo"), as well as the URL of the server component. The only purpose
of the server component is to provide a value for display. We're mainly
interested in dynamically generating styles for any type of server information your applications could acquire via Ajax and the request object.

The purpose of the setSpan( ) function defined within the
web page's script tags is to give some instructions ("press
tab or click outside the field when finished editing") a yellow background when the user passes the mouse pointer
over them.

Figure 1-18 shows what the page looks like in a web browser prior to the
sending of the HTTP request.

Figure 1-19 depicts what the page looks like when the user optionally selects
a style name, completes the URL in the text field, and presses Tab.

None of these web page changes involves waiting for the server to deliver a
new page. The request object fetches the data from the server in the background, and the client-side JavaScript styles the displayed information.
Voilà, Ajax!

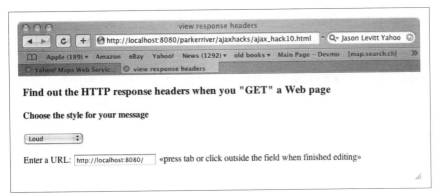

Figure 1-18. Choose a style for dynamic generation

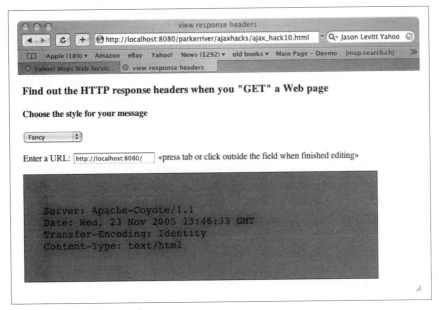

Figure 1-19. Styled server data

CHAPTER 2

Web Forms
Hacks 12–21

Almost everyone who has used the Web has encountered an HTML form. When users buy books or DVDs online, or log into discussion lists or other web communities, inevitably they are typing information into text fields or choosing options in select lists, and then submitting the forms by clicking a button. The purpose of these forms is to upload user- or client-related data to a server component, which then implements a task such as logging the user into an application.

Web applications that use Ajax-related techniques, however, can provide a different mechanism for submitting web-form information. JavaScript code can submit discrete values from only certain widgets or fields, for instance, without requiring the user to click the classic Submit button. This application model has transformed the web form into a "rich user interface" similar to a desktop application, where the code can send data over the network in response to click or blur events without refreshing the entire web page. The following hacks illustrate how to send selection and text-field values using XMLHttpRequest, and how to dynamically generate the content of display widgets from server data.

 HACK **Submit Text Field or textarea Values to the Server**
#12 **Without a Browser Refresh**
Create a smooth transition between entering information into a textarea or text field and instantly transferring the data to the server.

Ajax applications can automatically send to a server program the information that the user has entered into a text field or textarea. The application code waits for the text widget's onblur event to occur, then uses the request object to send just the data from that field or textarea. In many applications, this technique is preferable to requiring the user to click a Submit button, then sending all of the form's values to the server in a big clump. It is also much snappier in terms of the application's responsiveness. For example, an online quiz or teaching application can fetch and display the correct answer to a question as soon as the user has moved away from the field, instead of requiring the user to click a button and refresh the page just to see specific answers. Real-time language translation is another possible application for this user-interface behavior.

> The onblur event is triggered when a web form control such as a text field loses the keyboard focus, which is typically caused by the user pressing the Tab key or clicking outside of the field. You can also use the onkeypress, onkeydown, or onkeyup event handlers to respond to user interaction with a text widget.

Here is this hack's sequence of events for sending text to the server:

1. The user tabs into the field or clicks in a textarea.
2. The user types some text.
3. The user then presses Tab or clicks on another part of the page to exit the text field or textarea.

> One issue with intervention-less form sending is that users are not accustomed to this kind of behavior from web forms. A user might be put off or confused by web-form controls such as text fields that dynamically submit their own data. The user interface should make it clear that "something is going to happen" when the user is finished with the text field, or display a message or progress indicator when the request object is sending the data. In addition, depending on the sensitivity of the task, you may want to add another layer of communication with the user, such as an alert window asking "Are you sure you want to submit the information?"

This hack includes a text field and a textarea that send HTTP requests with their values when the user is finished with them. Figure 2-1 shows the web page loaded into a browser window.

The user types some information into the text field or textarea (the larger data-entry box) and then exits the control, and the application automatically sends what the user typed to a server component. Here is the HTML code for this page:

```
<!DOCTYPE html PUBLIC "-//W3C//DTD XHTML 1.0 Strict//EN"
 "http://www.w3.org/TR/2000/REC-xhtml1-20000126/DTD/xhtml1-strict.dtd">
<html xmlns="http://www.w3.org/1999/xhtml" xml:lang="en" lang="en">
<head>
```

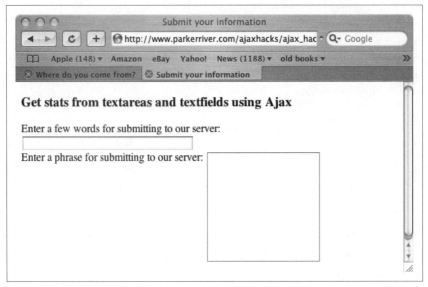

Figure 2-1. No buttons need apply

```
<meta http-equiv="content-type" content="text/html; charset=utf-8" />
<script type="text/javascript" src="js/hacks_2_1.js"></script>
<link rel="stylesheet" type="text/css" href="/css/hacks.css" />
<title>Submit your information</title>
</head>
<body>
<h3>Get stats from textareas and textfields using Ajax</h3>
<form action="javascript:void%200" >
<div id="textf">
Enter a few words for submitting to our server:
<input type="text" name="tfield" id="tfield" size="35" />
</div>
<div id="texta">
<span style="vertical-align: top">Enter a phrase for submitting to our
 server:</span> <textarea name="tarea" rows="20" id="tarea" cols="20">
</textarea>
</div>
</form>
</body>
</html>
```

Instead of a user clicking a button to send the form information, each text control sets the action in motion itself.

When the user presses Tab or clicks outside of one of the text widgets, the code specified by the widget's onblur event handler is executed. The upcoming code sample shows how this event handler is set up after the browser has finished loading the page.

The script tag in the HTML imports a JavaScript file, *hacks_2_1.js*. This file contains all the code necessary for running this hack. The following sample includes all the code for sending a request and handling the return value (in the handleResponse( ) function). "Display Text Field or textarea Values Using Server Data" **[Hack #13]** explains the related technique of inserting the server's response into text controls, but that shouldn't prevent you from peeking at handleResponse( ) if you want! Here's the relevant JavaScript code:

```
var formObj = null;
var formObjTyp = "";
var request=null;

//input field's event handlers
window.onload=function( ){
    var txtA = document.getElementById("tarea");
    if(txtA != null){
        txtA.onblur=function( ){if (this.value) { getInfo(this);}};  }

    var tfd = document.getElementById("tfield");
    if(tfd != null){
        tfd.onblur=function( ){if (this.value) { getInfo(this);}};  }
}

function getInfo(obj){
    if (obj == null ) { return; }
    formObj=obj;
    formObjTyp =obj.tagName;
    if(formObjTyp == "input" || formObjTyp == "INPUT"){
        formObjTyp = formObjTyp + " "+formObj.type;
    }
    formObjTyp = formObjTyp.toLowerCase( );
    var url = "http://www.parkerriver.com/s/webforms?objtype="+
            encodeURIComponent(formObjTyp)+"&val="+ encodeURIComponent(obj.
value);
    httpRequest("GET",url,true);
}

//event handler for XMLHttpRequest
function handleResponse( ){
    try{
        if(request.readyState == 4){
            if(request.status == 200){
                var resp = request.responseText;
                var func = new Function("return "+resp);
                var objt = func( );
                if(formObjTyp == "textarea"){
                    if(formObj != null){
                        formObj.value = objt.Form_field_type +
                                " character count: "+objt.Text_length+
                                "\nWord count: "+
```

```
                                objt.Word_count+"\nServer info: "+
                                objt.Server_info;
                    }
                } else if(formObjTyp == "input text"){
                    if(formObj != null){
                        formObj.value = objt.Form_field_type +
                                " # characters: "+objt.Text_length+
                                " Word count: "+objt.Word_count; }
                }
            } else {
                //request.status is 503
                //if the application isn't available;
                //500 if the application has a bug
                alert(
                        "A problem occurred with communicating between the
"+
                        "XMLHttpRequest object and the server program.");
            }
        }//end outer if
    } catch (err) {
        alert("It does not appear that the server is available "+
                "for this application. Please"+
                " try again very soon. \nError: "+err.message);


    }
}


/* Initialize a request object that is already constructed */
function initReq(reqType,url,bool){
    try{
        /* Specify the function that will handle the
        HTTP response */
        request.onreadystatechange=handleResponse;
        request.open(reqType,url,bool);
        request.send(null);
    } catch (errv) {
        alert(
                "The application cannot contact the server "+
                "at the moment. "+
                "Please try again in a few seconds." );
    }
}
/* Wrapper function for constructing a request object.
 Parameters:
  reqType: The HTTP request type, such as GET or POST.
  url: The URL of the server program.
  asynch: Whether to send the request asynchronously or not. */
function httpRequest(reqType,url,asynch){
    //Mozilla-based browsers
    if(window.XMLHttpRequest){
```

```
        request = new XMLHttpRequest( );
    } else if (window.ActiveXObject){
        request=new ActiveXObject("Msxml2.XMLHTTP");
        if (! request){
            request=new ActiveXObject("Microsoft.XMLHTTP");
        }
    }
    //the request could still be null if neither ActiveXObject
    //initialization succeeded
    if(request){
        initReq(reqType,url,asynch);
    } else {
        alert("Your browser does not permit the use of all "+
            "of this application's features!");}
}
```

The code declares two top-level JavaScript variables: formObj and
formObjTyp. The former variable holds the input or textarea object (other
functions in the code will need access to it later), and the latter holds a
string representing a form object tag name, such as "INPUT" or
"TEXTAREA." This string is one of the parameters that the server component requires (see the formatted URL that appears at the end of the next section, "Get the First Serve In").

These variables are simply part of this hack's behavior and,
in general, are not required for sending form values with the
request object.

As mentioned previously, the code sets up the text widgets' onblur event
handlers when the browser finishes loading the page. You can accomplish
this task in JavaScript by assigning a function to the window's onload event
handler. Using the window.onload code, as follows, is an alternative to calling the JavaScript functions from within an HTML element's onblur
attribute:

```
window.onload=function( ){
    var txtA = document.getElementById("tarea");
    if(txtA != null){
        txtA.onblur=function( ){if (this.value) { getInfo(this);}};  }
    var tfd = document.getElementById("tfield");
    if(tfd != null){
        tfd.onblur=function( ){if (this.value) { getInfo(this);}};  }
}
```

These text fields are now *hot*. Once the user types a value and exits a control, the information entered is off and running to the server; the user
doesn't have to click another button to send it.

Event handlers are simply attributes of an object to which your code can assign a function or block of code that defines some behavior. So, if you want to control how a radio button behaves when it's clicked, set up its onclick event handler. For example:

```
//Get a reference to a radio button element
//on a web page
var rad = document.getElementById("radio1");
//display a pop-up dialog window when it's clicked
rad.onclick=function( ){ alert("I was clicked!");};
```

Get the First Serve In

The main job of the text-field event handlers is to call the getInfo( ) function. This function grabs whatever the user typed into the text widget and sends this value to the server:

```
function getInfo(obj){
    if (obj == null ) { return; }
    formObj=obj;
    formObjTyp =obj.tagName;
    if(formObjTyp == "input" || formObjTyp == "INPUT"){
        formObjTyp = formObjTyp + " "+formObj.type;
    }
    formObjTyp = formObjTyp.toLowerCase( );
    var url = "http://www.parkerriver.com/s/webforms?objtype="+
            encodeURIComponent(formObjTyp)+"&val="+
            encodeURIComponent(obj.value);
    httpRequest("GET",url,true);
}
```

The getInfo( ) function takes as a parameter an object that represents the text field or textarea. We pass in references to the input or textarea objects so that the JavaScript code can use them to handle the server return value.

"Display Text Field or textarea Values Using Server Data" [Hack #13] shows how to display the server's return value inside these text widgets. Because a textarea generally holds more information than a text field, the server sends back more data if the original object was a textarea as opposed to a text field.

The last part of the previous code, httpRequest("GET",url,true), is the function call that actually sends the user's information to the server.

However, a few things have to occur before the code calls that function, such as putting together a proper URL (the server's address on the Internet). The server component is expecting a string describing the kind of form object from which the data derives. In this application, the string is formulated from the tagName property of the Element object (returning INPUT or TEXTAREA).

> The code needs this value to tell the server whether its return value will be inserted into a text field or a textarea. Again, this is described in "Display Text Field or textarea Values Using Server Data" [Hack #13].

The code further refines the input object's description by what input sub-type it represents (text input, radio button, etc.). This is accomplished by appending the value of the input object's type property (text, in this case) to the string input, which creates the final string input text.

In other words, this type property returns "text" only if the object represents an <input type="text" ...> HTML element. Then the string is forced to lowercase and submitted to the server with the user's content:

```
formObjTyp =obj.tagName;
if(formObjTyp == "input" || formObjTyp == "INPUT"){
    formObjTyp = formObjTyp + " "+formObj.type;
}
formObjTyp = formObjTyp.toLowerCase();
var url = "http://www.parkerriver.com/s/webforms?objtype="+
          encodeURIComponent(formObjTyp)+"&val="+ encodeURIComponent(val);
httpRequest("GET",url,true);
```

The global JavaScript function encodeURIComponent() is a method for ensuring that certain characters, such as spaces, are encoded when they are included in URLs. Otherwise, your program may send a partial or truncated URL to the server and generate an error. The entire URL might look like this in a real case:

```
http://www.parkerriver.com/s/webforms?objtype=input%20text&
val=Hello%20There!
```

What's Next?

The httpRequest() function wraps the code that initializes and uses the request object, which works behind the scenes so that the user doesn't have to manually send the data. "Use the Request Object to POST Data to the Server" [Hack #2], among others, describes this function in detail.

So what happens to the submitted data next? That depends on your application. The next hack explores a related but different topic: using JavaScript and Ajax to take an HTTP response and insert data into an existing text field or textarea.

Users can put tons of information in a large textarea, so in these cases use the POST method rather than GET with the request object. For example, you can write the httpRequest( ) function as httpRequest("POST",url,true), and the request object's send( ) method will have the POST querystring as a parameter:

```
request.
send(val=Hello%20there%20and%20a%20lot%20of%20other%
20stuff);
```

HACK #13 Display Text Field or textarea Values Using Server Data

Have server information magically appear in text boxes without the web page refreshing.

You can have a server component interact with information that the user enters in a text box, without the jarring effect of the page reconstituting every time the user enters new information. A typical example is a spell checker or auto-complete field [Hack #78]. Using the request object as an intermediary, a server component can respond in real time to what the user types.

This hack displays an automatic server response, so that the response appears as if by magic in the text control, without anything else changing in the web page. The hack is an extension of "Submit Text Field or textarea Values to the Server Without a Browser Refresh" [Hack #12], which used the request object to submit textarea or text field values to a server component behind the scenes.

This hack takes the information the user has submitted and displays a character count and word count in the same field. You can accomplish the same thing with client-side JavaScript, of course, but just to prove that a server component is doing the work, the hack displays some information about the server in the textarea.

Figure 2-2 shows the web page after the user has entered some data into the text field.

Figure 2-3 shows the browser window after the user has entered data in both fields and then clicked Tab.

The following code is the HTML for the page. It imports a JavaScript file named *hacks_2_1.js*, which contains the code that does most of the work:

```
<!DOCTYPE html PUBLIC "-//W3C//DTD XHTML 1.0 Strict//EN"
        "http://www.w3.org/TR/2000/REC-xhtml1-20000126/DTD/xhtml1-strict.
dtd">
```

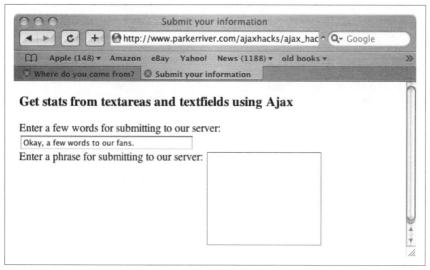

Figure 2-2. Enter data and elicit a response

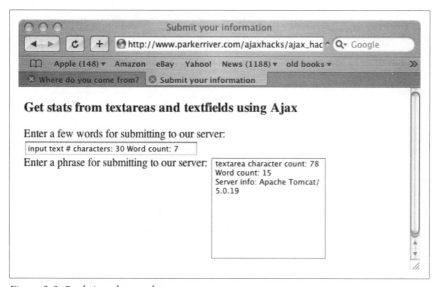

Figure 2-3. Real-time data updates

```
<html xmlns="http://www.w3.org/1999/xhtml" xml:lang="en" lang="en">
<head>
    <meta http-equiv="content-type" content="text/html; charset=utf-8" />
    <script type="text/javascript" src="js/hacks_2_1.js"></script>
    <link rel="stylesheet" type="text/css" href="/css/hacks.css" />
    <title>Submit your information</title>
</head>
<body>
```

```
<h3>Get stats from textareas and textfields using Ajax</h3>
<form action="javascript:void%200" >
<table border="0"><tr>
<td>Enter a few words for submitting to our server:
<input type="text" name="tfield" size="35"/></td></tr>
<tr><td valign="top">Enter a phrase for submitting to our server:
<textarea name="tarea" rows="20" cols="20">
</textarea></td>   </tr>
</table></form>
</body>
</html>
```

The last hack explained how the code submits the user's information without refreshing the web page. In other words, after the user has typed in some information and pressed Tab or clicked outside of the field, just the piece of data that user added to the text field or textarea is sent in an HTTP request to the server.

An onblur event handler calls the getInfo( ) function, passing in the text field or textarea object as a parameter.

The entire code for this behavior appears in "Submit Text Field or textarea Values to the Server Without a Browser Refresh" [Hack #12], so it's not reproduced in full here. However, I will show the code for the getInfo( ) and handleResponse( ) functions, which do the work of sending the server component the information it needs and then handling the server's response. First, let's take a look at the getInfo( ) function:

```
function getInfo(obj){
    if (obj == null ) { return; }
    formObj=obj;
    formObjTyp =obj.tagName;
    if(formObjTyp == "input" || formObjTyp == "INPUT"){
        formObjTyp = formObjTyp + " "+formObj.type;
    }
    formObjTyp = formObjTyp.toLowerCase( );
    var url = "http://www.parkerriver.com/s/webforms?objtype="+
            encodeURIComponent(formObjTyp)+"&val="+
            encodeURIComponent(obj.value);
    httpRequest("GET",url,true);
}
```

This function passes along to the server component the user's typed-in information as part of the val parameter. In addition, the obj parameter holds a reference to the text control in which the information was entered, such as a text field or textarea. The reference is specifically a DOM object, such as an HTMLInputElement or HTMLTextAreaElement.

You do not have to worry about the DOM object tree at this point (although it is interesting!). The HTML code for this hack refers to the particular text control using the this keyword in the onblur event handler. The getInfo( ) function can determine exactly what kind of text control the user is interacting with—a text field or a textarea—by accessing the object's tagName property. You can learn more about DOM object programming in David Flanagan's *JavaScript: The Definitive Guide* (O'Reilly).

Instant Server Messaging

The server program takes the information typed in by the user and sends back the associated number of characters and words. To make this response information palatable to our receiving code, the server returns its information in JavaScript Object Notation (JSON) format [Hack #7]. JSON is similar to XML in that it structures data to make it easier for software to digest and work with.

Your own program could simply return data in XML format or as a simple string. Using JSON for the return value is this programmer's personal preference. It is particularly useful if the server client is composed of JavaScript code.

This code shows a typical JSON server return value, if the user typed 55 words into a textarea:

```
{
Form_field_type: "textarea",
Text_length: "385",
Word_count: "55",
Server_info: "Apache Tomcat/5.0.19"
}
```

This code represents a JavaScript object with four different properties: Form_field_type, Text_length, Word_count, and Server_info. An explanation of how these properties are used is provided after the next code sample.

Now the hack takes this information and plugs it back into the textarea. This is the job of the handleResponse( ) function:

```
//event handler for XMLHttpRequest
function handleResponse( ){
    try{
        if(request.readyState == 4){
            if(request.status == 200){
                var resp = request.responseText;
                if(resp != null){
```

```
                              var func = new Function("return "+resp);
                              var objt = func( );
                              if(formObjTyp == "textarea"){
                                  if(formObj != null){
                                    formObj.value = objt.Form_field_type +
                                            " character count: "+objt.Text_length+
                                            "\nWord count: "+
                                            objt.Word_count+"\nServer info: "+
                                            objt.Server_info;
                                  }
                              } else if(formObjTyp == "input text"){
                                  if(formObj != null){
                                      formObj.value = objt.Form_field_type +
                                          " # characters: "+objt.Text_length+
                                          " Word count: "+objt.Word_count; }
                                  }
                              }
                          } else {
                              //request.status is 503
                              //if the application isn't available;
                              //500 if the application has a bug
                              alert(
                                  "A problem occurred with communicating "+
                                  "between the XMLHttpRequest object and "+
                                  "the server program.");
                          }
                      }//end outer if
                  } catch (err) {
                      alert(err.name);
                      alert("It does not appear that the server "+
                          "is available for this application. Please"+
                          " try again very soon. \nError: "+err.message);
                  }
              }
```

This code grabs the response as text. Since the text is already formatted in
JSON syntax (as an object literal in JavaScript), the code uses the special
technique described in "Receive Data in JSON Format" [Hack #7]. A Function
constructor returns the text as a JavaScript object. In this case, the variable
objt now refers to the server component's response in an object-centric way,
so you can access the server information with syntax such as objt.Server_
info.

The latter code piece accesses the Server_info property of the object referred
to by the variable objt:

```
var resp =  request.responseText;
var func = new Function("return "+resp);
//call the function and return the object to which
//the objt variable now points
var objt = func( );
```

The rest of the code goes about inserting this information back into the textarea using this syntax:

```
if(formObjTyp == "textarea"){
    if(formObj!= null){
        formObj.value = objt.Form_field_type +
                " character count: "+objt.Text_length+
                "\nWord count: "+
                objt.Word_count+"\nServer info: "+
                objt.Server_info;
    }
}
```

To see what the textarea looks like after the information is placed inside it, refer back to Figure 2-3.

You can access the textarea because a top-level JavaScript variable, formObj, refers to it. One of the keys to this code is setting the value of a textarea or text field with the "dot property-name" syntax common to JavaScript, as in formObj.value.

> The server program sends more information back to a textarea than it does to a text field, including line breaks (\n in JavaScript) because the textarea is a big box that can hold more text. You cannot include line breaks in a text field, for instance, because it holds only one line (even if that line can have numerous characters).

The code formats the value of the textarea by connecting strings to the properties of the object the server returned, as in " character count: "+objt. Text_length.

Although in a conventional web interface users expect textareas and text fields to be reserved for their own data entry, this hack demonstrates how to provide direct feedback related to what the user types into a particular field.

HACK #14 Submit Selection-List Values to the Server Without a Round Trip

Whisk the user's multiple list choices off to the server without delay.

Many web developers will see the advantage of sending a user's multiple choices in a radio button or select list directly to a server program using the request object, rather than requiring the user to click a button and send the entire form. This gives the application greater responsiveness and increases efficiency by sending discrete values rather than clumps of information.

This hack sends the user's choices of U.S. states to a server program when the keyboard focus is moved away from the select list. The select element looks like this in the HTML code that underlies the web page:

```
<select name="_state" multiple="multiple" size="4">
```

This is a selection list that allows the user to choose more than one item. When the keyboard focus moves from the select list (because the user presses the Tab key or clicks elsewhere on the page), the code defined by the element's onblur event handler executes. (This code is shown in an upcoming section.) The size=4 part indicates that four state names can be displayed at a time in the select list. Figure 2-4 shows the page loaded into the Safari browser.

Figure 2-4. Multiple choices for immediate delivery

A JavaScript file named *hacks_2_4.js* declares all the code this hack needs. Here is the HTML for the web page, which imports this file:

```
<!DOCTYPE html PUBLIC "-//W3C//DTD XHTML 1.0 Strict//EN"
        "http://www.w3.org/TR/2000/REC-xhtml1-20000126/DTD/xhtml1-strict.
dtd">
<html xmlns="http://www.w3.org/1999/xhtml" xml:lang="en" lang="en">
<head>
    <meta http-equiv="content-type" content="text/html; charset=utf-8" />
    <script type="text/javascript" src="js/hacks_2_4.js"></script>
    <link rel="stylesheet" type="text/css" href="/css/hacks.css" />
```

```
    <title>Alter select lists</title>
  </head>
  <body>
  <h3>Create or Alter a Select List</h3>
  <form action="javascript:void%200" >
      <table border="0">
          <tr><td>Choose one or more states: </td><td>
          <select name="_state" multiple="multiple" size="4">
              <option value="al">Alabama</option>
              <option value="ak">Alaska</option>
              <option value="az">Arizona</option>
              <option value="ar">Arkansas</option>
              <option value="ca">California</option>
              <option value="co">Colorado</option>
              <option value="ct">Connecticut</option>
              <option value="de">Delaware</option>
              <option value="dc">District of Columbia</option>
              <option value="fl">Florida</option>
              <option value="ga">Georgia</option>
              <option value="hi">Hawaii</option>
              <!-snipped...-->
          </select></td></tr>
          <tr><td><span id="select_info" class=
                  "message">The server reports that you have chosen the
                  following abbreviated states: </span>
          <tr><td>Choose your list content:</td>
          <td>European countries:
          <input type="radio" name="countryType" id="euro" value="euro" />
          South American countries:
          <input type="radio" name="countryType" id="southam" value="southam"
/>
          </td></tr>
          <tr><td><div id="newsel"></div></td></tr>
      </table></form>
  </body>
  </html>
```

A span element contains a message the user sees after making some choices
in the select list. This message is styled by a CSS rule in the file *hacks.css*.
We'll take a look at the message returned to the user momentarily, but first
let's examine the code that submits the user's choices to a server. The code
is a little complicated at first glance, but stay with it because what it accomplishes is really quite simple:

```
function getSelectInfo(selectObj){
    if (selectObj == null) { return; }
    formObj=selectObj;
    formObjTyp =formObj.tagName.toLowerCase();
    var optsArray = formObj.options;
    var selectedArray = new Array();
    var val = "";
    //store selected options in an Array
```

```
for(var i=0,j=0; i < optsArray.length; i++){
    if(optsArray[i].selected) {
        selectedArray[j]=optsArray[i].value;
        j++;
    }

}
//create a comma-separated list of each
//selected option value
for(var k = 0; k < selectedArray.length; k++){
    if(k !=selectedArray.length-1 ) { val +=selectedArray[k]+",";}
    else {val +=selectedArray[k]; }
}
var url = "http://www.parkerriver.com/s/webforms?objtype="+
        encodeURIComponent(formObjTyp)+"&val="+
encodeURIComponent(val);
httpRequest("GET",url,true);
}
```

The code takes all of the options associated with the select element and determines which of them the user has selected. These options represent the user's choice(s) of U.S. states. The code takes each selected option and stores it in a string, separated by commas (if there is more than one choice), as follows: ma,nh,vt.

This task would be easier if the browser stored the selected values in one convenient place, such as a value property of the select object, but this isn't the case! You have to grab all the options, determine which ones were selected, and store those somewhere, such as in a JavaScript array.

A select element contains option elements, as in:

```
<select name="_states">
<option value="vt">Vermont</option>
...
</select>
```

In the DOM, the select element is represented by a select object that has an options property, an array of option objects. You get the value of each option, which the user sees as words in a list (e.g., "Vermont") using the value property of an option object. Phew—fun to code, but it involves endless objects and properties!

The server component is expecting an objtype parameter, which in this case equals "select." We are also sending the string of comma-separated choices, pointed to by the val parameter (we could just as easily have used spaces, colons, or some other delimiter to separate each choice). Because we are using JavaScript's global function encodeURIComponent( ), each comma is encoded into %2C, since certain punctuation marks are not allowed in the character strings that are sent to server components.

> encodeURIComponent() is a global function that is designed to encode portions of a uniform resource indicator (URI), which is a fancy name for the addresses you enter into a browser's location field to download a web page. This function encodes punctuation characters that have special purposes in URIs, such as /, :, @, and ;, as well as space characters, into their hexadecimal equivalents. For example, a ; character is encoded into %3B. encodeURIComponent() does not encode ASCII numbers or letters. Use encodeURIComponent() to encode query strings or path information that your JavaScript code is handling.

Here is an example of a URL sent by the previous JavaScript:

```
http://www.parkerriver.com/s/webforms?objtype=select&val=ma%2Cvt%2Cny
```

This URL contains ma, vt, and ny as choices; after the val parameter is decoded, it will read ma,vt,ny.

Now What Happens?

The server grabs the selected values and redirects them back to the application, with some extra information. This is where the displayed message comes to the fore. It displays the user's current choices and some information about the server with which the application is connected. Figure 2-5 shows the web page after the user has made some choices and moved the keyboard focus from the select list.

The message changes dynamically without anything else being rebuilt or refreshed on the web page. It gives the user instant feedback while connected to a server, without any browser round trips. How does this work? Here is the JavaScript for the handleResponse() function, which deals with the server return value. I have highlighted only the code that converts the return value into the user message:

```
//event handler for XMLHttpRequest
function handleResponse(){
    try{
        if(request.readyState == 4){
            if(request.status == 200){
                if(formObjTyp.length > 0 && formObjTyp == "input"){
                //working with existing radio button
                    var resp = request.responseText;
                    //return value is an array
                    var func = new Function("return "+resp);
```

Figure 2-5. Instant feedback on list choices

```
            var objt = func();
            var sel = document.createElement("select");
            sel.setAttribute("name","countries");
            createOptions(sel,objt);
            var newsel = document.getElementById("newsel");
            reset(newsel);
            newsel.appendChild(sel);
        } else  if(formObjTyp.length > 0 && formObjTyp == "select"){
            var resp =  request.responseText;
            //return value is a JSON object literal
            var func = new Function("return "+resp);
            var objt = func();
            var fld = document.getElementById("select_info");
            if(fld != null){
                fld.innerHTML = "The server <strong>"+
                    objt.Server_info+
                    "</strong> reports that you have chosen"+
                    "<br /> the following "+
                    "abbreviated states: <strong>"+
                    objt.Selected_options+"</strong>";
            }
        }
    } else {
        //request.status is 503
        //if the application isn't available;
        //500 if the application has a bug
```

```
            alert(
                    "A problem occurred with communicating "+
                    "between the XMLHttpRequest object and the "+
                    "server program.");
        }
    }//end outer if
} catch (err) {
    alert("It does not appear that the server "+
        "is available for this application. Please"+
        " try again very soon. \nError: "+err.message);
    }
}
```

Hello Again, JSON

The server provides its answer in JSON format **[Hack #7]** as a string that can easily be converted by the client-side browser code into a JavaScript object. An example of a server return value, which some readers may recognize as an object literal, is:

```
{
Server_info: "Apache Tomcat/5.0.19",
Selected_options: "vt ny nh ma"
}
```

This code represents an object that has two properties, Server_info and Selected_options. To derive the property values from the object, you use the "dot" syntax, as in obj.Selected_options. If the obj variable is set to the prior code's object literal, the latter code line returns "vt ny nh ma". ("Receive Data in JSON Format" **[Hack #7]** describes the JavaScript code to use for sending and handling JSON syntax.)

A Dabble of Server-Side

For those interested in one method of sending JSON-formatted values back to Ajax, here is a Java method that is used for this hack. This method takes as parameters the property names and values in a string, and the character, such as a comma, that separates the property names from the values:

```
public static String getJsonFormat(String propValues, String delim) {
    if(propValues == null || propValues.length()==0) { return "";}

    StringBuffer structure = new StringBuffer("");
    structure.append("{\n");
    if (delim == null || delim.length() == 0) { delim = ",";}
    /* We're expecting comma-separated values such as prop1,val1,
    prop2,val2, etc. */
    StringTokenizer toke = new StringTokenizer(propValues,delim);
    int j = 0;
    int c =  toke.countTokens();
```

```
for(int i = 1; i <=c; i++) {
    j = i%2;
    if(j != 0) { structure.append(toke.nextToken( )).
        append(": ");    } //it's a property name
    else { structure.append("\"").append(toke.nextToken( )).
        append("\""); //it's a property value
        if(i != c){structure.append(",");}
        structure.append("\n");
    }
}
structure.append("}");
return structure.toString( );
}
```

If the Java servlet calls the method this way:

```
getJsonFormat("Server_info,Apache Tomcat,Selected_options,ca ma nh ny",",")
```

the method returns:

```
{
Server_info: "Apache Tomcat",
Selected_options: "ca ma nh ny"
}
```

The DOM API

This hack's next step is to store this return value in a variable, so the JavaScript can display its value to the user:

```
var func = new Function("return "+resp);
var objt = func( );
var fld = document.getElementById("select_info");
```

"Receive Data in JSON Format" [Hack #7] explains this use of the Function constructor to take advantage of the JSON format. Here, suffice it to say that the variable objt now contains the properties/values that interest us.

The variable fld represents the div element we reserved on the HTML page for containing this user message from the server. getElementById( ) is a DOM API method for getting a reference to a tag in HTML code, so the code can change its behavior or alter its appearance:

```
if(fld != null){
    fld.innerHTML = "The server <strong>"+objt.Server_info+
                    "</strong> reports that you have chosen"+
                    "<br /> the following "+
                    "abbreviated states: <strong>"+
                    objt.Selected_options+"</strong>";
}
```

Easily display the object's information using syntax such as objt.Selected_ options. As you saw in Figure 2-4, the states that the user has chosen and the name of the server software are displayed dynamically. The message changes automatically as the user makes different selections in the list. The information is derived from a server rather than just being generated by client-side JavaScript.

HACK #15 Dynamically Generate a New Selection List Using Server Data

Create a list of choices on a web page that automatically branches into a new selection list without the entire page being refreshed.

Sometimes a choice in a user interface naturally leads to a subsequent set of choices. An example is a support page for computer hardware, where one select list has a choice for hardware platform, such as Apple or HP, which generates (when the user makes a choice) a second list of related operating systems, and so on. Ajax can shine in these situations where the user interface can automatically be customized for the browser user, as well as where the content for the select list must come from a server.

You could set up this page using only dynamic HTML, with JavaScript creating the new select list. However, the choices for the new list would have to be hardcoded into the JavaScript. Ultimately, this content for new lists will change, creating an awkward situation in which developers have to constantly add persistent lists to an existing JavaScript file. Without being able to store these values in a sensible location such as a database or other persistent store, this application model becomes unwieldy.

This hack displays two radio buttons on a web page, offering users the choice of displaying either European countries or South American countries. Either choice results in the display of a new selection list with different content. Figure 2-6 shows the web page for the hack.

Here is the HTML code underlying the web page. I removed most of the long select list above the radio buttons because that code appears in the previous hack:

```
<!DOCTYPE html PUBLIC "-//W3C//DTD XHTML 1.0 Strict//EN"
      "http://www.w3.org/TR/2000/REC-xhtml1-20000126/DTD/xhtml1-strict.
dtd">
<html xmlns="http://www.w3.org/1999/xhtml" xml:lang="en" lang="en">
<head>
    <meta http-equiv="content-type" content="text/html; charset=utf-8" />
    <script type="text/javascript" src="js/hacks_2_4.js"></script>
    <link rel="stylesheet" type="text/css" href="/css/hacks.css" />
    <title>Alter select lists</title>
</head>
<body>
<h3>Create or Alter a Select List</h3>
```

Figure 2-6. Dynamically generate a list widget by selecting a radio button

```
<form action="javascript:void%200" >
    <table border="0">
        <tr><td>Choose one or more states: </td>
        <td><select name="_state" multiple="multiple" size="4">
            <option value="al">Alabama</option>
            <!--more options... -->
        </select></td></tr>
        <tr><td><span id="select_info" class="message">
        The server reports that you have chosen the following abbreviated
        states:
        </span>
        <tr><td>Choose your list content:</td><td>European countries:
        <input type=
        "radio" name="countryType" id="euro" value=
        "euro" /> South American countries:
        <input type="radio" name=
        "countryType" id="southam" value="southam" /></td></tr>
        <tr><td><div id="newsel"></div></td></tr>
    </table>
</form>
</body>
</html>
```

The purpose of this code is to create a new select list whenever the browser
user clicks on a radio button. With radio buttons on a web page, only one
can be selected at a time. If you select a certain button, the other one(s) are
automatically deselected.

Central to this hack is each radio button's onclick event handler. This is an attribute of an HTML element that points to a JavaScript function. The function's code executes each time the user clicks on a radio button. In other words, if a button is deselected and the user clicks it, the code calls the function named generateList( ).

The code appears in the file that the web page imports, *hacks_2_4.js*. Here is the code that controls the response to the user's radio-button clicks:

```
//input field's event handlers
window.onload=function( ){
    var eur = document.getElementById("euro");
    if(eur != null){
        eur.onclick=function( ){generateList(this);  };}
    var southa = document.getElementById("southam");
    if(southa != null){
        southa.onclick=function( ){generateList(this);  };}
}
```

Each onclick event handler points to a function that simply calls generateList( ). You will notice that the this keyword is used as a parameter. That holds a reference to each radio button that is clicked, so that the function's code can grab the button's value and send the value to a server component.

Presto, New Lists

The generateList( ) function is defined in a file named *hacks_2_4.js*. The HTML code for the web page imports this file using a script element. Here are the highlights of this file, with the emphasis on the functions used to generate a new list:

```
var formObj = null;
var formObjTyp = "";
var request=null;

function generateList(obj){
    if (obj == null ) { return; }
    if(obj.checked) {
        formObj=obj;
        formObjTyp =formObj.tagName.toLowerCase( );
        var url = "http://www.parkerriver.com/s/select1?countryType="+
                  encodeURIComponent(obj.value);
        httpRequest("GET",url,true);
    }
}

//event handler for XMLHttpRequest
function handleResponse( ){
    try{
```

```
            if(request.readyState == 4){
                if(request.status == 200){
                    if(formObjTyp.length > 0 && formObjTyp == "input") {
                        if (resp != null){
                            //return value is an array
                            var objt = eval(resp);
                            //create a new select element
                            var sel = document.createElement("select");
                            sel.setAttribute("name","countries");
                            //give the select element some options based
                            //on a list of countries from the server
                            createOptions(sel,objt);
                            //the div element within which the select appears
                            var newsel = document.getElementById("newsel");
                            reset(newsel);
                            newsel.appendChild(sel);
                        }
                    } else if(formObjTyp.length > 0 && formObjTyp == "select"){
                        //code edited out here for the sake of brevity...
                    }
                } else {
                    //request.status is 503 if the application isn't available;
                    //500 if the application has a bug
                    alert("A problem occurred with communicating between "+
                            "the XMLHttpRequest object and the server program.");
                }
            }//end outer if
        } catch (err) {
            alert("It does not appear that the server is available"+
                    " for this application. Please"+
                    " try again very soon. \nError: "+err.message);

        }
    }


function createOptions(sel,_options) {
    //_options is an array of strings that represent the values of
    //a select list, as in each option of the list.
    //sel is the select object
    if(_options == null || _options.length==0) { return;}
    var opt = null;
    for(var i = 0; i < _options.length; i++) {
        opt = document.createElement("option");
        opt.appendChild(document.createTextNode(_options[i]));
        sel.appendChild(opt);
    }
}
//remove any existing children from an Element object
function reset(elObject){
    if(elObject != null && elObject.hasChildNodes( )){
        for(var i = 0; i < elObject.childNodes.length; i++){
            elObject.removeChild(elObject.firstChild);
        }
```

```
        }
    }
    /* Initialize a request object; code omitted, see Hack #1 or #2. */
```

When the user clicks on a radio button, the control either indicates a selected state or, if it is already selected, or deselects the button. The onclick event handler does not differentiate between checked or unchecked radio buttons; it is designed simply to react when the button has been clicked. Just to make sure the radio button is selected (even though the button is designed to be selected based on a click event), the code first checks whether the object was in a checked state before it begins creating a new select list:

```
function generateList(obj){
    if (obj == null ) { return; }
    if(obj.checked) {
        formObj=obj;
        formObjTyp =formObj.tagName.toLowerCase( );
        var url = "http://www.parkerriver.com/s/selectl?countryType="+
                encodeURIComponent(obj.value);
        httpRequest("GET",url,true);
    }
}
```

Querying the Server

The code queries a server with the value of the checked radio button. Recall that the new select list contains choices (the words the user sees, such as "United Kingdom") that are stored on the server side. To determine which set of values to acquire from the server—the European or South American countries—you include in the request URL a parameter named countryType. The value for this parameter derives from the radio button's value attribute, as in:

```
<input type="radio" name="countryType" id="southam" value="southam" />
```

The code sends this information to the server using the request object and the httpRequest( ) function. "Use the Request Object to POST Data to the Server" [Hack #2] and "Submit Text Field or textarea Values to the Server Without a Browser Refresh" [Hack #12] (among others) describe this function, which wraps the initialization of the request object and the calling of its methods. The URL the request object uses to connect with the server might look like *http://www.parkerriver.com/s/selectl?countryType=euro*.

The code then receives the response and builds the new select list. It pulls the values out of the response using the familiar handleResponse( ) function, which shows up in most of the other hacks. Here are the key lines of JavaScript for this hack:

```
if(request.readyState == 4){
    if(request.status == 200){
```

```
if (resp != null){
//return value is a JSON array
var objt = eval(resp);
//create a new select element
var sel = document.createElement("select");
sel.setAttribute("name","countries");
//give the select element some options based
//on a list of countries from the server
createOptions(sel,objt);
//the div element within which the select appears
var newsel = document.getElementById("newsel");
reset(newsel);
newsel.appendChild(sel);
```

The server's return value looks like ["Spain","Germany","Austria"]. The code takes the string return value and converts it to an array with eval( ), as discussed in "Receive Data in JSON Format" [Hack #7]. The JavaScript then uses the DOM API to create a new select element. It's a good idea to give the newly generated HTML element a name and a value, in case your application calls for submitting these values to a server component:

```
var sel = document.createElement("select");
sel.setAttribute("name","countries");
```

Using the array of values returned by the server, the createOptions( ) function populates the select element with a new option element pointing at each array member. The end result is a new select element built from scratch that looks like this:

```
<select name="countries">
    <option>United Kingdom</option>
    ...
</select>
```

Here is the code for the createOptions( ) function:

```
function createOptions(sel,_options) {
    //_options is an array of strings that represent the values of
    //a select list, as in each option of the list.
    //sel is the select object
    if(_options == null || _options.length==0) { return;}
    var opt = null;
    for(var i = 0; i < _options.length; i++) {
        opt = document.createElement("option");
        opt.appendChild(document.createTextNode(_options[i]));
        sel.appendChild(opt);
    }
}
```

The _options variable contains all the country names. The code uses the DOM API to create each new option element, call the element's appendChild( ) method to add the country name to the option, and finally call the select element's appendChild( ) method to add the option to the select list.

The Final Step

We have to figure out which block-level element in the HTML will hold the new select element, rather than just throwing the select element somewhere within the body tag, willy-nilly. A div element with the id newsel serves this purpose:

```
<div id="newsel"></div>
```

The div element appears beneath the radio buttons on the page, but since it initially does not contain any visible HTML elements, the user will not be aware of it. The code uses another popular DOM method, getElementById( ), to get a reference to this div, and then appends the select element to it as a node:

```
var newsel = document.getElementById("newsel");
reset(newsel);
newsel.appendChild(sel);
```

To prevent users from continuously clicking the radio buttons and generating a million new lists, another method named reset( ) first checks the div for any existing child nodes, which would represent a previously created select element. The function deletes any existing nodes before the code adds a new select list inside the div:

```
function reset(elObject){
    if(elObject != null && elObject.hasChildNodes( )){
        for(var i = 0; i < elObject.childNodes.length; i++){
            elObject.removeChild(elObject.firstChild);
        }
    }
}
```

Figure 2-7 shows the web page after the user has clicked one of the radio buttons. The choice of South American countries has generated a new select list beginning with Brazil.

Extend an Existing Selection List

Give browser users the option to modify an existing list before making and submitting their choices.

Imagine that you have a list of U.S. states, as in the select element used in "Submit Selection-List Values to the Server Without a Round Trip" [Hack #14]. As part of the customer-registration process, you ask what state your customers live in (for sales-tax purposes, say). However, you want to be able

Figure 2-7. Choose a radio button to create a new list

register customers from other countries too, because your product can now be distributed overseas. You do not want to include every country on earth in the select list, though, both for geo-political reasons (countries frequently change, as in the case of the former Yugoslavia) and because the select list would be too big to fit nicely on the page. Thus, you want your users to be able to choose (when applicable) a continent, making a selection that adds a subset of select options to the page. Your application will pass the name of the selected continent to the server program and query the server for the specific countries associated with that continent.

To begin with, you'll provide a select list of continents. When the user makes a selection, the names of the countries within that continent are derived from the server and automatically added to an existing select list, without the page being refreshed. Figure 2-8 shows the web page for this hack, which is based on the previous hack containing the select list of U.S. states.

The user selects a continent in the top-level select list. This action triggers the onclick event for the select element. Here is the HTML code for the page:

```
<!DOCTYPE html PUBLIC "-//W3C//DTD XHTML 1.0 Strict//EN"
        "http://www.w3.org/TR/2000/REC-xhtml1-20000126/DTD/xhtml1-strict.
dtd">
```

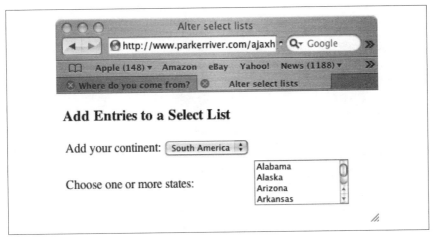

Figure 2-8. Add options to a list

```html
<html xmlns="http://www.w3.org/1999/xhtml" xml:lang="en" lang="en">
<head>
    <meta http-equiv="content-type" content="text/html; charset=utf-8" />
    <script type="text/javascript" src="js/hacks2_6.js"></script>
    <link rel="stylesheet" type="text/css" href="/css/hacks.css" />
    <title>Alter select lists</title>
</head>
<body>
<h3>Add Entries to a Select List</h3>
<form action="javascript:void%200">
    <table border="0">
        <tr><td>Add your country: <select id="cts" name="_continents">
            <option value="southam">South America</option>
            <option value="euro">Europe</option>
        </select></td></tr><tr><td>Choose one or more states: </td>
        <td> <select id="sts" name="_state" multiple="multiple" size="4">
            <option value="al">Alabama</option>
            <option value="ak">Alaska</option>
            <option value="az">Arizona</option>
            <option value="ar">Arkansas</option>
            <option value="ca">California</option>
            <option value="co">Colorado</option>
            <option value="ct">Connecticut</option>
            <option value="de">Delaware</option>
            <option value="dc">District of Columbia</option>
            <option value="fl">Florida</option>
            <option value="ga">Georgia</option>
            <option value="hi">Hawaii</option>
            <!--snipped here...-->
        </select></td></tr>

    </table>
</form>
```

```
</body>
</html>
```

All of the JavaScript appears in the file *hacks2_6.js*. Here are the contents of
this file (omitting the creation and initialization of the request object, which
the first hack in this chapter and several other hacks show):

```javascript
var origOptions = null;
var request=null;
/* Set up the onclick event handler for the "countries"
select list */
window.onload=function( ){
    var sel = document.getElementById("cts");
    var sel2 = document.getElementById("sts");
    if(sel != null){
        sel.onclick=function( ){
            addCountries(this)};
    }
    origOptions = new Array( );
    //save the original select list of states so that
    //it can be reconstructed with just the original states
    //and the newly added countries
    for(var i = 0; i < sel2.options.length; i++){
        origOptions[i]=sel2.options[i];
    }
}

function addCountries(obj){
    if (obj == null ) { return; }
    var url = "";
    var optsArray = obj.options;
    var val = "";
    for(var i=0; i < optsArray.length; i++){
        if(optsArray[i].selected) {
            val=optsArray[i].value; break;
        }

    }
    url = "http://www.parkerriver.com/s/select1?countryType="+
            encodeURIComponent(val);
    httpRequest("GET",url,true);

}

//event handler for XMLHttpRequest
function handleResponse( ){
    try{
        if(request.readyState == 4){
            if(request.status == 200){
                var resp =  request.responseText;
                if(resp != null){
                    //return value is an array
                    var objt = eval(resp);
```

```
                    addToSelect(objt);
                }
            } else {
                //request.status is 503 if the application isn't available;
                //500 if the application has a bug
                alert(
                        "A problem occurred with communicating between"+
                        " the XMLHttpRequest object and the server program.
");
            }
        }//end outer if
    } catch (err) {
        alert("It does not appear that the server "+
                "is available for this application. Please"+
                " try again very soon. \nError: "+err.message);

    }
}
/* Take an array of string values (obj) and add an option
for each of the values to a select list */
function addToSelect(obj){
    //contains the U.S. states
    var _select = document.getElementById("sts");
    var el;
    //first remove all options, because the select could include
    //newly added countries from previous clicks
    while(_select.hasChildNodes( )){
        for(var i = 0; i < _select.childNodes.length; i++){
            _select.removeChild(_select.firstChild);
        }
    }
    //now add just the original options: 52 states
    for(var h=0; h < origOptions.length;h++) {
        _select.appendChild(origOptions[h]);
    }
    //obj is an array of new option values
    for(var i=0; i < obj.length;i++) {
        el = document.createElement("option");
        el.appendChild(document.createTextNode(obj[i]));
        _select.insertBefore(el,_select.firstChild);
    }
}

    /* Create and initialize a request object; see Hack #1 or #2. */
```

When the browser first loads the web page, the code defines an onclick event handler for the select list containing the U.S. states. This event is triggered whenever users click on the select widget, whether or not they change the value in the list. The event handler calls a function named addCountries( ), passing in as a parameter a reference to the select object that was clicked:

```
window.onload=function( ){
    var sel = document.getElementById("cts");
```

```
    var sel2 = document.getElementById("sts");
    if(sel != null){
        sel.onclick=function( ){
                addCountries(this)};
    }
    origOptions = new Array( );
    //save the original select list of states so that
    //it can be reconstructed with just the original states
    //and the newly added countries
    for(var i = 0; i < sel2.options.length; i++){
        origOptions[i]=sel2.options[i];
    }
}
```

The code also saves the original contents of the U.S. states list in an `Array` object. Otherwise, as the user clicked in the upper select list, the same countries could be added to the second select list over and over again. Because the `origOptions` `Array` variable caches the original list, each time the user clicks the top-level select list, the bottom select list is rebuilt with the new countries added in front of the original list of states.

Next up is the `addCountries( )` function. You don't need to show this function again, because what it accomplishes is fairly simple. The function cycles through the `options` in the continents select list, and if an `option` is checked (i.e., is the selected `option`), its value is submitted to a Java servlet. The servlet program returns an `array` of countries associated with the continent, and the code adds those countries to the other select list.

> My apologies to all those other global citizens who are not represented by these continent choices. For the sake of brevity, I stopped at Europe and South America. A "real-world" (pun intended!) application would represent all of the world's continents, except perhaps Antarctica.

Figure 2-9 shows the web page after the user has chosen South America.

New Select List or Mirage?

The code receives the return value in as a string that can be converted to a JavaScript array. The return value takes the form of `["Brazil", "Ecuador",etc.]`. It is a `string` that is evaluated as a JavaScript `array` using the `eval( )` function. In the next step, as if by magic, the new countries appear at the top of the second select list. Here is the responsible `addToSelect( )` function:

```
function addToSelect(obj){
    //contains the U.S. states
    var _select = document.getElementById("sts");
```

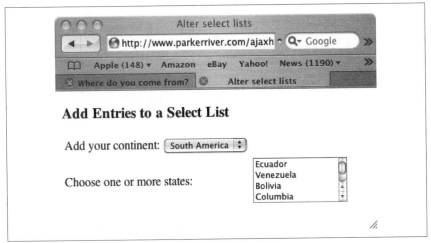

Figure 2-9. Add countries to the select list without a round trip

```
var el;
//first remove all options, because the select could include
//newly added countries from previous clicks
while(_select.hasChildNodes()){
    for(var i = 0; i < _select.childNodes.length; i++){
        _select.removeChild(_select.firstChild);
    }
}
//now add just the original options: 52 states
for(var h=0; h < origOptions.length;h++) {
    _select.appendChild(origOptions[h]);
}
//obj is an array of new option values
for(var i=0; i < obj.length;i++) {
    el = document.createElement("option");
    el.appendChild(document.createTextNode(obj[i]));
    _select.insertBefore(el,_select.firstChild);
}
}
```

This function involves basic DOM API programming, representing a select
list as a parent node of several option-related child nodes. First, the code
clears the select list and repopulates it with the original states. This is a rule
for the application; the user can add new countries on top of the original
list, but the countries won't pile up in the list repetitively. The code then creates a new option element for each member of the array derived from the
server, which is a country name (such as "Brazil"). Finally, the code uses the
Node.insertBefore( ) method to insert each new option before the first
option in the select list.

The _select.firstChild node keeps changing in the for loop. For example, if Alabama is at the top of the list, _select. firstChild returns the option node containing the "Alabama" value. The loop then inserts "Brazil" before "Alabama," and the option representing Brazil becomes the firstChild node.

Hacking the Hack

Naturally, the next step in this hack is to allow the user to dynamically submit the new country name from the second select element. "Submit Selection-List Values to the Server Without a Round Trip" [Hack #14] shows you how to add this behavior to a select list.

HACK #17 Submit Checkbox Values to the Server Without a Round Trip

Generate immediate interaction with a server program when the browser user clicks a checkbox.

Checkboxes are those little squares or buttons that allow users to make choices among multiple options. The conventional setup is for users to check one or more checkboxes as part of a form that they have to submit later. But what if you want your application to submit only the checkbox values, rather than the whole form, and have that submission take place when the user clicks the checkbox and not at some indeterminate time in the future?

This hack represents a poll in which users vote for their favorite team and individual sports. When the browser user selects any of the checkboxes, this action triggers an event that submits this value to a server program and then displays the poll results. Figure 2-10 shows what the page looks like in a browser.

The server program has a database that captures the poll results; the program updates and then returns those results. This hack uses the XMLHttpRequest object to send the sport choices and handle the server's response, and it uses DOM programming and CSS to display the poll results. Here is the HTML code for the page:

```
<!DOCTYPE html PUBLIC "-//W3C//DTD XHTML 1.0 Strict//EN"
        "http://www.w3.org/TR/2000/REC-xhtml1-20000126/DTD/xhtml1-strict.
dtd">
<html xmlns="http://www.w3.org/1999/xhtml" xml:lang="en" lang="en">
<head>
    <meta http-equiv="content-type" content="text/html; charset=utf-8" />
    <script type="text/javascript" src="js/hacks2_5.js"></script>
```

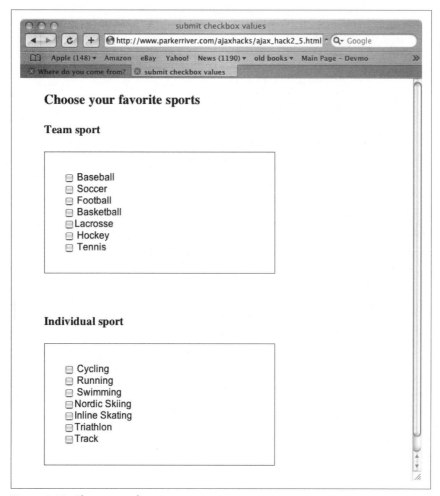

Figure 2-10. Choose your favorite sports

```
<link rel="stylesheet" type="text/css" href="/css/hacks2_5.css" />
  <title>submit checkbox values</title>
</head>
<body>
<h3>Choose your favorite sports</h3>
<h4>Team sport</h4>
<form id="team" action="javascript:void%200" method="get">
<div id="team_d" class="team">
<input type="checkbox" name="team_sports" id=
"baseball" value="baseball" /> Baseball <br />
<input type="checkbox" name="team_sports" id=
"soccer" value="soccer"  /> Soccer  <br />
<input type="checkbox" name="team_sports" id=
"football" value="football"  /> Football  <br />
```

```
<input type="checkbox" name="team_sports" id=
"basketball" value="basketball" /> Basketball  <br />
<input type="checkbox" name="team_sports" id=
"lacrosse" value="lacrosse" />Lacrosse  <br />
<input type="checkbox" name="team_sports" id=
"hockey" value="hockey" /> Hockey  <br />
<input type="checkbox" name="team_sports" id=
"tennis" value="tennis" /> Tennis  <br />
</div>
</form>
<div id="team_poll" class="poll">
    <span id="t_title" class="p_title"></span>
    <span id="t_results" class="p_results"></span></div>
<h4>Individual sport</h4>
<form  id="ind" action="javascript:void%200" method="get">
<div id="ind_d" class="ind">
<input type="checkbox" name="individual_sports" id=
"cycling" value="cycling" /> Cycling  <br />
<input type="checkbox" name="individual_sports" id=
"running" value="running"  /> Running  <br />
<input type="checkbox" name="individual_sports" id=
"swimming" value="swimming"  /> Swimming <br />
<input type="checkbox" name="individual_sports" id=
"nordic_skiing" value="nordic_skiing"  />Nordic Skiing  <br />
<input type="checkbox" name="individual_sports" id=
"inline_skating" value="inline_skating"  />Inline Skating <br />
<input type="checkbox" name="individual_sports" id=
"triathlon" value="triathlon"  />Triathlon <br />
<input type="checkbox" name="individual_sports" id=
"track" value="track"  />Track <br />
</div>
</form>
<div id="individual_poll" class="poll">
    <span id="i_title" class="p_title"></span>
    <span id="i_results" class="p_results"></span></div>
</body>
</html>
```

This page first imports the JavaScript code that performs all of the application's work from a file named *hacks2_5.js*. This HTML also imports a stylesheet (*hacks2_5.css*) to control the page's appearance and makes the poll results invisible until the user is ready to see them.

The HTML page includes two div elements, each containing a set of checkbox elements that specify the various team and individual sports. Here is the JavaScript code underlying this hack:

```
var sportTyp = "";
var request=null;

window.onload=function( ){
    var allInputs = document.getElementsByTagName("input");
```

```
if(allInputs != null){
    for(var i = 0; i < allInputs.length;i++) {
        if(allInputs[i].type == "checkbox"){
            allInputs[i].onchange=function( ){
                sendSportsInfo(this)};
        }
    }
}
}

function sendSportsInfo(obj){
    if (obj == null ) { return; }
    var url = "";
    var nme = "";
    if(obj.checked) {
        nme = obj.name;
        var sub = nme.substring(0,nme.indexOf("_"));
        sportTyp=sub;
        url = "http://www.parkerriver.com/s/fav_sports?sportType="+nme+
            "&choices="+obj.value;
        httpRequest("GET",url,true);
    }
}

//event handler for XMLHttpRequest
function handleResponse( ){
    try{
        if(request.readyState == 4){
            if(request.status == 200){
                var resp =  request.responseText;
                if(resp != null){
                    //return value is a JSON object
                    var func = new Function("return "+resp);
                    displayPollResults(func( ));
                }
            } else {
                //request.status is 503
                //if the application isn't available;
                //500 if the application has a bug
                alert(
                    "A problem occurred with communicating between"+
                    " the XMLHttpRequest object and the server program.
");
            }
        }//end outer if
    } catch (err) {
        alert("It does not appear that the server "+
            "is available for this application. Please"+
            " try again very soon. \nError: "+err.message);

    }
}
```

```
function displayPollResults(obj){
    var div = document.getElementById(sportTyp+"_poll");
    var spans = div.getElementsByTagName("span");
    for(var i = 0; i < spans.length; i++){
        if(spans[i].id.indexOf("title") != -1){
            spans[i].innerHTML = "<strong>Here are the latest poll "+
                        "results for "+sportTyp+
                        " sports</strong>"
        } else {
            //use the object and its properties
            var str ="<br />";
            for(var prop in obj) { str += prop + " : "+obj[prop]+"<br />";}
            spans[i].innerHTML = str;
        }
    }
    div.style.visibility="visible";
}
```

I have omitted the code for creating and initializing the
request object, such as the httpRequest( ) function, since so
many of the other hacks have already included this code. See
"Detect Browser Compatibility with the Request Object"
[Hack #1] or "Use Your Own Library for XMLHttpRequest"
[Hack #3] if you need another look!

The first task of this code is to assign a function to execute when the checkbox's state changes (from unchecked to checked). This is the responsibility of
the window.onload event handler, which the browser calls after the page has
been completely loaded:

```
window.onload=function( ){
    var allInputs = document.getElementsByTagName("input");
    if(allInputs != null){
        for(var i = 0; i < allInputs.length;i++) {
            if(allInputs[i].type == "checkbox"){
                allInputs[i].onchange=function( ){
                    sendSportsInfo(this)};
            }
        }
    }
}
```

The code first stores an Array of all the page's input elements in an
allInputs variable. If the input is of a checkbox type, as in <input
type="checkbox" .../>, its onchange property refers to a function that calls
sendSportsInfo( ). The code sets all the checkbox's onchange event handlers
at once; it will not affect any other input elements a page designer adds to
the page later.

Using this as a parameter to sendSportsInfo( ) is a handy mechanism for passing a reference to the exact input element whose state has changed.

Vote Early and Often

Let's look at the sendSportsInfo( ) function more closely. This function constructs a URL or web address to send the user's sports choices to a server program:

```
function sendSportsInfo(obj){
    if (obj == null ) { return; }
    var url = "";
    var nme = "";
    if(obj.checked) {
        formObj=obj;
        nme = obj.name;
        var sub = nme.substring(0,nme.indexOf("_"));
        sportTyp=sub;
        url = "http://www.parkerriver.com/s/fav_sports?sportType="+nme+
            "&choices="+obj.value;
        httpRequest("GET",url,true);
    }
}
```

Since we used the this keyword as a parameter to sendSportsInfo( ), the obj variable refers to an HTML input element. We are only going to hit the server if the input checkbox is selected, so the code checks for that state. The name of each input element in the form is set in the HTML to team_ sports or individual_sports, so the code captures the name and the name substring preceding the "_" character (we need that for the code that displays the poll results).

> The code obj.name accesses the name property of an HTMLInputElement, which is part of the DOM API. This property refers to the name in the HTML element code, as in <input name="myname".../>.

The URL requires the sport type and the value of the checkbox. A typical URL example looks like *http://www.parkerriver.com/s/fav_sports?sportType= individual_sports&choices=soccer*. The httpRequest( ) method uses the request object to query the server with these values.

Poll Vault

The server returns an HTTP response representing the latest poll results, after it stores the user's vote. The code has designated the handleResponse( )

function for dealing with the response and calling another function to display the results:

```
if(request.readyState == 4){
    if(request.status == 200){
        var resp = request.responseText;
        if(resp != null){
            //return value is a JSON object
            var func = new Function("return "+resp);
            displayPollResults(func());
        }
    }
}
```

The server returns the result not as XML but in JSON format, a form of plain text that can easily be converted by JavaScript to an object. This is a useful way of enclosing the results. A typical server return value looks like:

```
{
nordic_skiing: "0",
inline_skating: "0",
cycling: "2",
track: "2",
swimming: "0",
triathlon: "0",
running: "3"
}
```

The code uses the technique described in "Receive Data in JSON Format" [Hack #7] to evaluate this text as a JavaScript object. The code then calls displayPollResults(), which, as you've probably figured out, shows the results in the browser. Figure 2-11 shows what the results look like in Safari.

The displayPollResults() function uses the DOM to generate a colorful display of the results in the browser:

```
function displayPollResults(obj){
    var div = document.getElementById(sportTyp+"_poll");
    var spans = div.getElementsByTagName("span");
    for(var i = 0; i < spans.length; i++){
        if(spans[i].id.indexOf("title") != -1){
            spans[i].
            innerHTML = "<strong>Here are the latest "+
            "poll results for "+sportTyp+" sports</strong>"
        } else {
            //use the object and its properties
            var str ="<br />";
            for(var prop in obj) { str += prop + " : "+
                    obj[prop]+"<br />";}
            spans[i].innerHTML = str;
        }
    }
    div.style.visibility="visible";
}
```

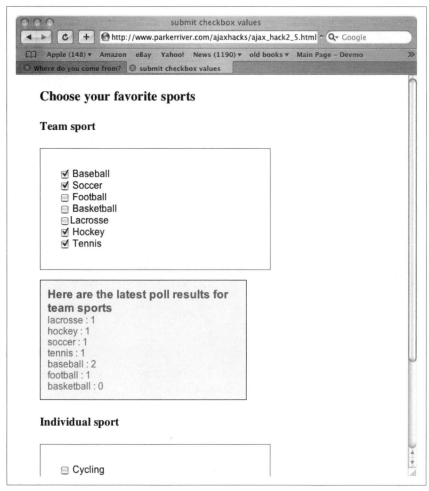

Figure 2-11. Which sports are favored?

The poll results are displayed inside div elements, which have ids of team_
poll or individual_poll. Each div contains two span elements. The span elements are responsible for the result titles and the actual data.

At this point, it is helpful to look at the CSS file that specifies various rules
for the appearance of our poll results. The divs and their contents are initially hidden (with the visibility CSS property), until the user clicks a
checkbox:

```
.p_title {font-size: 1.2em; color: teal }
h3 { margin-left: 5%; font-size: 1.4em; }
h4 { margin-left: 5%; font-size: 1.2em; }
div.poll { margin-left: 5%; visibility: hidden; border: thin solid black;
```

```
padding: 2%; font-family: Arial, serif;
color: gray; background-color: yellow}

div.team { margin-left: 5%; border: thin solid green; padding: 5%;
    font-family: Arial, serif}

div.ind { margin-left: 5%; border: thin solid green; padding: 5%;
    font-family: Arial, serif }

div { max-width: 50% }
```

One of the cool aspects of DOM and Ajax mechanisms is that CSS properties are programmable too. When the page view is ready to show the poll results, the visibility property of the divs that hold these results is set to visible. This is accomplished with the code div.style.visibility = "visible".

In the displayPollResults( ) function, the code sets the innerHTML property for the span elements responsible for displaying a title about the poll results. In addition, the poll results derived from the server are stored in a string and displayed in this manner:

```
var str ="<br />";
for(var prop in obj) { str += prop + " : "+
    obj[prop]+"<br />";}
    spans[i].innerHTML = str;
```

The obj variable is a JavaScript object. The for(property in object) expression then generates a string that looks like this:

```
<br />baseball : 2<br />soccer : 3...
```

If you keep clicking on checkboxes, you can watch the votes increment without anything else changing in the browser. This is a useful design for applications that collect discrete feedback from users and instantaneously display the results.

HACK #18   Dynamically Generate a New Checkbox Group with Server Data

Let a web page's checkbox content evolve from a user's interaction with an application.

Most web forms are static, meaning the text labels and entry widgets (e.g., textareas, checkboxes, and radio buttons) are hardcoded into the HTML. Lots of applications, however, can benefit from the ability to whip together form elements on the fly, based on the user-interface widgets the user is clicking. The content for the forms, if necessary, can even be derived from a server, such as questions for various types of quizzes and polls.

"Dynamically Generate a New Selection List Using Server Data" [Hack #15] showed how to do this with a select list widget, so why don't we auto-generate a bunch of checkboxes?

This hack gives users a choice of "Team Sports" or "Individual Sports" in two radio buttons and then, when they click either button, grabs the sports categories from a server component and creates a new group of checkboxes.

Choose Your Activity

Figure 2-12 shows our barebones web page to begin with, before the DOM magic starts.

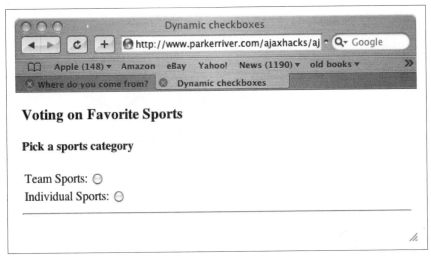

Figure 2-12. Let the web form evolve

What follows is the HTML for the form. The dynamic behavior for this page is all contained in the JavaScript file *hacks2_7.js*. The two radio buttons that the users can click to get things going are represented by the two input elements, and the newly generated checkboxes appear within the div element with the id checks:

```
<!DOCTYPE html PUBLIC "-//W3C//DTD XHTML 1.0 Strict//EN"
        "http://www.w3.org/TR/2000/REC-xhtml1-20000126/DTD/xhtml1-strict.
dtd">
<html xmlns="http://www.w3.org/1999/xhtml" xml:lang="en" lang="en">
<head>
    <meta http-equiv="content-type" content="text/html; charset=utf-8" />
    <script type="text/javascript" src="js/hacks2_7.js"></script>
    <title>Dynamic checkboxes</title>
</head>
<body>
```

```
<h3>Voting on Favorite Sports</h3>
<h4>Pick a sports category</h4>
<form action="javascript:void%200">
    <table border="0">
        <tr><td>
        Team Sports:
        <input type="radio" name="_sports" value="team" />
        </td></tr>
        <tr><td>  Individual Sports:
        <input type="radio" name="_sports" value="individual" />
        </td></tr>
    </table>
    <hr />
    <div id="checks"></div>
</form>
</body>
</html>
```

When the user clicks a checkbox, the page instantly displays either of two different sets of new checkboxes, representing either individual sports or team sports. The actual lists of sports that make up the checkboxes are arrays of strings that the server returns. They obviously could be hard-coded into the JavaScript to prevent a network hit, but the approach discussed in this hack is useful if the checkbox widgets represent values that change frequently and/or must be derived from persistent storage on the server (think product information, or complex multiple-choice questions in a questionnaire).

Figure 2-13 shows the web page after the user has clicked a radio button. This action submits only the value associated with the radio button that the user clicked, not the entire form.

Okay, Where's the Code?

The JavaScript contained in the file *hacks2_7.js* is reproduced below. I've omitted the code that creates and initializes the request object, which you can review in "Detect Browser Compatibility with the Request Object" [Hack #1] and several other earlier hacks. The first thing you may notice in the code is that it assigns a function to handle the radio buttons' onclick event handlers. The user triggers these events by clicking either radio button.

> An *event handler* such as onclick or onchange is an attribute of an HTML element that can be assigned to the code that is executed whenever the user clicks that element on the page, for example.

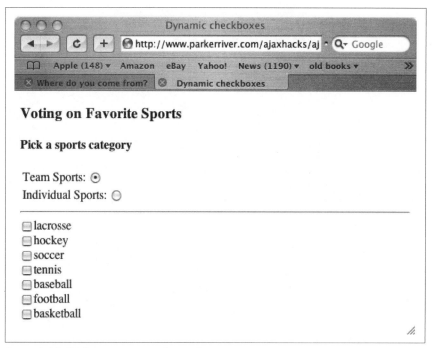

Figure 2-13. Widgets spawning other widgets

This assignment begins in the window's onload event handler. This event takes place when the browser has finished loading all the elements in the HTML page:

```
var sportType="";
var request=null;
window.onload=function( ){
    var rads = document.getElementsByTagName("input");
    if(rads != null) {
        for(var i = 0; i < rads.length; i++) {
            if(rads[i].type=="radio"){ rads[i].onclick=function( ){
                getSports(this)};}
        
        }
    }
}

function getSports(obj){
    if (obj == null ) { return; }
    var url = "";
    var val = "";
    if(obj.checked) {
        val=obj.value;
        sportType=val;
        url = "http://www.parkerriver.com/s/fav_sports"+
```

```
                   "?sportType="+encodeURIComponent(val)+"&col=y";
        httpRequest("GET",url,true);
    }
}

//event handler for XMLHttpRequest
function handleResponse( ){
    try{
        if(request.readyState == 4){
            if(request.status == 200){
                var resp =  request.responseText;
                if(resp != null){
                    //return value is an array
                    var objt = eval(resp);
                    createChecks(objt);
                }
            } else {
                //request.status is 503
                //if the application isn't available;
                //500 if the application has a bug
                alert(
                    "A problem occurred with communicating between"+
                    " the XMLHttpRequest object and the server program.");
            }
        }//end outer if
    } catch (err)    {
        alert("It does not appear that the server "+
            "is available for this application. Please"+
            " try again very soon. \nError: "+err.message);

    }
}

function createChecks(obj){
    var _div = document.getElementById("checks");
    var el;
    //first remove all existing checkboxes
    while(_div.hasChildNodes( )){
        for(var i = 0; i < _div.childNodes.length; i++){
            _div.removeChild(_div.firstChild);
        }
    }
    //obj is an array of new sports names
    for(var i=0; i < obj.length;i++) {
        el = document.createElement("input");
        el.setAttribute("type","checkbox");
        el.setAttribute("name",sportType);
        el.setAttribute("value",obj[i]);
        _div.appendChild(el);
        _div.appendChild(document.createTextNode(obj[i]));
        _div.appendChild(document.createElement("br"));
    }
}
```

```
/* httpRequest( ) and related code omitted for the sake of brevity;
see Hack #1 or #2. */
```

The first stage in generating the checkboxes is to send the request that fetches the values for each widget. When the user clicks a radio button, the code calls getSports( ). This function formats a URL based on the value it receives from the checkbox, then sends a request to a server component for a list of related sports.

Array Return Value

The response comes back from the server in a string formatted as a JavaScript array. A response might look like:

```
["football","soccer","tennis", etc.]
```

You get the response from the request object's responseText property and then convert the response to a JavaScript array using the eval( ) global function. Phew, that was a mouthful!

> Make sure that production applications handling return values with eval( ) protect against any cross-site scripting (XSS) attacks. See the following URL: *http://en.wikipedia.org/wiki/Cross-site_scripting.*

Once the code has this array of values from the server, it passes the array along to createChecks( ). This function uses the DOM API to create the checkboxes. It creates one checkbox for each value in the array (a checkbox for tennis, another for soccer, and so on). Here is the code for this function:

```
function createChecks(obj){
    var _div = document.getElementById("checks");
    var el;
    //first remove all existing checkboxes
    while(_div.hasChildNodes( )){
        for(var i = 0; i < _div.childNodes.length; i++){
            _div.removeChild(_div.firstChild);
        }
    }
    //obj is an array of new sports names
    for(var i=0; i < obj.length;i++) {
        el = document.createElement("input");
        el.setAttribute("type","checkbox");
        el.setAttribute("name",sportType);
        el.setAttribute("value",obj[i]);
        _div.appendChild(el);
        _div.appendChild(document.createTextNode(obj[i]));
        _div.appendChild(document.createElement("br"));
    }
}
```

The function gets a reference to the div element on the HTML page that will enclose the checkboxes. The code then removes any existing checkboxes, because if it didn't, the user could keep clicking the radio buttons and generate several duplicate checkboxes appended on the end of the web page (an outcome you want to avoid). Finally, the code creates a new input element for each sport, so that each of these widgets looks like:

```
<input type="checkbox" name=
"team_sports" value="baseball" /> baseball<br />
```

As soon as this function finishes executing, the checkboxes appear on the web page without any visible refresh. Like magic!

Hacking the Hack

Naturally, you want the user to select one or more of these generated checkboxes for some purpose. Maybe to generate another subset of widgets or checkboxes? Or to send the values from the new checkboxes, when the user clicks them, to a server component? You can adapt the code from "Submit Checkbox Values to the Server Without a Round Trip" [Hack #17] to accomplish the latter task, as well as create onclick event handlers for the new checkboxes (as in this hack) to give them some behavior.

HACK #19 Populate an Existing Checkbox Group from the Server
Dynamically add widgets to an existing group of checkboxes.

This hack deals with another type of adaptive web form, where a group of widgets can change based on the preferences of the user that accesses the web page. In "Submit Checkbox Values to the Server Without a Round Trip" [Hack #17], the code submitted a clicked checkbox value right away to a server program. This hack allows users to add new choices to the same bunch of checkboxes before they choose among those widgets. The web page has a select list including the choices Team or Individual. It shows two groups of checkboxes representing team sports and individual sports. Choosing either Team or Individual from the first pop-up menu or select list expands the existing checkboxes for the selected group by getting new content from a server. Choosing one value from the second pop-up menu restores the original checkboxes for either the Team or Individual list.

Figure 2-14 shows the web page before the user makes a choice.

Figure 2-15 depicts the same page after the user chooses Team from the pop-up menu at the top of the page, thus expanding the choices of team sports.

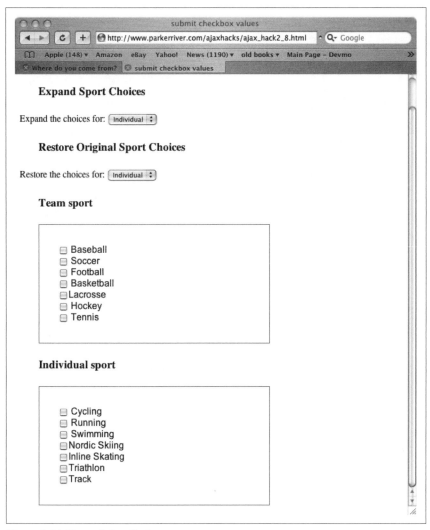

Figure 2-14. Expand the offerings

How Does It Work?

We are assuming that the content for the new checkboxes must come from the server, because it changes often and/or derives from the organization's database. Otherwise, an application like this can just include a JavaScript array of new content and never touch the server program. When the user makes a choice from the first pop-up menu or select list, this action sends the choice of Team or Individual to a server program. The code uses the request object to connect with the server the Ajax way.

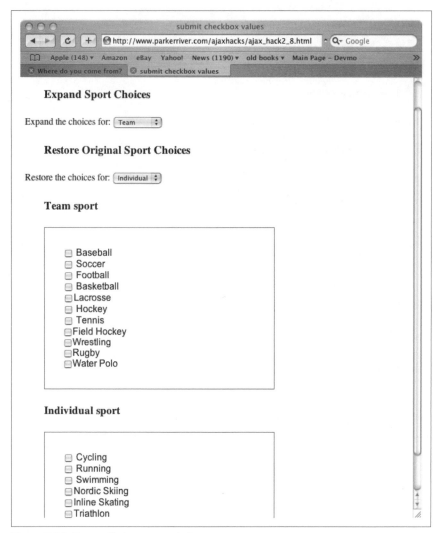

Figure 2-15. Team offerings expanded

The server replies with an `array` of titles for new checkboxes. Flipping the choices in the `select` list launches an `onclick` event handler in the JavaScript code, which the upcoming code sample shows.

I won't take up space with the HTML code, because the page is almost exactly the same as the one in "Submit Checkbox Values to the Server Without a Round Trip" [Hack #17]. The page uses a `script` tag to import all its Ajax-related JavaScript in a file named *hacks2_8.js*. You can read through the code comments right now to get a feel for what the code does.

Generally, a single-line JavaScript comment begins with //
while a multiline comment is bracketed by /* */. You can,
of course, have lots of consecutive //-style comments if you
prefer to comment that way.

Here is the relevant JavaScript code:

```javascript
var sportTyp = "";
var checksArray = null;
var request=null;

window.onload=function( ){
    //the 'expanding checkboxes' select pop-up
    var sel = document.getElementById("expand");
    //bind onclick event handler to a function
    if(sel != null){
        sel.onclick=function( ){
                getMoreChoices(this)};
    }
    //the 'restoring checkboxes' select pop-up
    var selr = document.getElementById("restore");
    //bind onclick event handler to the function
    if(selr != null){
        selr.onclick=function( ){
                restore(this)};
    }
    //Place all existing checkbox elements in two arrays
    //for restoring the original checkbox lists
    checksArray = new Object( );
    checksArray.team = new Array( );
    checksArray.individual = new Array( );
    var ckArr = document.getElementsByTagName("input");
    populateArray(ckArr,"team");
    populateArray(ckArr,"individual");
}

function populateArray(arr,typ)  {
    var inc = 0;
    for(var i = 0; i < arr.length; i++){
        if(arr[i].type == "checkbox") {
            if(arr[i].name.indexOf(typ) != -1) {
                checksArray[typ][inc] = arr[i];
                inc++;
            }
        }
    }
}

//Return the number of input checkbox elements contained
//by a div element
function getCheckboxesLength(_sportTyp){
```

```
        var div = document.getElementById(_sportTyp+"_d");
        var len=0;
        for(var i =0; i < div.childNodes.length; i++){
            if(div.childNodes[i].nodeName == "INPUT" ||
                    div.childNodes[i].nodeName == "input" ){
                len++;
            }
        }
        return len;
}
/* Use the request object to fetch an array of
titles for new checkboxes.
The obj parameter represents a select element; get the
value of this element, then hit the server with this value
to request the new titles, but only if the
checkbox hasn't already been expanded */
function getMoreChoices(obj){
    if (obj == null ) { return; }
    var url = "";
    var optsArray = obj.options;
    var val = "";
    for(var i=0; i < optsArray.length; i++){
        if(optsArray[i].selected) {
            val=optsArray[i].value;   break;
        }
    }
    sportTyp=val;
    //determine whether the checkboxes have already been expanded
    if(checksArray[sportTyp].length < getCheckboxesLength(sportTyp)) {
        return;
    }
    url = "http://www.parkerriver.com/s/expand?expType="+val;
    httpRequest("GET",url,true);
}
/* Add new checkboxes to either of the original checkbox lists.
Only add the new checkboxes if the list hasn't been expanded yet.
Just return from this function and don't hit the network
if the list has already been expanded.
 Parameter:
   obj: An array of new titles, like ["Field Hockey","Rugby"] */
function addToChecks(obj){
    //div element that contains the checkboxes
    var div = document.getElementById(sportTyp+"_d");
    var el = null;
    //now add the new checkboxes derived from the server
    for(var h = 0; h < obj.length; h++){
        el = document.createElement("input");
        el.type="checkbox";
        el.name=sportTyp+"_sports";
        el.value=obj[h];
        div.appendChild(el);
        div.appendChild(document.createTextNode(obj[h]));
        div.appendChild(document.createElement("br"));
```

```
        }
    }
    //restore the original list of checkboxes, using
    //the checksArray object containing the
    //original checkboxes
    function restore(_sel) {
        var val;
        var opts = _sel.options;
        for (var i = 0; i < opts.length; i++){
            if(opts[i].selected) { val=opts[i].value; break;}
        }
        //only restore if the checkboxes have
        //already been expanded
        if(checksArray[sportTyp].length < getCheckboxesLength(sportTyp)) {
            var _div = document.getElementById(val+"_d");
            if(_div != null) {
                //rebuild the list of original checkboxes
                _div.innerHTML="";
                var tmpArr = checksArray[val];
                for(var j = 0; j < tmpArr.length; j++){
                    _div.appendChild(tmpArr[j]);
                    _div.appendChild(document.createTextNode(tmpArr[j].value));
                    _div.appendChild(document.createElement("br"));
                }
            }
        }
    }
    //event handler for XMLHttpRequest
    function handleResponse( ){
        try{
            if(request.readyState == 4){
                if(request.status == 200){
                    var resp = request.responseText;
                    if(resp != null){
                        //return value is an array
                        addToChecks(eval(resp));
                    }
                } else {

    /* Create and initialize a request object; not included.
    See Hack #1 or #2. */
```

Most of the code is involved with capturing and restoring the checkboxes's original state, and the comments contained in the latter code sample should make it clear what this code is accomplishing. This code is included to prevent the same set of new checkboxes from being appended to the list multiple times if the user chooses the same value repeatedly from the pop-up list.

The code checks whether the list has already been expanded, by comparing the number of checkboxes in the cached array with number in the existing checkbox group. If the existing group has more checkboxes than the original group, the list has already been expanded. If the user tries to expand the list twice, the second click is ignored, thus sparing the network from a needless hit.

Ajax Requests

getMoreChoices( ) makes a server request using the request object to acquire titles for new checkboxes. (See "Detect Browser Compatibility with the Request Object" **[Hack #1]** or "Submit Text Field or textarea Values to the Server Without a Browser Refresh" **[Hack #12]** if you have not been introduced to the request object.) The first select list's onclick event handler, which is set up when the browser window first loads the web page (window.onload), launches this function, passing in a reference to the select element.

The select element in our page can only have the values Team or Individual. The code appends the value (Team or Individual) onto the end of the URL reflecting the server program. Finally, the httpRequest( ) function sets up and launches the request:

```
function getMoreChoices(obj){
    if (obj == null ) { return; }
    var url = "";
    var optsArray = obj.options;
    var val = "";
    for(var i=0; i < optsArray.length; i++){
        if(optsArray[i].selected) {
            val=optsArray[i].value;   break;
        }
    }
    sportTyp=val;
    //determine whether the checkboxes have already been expanded
    if(checksArray[sportTyp].length < getCheckboxesLength(sportTyp))  {
        return;
    }
    url = "http://www.parkerriver.com/s/expand?expType="+val;
    httpRequest("GET",url,true);
}
```

Here Comes an Array

The server sends back the HTTP response as a string that can be converted to a JavaScript array:

```
if(request.readyState == 4){
    if(request.status == 200){
        var resp =  request.responseText;
        if(resp != null){
            //return value is an array
            addToChecks(eval(resp));
        }
    } else {...}
```

The return value represented by the variable resp is a string, such as ["Field Hockey","Rugby"]. The code passes this string to the eval( ) global function, which returns a JavaScript array. The addToChecks( ) function then creates new checkboxes from this array:

```
function addToChecks(obj){
    //div element that contains the checkboxes
    var div = document.getElementById(sportTyp+"_d");
    var el = null;
    //now add the new checkboxes derived from the server
    for(var h = 0; h < obj.length; h++){
        el = document.createElement("input");
        el.type="checkbox";
        el.name=sportTyp+"_sports";
        el.value=obj[h];
        div.appendChild(el);
        div.appendChild(document.createTextNode(obj[h]));
        div.appendChild(document.createElement("br"));
    }
}
```

This function uses the DOM API to create new input elements and add them to the end of the div element containing the checkboxes. The user sees the checkbox list grow, but nothing else changes on the page. Nifty!

> You may want to take a look at the restore( ) function, which takes an expanded checkbox list and restores it to its original content, without any network hits.

HACK #20 Change Unordered Lists Using an HTTP Response

Change static unordered lists based on content derived from a server.

One of the most common tags found on web pages is the unordered list (ul) tag, which browsers usually render as a list of bullets accompanied by labels. This hack allows the web page user to change an unordered list by adding items to it. The content for the items derives from a server program. This hack is very similar to the previous one, in which the user was able to add items to two lists of checkboxes. The main difference is that this hack deals with unordered lists, which are designed to *display* information rather than to provide a selection widget (such as a list of checkboxes).

> Go ahead and skip this hack if you are not interested in playing with unordered lists because the code is a revised version of the previous hack.

Figure 2-16 shows this hack's web page before the user chooses to expand either of two lists. The lists involve team sports and individual sports. When the user chooses an expansion option from the pop-up list at the top of the page, the indicated list grows by a few items without anything else on the page changing. As in the last hack, each list can be restored to its original contents by choosing the appropriate option from the second pop-up list. The speed with which the lists grow and shrink is quite impressive, particularly considering that the "growth" content comes from a server.

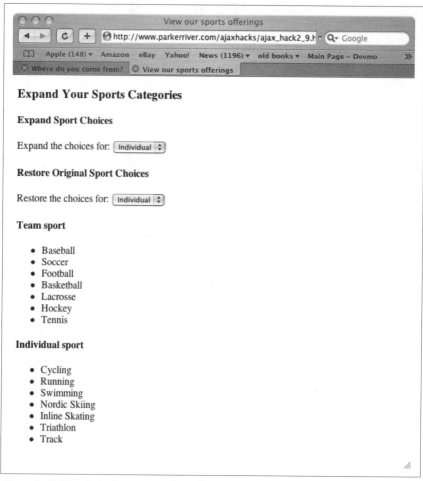

Figure 2-16. Watch the list grow and shrink

Figure 2-17 shows the web page after the user has expanded the team sports category.

Figure 2-17. Expanding the menu of team sports

Here's the code for the web page:

```
<!DOCTYPE html PUBLIC "-//W3C//DTD XHTML 1.0 Strict//EN"
        "http://www.w3.org/TR/2000/REC-xhtml1-20000126/DTD/xhtml1-strict.
dtd">
<html xmlns="http://www.w3.org/1999/xhtml" xml:lang="en" lang="en">
<head>
    <meta http-equiv="content-type" content="text/html; charset=utf-8" />
    <script type="text/javascript" src="js/http_request.js"></script>
    <script type="text/javascript" src="js/hacks2_9.js"></script>
    <title>View our sports offerings</title>
</head>
<body>
<h3>Expand Your Sports Categories</h3>
<h4>Expand Sport Choices</h4>
```

```
<form action="javascript:void%200">
    <div id="exp">
    Expand the choices for:
    <select name="_expand" id="expand">
        <option value="individual">Individual</option>
        <option value="team">Team</option>
    </select>
    </div>
</form>
<h4>Restore Original Sport Choices</h4>
<form action="javascript:void%200">
    <div id="rest">
    Restore the choices for:
    <select name="_restore" id="restore">
        <option value="individual">Individual</option>
        <option value="team">Team</option>
    </select>
    </div>
</form>
<h4>Team sport</h4>
    <ul id="team_u">
        <li>Baseball</li>
        <li>Soccer</li>
        <li>Football</li>
        <li>Basketball</li>
        <li>Lacrosse</li>
        <li>Hockey</li>
        <li>Tennis </li>
    </ul>
<h4>Individual sport</h4>
    <ul id="individual_u">
        <li>Cycling</li>
        <li>Running</li>
        <li>Swimming</li>
        <li>Nordic Skiing</li>
        <li>Inline Skating</li>
        <li>Triathlon</li>
        <li>Track</li>
    </ul>
</body>
</html>
```

The key to this code is giving the ul tags their own id values. The JavaScript code can then access the tags, as shown in the following example:

```
var ul = document.getElementById(sportTyp+"_u");
```

The ul elements contain the list items; therefore, the code increases the number of items in each list by appending child nodes or elements to the ul elements and restores the lists to their original states by removing those child elements. Of course, in this hack, the content for the new list items derives from a server. As a result, the code first must use the request object to fetch the new values.

The web page imports two JavaScript files, *http_request.js* and *hacks2_9.js*. The first file creates and sets up the XMLHttpRequest object. (See "Use Your Own Library for XMLHttpRequest" [Hack #3] for a description of a JavaScript file that manages the request object.) *hacks2_9.js* contains the code that grows and restores the unordered lists:

```javascript
var sportTyp = "";
var itemsArray = null;
//define Object for caching li items
//this is a workaround for IE 6, which
//doesn't save the li element's text node
//or label when you cache it
function CachedLiItem(liElement,liLabel){
    //an li element object
    this.liElement=liElement;
    //a string representing the li text node or label
    this.liLabel=liLabel;
}
window.onload=function( ){
    var sel = document.getElementById("expand");
    //bind onclick event handler to a function
    if(sel != null){
        sel.onclick=function( ){
                getMoreChoices(this)};
    }
    var selr = document.getElementById("restore");
    //bind onclick event handler to a function
    if(selr != null){
        selr.onclick=function( ){
                restore(this)};
    }
    //place all existing bullet items in two arrays
    //for restoring later
    itemsArray = new Object( );
    itemsArray.team = new Array( );
    itemsArray.individual = new Array( );
    var bulletArr = document.getElementsByTagName("li");
    populateArray(bulletArr,"team");
    populateArray(bulletArr,"individual");
}

//create Arrays of CachedLiItem objects for
//restoring the unordered lists later
function populateArray(arr,typ) {
    var inc = 0;
    var el = null;
    var liObj=null;
    for(var i = 0; i < arr.length; i++){
        el = arr[i].parentNode;
```

```
                if(el.id.indexOf(typ) != -1) {
                    liObj=new CachedLiItem(arr[i],arr[i].childNodes[0].nodeValue);
                    itemsArray[typ][inc] = liObj;
                    inc++;
                }
            }
        }
        //return the number of li elements contained
        //by a ul element
        function getULoptionsLength(_sportTyp){
            var ul = document.getElementById(_sportTyp+"_u");
            var len=0;
            for(var i =0; i < ul.childNodes.length; i++){
                if(ul.childNodes[i].nodeName == "LI" ||
                    ul.childNodes[i].nodeName == "li" ){
                    len++;
                }
            }
            return len;
        }
        function getMoreChoices(obj){
            if (obj == null ) { return; }
            var url = "";
            var optsArray = obj.options;
            var val = "";
            for(var i=0; i < optsArray.length; i++){
                if(optsArray[i].selected) {
                    val=optsArray[i].value;  break;
                }
            }
            sportTyp=val;
            //determine whether the bullets have already been expanded
            if(itemsArray[sportTyp].length < getULoptionsLength(sportTyp)) {
                return;
            }
            url = "http://www.parkerriver.com/s/expand?expType="+val;
            httpRequest("GET",url,true,handleResponse);
        }
        function addToBullets(obj){
            //ul element that contains the bullet items
            var ul = document.getElementById(sportTyp+"_u");
            var el = null;
            //now add the new items derived from the server
            for(var h = 0; h < obj.length; h++){
                el = document.createElement("li");
                el.appendChild(document.createTextNode(obj[h]));
                ul.appendChild(el);
            }
        }

        function restore(_sel) {
            var val;
            var opts = _sel.options;
```

```
    for (var i = 0; i < opts.length; i++){
        if(opts[i].selected) { val=opts[i].value; break;}
    }
    sportTyp=val;
    //only restore the lists if the bullets have
    //already been expanded
    if(itemsArray[sportTyp].length < getULoptionsLength(sportTyp)) {
        var ul = document.getElementById(val+"_u");
        if(ul != null) {
            //rebuild the list of original bullets
            ul.innerHTML="";
            var tmpArr = itemsArray[val];
            var tmpLiElement = null;
            for(var j = 0; j < tmpArr.length; j++){
                tmpLiElement=tmpArr[j].liElement;
                //workaround for IE6
                if(tmpLiElement.hasChildNodes( )){tmpLiElement.
                        removeChild(tmpLiElement.firstChild);}
                tmpLiElement.appendChild(document.
                        createTextNode(tmpArr[j].liLabel))
                ul.appendChild(tmpLiElement);
            }
        }
    }
}
//event handler for XMLHttpRequest
function handleResponse( ){
    try{
        if(request.readyState == 4){
            if(request.status == 200){
                var resp =  request.responseText;
                if(resp != null){
                    //return value is an array
                    addToBullets(eval(resp));
                }
            } else {
                //snipped for the sake of brevity
            }
        }//end outer if
    } catch (err)   {
        alert("It does not appear that the server "+
            "is available for this application. Please"+
            " try again very soon. \nError: "+err.message);

    }
}
```

The populateArray( ) and getMoreChoices( ) functions are almost exactly the
same as in the previous hack's code, so I won't take up space here explaining them in detail. The former function caches the original unordered list in
an array, so that it can be restored later. getMoreChoices( ) hits the server for

more sport types using the request object, but only if the unordered list has not yet been expanded.

Next, the code gets the server's return value so that the code can grow either the team sport list or the individual sport list:

```
var resp = request.responseText;
if(resp != null){
    //return value is an array
    addToBullets(eval(resp));
}
```

The return value is a string in array syntax, as in ["Field Hockey","Rugby"]. The code uses the eval( ) global function to convert the string to a JavaScript array. It then passes this array to addToBullets( ):

```
function addToBullets(obj){
    //ul element that contains the bullet items
    var ul = document.getElementById(sportTyp+"_u");
    var el = null;
    //now add the new items derived from the server
    for(var h = 0; h < obj.length; h++){
        el = document.createElement("li");
        el.appendChild(document.createTextNode(obj[h]));
        ul.appendChild(el);
    }
}
```

This function initiates some DOM programming to create new list items and append them as children of a ul tag. The existing ul tag has an id like team_u. The code uses document.getElementById(sportTyp+"_u") to get a reference to the ul tag, then appends a new li element to the ul for each value in the array.

restore( ) comes into play if the user wants to restore the original lists:

```
//only restore the lists if the bullets have
//already been expanded
    if(itemsArray[sportTyp].length < getULoptionsLength(sportTyp)) {
        var ul = document.getElementById(val+"_u");
        if(ul != null)  {
            //rebuild the list of original bullets
            ul.innerHTML="";
            var tmpArr = itemsArray[val];
            var tmpLiElement = null;
            for(var j = 0; j < tmpArr.length; j++){
                tmpLiElement=tmpArr[j].liElement;
                //workaround for IE6
                if(tmpLiElement.hasChildNodes( )){tmpLiElement.
                        removeChild(tmpLiElement.firstChild);}
                tmpLiElement.appendChild(document.
                        createTextNode(tmpArr[j].liLabel))
                ul.appendChild(tmpLiElement);
            }
```

This code uses a cache of original list items to rebuild the restored unordered list. When the web page loads, the code uses a simple JavaScript object to represent each li element:

```
function CachedLiItem(liElement,liLabel){
    //an li element object
    this.liElement=liElement;
    //a string representing the li text node or label
    this.liLabel=liLabel;
}
```

The object has two properties: the li element itself, and the string that specifies its label (the text that you see next to the bullet). When you cache an li element in an array, for instance, Internet Explorer 6 will not save the li element's internal text node, so we use this workaround object. The code empties the ul element first by setting its innerHTML property to the empty string. Then the code uses appendChild( ) from the DOM API to embed the original list items within this ul parent element.

Parting Shots

Your application never has to hit the network if it has a well-defined list of items that can just be hard-coded into the client-side JavaScript as arrays. But if the task calls for expanding web lists from server databases, and this persistent information changes often, this hack's approach can come through for the developers.

HACK #21 Submit Hidden Tag Values to a Server Component

Send the values of hidden form fields to the server whenever you want.

The use of hidden form fields to connect one request from the same user to another may be less compelling these days, as newer approaches (such as cookies and sessions) have evolved. However, your application might have other reasons for using an `<input type="hidden">` element.

A hidden field contains a value that users do not see, unless they peek at the page's source code. It can be used to send the server some extra identifying information along with the rest of the form input.

Unless the server specifies with various HTTP response headers that a web page shouldn't be cached, the browser will cache, or keep a local copy of, each page a user requests. The purpose of this caching strategy is to improve performance and prevent unnecessary network requests for the same page if it hasn't changed. But what if you want to track the number of times a user opens up a page, even if the page derives from that user's client-side cache. This hack sends a server component the value of a hidden input field whenever the page is loaded into a browser, letting it know when the page is loaded from the cache as well as when it is downloaded from the server.

 You could use such a strategy for web user *testing* within an application. However, you would probably bombard a network with many wasteful requests if you included this feature in a production application. In addition, any kind of automated submission of this nature could raise privacy issues with web users or violate online privacy policies. This type of web-application behavior should be checked against user expectations and site policies before it is ever used in a production site.

Dynamo

The HTML for the web page in this hack is minimal, but it includes a hefty hidden value tucked inside of it. The value of the hidden field is dynamically generated when the browser loads the page. Here's the code:

```
<!DOCTYPE html PUBLIC "-//W3C//DTD XHTML 1.0 Strict//EN"
        "http://www.w3.org/TR/2000/REC-xhtml1-20000126/DTD/xhtml1-strict.
dtd">
<html xmlns="http://www.w3.org/1999/xhtml" xml:lang="en" lang="en">
<head>
    <script type="text/javascript" src="js/http_request.js"></script>
    <script type="text/javascript" src="js/hacks2_11.js"></script>
    <meta http-equiv="content-type" content="text/html; charset=utf-8" />
    <title>hidden hacks</title>
</head>
<body>
<h3>Delving into some navigator properties</h3>
<div id="content">
These include:   navigator.appName, navigator.platform,
navigator.language, and navigator.userAgent.
</div>
<form action="javascript:void%200">
    <script type="text/javascript" src="js/innerInput.js"></script>
</form>
</body>
</html>
```

When the page is loaded into the browser, the JavaScript file *innerInput.js* dynamically creates a hidden input tag and populates that tag with useful information, such as the name of the page, when it was accessed, the computing platform of the user, the default language for the browser, as well as the User Agent string associated with the user's browser. Code can access most of these properties via the navigator client-side object in JavaScript.

For example, accessing navigator.platform returns MacPPC for my computer; navigator.userAgent provides the content of the User Agent request header from my browser.

Now the hidden tag has a lot of meaningful information for its value attribute. *inner_input.js* contains:

```
var delim = ":::";
document.write(
        "<input type=\"hidden\" id=\"hid\" name=\"data\"  value=\"\""+
        location.pathname+delim+new Date( )+
        delim+navigator.appName+delim+navigator.platform+
        delim+navigator.language+delim+navigator.userAgent+"\" />");
```

The document.write( ) method can dynamically write part of the page as the browser loads the HTML. The code creates a hidden tag with the id hid. The user does not see the value of this tag, but the value is available to JavaScript code. The values of the various properties (navigator.userAgent, etc.) are separated by the characters :::. For example:

```
/ajaxhacks/ajax_hack2_11.html:::
Thu Oct 27 2005 10:37:15 GMT-0400:::
Netscape:::MacPPC:::en:::Mozilla/5.0 (Macintosh; U;
PPC Mac OS X; en) AppleWebKit/412.6
(KHTML, like Gecko) Safari/412.2
```

Notifying Home

Now we want to send this information to a server, so it can be logged. For this task, the application requires more JavaScript. The page imports (with script tags) two more JavaScript files. *http_request.js* (see "Use Your Own Library for XMLHttpRequest" [Hack #3]) sets up the request object to talk with the server. *hacks2_11.js* contains the code that accesses the input tag's value and sets up a request to POST it to the server as soon as the browser loads the page:

```
window.onload=function( ){
    var hid = document.getElementById("hid");
    var val = "navprops="+encodeURIComponent(hid.value);
    url = "http://www.parkerriver.com/s/hid";
    httpRequest("POST",url,true, handleResponse,val);
}
//event handler for XMLHttpRequest
function handleResponse( ){
    try{
        if(request.readyState == 4){
            if(request.status == 200){
                //commented out now: alert(
                //"Request went through okay...");
            } else {
                //request.status is 503
```

```
                        //if the application isn't available;
                        //500 if the application has a bug
                        alert(
                                "A problem occurred with communicating between"+
                                " the XMLHttpRequest object and "+
                                "the server program.");
                    }
                }//end outer if
            } catch (err) {
                alert("It does not appear that the server "+
                    "is available for this application. Please"+
                    " try again very soon. \nError: "+err.message);

            }
        }
```

The code gets the value of the input element and encodes the value's characters so that they can be properly transferred over the network. The code then sends a POST request because of the volume of this server message.

> A GET request appends the parameters to the end of the URL, whereas a POST request sends the parameter data as a block of characters following the request headers.

The httpRequest() function is a wrapper around the code that sets up an XMLHttpRequest object and sends the message.

The httpRequest() function does a browser compatibility check [Hack #1]. This function also checks for any data that is designed to be posted. This data will appear as the fifth parameter to the function.

> JavaScript allows code to define a function, and client code may then pass variable arguments to the function. These parameters can be accessed within the defined function as part of an arguments array, which every JavaScript function has built in. Therefore, arguments[4] represents the fifth parameter passed into a function (the array is zero-based).

http_request.js uses the request object's setRequestHeader() function to convey to the server component the content type of the sent data:

```
request.setRequestHeader("Content-Type",
        "application/x-www-form-urlencoded; charset=UTF-8");
```

The HTTP POST request will not succeed with Firefox, for instance, unless you include this request header (see "Use the Request Object to POST Data to the Server" [Hack #2] for details).

Logging

The server component can log the posted data, or do whatever the application calls for. Here is an example log entry after a couple of requests with Firefox and Safari (with some of the logged text removed and/or edited for readability):

```
/ajaxhacks/ajax_hack2_11.html:::
Thu Oct 27 2005 10:37:15 GMT-0400:::
Netscape:::MacPPC:::en:::
Mozilla/5.0 (Macintosh; U; PPC Mac OS X; en) AppleWebKit/412.6
(KHTML, like Gecko) Safari/412.2

/ajaxhacks/ajax_hack2_11.html:::
Thu Oct 27 2005 10:49:24 GMT-0400 (EDT):::
Netscape:::MacPPC:::en-US:::Mozilla/5.0 (Macintosh; U;
PPC Mac OS X Mach-O; en-US; rv:1.7.12)
Gecko/20050915 Firefox/1.0.7
```

You can see that the name of the file is included, followed by the date and time when it was requested, then some browser-specific data such as the default locale (en-US, or U.S. English) and the value of the User Agent request header.

> In JavaScript, the User Agent header data is accessed from the navigator.userAgent property.

CHAPTER 3

Validation
Hacks 22–27

Validating the data that users provide in web forms is an important step in exchanging information with them. Web applications should not hit the network with blank form information or fields that contain nonnumeric characters where numbers (such as a credit card number or ZIP Code) are required. To prevent this, JavaScript provides an option to implement *client-side validation*: a form can self-check before the code connects with the server and submits the data. The client represents the first layer of validation an application can implement. A second layer of validation on the server is critically important, for example, when the data involves financial or other private information, or if JavaScript is disabled in the user's browser. Server-side validation is required to ensure that the application handles valid data. The following hacks demonstrate validation techniques for blank text controls, email addresses, credit card numbers, and U.S. ZIP Codes.

HACK #22 Validate a Text Field or textarea for Blank Fields
Spare the network an unnecessary hit if the user leaves any required form fields blank.

No web developers want their Ajax applications to hit the network with requests if the users leave necessary text fields blank. Thus, checking that input elements of type text and the large boxes called textareas in HTML contain values is one of the most common forms of validation.

This hack shows the code for checking if a text control is blank. The *inline* way of doing this is by assigning a check for the field's value in the text field's event handler:

```
<input type="text" name="firstname" id="tfield" onblur=
"if (this.value) {doSomething();}" />
```

or in the textarea's event handler:

```
<textarea name="tarea" rows="20" id="question" cols="20" onblur=
"if (this.value) {doSomething( );}">
```

The JavaScript phrase if (this.value) {...} returns false if the user leaves a field blank, so the function call doSomething( ) will never occur. JavaScript evaluates a blank web-form text field as the empty string or "", which evaluates to false when it's used in the context of a programming test. The this keyword is a nice generic way of referring to the form field that contains the event handler attribute. For example, onblur. this.value returns the text field's value, which in our case is the empty string.

> onblur captures the event involving the transfer of keyboard focus away from a form field. For example, users trigger onblur event handlers when they type in a text field and then click in another form field or press the Tab key.
>
> If you use the onchange event handler, the browser calls the onchange-related function only if the field's value changes. In other words, the change event will not capture an instance if the user leaves the text field blank.

Separating the Logic from the View

Probably a better way of going about your event-handling tasks is to separate the logic of your code from the HTML or template text that comprises the application's visual aspects. The JavaScript goes into an external file that the HTML page imports with a script tag. Inside the external file, the code binds a field's various event handlers to a function or the code that represents your application's behavior.

Let's take the following web page, *myapp.html*, which includes the following HTML in its header:

```
<html xmlns="http://www.w3.org/1999/xhtml" xml:lang="en" lang="en">
<head>
    <meta http-equiv="content-type" content="text/html; charset=utf-8" />
    <script type="text/javascript" src="js/hacks_method.js"></script>
    <title>Cool Ajax application</title>
</head>
```

The file *hacks_method.js* is located in a directory *js*, which is in the same directory as the HTML file. The HTML file contains the same textarea and text field as mentioned earlier, except these fields no longer have an onblur attribute. The JavaScript file includes this code:

```
window.onload=function( ){
    var txtA = document.getElementById("tarea");
    if(txtA != null){
```

```
            txtA.onblur=function( ){
                if (this.value) { doSomething( );}
            };
        }
        var tfd = document.getElementById("tfield");
        /* An alternative:
        if(tfd != null && txtA != null){tfd.onblur = txtA.onblur; }
        */
        if(tfd != null){
            tfd.onblur=function( ){
                if (this.value) { doSomething( );}
            };
        }
    }
```

window.onload involves the binding of the load event to your blank-field checks. load occurs when the browser has completed loading the web page, so when that happens, all the stuff after window.onload= follows.

The getElementById( ) method returns a reference to an HTML element, such as the textarea reference stored in txtA. The code then binds the textarea's onblur event handler to a function, which checks for blank field values *before* it calls doSomething( ). The code initiates the same behavior for the text field referred to by the variable tfd.

> If the web designers leave out the text fields with the id tarea or tfield, nothing will happen because the getElementById( ) method returns null, and the code includes a check for that occurrence.

Another way to bind an event handler to a function is to declare the function somewhere and then use the function name:

```
window.onload=function( ){
    var txtA = document.getElementById("tarea");
    txtA.onblur=doSomething;//no parens...
}
function doSomething( ){ //... }
```

> When the code binds an event handler to a previously defined function, leave the parentheses off the function name.

Programmers often consider placing the definition of the blank-field checks and other coding stuff in an external file to be a better way of organizing any but the most trivial web applications.

Validate Email Syntax

#23 Check email syntax on the client side before the server component takes over.

Many web sites ask their users to register their email addresses as usernames. This hack makes sure the syntax of the entered email address is valid, before the server component finds out whether the email address has already been used as a user identifier. "Validate Unique Usernames" [Hack #24] takes care of the second step of this task.

> The server component that receives the email address should *always* implement its own validation step, in order to deal with, for example, the disabling of JavaScript in the user's browser or a direct connection with the server by a hacker.

The Longest Wait

When registering with a web site, users typically type in an email address, make up a password, click Submit, and then often experience a long wait staring at the browser as the page is slowly reconstructed (if they're lucky). To add insult to injury, even though email addresses are supposed to be unique, sometimes the address is rejected—people often try to register at a site more than once with the same email address (guilty as charged!), forgetting that they've already visited. Therefore, the application often has to check both the email syntax *and* whether the identifier is already being used.

Ajax techniques can validate the email address on the client side and initiate a trip to the server behind the scenes to find out whether it is already in use, without disrupting the current view of the page. "Validate Unique Usernames" [Hack #24] ensures the uniqueness of the username. Both hacks share the same code base, a mix of JavaScript and other Ajax techniques.

Checking Out the Email Syntax

Web sites often use email addresses as usernames because they are guaranteed to be unique, as long as they are valid. In addition, the organizations can use the email addresses to communicate with their users later. You do not have to initiate a server round trip just to validate an email address, however. This task can be initiated in the client, which cancels the submission of the username to the server if the email syntax is invalid.

What criteria can you use for validation? A fairly dry technical document, RFC 2822 is a commonly accepted guideline from 2001 that organizations can use to validate email addresses. Let's look at an example email address to briefly summarize the typical syntax: *hackreader@oreilly.com*. Here, *hackreader* is the *local part* of the address, which typically identifies the user. This is followed by the *commercial at sign* (@), which precedes the *Internet domain*. Internet domains are those often well-known addresses of computer locations that handle in-transit emails; *google.com* and *yahoo.com* come to mind.

All of this is common knowledge. However, you may *not* know that RFC 2822 specifies that the local part cannot contain spaces (unless it's quoted, which is rare, as in *"bruce perry"@gmail.com*). The local part also cannot contain various special characters, such as the following: ( ) < > , ' @ : ; \ [ ]. Maybe if someone tries to create an email address that looks like *<((([))>@yoursite.com* you should reject it outright, rather than give points for originality!

The local part can and often does contain period characters, as in *bruce.perry@google.com*, but the periods have to be preceded and followed by alphanumeric characters (i.e., you cannot use an email address such as *bruce.@google.com*). The domain can contain more than one period, as in *bruce@lists.myorg.net*, but it cannot begin or end with a period (as in *bruce@.lists.myorg.net*). Finally, the guidelines permit but discourage a *domain literal*, as in *bruce@[192.168.0.1]*. These are the criteria you can check for in your validation code.

Looking at the Code

First, take a look at the page that imports the JavaScript code:

```
<!DOCTYPE html PUBLIC "-//W3C//DTD XHTML 1.0 Strict//EN"
        "http://www.w3.org/TR/2000/REC-xhtml1-20000126/DTD/xhtml1-strict.
dtd">
<html xmlns="http://www.w3.org/1999/xhtml" xml:lang="en" lang="en">
<head>
<script type="text/javascript" src="js/http_request.js"></script>
<script type="text/javascript" src="js/email.js"></script>
<meta http-equiv="content-type" content="text/html; charset=utf-8">
<title>Enter email</title>
</head>
<body>
<form action="javascript:void%200">
<div id="message"></div>
Enter email: <input type="text" name="email" size="25"><br />
<button type="submit" name="submit" value="Send">Send</button>
</form>
</body>
</html>
```

Figure 3-1 shows a simple web page with a text field for entering an email address and a Send button.

Figure 3-1. Enter your email address, please

The user types an email address into the text field and then clicks the Send button. This action does not send the email address to a server component yet, though. First, the code has to validate the syntax. The HTML code for the page imports two JavaScript files with the script tag. *email.js* is responsible for a thorough email-syntax check. *http_request.js* sends the email address to a server component as a username, but you can find this bit of Ajax in "Validate Unique Usernames" [Hack #24].

Figure 3-2 shows what the browser window looks like if the user types in an invalid email address. The page dynamically prints out a red message summarizing what appears to be wrong with the entered email address.

If, on the other hand, the email address is okay, the application sends it to a server component to determine if the address has already been used as a username. Here is the code from *email.js*:

```
var user,domain, regex, _match;

window.onload=function( ){
    document.forms[0].onsubmit=function( ) {
        checkAddress(this.email.value);
        return false;
    };
};
/* Define an Email constructor */
function Email(e){
    this.emailAddr=e;
    this.message="";
    this.valid=false;
}

function validate( ){
    //do a basic check for null, zero-length string, ".", "@",
    //and the absence of spaces
```

```
    if (this.emailAddr == null || this.emailAddr.length == 0 ||
    this.emailAddr.indexOf(".") == -1 ||
    this.emailAddr.indexOf("@") == -1 ||
    this.emailAddr.indexOf(" ") != -1){
    this.message="Make sure the email address does " +
    "not contain any spaces "+
    "and is otherwise valid (e.g., contains the \"commercial at\" @ sign).";
        this.valid=false;
        return;
    }

    /* The local part cannot begin or end with a "."
    Regular expression specifies: the group of characters before the @
    symbol must be made up of at least two word characters, followed by zero
    or one period char, followed by at least 2 word characters. */
    regex=/(^\w{2,}\.?\w{2,})@/;
    _match = regex.exec(this.emailAddr);

    if ( _match){
        user=RegExp.$1;
        //alert("user: "+user);
    } else {
        this.message="Make sure the user name is more than two characters, "+
            "does not begin or end with a period (.), or is not otherwise "+
            "invalid!";
        this.valid=false;
        return;
    }
    //get the domain after the @ char
    //first take care of domain literals like @[19.25.0.1], however rare
    regex=/@(\[\d{1,3}\.\d{1,3}\.\d{1,3}.\d{1,3}\])$/;
    _match = regex.exec(this.emailAddr);

    if( _match){
        domain=RegExp.$1;
        this.valid=true;
    } else {
    /* The @ character followed by at least two chars that are not a period (.),
    followed by a period, followed by zero or one instances of two or more
    characters ending with a period, followed by two-three chars that are
    not periods */
        regex=/@(\w{2,}\.(\w{2,}\.)?[a-zA-Z]{2,3})$/;
        _match = regex.exec(this.emailAddr);
        if( _match){
            domain=RegExp.$1;
            //alert("domain: "+domain);
        } else {
            this.message="The domain portion of the email had less than 2
                        chars "+
                        "or was otherwise invalid!";
            this.valid=false;
```

```
                return;
            }
        }//end domain check
        this.valid=true;

    }

    //make validate( ) an instance method of the Email object
    Email.prototype.validate=validate;

    function eMsg(msg,sColor){
        var div = document.getElementById("message");
        div.style.color=sColor;
        div.style.fontSize="0.9em";
        //remove old messages
        if(div.hasChildNodes( )){
            div.removeChild(div.firstChild);
        }
        div.appendChild(document.createTextNode(msg));

    }
    //a pull-it-all-together function
    function checkAddress(val){
        var eml = new Email(val);
        var url;
        eml.validate( );
        if (! eml.valid) {eMsg(eml.message,"red")};
        if(eml.valid)
        {
            //www.parkerriver.com
            url="http://www.parkerriver.com/s/checker?email="+
                encodeURIComponent(val);
            httpRequest("GET",url,true,handleResponse);
        }
    }
    //event handler for XMLHttpRequest
    //see Hack #24
    function handleResponse( ){
        //snipped...
    }
```

First, the code sets up the handling for the user's click on the Send button.
window.onload specifies an event handler that is called when the browser
completes the loading of the web page:

```
window.onload=function( ){
    document.forms[0].onsubmit=function( ) {
        checkAddress(this.email.value);
        return false;
    };
};
```

The reason the code uses `window.onload` is that for the code to control form-related behavior, the `form` tag has to be able to be referenced from JavaScript—that is, fully loaded into the browser.

> Event handlers are designed to assign functions or blocks of code that specify the application's behavior (i.e., "Take this action when this happens in the browser."). For example, the onsubmit event handler indicates which function should be called when the user submits the form.

The previous code also sets up the `form` element's `onsubmit` event handler, a function that calls `checkAddress()`. The onsubmit event handler intercepts the form submission because you want to validate what the user entered into the text field before the application does anything else. `checkAddress()` takes as a parameter the address that the user typed (if anything).

Checking Email at the Door

Let's take a closer look at the `checkAddress()` function:

```
function checkAddress(val){
    var eml = new Email(val);
    var url;
    eml.validate();
    if (! eml.valid) {eMsg(eml.message,"red")};
    if(eml.valid)
    {
        url="http://www.parkerriver.com/s/checker?email="+
            encodeURIComponent(val);
        httpRequest("GET",url,true,handleResponse);
    }
}
```

This function creates a new `Email` object, validates the user's email address, and, if it's valid, submits it to a server component. You may be wondering, what the heck is an `Email` object? An `Email` object is a code template you can use over and over again every time you want to check the syntax of an email address. In fact, if you write a lot of JavaScript that handles email addresses, you'd likely break this code off into its own file (say, *emailObject.js*) so that it isn't tangled up with hundreds of lines of additional complex code in future applications. Here is the `Email` object definition:

```
/* Define an Email constructor */
function Email(e){
    this.emailAddr=e;
    this.message="";
    this.valid=false;
}
```

An `Email` object is constructed using a JavaScript function definition that takes the email address as the one function parameter, stored here as e.

> This is a special kind of function that is called a *constructor* in object-oriented parlance, because it is used to construct an object.

An `Email` object has three properties: an email address (`emailAddr`), a `message`, and a boolean or true/false property named `valid`. When you use the `new` keyword in JavaScript to create a new `Email` object, as follows, the `emailAddr` property is set to the passed-in email address (stored in e):

```
var email = new Email("brucew@yahoo.com");
```

The message is initialized to the empty `string` because new `Email` objects do not have any special messages associated with them. The validity of the email address, somewhat pessimistically, is initialized as `false`. The `this` keyword refers to the *instance* of `Email` that the browser creates in memory when the code generates a new `Email` object. To look at this in a different way, a bicycle company might create a mold for new bicycle helmets. Conceptually, the mold is like our `Email` constructor. When the company makes new helmets, these helmets are instances of the mold or template that was developed for them.

On to Validation

An `Email` object validates the email address it is passed, which in our application takes place when the user clicks the Send button. The `checkAddress( )` function contains code such as `eml.validate( )` and `if(eml.valid)`, indicating that our application validates individual email addresses and checks their `valid` properties. This happens because the code defines a `validate( )` function and then signals that the `Email` object owns or is linked with that function.

> Using code such as `Email.prototype.validate=validate;` is a special way in JavaScript to specify that you've defined this function, `validate( )`, and that every new `Email` object has its own `validate( )` method. Using object-oriented techniques is not mandated, but it makes the code a little more tidy, concise, readable, and potentially reusable.

Now let's examine the validation code, which contains a few regular expressions for checking email syntax. The code, included in the prior code sample for *email.js*, is fairly complex, but the embedded comments are designed to help you along the way in figuring out what the code accomplishes. In order, here are the rules for our validation logic (partly based on RFC 2822 and partly on our own criteria for proper email syntax):

1. If the email address is the empty string, if the emailAddr property value is null, or if the email address does not contain an @ character or any periods at all, it is rejected. No surprises there.

2. The code then uses a regular expression to grab the local part of the email, which is the username, or the chunk of characters preceding the @. This regular expression checks for at least two "word characters" (the \w predefined character class; i.e., [a–zA–Z_0–9]), followed by zero or one period characters, followed by at least two word characters.

3. The code then grabs all characters after the @ and checks whether the character string represents either a domain literal (however rare that is) or a typical domain syntax. The rule for the latter syntax is expressed as "the @ character followed by at least two word characters, followed by a period, followed by zero or one instances of at least two characters ending with a period, followed by two to three characters that fall into the character class [a–zA–Z]."

JavaScript's built-in RegExp object's exec( ) method returns an array if it finds a match, or null otherwise. The RegExp.$1 part contains the first group of parenthesized matched characters after exec( ) is called—in this case, the local part/username before the @ character.

You can try different email addresses with the validation code and look at the returned values for debugging purposes.

The User Message

If users include illegal characters, type in otherwise invalid addresses, or leave the text field blank, they are greeted with a message like the one shown in Figure 3-2.

The following code inside validate( ) creates another such message if the email address does not include a domain (the part after the @) that matches the regular expression:

```
/* The @ character followed by at least two chars that are not a period (.),
followed by a period, followed by zero or one instances of at least two
characters ending with a period, followed by two-three chars that are
not periods */
regex=/@(\w{2,}\.(\w{2,}\.)?[a-zA-Z]{2,3})$/;
_match = regex.exec(this.emailAddr);
if( _match){
    domain=RegExp.$1;
} else {
```

Figure 3-2. Communicating with the user

```
    this.message="The domain portion of the email had less than 2 chars "+
            "or was otherwise invalid!";
    this.valid=false;
    return;
}
```

Notice that the code also sets the Email object's valid property to false. checkAddress( ) then checks the valid property before the email address heads off to the server (we'll look at that part in "Validate Email Syntax" [Hack #23]):

```
//inside checkAddress( )...
eml.validate( );
if (! eml.valid) {eMsg(eml.message,"red")};
if(eml.valid)
{
    url="http://www.parkerriver.com/s/checker?email="+
        encodeURIComponent(val);
    httpRequest("GET",url,true,handleResponse);
}
```

The eMsg( ) function generates the message. eMsg( ) uses a little DOM, a little dynamic CSS programming, and some JavaScript:

```
function eMsg(msg,sColor){
    var div = document.getElementById("message");
    div.style.color=sColor;
    div.style.fontSize="0.9em";
    //remove old messages
    if(div.hasChildNodes( )){
        div.removeChild(div.firstChild);
    }
    div.appendChild(document.createTextNode(msg));

}
```

The parameters to this function are the text message and the color of the text. The application uses red for error messages and blue for notifications about usernames (this is discussed in the next hack). The code dynamically generates the message inside a div that the HTML reserves for that purpose:

```
var div = document.getElementById("message");
```

On Deck

As the user attempts to enter an email address with valid syntax, the page itself doesn't change; only the message shows different content. During the syntax validation step, the application responds rapidly because the work is done on the client side, and the server component does not participate (although a server role does come into play when the email address is valid).

Although we have not gone into very much detail about what's happening on the server end, the server component keeps a database of unique usernames for its web application. Once this hack gives the green light on the syntax, the application sends the email address to the server, which checks to see whether that address is already in its database. "Validate Email Syntax" [Hack #23] dives into this related functionality.

 ## HACK #24 Validate Unique Usernames

Ensure that an email address used as a username is unique but do not submit anything else on the page.

The email-address validation performed in "Validate Email Syntax" [Hack #23] allows you to safely send the email address off to the server-side program, where it will be checked against an existing database to see if it has already been used. This hack does that checking.

Figure 3-2 in "Validate Email Syntax" [Hack #23] shows what the web page looks like when the user types an entry that breaks our validity check. If the user enters an address with valid syntax, that address is sent to the server component. Depending on whether it passes the server-side check, the user then sees a message conveying either that the specified username has already been taken or that they have provided a unique email address, and it has been saved (Figure 3-3). "But all email addresses are unique," you might declare. That's true, but web users often try to register more than once at the same site—who remembers all the tedious details about registering at the countless web sites we typically use? If you try to register twice with the same email address, the application responds that your username is already taken.

If the email address is just one element on a lengthy registration form, a non-Ajax web application will submit all the form values at once when a user

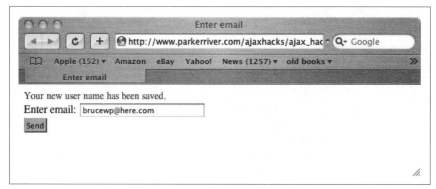

Figure 3-3. Unique name passes muster

registers, and often painstakingly reconstruct the page just to instruct the user to try again. This hack submits only the email address and does not evaluate or refresh other page elements.

How It Works

Here is the HTML code, which "Validate a Text Field or textarea for Blank Fields" [Hack #22] also uses:

```
<!DOCTYPE html PUBLIC "-//W3C//DTD XHTML 1.0 Strict//EN"
        "http://www.w3.org/TR/2000/REC-xhtml1-20000126/DTD/xhtml1-strict.
dtd">
<html xmlns="http://www.w3.org/1999/xhtml" xml:lang="en" lang="en">
<head>
<script type="text/javascript" src="js/http_request.js"></script>
<script type="text/javascript" src="js/email.js"></script>
<meta http-equiv="content-type" content="text/html; charset=utf-8">
<title>Enter email</title>
</head>
<body>
<form action="javascript:void%200">
<div id="message"></div>
Enter email: <input type="text" name="email" size="25"><br />
<button type="submit" name="submit" value="Send">Send</button>
</form>
</body>
</html>
```

The JavaScript in *email.js* sends the validated email address to the server, which checks an existing database of usernames and responds with a "1" if the address is already in use (details on email validation were provided in "Validate Email Syntax" [Hack #23]). The simple XML response output looks like `<is_used>1</is_used>`. Here is the code from the `checkAddress()` function, contained in *http_request.js*, that sends the validated email address:

```
if(eml.valid)
{
    url="http://www.parkerriver.com/s/checker?email="+
        encodeURIComponent(val);
    httpRequest("GET",url,true,handleResponse);
}
```

The code uses `XMLHttpRequest` to send the email address to the server component. The `httpRequest()` function wraps the creation and initialization of the request object. `httpRequest()` takes as parameters:

- The type of request, as in GET or POST
- The URL or server web address
- A Boolean indicating whether the request is asynchronous or not
- The name of a function or a function literal that handles the server response

The Server Handshake

The server then returns some XML indicating whether it has found the username or not. Here's the code for `handleResponse()`, which appears in *email.js*:

```
//event handler for XMLHttpRequest
function handleResponse( ){
    var usedTag, answer,xmlReturnVal;
    if(request.readyState == 4){
        if(request.status == 200){
            //implement Document object in DOM
            xmlReturnVal = request.responseXML;
            usedTag = xmlReturnVal.getElementsByTagName("is_used")[0];
            //the data will be 0 or 1
            answer= usedTag.childNodes[0].data;
            if(answer==true){
                eMsg("This user name is not available. Kindly try again.",
                    "red");  }
            else { eMsg("Your new user name has been saved.","blue"); }
        } else {
            alert("A problem occurred with communicating between the "+
                "XMLHttpRequest object and the server program.");
        }
    }//end outer if
}
```

`handleResponse()` gets the XML by accessing the `responseXML` property of `XMLHttpRequest`. The code calls the DOM `Document` method `getElementsByTagName()`, which returns a `nodeList` (just like an `array`) of nodes that have the specified tag name. The tag name is is_used, as in `<is_used>0</is_`

used>. Since the return value is an `array` structure, the code gets the first and only array member using [0]:

```
xmlReturnVal.getElementsByTagName("is_used")[0];
```

The code then accesses the text contained by the is_used tag and generates a user message. "Validate Email Syntax" **[Hack #23]** shows the eMsg( ) code.

For Those Server Hackers...

The code for the server-side component, which is a Java servlet that mimics a database, is shown below. It uses a `Map` type, a kind of `Hashtable` object, to contain the stored usernames; however, a full-fledged production application would use middleware to connect with a database and check on usernames.

> A production application would also use a server compo-
> nent to implement a second layer of email validation, before
> it interacted with any stored email addresses. The server
> would also implement security measures to prevent any tam-
> pering with or mining of the email database.

Here is the server-side code:

```
public class EmailChecker extends HttpServlet{
    //pretend this is the database!
    private static List USERS;
    static{
        USERS=Collections.synchronizedList(new ArrayList( ));
        USERS.add("bruceperry@gmail.com");
        USERS.add("johnjsmith@gmail.com");
        USERS.add("teddyroosevelt@gmail.com");
        USERS.add("janejsmith@gmail.com");

    }
    protected void doGet(HttpServletRequest httpServletRequest,
                    HttpServletResponse httpServletResponse) throws
                    ServletException, IOException {
        String email=null;
        email = httpServletRequest.getParameter("email");
        //we make this an int, because JavaScript converts
        //a valid String such as "false" to true
        int bool = 0;
        if(email != null){

            if(USERS.contains(email)){
                bool=1;
            } else {
                USERS.add(email);    }
        } else {
```

```
        //throw ServletException signaling a null or
        //absent parameter
    }
    sendXML(httpServletResponse,bool);

    }

    protected void doPost(HttpServletRequest httpServletRequest,
                          HttpServletResponse httpServletResponse) throws
                          ServletException, IOException {
        doGet(httpServletRequest, httpServletResponse);
    }

    private void sendXML(HttpServletResponse response,
                         int emailUsed) throws IOException {
        response.setContentType("text/xml; charset=UTF-8");
        String content = "<?xml version=\"1.0\" encoding=\"UTF-8\"?>"+
                         "<is_used>"+emailUsed+"</is_used>";
        response.getWriter( ).write(content);
    }
}
```

The server component can also check the email address's validity, as mentioned in the Note above the code, using another component designed for this purpose.

HACK #25 Validate Credit Card Numbers

Validate credit card numbers without submitting and refreshing the entire web page.

Entering a credit card number on a web page has become commonplace. This hack verifies the entered credit card number, then submits it to the server component only if the number is valid. Nothing else changes on the page except for a user message, which notifies the user of any error conditions or that the credit card has passed muster and has been sent to the server to be processed. (Although we won't discuss them here, as in "Validate Email Syntax" [Hack #23], the server component then implements its own credit card validation routines.)

The server connection will likely be initiated over Secure Sockets Layer (SSL), such as with the HTTPS protocol, and be involved with an e-commerce component that further verifies the purchase information with a merchant bank. This hack, however, just verifies the number, generates a message, and makes an HTTP request using Ajax techniques.

Figure 3-4 shows what the web page looks like.

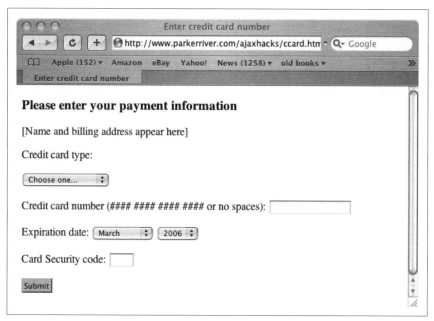

Figure 3-4. Enter a credit card number for verification

This is the web page code. It imports two JavaScript files, *http_request.js* and *cc.js*:

```
<!DOCTYPE html PUBLIC "-//W3C//DTD XHTML 1.0 Strict//EN"
        "http://www.w3.org/TR/2000/REC-xhtml1-20000126/DTD/xhtml1-strict.
dtd">
<html xmlns="http://www.w3.org/1999/xhtml" xml:lang="en" lang="en">
<head>
    <script type="text/javascript" src="js/http_request.js"></script>
    <script type="text/javascript" src="js/cc.js"></script>
    <meta http-equiv="content-type" content="text/html; charset=iso-8859-1"
/>
    <title>Enter credit card number</title>
</head>
<body>
<h3>Please enter your payment information</h3>
<div id="message"></div>
<p>
    [Name and billing address appear here]
</p>
<p>
    Credit card type:
</p>
<form action="javascript:void%200">
    <p>
        <select name="cctype">
            <option value="Choose one...">Choose one...</option>
```

```
            <option value="Mastercard">Mastercard</option>
            <option value="Visa">Visa</option>
            <option value="American Express">American Express</option>
            <option value="Discover">Discover</option>
        </select>
    </p>
    <p>
        Credit card number (#### #### #### #### or no spaces):
        <input type="text" name="cc" size="16" maxlength="19" />
    </p>
    <p>Expiration date:
        <select name="exp_month">
            <option>January</option>
            <option>February</option>
            <option>March</option>
            <!--etc...-->
        </select>
        <select name="exp_year">
            <option>2005</option>
            <option>2006</option>
            <option>2007</option>
            <!--etc...-->
        </select>
    </p>
    <p>
        Card Security code:
        <input type="text" name="scode" size="4" maxlength="4" />
    </p>
    <p>
        <button type="submit" name="submit" value="Submit">Submit</button>
    </p>
</form>
</body>
</html>
```

The user chooses a credit card type (e.g., "Mastercard"); enters the card number, expiration date, and card security code (CSC); and clicks the Submit button. However, instead of having the page dissolve and the values depart immediately for the server, the application verifies a few conditions first. The JavaScript makes sure that the fields are not blank and contain the required minimum number of characters (such as three for the CSC), and then it verifies the card number using the Luhn formula or algorithm.

The Luhn forumla is a well-known algorithm used to verify ID numbers like credit card numbers. See *http://en.wikipedia.org/wiki/Luhn_formula* for details.

If one of these checks fails, the hack displays an error message in red. Figure 3-5 shows one of these messages.

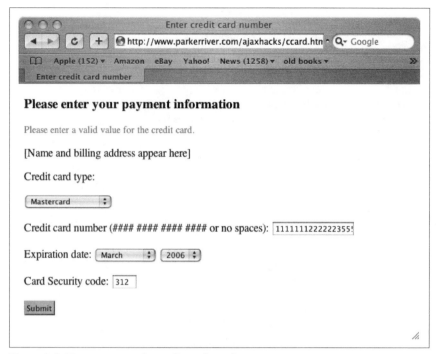

Figure 3-5. Time to reenter the credit card number

If the credit card number is verified and everything else has been correctly entered, the hack uses XMLHttpRequest to send this information to a server.

> We are not strictly making a secure connection in this hack, but a real application would not send any purchase information unencrypted over a network. In addition, it is worth mentioning a second time that the main job of validating a credit card rests with the processing server component(s).

A message in blue notifies the user that the organization is processing the credit card.

Verifying the Card Number

cc.js contains the code for responding to the user's button click, as well as for verifying the information and generating a user message. *http_request.js* (see "Use Your Own Library for XMLHttpRequest" [Hack #3]) creates and calls the methods of XMLHttpRequest. Here is the code contained in *cc.js*:

```
var finalCnumber;

window.onload=function( ){
```

```
        document.forms[0].onsubmit=function( ){
            verify(this.cc.value,this.scode.value,this.cctype.value,
                this.exp_month.value+" "+this.exp_year.value);
            return false;
        };
    }

    //credit card number, security code, credit card type, and expiration date
    function verify(ccard,secure_code,cctype,ccexp){
        if(secure_code.length < 3) {
            eMsg("Please enter a valid value for the security code.","red");
            return;}
        if(cctype=="Choose one...") {
            eMsg("Please enter a valid value for the credit card type.","red");
            return;}
        if (! clientsideVerify(ccard)) {
            eMsg("Please enter a valid value for the credit card.","red");}
        else{
            eMsg("Please wait while we process the credit card.","blue");
            ccard=remDashSpace(ccard);
            url="http://www.parkerriver.com/s/verify?cc="+
                encodeURIComponent(ccard)+"&scode="+
                encodeURIComponent(secure_code)+"&type="+
                encodeURIComponent(cctype)+"&exp="+
                encodeURIComponent(ccexp);
            httpRequest("GET",url,true,handleCheck);
        }
    }
    /* Check whether the credit card entry is null, is not lengthy enough,
    or contains any letters. Remove any dashes or spaces from the entry,
    then run the Luhn algorithm on the resulting number. */
    function clientsideVerify(ccVal){
        if(ccVal == null || ccVal.length < 13 ||
            ccVal.search(/[a-zA-Z]+/) != -1){ return false; }
        ccVal=remDashSpace(ccVal);
        return (applyLuhn(ccVal) % 10) == 0;

    }
    //http://en.wikipedia.org/wiki/Luhn_formula
    function applyLuhn(cc){
        //reverse the String
        var rev = reverse(cc);
        //get array of character Strings
        var revArr = rev.split("");
        var total = 0;
        var tmp = 0;
        //add up the numbers
        for(var i = 0; i < revArr.length; i++){
            if((i % 2) > 0){
                tmp = revArr[i]*2;
                tmp= (tmp < 9 ? tmp : (tmp - 9) );
                total += tmp;
            } else {
```

```
            total += Number(revArr[i]);
        }
    }//end for
    return total;
}
//event handler for XMLHttpRequest
function handleCheck(){
    var sTag,answer,xmlReturnVal;
    if(request.readyState == 4){
        if(request.status == 200){
            //implement Document object in DOM
            xmlReturnVal = request.responseXML;
            sTag = xmlReturnVal.getElementsByTagName("cc_status")[0];
            answer= sTag.childNodes[0].data;
            if(answer=="okay"){
                eMsg("Your purchase information has"+
                    " been submtted to our online store.","blue"); }
            else {
                eMsg("There was a problem with processing "+
                    "the credit card.","red"); }
        } else {
            alert("A problem occurred with communicating "+
                "between the XMLHttpRequest object and the server program.
            ");
        }
    }//end outer if
}
/* Utility functions:
reverse a string. */
function reverse(str){

    var sArray = str.split("");
    var newS="";
    for(var i = sArray.length-1; i >= 0; i--){
        newS += sArray[i];
    }
    return newS;
}
//generate a styled message
function eMsg(msg,sColor){
    var div = document.getElementById("message");
    div.style.color=sColor;
    div.style.fontSize="0.9em";
    //remove old messages
    if(div.hasChildNodes()){
        div.removeChild(div.firstChild);
    }
    div.appendChild(document.createTextNode(msg));

}
//remove dashes or spaces
function remDashSpace(_number){
    number = _number.replace(/-/g,"");
```

```
number = _number.replace(/ /g,"");
return _number;
}
```

There is a lot of functionality to absorb here, so first we will discuss the button click. When the browser completes loading the web page, this event is captured by the code window.onload. This event handler is a sensible place to set up other event handlers, because the browser is guaranteed to have finished loading any other HTML tags that might be used by these handlers. Next, the code sets up an event handler for when the user submits the form:

```
document.forms[0].onsubmit=function(){
    verify(this.cc.value,this.scode.value,this.cctype.value,
        this.exp_month.value+" "+this.exp_year.value);
    return false;
};
```

The form's onsubmit event handler points to a function that calls verify( ), then returns false, which effectively cancels the browser's form submission. We are using the request object to send the form values only after verifying that the submissions are valid. Let's look at the verify( ) function:

```
function verify(ccard,secure_code,cctype,ccexp){
    if(secure_code.length < 3) {
        eMsg("Please enter a valid value for the security code.","red");
        return;}
    if(cctype=="Choose one...") {
        eMsg("Please enter a valid value for the credit card type.","red");
        return;}
    if (! clientsideVerify(ccard)) {
        eMsg("Please enter a valid value for the credit card.","red");}
    else {
        eMsg("Please wait while we process the credit card.","blue");
        ccard=remDashSpace(ccard);
        url="http://www.parkerriver.com/s/verify?cc="+
            encodeURIComponent(ccard)+"&scode="+
            encodeURIComponent(secure_code)+"&type="+
            encodeURIComponent(cctype)+"&exp="+
            encodeURIComponent(ccexp);
        httpRequest("GET",url,true,handleCheck);
    }
}
```

This function includes a number of common-sense checks before it validates the credit card number using another function, clientsideVerify( ). If the latter function returns true, the code builds a URL for the server component and then uses XMLHttpRequest to send the card information.

The httpRequest( ) function is responsible for setting up XMLHttpRequest and connecting with the server. Again, this function takes four parameters:

- The type of request, as in GET or POST
- The URL or server web address
- A Boolean indicating whether the request is asynchronous or not
- The name of a function or a function literal that handles the server response

The function name should be passed in without the following parentheses, as in handleCheck. It can also be a function literal, as in

```
httpRequest("GET",url,true,function(){ //...});
```

The httpRequest( ) code appears in the file *http_request.js* (see "Use Your Own Library for XMLHttpRequest" [Hack #3]).

Shooting the Luhn

The clientsideVerify( ) function verifies that the credit card number is at least 13 characters long and does not contain any letters. If the credit card number passes these checks, the code removes any spaces or dashes from the string and calls a function that uses the Luhn formula:

```
function clientsideVerify(ccVal){
    if(ccVal == null || ccVal.length < 13 ||
        ccVal.search(/[a-zA-Z]+/) != -1){ return false; }
    ccVal=remDashSpace(ccVal);
    return (applyLuhn(ccVal) % 10) == 0;

}
```

Here is the code for the applyLuhn( ) function:

```
function applyLuhn(cc){
    //reverse the String
    var rev = reverse(cc);
    //get array of character Strings
    var revArr = rev.split("");
    var total = 0;
    var tmp = 0;
    //add up the numbers
    for(var i = 0; i < revArr.length; i++){
        if((i % 2) > 0){
            tmp = revArr[i]*2;
            tmp= (tmp < 9 ? tmp : (tmp - 9) );
            total += tmp;
        } else {
            total += Number(revArr[i]);
        }
    }//end for
    return total;
}
```

Information on the Luhn formula or algorithm is easily found on the Web, so we will not take up a lot of space describing it here.

This function takes a `string` of numbers, applies the formula to the numbers, and returns the sum to `clientsideVerify( )`. If the total can be evenly divided by 10, the credit card number is valid. Here is the piece of code from `clientsideVerify( )` that makes this determination:

```
return (applyLuhn(ccVal) % 10) == 0;//returns true or false
```

The server component returns a bit of XML indicating success or failure, mimicking the processing of a purchase order (as in `<cc_status>okay</cc_status>`). The `handleResponse( )` function generates a user message from this return value:

```
xmlReturnVal = request.responseXML;
sTag = xmlReturnVal.getElementsByTagName("cc_status")[0];
answer= sTag.childNodes[0].data;
if(answer=="okay"){
  eMsg("Your purchase information has"+
  " been submtted to our online store.","blue");  }
```

The `eMsg( )` function is responsible for generating a styled user message in red, in the event of an error in handling the purchase information, or in blue otherwise. However, the entire process takes place backstage; the web page never refreshes, and only small parts of the user interface change as the user interacts with the application.

HACK #26 Validate Credit Card Security Codes

Make sure the security code is entered correctly in your Ajax credit card application.

The *card security code*, or CSC, is the three- or four-digit number that is printed on the back of a credit card, along with the card number (see *http://en.wikipedia.org/wiki/Card_Security_Code*). The CSC is designed to augment the authentication of the credit card user. In addition to the card number, many online stores that take credit cards also request that the user provide the CSC associated with the card. This act in itself, however, puts in jeopardy the secure identity of the CSC, so this authentication technique is far from airtight.

The only entity that can *validate* a CSC is the merchant bank that has the responsibility for processing the credit card. There isn't a special formula like the Luhn algorithm to validate it (it's only three or four numbers long, anyway!). However, this hack verifies that the user has entered the CSC correctly, using the following criteria:

- The field contains only numbers.
- If the credit card type is Mastercard, Visa, or Discover, the field has exactly three numbers.
- If the credit card type is American Express, the field has exactly four numbers.

Figure 3-6 shows a web page that requests a CSC and other information (you may recognize it from "Validate Credit Card Numbers" [Hack #25]).

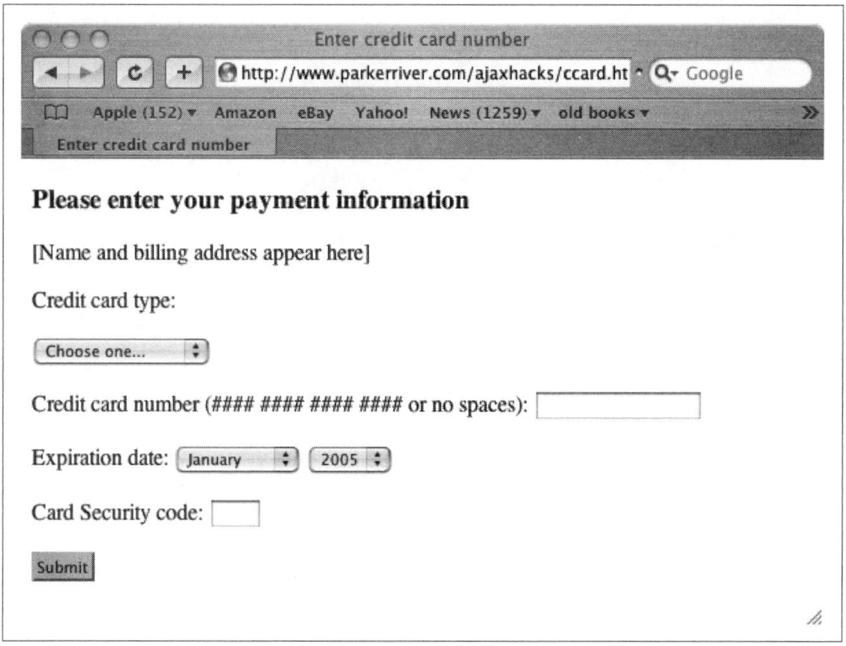

Figure 3-6. Validate card security codes

This hack sets up the CSC validation so that when the user types in the text field and then clicks outside of the field or presses the Tab key, JavaScript code ensures that the criteria described earlier are met before continuing with the rest of the application. Here is the HTML for the web page:

```
<!DOCTYPE html PUBLIC "-//W3C//DTD XHTML 1.0 Strict//EN"
        "http://www.w3.org/TR/2000/REC-xhtml1-20000126/DTD/xhtml1-strict.
dtd">
<html xmlns="http://www.w3.org/1999/xhtml" xml:lang="en" lang="en">
<head>
    <script type="text/javascript" src="js/http_request.js"></script>
    <script type="text/javascript" src="js/cc.js"></script>
    <meta http-equiv="content-type" content="text/html; charset=iso-8859-1"
/>
    <title>Enter credit card number</title>
```

Validate Credit Card Security Codes

```
    </head>
    <body>
    <h3>Please enter your payment information</h3>
    <div id="message"></div>
    <p>
        [Name and billing address appear here]
    </p>
    <p>
        Credit card type:
    </p>
    <form action="javascript:void%200">
        <p>
            <select name="cctype" id="cctype">
                <option value="Choose one...">Choose one...</option>
                <option value="Mastercard">Mastercard</option>
                <option value="Visa">Visa</option>
                <option value="American Express">American Express</option>
                <option value="Discover">Discover</option>
            </select>
        </p>
        <p>
            Credit card number (#### #### #### #### or no spaces):
            <input type="text" name="cc" size="16" maxlength="19" />
        </p>
        <p>Expiration date:
            <select name="exp_month" id="exp_month">
                <option>January</option>
                <option>February</option>
                <option>March</option>
                <option>April</option>
                <option>May</option>
                <option>June</option>
                <option>July</option>
                <option>August</option>
                <option>September</option>
                <option>October</option>
                <option>November</option>
                <option>December</option>
            </select>
            <select name="exp_year" id="exp_year">
                <option>2005</option>
                <option>2006</option>
                <option>2007</option>
                <option>2008</option>
                <option>2009</option>
                <option>2010</option>
            </select>
        </p>
        <p>
            Card Security code:
            <input type="text" name="scode" id="csc" size="4" maxlength="4" />
        </p>
        <p>
```

```
            <button type="submit" name="submit" id="submit" value=
                "Submit">Submit</button>
      </p>
   </form>
   </body>
   </html>
```

The web page imports a JavaScript file called *cc.js*. Here is the code in *cc.js* that handles the CSC text field:

```
var csc = document.getElementById("csc");
   if(csc != null) {
       csc.onblur=function( ){
           var typ = document.getElementById("cctype");
           if(typ != null){
               if(csc.value.indexOf("Choose") == -1 &&
                    ! checkCSC(typ.value, csc.value.
                    replace(/\s/,""))) {
                   eMsg("Please enter a valid value for the security code.
                   ","red");
                   csc.focus( );
                   document.getElementById("submit").disabled=true;
               } else {
                   clearMsg( );
                   document.getElementById("submit").disabled=false;

               }
           }
       };
   }
```

The variable csc refers to the text field where the user is supposed to enter the CSC. The code sets the field's onblur event handler to a function that checks the security code value. The function then generates a user message and disables the Submit button if the value is invalid. You want to disable this button because the application should prevent the running of the form's onsubmit event handler until the security code text field contains a valid value.

checkCSC( ) validates the CSC field using regular expressions:

```
function checkCSC(cardTyp,fldValue){
   var re = null;
   if(cardTyp != null){
       if(cardTyp == "American Express"){
           re = /^\d{4}$/;
           return re.test(fldValue);
           //Mastercard, Visa, Discover
       } else {
           re = /^\d{3}$/;
           return re.test(fldValue);

       }
```

```
        }

    }
```

If the card is American Express, the regular expression looks for a `string` containing four digits. The `RegExp` object's `test( )` method returns `true` if its string parameter returns a match:

```
re = /^\d{4}$/;
return re.test(fldValue);
```

Similarly, the code checks the value associated with the three other major credit card types for a `string` containing three digits. A `false` return value from this method indicates an invalid value; in this case, the user will see a red message and a disabled Submit button, as in Figure 3-7.

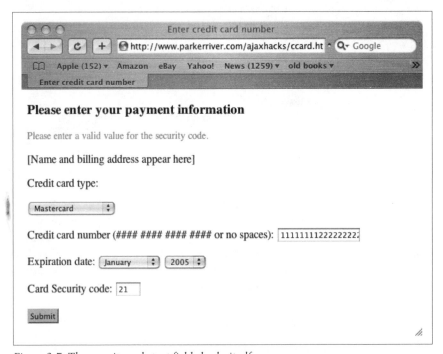

Figure 3-7. The security code text field checks itself

> You should trim the value in the security code text field, because if the user inadvertently types a space and three numbers (and is using, say, Mastercard) the regular expression will not find a match, because the searched string will be " 123" instead of "123". The user, who will see the correct number in the field, will be irritated. You can use the string method `replace(/\s/,"")`, which replaces any space characters in the `string` with the empty `string`.

When the application has finished checking the card security code, the user can click the Submit button. Then an onsubmit event handler will verify the credit card number, as in the previous hack, before sending a valid number to a server component to process the purchase order.

Validate a Postal Code
#27

Implement a client-side format validation for a ZIP Code.

This hack checks what the user has entered in a text field and makes sure that the value represents the proper format for a U.S. ZIP Code. We'll only look at the basics of validating a ZIP Code here. If you want to take it beyond just validating the *format* of a ZIP, you can use the code in "Fetch a Postal Code" [Hack #34], in the next chapter, as a secondary step to determine if the ZIP Code is actually the correct one for the specified city and state.

Figure 3-8 shows what this hack's web page looks like. It is a subset of the typical form that asks for the user's address information.

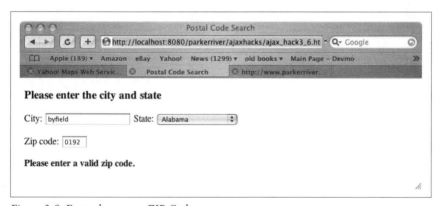

Figure 3-8. Enter the correct ZIP Code

The user enters zero to five digits in the text field (this hack tests only the first five digits of a ZIP Code), then presses Tab or clicks outside of the field. The application's code then automatically validates what the user typed.

The code makes sure that the user entered five digits, and only five digits, into the field. The web page imports a JavaScript file named *hacks3_7.js*, which contains the following code:

```
window.onload=function( ){
    var zip = document.getElementById("zip5");
    var cit = document.getElementById("city");
    zip.onblur=function( ){
        if(this.value && cit.value) {chkZipcode(zip.value);}
        //validate actual zip code:
```

```
            // httpRequest("GET","http://www.parkerriver.com/s/zip?city="+
            //                      encodeURIComponent(cit)+"&state="+
            //                      encodeURIComponent(_st),
            //              true,handleResponse);
      };
   };

   function chkZipcode(zipVal){
       var re = /^\d{5}$/;
       if(! re.test(zipVal)) {
          document.getElementById("message").
                 innerHTML="<strong>Please enter a valid zip code.</strong>";
       }
   }

   function handleResponse( ){
       var xmlReturnVal;
       try{
          if(request.readyState == 4){
             if(request.status == 200){
                xmlReturnVal=request.responseXML;
                if(xmlReturnVal != null) {
                   //validate entered zip code against this value
                }
             } else {
                //request.status is 503
                //if the application isn't available;
                //500 if the application has a bug
                alert(
                      "A problem occurred with communicating between"+
                      " the XMLHttpRequest object and the server program.
                   ");
             }
          }//end outer if
       } catch (err) {
          alert("It does not appear that the server "+
                "is available for this application. Please"+
                " try again very soon. \nError: "+err.message);

       }
   }
```

The `window.onload` event handler, triggered when the browser finishes loading the web page, sets up the behavior for the application. Within the
`window.onload` event handler is an onblur event handler for the ZIP Code text
field. This event handler is triggered when the user presses Tab or clicks outside of the ZIP Code field. The code verifies that the user has typed values
into the city and ZIP Code text fields (`if(cit.value && zip.value)`), and, if
so, validates the format of the ZIP Code value using `chkZipcode( )`.

This function uses a regular expression that represents a phrase made up of five numbers. The code tests the entered ZIP Code value against this regular expression to determine if the ZIP Code's format is correct.

 A regular expression represents a template for testing strings of characters. The regular expression used here looks for a line of text made up of just five numbers (the ^ means "beginning of the line," and $ is a special symbol for "end of the line"). \d is a predefined character class for a digit [0–9].

If the format is not correct, the code generates a user message. The web page code includes a div element with an id of message to contain these notifications:

```
var re = /^\d{5}$/;
if(! re.test(zipVal)) {
    document.getElementById("message").
            innerHTML="<strong>Please enter a valid zip code.</strong>";
}
```

Hacking the Hack

If you want to ensure that the five numbers represent a *real* ZIP Code, you can use the code in "Fetch a Postal Code" [Hack #34] to request a postal code for a certain city and state. That hack requests the ZIP from a web service; your code can then compare this value with the value entered by the user.

 Some cities have multiple ZIP Codes, and "Fetch a Postal Code" [Hack #34] returns only the first ZIP Code found for a city/state combination. Therefore, this method is not a fool-proof way of validating every ZIP Code value. You could alter the server component that connects with the web service to return all ZIP Codes found for a specified city, but this method would still require more user interaction to narrow down the choices to one ZIP Code.

## CHAPTER 4

Power Hacks for Web Developers
Hacks 28–42

Web development these days increasingly involves making connections with cool and useful web APIs, such as Google Maps, Yahoo! Maps, and Weather.com. The first five hacks in this chapter cover some uses of these APIs; "Use Ajax with a Yahoo! Maps and GeoURL Mash-up" [Hack #32] integrates data from the GeoURL service. The growth of Ajax techniques also makes it necessary to take some applications off-line (for example, when moving from the terminal to an airliner with a laptop), and thus requires persistent storage of data on the client side. To this end, this chapter includes a hack describing the new open source client storage tool called AMASS. It also delves into the typical tasks that inhabit a web developer's calendar, such as adding email capabilities to Ajax applications, accessing and creating HTTP cookies, debugging the DOM objects in Ajax software, and finding out the browser's locale information. Finally, this chapter's last hack creates an "Ajaxy" RSS feed reader. (RSS—Really Simple Syndication, in one of its flavors—is an XML file format that plays an important role at a number of news- and issue-oriented web sites.)

Get Access to the Google Maps API
#28   Create applications that combine Google Maps and your own server components.

For map lovers and developers, perhaps the only thing cooler than Google Maps is the Google Maps API. The API allows developers to invent new Ajax-style applications with Google Maps. It is made up of JavaScript objects and methods that let you control the appearance of maps on web pages, add controls to them, and create new clickable behaviors.

To use the API, you have to first obtain a developer's key from Google. This is very easy. Simply go to *http://www.google.com/apis/maps/*, specify the web site that will use Google Maps (such as *http://www.parkerriver.com*), and click on a form button, and Google generates a key for you. This is a long bunch of alphanumeric characters, such as:

```
CDROAAAANJd_PEMs2vnU_fo4htHhZhSa_9HZXsWbc66iRLah8f17kmN8QRSryZ54UMgeX7XabY
zm82xuubmjRb
```

Google Objects

You specify the key in your web page when your `script` tag imports Google's JavaScript library for Google Maps. Here is what the top part of an HTML page looks like when enabling the Google Maps API, including the key specification:

```
<!DOCTYPE html PUBLIC "-//W3C//DTD XHTML 1.0 Strict//EN"
"http://www.w3.org/TR/xhtml1/DTD/xhtml1-strict.dtd">
<html xmlns="http://www.w3.org/1999/xhtml">
<head>
<script src="http://maps.google.com/maps?file=api&v=1&key=ABQIAAAANJd_
PEMs2vnU_fORhwHhZhSa_9HZXsWbc66iRLah8f17kmN8QRSryZ54UMgeX8GjfYzm82xuubmjRw"
type="text/javascript"></script>
```

The result of importing this script with a proper key is that your own JavaScript code can now access the objects that are part of the Google Maps API. These include the following:

- `GMap`, an object that allows you to embed a digital map with zooming controls inside of a block-type HTML element, such as a `div`
- `GMarker`, an icon that points to a specific place on the map
- `GPolyline`, which can overlay shapes onto a map
- `GPoint`, representing a map coordinate
- `GXmlHttp`, a "wrapper object" for our familiar `XMLHttpRequest` object

All these objects except for `GPolyline` are used in the next two hacks. In addition, the API includes `GXml` and `GXslt` objects for parsing XML and using XSLT technology.

 As mentioned in Chapter 1, XSLT is a templating language for transforming the information embedded in XML files.

The API also includes a general-purpose function, `GBrowserIsCompatible()`, which returns true if the user's browser supports Google Maps. As of November 2005, according to the Google documentation, Google Maps supported recent versions of Firefox/Mozilla, IE 5.5+, and Safari 1.2+, and "sort of" supported Opera. It did not support IE 5.0.

"Use the Google Maps API Request Object" **[Hack #29]** and "Use Ajax with a Google Maps and Yahoo! Maps Mash-up" **[Hack #30]** show how to use the Google Maps API. Visit the above-mentioned URL to obtain an API key, take a look at the developer's documentation at *http://www.google.com/apis/ maps/documentation/*, and start cracking!

HACK #29 Use the Google Maps API Request Object

The Google Maps API comes with its own request object for making HTTP requests from JavaScript code.

This hack initially displays a Google Map based on a user's preferences. These include the latitude/longitude at which the map should be centered, and the *zoom level* or magnification of the map when it is first displayed on the web page. An application typically obtains user-specific properties by reading a *cookie*, a small piece of data saved on a user's hard drive, or having a user sign in. This hack skips this opening step in order to focus on the gist of the hack's technology: obtaining user preferences from a server component to control a Google Map display.

"Send Cookie Values to a Server Program" **[Hack #38]** discusses reading cookies in an Ajax application.

Personal Googling

This hack displays a 500-by-300-pixel U.S. map on a web page, which also shows the user's preferred coordinates for centering the map and preferred zoom level (a two-digit number from the highest zoom level of 1 to around 18). A zoom level of 18, for instance, shows the continents and oceans, whereas a zoom level of 1 displays a town's streets.

As mentioned previously, when the user requests this web page, the application can either obtain the user's username from a previously generated cookie, or ask the user to sign in and fetch the preferences from a database. However, we are not going to show that step (even though it is important in a real-world application) because we surmise that the reader is more interested in the API's Ajax-related objects and the map-display code.

Here is the HTML for the hack:

```
<!DOCTYPE html PUBLIC "-//W3C//DTD XHTML 1.0 Strict//EN"
"http://www.w3.org/TR/xhtml1/DTD/xhtml1-strict.dtd">
<html xmlns="http://www.w3.org/1999/xhtml" xmlns:v=
"urn:schemas-microsoft-com:vml">
<head>
<script src="http://maps.google.com/maps?file=api&v=1&key=ABQIAAAANJd_
```

```
PEMs2vnU_foRhwHhZhQ6pfwiB1eVXKVVHswEcdvw4p5NixS195EO7O7VmH483DMzOQiZbIlbIf"
type="text/javascript"></script>
<script src="js/hacks4_1a.js" type="text/javascript"></script>
<title>View Map</title>
</head>
<body>
<h3>Your Google Map</h3>
<div id="map" style="width: 500px; height: 300px"></div>
<h4>Your specifications</h4>
<form action="javascript:void%200">
<p>
Latitude: <input type="text" name="_latitude" size="20" maxlength="20" />
</p>
<p>
Longitude: <input type="text" name="_longitude" size="20" maxlength="20" />
</p>
<p>
Zoom level: <input type="text" name="_zoomLevel" size="2" maxlength="2" />
</p>
</form>
</body>
</html>
```

This code imports the Google API library with the first script tag. This tag allows the application to use Google Maps API objects such as GMap and GXmlHttp (which represents the request object). The script src attribute includes the developer key, as described in "Get Access to the Google Maps API" [Hack #28]. Another script tag imports into the page a *hacks4_1a.js* Java-Script code file, which contains the custom code for our application.

> Google Maps requires a separate developer key for every URL directory containing Google Maps–related web pages. For example, I have a developer key that covers every web page in the *http://www.parkerriver.com/ajaxhacks/* directory. It is extremely easy to generate a developer key at *http:// www.google.com/apis/maps/signup.html*.

The map itself is displayed within a div tag that has an id of map. When the browser loads the page, the code first checks the compatibility of the browser using a Google global function, GBrowserIsCompatible( ). If this function returns true, the application calls a function named googleAjax( ). The window.onload event handler and googleAjax( ) appear inside the *hacks4_1a.js* file. googleAjax( ) queries a server for the user's specific preferences of a user by passing along the username ("bwperry," in this case). The application then uses the properties fetched by googleAjax( ) to display and zoom in on a map. Here is the code from *hacks4_1a.js*:

```
var map = null;
window.onload = function( ){
```

```
        if(GBrowserIsCompatible( )){
            googleAjax('http://www.parkerriver.com/s/gmap?user=bwperry');
        } else { alert('Your browser is not compatible with Google Maps!');}
};
function createMap(lat,lng,zoomLevel){
    map = new GMap(document.getElementById("map"));
    GEvent.addListener(map, 'click', function(overlay, point) {
        document.forms[0]._longitude.value=point.x;
        document.forms[0]._latitude.value=point.y;
        map.addOverlay(new GMarker(point));

    });
    map.addControl(new GLargeMapControl( ));
    map.addControl(new GMapTypeControl( ));
    if(lat != null && lat.length != 0 && lng != null && lng.
            length != 0 && zoomLevel != null && zoomLevel.length != 0){
        map.centerAndZoom(new GPoint(lng, lat), zoomLevel);
    } else {
        //center on roughly middle of USA
        map.centerAndZoom(new GPoint(-97.20703, 40.580584), 14);
    }
}

function googleAjax(url){

    var request = GXmlHttp.create( );
    request.open("GET", url, true);
    request.onreadystatechange = function( ) {
        if (request.readyState == 4) {
            if (request.status == 200) {
                var resp = request.responseXML;
                var rootNode = resp.documentElement;
                var zoom = rootNode.getElementsByTagName("zoomLevel")[0];
                var latLng = rootNode.
                getElementsByTagName("centerCoords")[0];
                var coordArr = latLng.firstChild.nodeValue.split(" ");
                var zoomLevel=zoom.firstChild.nodeValue;
                createMap(coordArr[0],coordArr[1],zoomLevel);
                alert(coordArr[0]+" "+coordArr[1]+" "+zoomLevel);
                document.forms[0]._latitude.value=coordArr[0];
                document.forms[0]._longitude.value=coordArr[1];
                document.forms[0]._zoomLevel.value=zoomLevel;
            } else {
                alert(
                        "The application had a problem communicating with "+
                        "the server. Please try again.");
            }//inner if
        }//outer if
    }//end function
    request.send(null);

}
```

It will probably help you visualize the application's purpose if I show you the map inside a browser window, before digging into the code. The page loads the map and displays the user's preferred coordinates and zoom level in text fields beneath it. Figure 4-1 shows the page displayed in a browser.

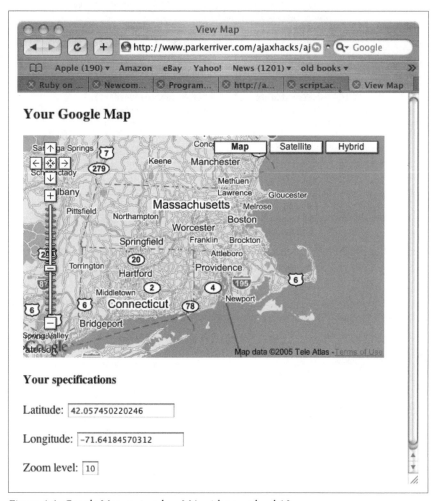

Figure 4-1. Google Map centered on MA with zoom level 10

Map Objects

Take a gander at the googleAjax( ) function and its creation of an object that makes HTTP requests:

```
function googleAjax(url){
    var request = GXmlHttp.create( );
    request.open("GET", url, true);
```

```
        request.onreadystatechange = function( ) {
            if (request.readyState == 4) {
                if (request.status == 200) {
                    var resp = request.responseXML;
                    var rootNode = resp.documentElement;
                    var zoom = rootNode.getElementsByTagName("zoomLevel")[0];
                    var latLng = rootNode.
                    getElementsByTagName("centerCoords")[0];
                    var coordArr = latLng.firstChild.nodeValue.split(" ");
                    var zoomLevel=zoom.firstChild.nodeValue;
                    createMap(coordArr[0],coordArr[1],zoomLevel);
                    document.forms[0]._latitude.value=coordArr[0];
                    document.forms[0]._longitude.value=coordArr[1];
                    document.forms[0]._zoomLevel.value=zoomLevel;
                } else {
                    alert(
                            "The application had a problem communicating with "+
                            "the server. Please try again.");
                }//inner if
            }//outer if
        }//end function
        request.send(null);
}
```

Remember all the code that created a request object in "Detect Browser Compatibility with the Request Object" **[Hack #1]** and "Use Your Own Library for XMLHttpRequest" **[Hack #3]**? All that's necessary with the Google Maps API is var request = GXmlHttp.create( ). You then call the open( ) and send( ) methods and point to a function that will be your onreadystatechange event handler, just as you would with a request object that you created with your own code.

 The onreadystatechange event handler specifies a JavaScript function that the code uses to handle an HTTP response. In Ajax, the request object queries a server, which typically sends back a response. You can have the event handler refer to a function literal (as in this code) or to the name of a function (without the ( ) characters) that you have defined elsewhere in the code (see "Detect Browser Compatibility with the Request Object" **[Hack #1]**).

This code fetches an XML document from the server that contains the user's map preferences:

```
var resp = request.responseXML;
```

The returned XML data might look like this:

```
<mapSetup>
<centerCoords>42.057450220246 -71.64184570312</centerCoords>
```

```
<zoomLevel>10</zoomLevel>
</mapSetup>
```

Remember that you are getting this XML information from the server. The data is specific to each user and can be stored in a database. This information represents the user's preferred latitude and longitude for the center point of the map, as well as the preferred zoom level.

In Google Maps, latitude is measured in the range 90 degrees north of the equator to –90 degrees south of the equator. Longitude is measured in a range of 180 degrees east of the Greenwich Meridian to –180 degrees west of the Greenwich Meridian.

The code then uses Document Object Model programming to pull the text values out of the XML document and use them for map display:

```
var rootNode = resp.documentElement;
var zoom = rootNode.getElementsByTagName("zoomLevel")[0];
var latLng = rootNode.getElementsByTagName("centerCoords")[0];
var coordArr = latLng.firstChild.nodeValue.split(" ");
var zoomLevel = zoom.firstChild.nodeValue;
createMap(coordArr[0],coordArr[1],zoomLevel);
document.forms[0]._latitude.value=coordArr[0];
document.forms[0]._longitude.value=coordArr[1];
document.forms[0]._zoomLevel.value=zoomLevel;
```

The root node is the top-level XML element, such as `mapSetup`. The DOM `Document` object has a `documentElement` property that returns a reference to this element. The code then stores references to the elements that hold the data on the coordinates for the center point of the map and the zoom level in variables named `latLng` and `zoom`, respectively.

How do you get the values of elements using DOM? The `latLng` variable, for instance, is of a `Node` type. The `Node` has a property named `firstChild`, which (phew!) returns the text node contained by the XML element. The code gets the text value of this `Node` using the `Node`'s `nodeValue` property.

The `centerCoords` element contains both latitude and longitude values, separated by a space character. Thus, calling the `string split( )` method returns an `array` that contains the latitude as the first `array` member and the longitude as the second member.

You can redesign the server component to return the latitude and longitude in separate XML elements.

Creating Your Own Map

The `createMap( )` function uses Google Maps objects to generate a map for the web page. The code calls this function with the user's preferred latitude, longitude, and zoom level as parameters, as in:

```
createMap(coordArr[0],coordArr[1],zoomLevel)
```

> The first two parameters are `array` members, which is why the code uses, for example, the `coordArr[0]` syntax.

Unlike in other Ajax libraries, when using the Google Maps API, the developer does not have to deal with the basics of `XMLHttpRequest`. However, if your application requires more control over the request object, you can initiate a setup like the one described in [Hack #3], which imports its own JavaScript file that handles HTTP requests.

HACK #30 Use Ajax with a Google Maps and Yahoo! Maps Mash-up

Use Google Maps in a web application with Yahoo! Maps and driving directions.

Both Google and Yahoo! provide developers with power tools for manipulating maps within their own web applications. "Get Access to the Google Maps API" [Hack #28] introduced readers to the Google Maps API; Yahoo! in turn provides the Yahoo! Maps API, which includes a specific API for Ajax developers (see *http://developer.yahoo.net/maps/ajax/index.html*).

Yahoo! Maps is very easy to get started with; just acquire an application ID from the above URL, then begin embedding Yahoo! Maps and controls inside your web pages. You have to include the application ID in the URL that embeds a map inside your web page, which you'll learn how to do in the upcoming hack description.

This hack uses both the Yahoo! Maps and Google Maps APIs. Combining two technologies in a web application is sometimes referred to as a *mash-up*, an expression that derives partly from the music industry. This way we can view a Google Map on the left side of the screen, perhaps in satellite view, and the same geographical region in a Yahoo! Map on the screen's right side. The mash-up also allows the user to click on a destination on a Google Map and access Yahoo's driving directions.

Use Ajax with a Google Maps and Yahoo! Maps Mash-up

HACK
#30

How It Works

This hack first sets up a Google Map on a web page using the Google Maps API. The application asks the user to click on the map to specify a map coordinate, and optionally, type in an origin address for driving directions. Users can zoom in on different map coordinates and areas prior to clicking a destination point.

The destination is specified in terms of latitude and longitude. A little balloon icon pops up on the Google Map wherever the mouse is clicked. When the user clicks the Yahoo! Map button, a Yahoo! Map appears on the screen's right side, centered on the specified latitude and longitude. The user can then optionally put the Google Map into satellite view, while manipulating the Yahoo! Map with its sophisticated controls.

To obtain driving directions, the user can enter an origin address in the left side text fields and then click the Yahoo! Directions button. The application uses the indicated latitude/longitude coordinates to scrape the driving directions off of a Yahoo! HTTP response. The hack then replaces the Yahoo! Map with the step-by-step driving directions.

Figure 4-2 shows what the application looks like in a web browser before the user clicks the Yahoo! Map button.

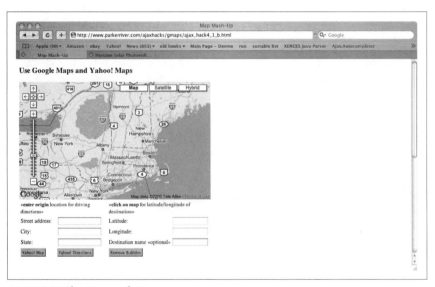

Figure 4-2. Choose your destination

The HTML page divides the application into two regions using div tags and CSS styles. The Google Map sits on the left side. Figure 4-3 shows the mashup after the user clicks on the Google Map to specify a coordinate, then clicks the Yahoo! Map button. The Yahoo! Map is shown on the right side of the screen.

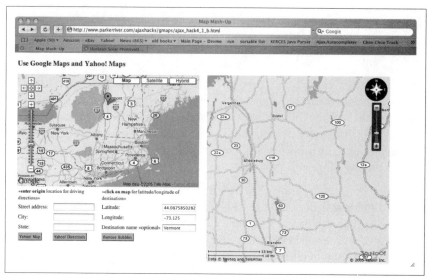

Figure 4-3. Google and Yahoo!, duking it out

Figure 4-4 shows the application when the user has changed to satellite mode in the Google Map and zoomed out a bit in the Yahoo! Map.

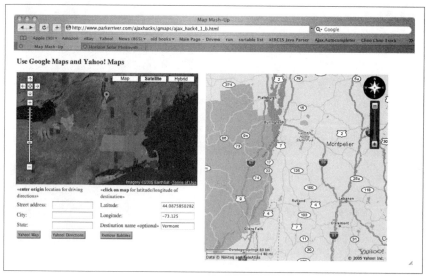

Figure 4-4. Changing to satellite mode

Use Ajax with a Google Maps and Yahoo! Maps Mash-up

HACK
#30

If the user requests driving directions, they appear in the right part of the screen, as in Figure 4-5.

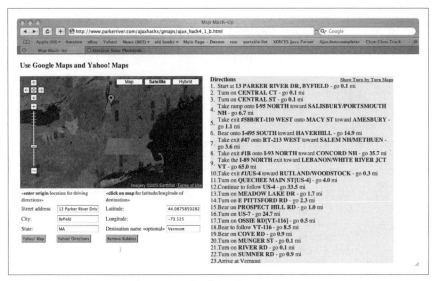

Figure 4-5. Marrying Google Maps and Yahoo! directions

 Google Maps provides latitude/longitude coordinates for anywhere on earth, but Yahoo!'s driving directions cannot presently provide directions between places that are separated by bodies of water such as oceans or bays. If you click on an island in a Google Map, for example, you will get the latitude/longitude point. However, the directions will be blank because Yahoo! driving directions, as of this writing, do not connect mainland origins with island destinations.

Fall Harvest

A good chunk of the work for the driving-directions mechanism is done by the server component, which harvests the directions from a Yahoo! page. Specifically, the Google request object sends along a Yahoo!-related URL that includes the user's chosen latitude and longitude coordinates. The server component then:

1. Makes a request to Yahoo! using the URL
2. Receives all the code for the Yahoo! page
3. Scrapes the driving directions from the page
4. Sends just this chunk of data back to the application, which displays the directions in the right frame

This chunk of data in the response is a div element containing a numbered list of driving directions, as in:

1. Take a right on Main Street and go 1.2 miles.
2. Go on the highway for another 680 miles....

HTML

Let's look at some of the HTML code for the page that's loaded into the mash-up user's browser. I'll just show the top part of the HTML code that sets this application in motion:

```
<!DOCTYPE html PUBLIC "-//W3C//DTD XHTML 1.0 Strict//EN"
        "http://www.w3.org/TR/xhtml1/DTD/xhtml1-strict.dtd">
<html xmlns="http://www.w3.org/1999/xhtml">
<head>
    <style type="text/css">
        .cont { float: left; height: 500px;
                width: 500px; }
        .instructions { font-size: 0.8em; }
        .label { font-size: 0.9em;}
    </style>
    <script src=
    "http://maps.google.com/maps?file=api&v=1&key=ABQIAAAANJd_PEMs2vnU_
    fORhwHhZhSkdb7FxCoFqdzTrRB9tjTtDcnrVRSo66iNyUFvtz5XXXXXXXXXXX"
    type="text/javascript"></script>
    <script src="/ajaxhacks/js/http_request.js" type=
    "text/javascript"></script>
    <script src="/ajaxhacks/js/hacks4_1_b.js" type=
    "text/javascript"></script>
    <script type="text/javascript" src=
    "http://api.maps.yahoo.com/ajaxymap?v=2.0&appid=YRXXXXXXXXXXX"></script>
    <title>Map Mash-Up</title>
</head>
<body>
<h3>Use Google Maps and Yahoo! Maps</h3>
<div id="gmap_container" class="cont">
<div id="map" style="width: 500px; height: 300px"></div>
...
```

The first script tag imports the Google Maps objects that we can use as official Google hackers. These are JavaScript objects such as GMap that allow the code to add and control maps on a web page. The src attribute of the script tag includes the long, involved URL for importing Google's special code, as well as the developer-specific key [Hack #28]. (The XXXs have been added because we shouldn't publish the exact keys we are using.)

The JavaScript code appears in the file *hacks4_1_b.js*. script tags import that code, which you'll see in an upcoming section, as well as the code that uses XMLHttpRequest [Hack #3]. Finally, the HTML code imports the Yahoo!

Use Ajax with a Google Maps and Yahoo! Maps Mash-up

HACK
#30

Maps–related code with another script tag. This code base is necessary for web pages that embed Yahoo! Maps. The URL for this purpose includes an appid parameter specifying your own application ID for Yahoo! Maps:

```
<script type="text/javascript" src=
"http://api.maps.yahoo.com/ajaxymap?v=2.0&appid=YRXXXXXXXXXXXX"></script>
```

Google and Yahoo!, Toe to Toe

Here is the JavaScript code in the *hacks4_1_b.js* file. The createMap( ) function does not need further explanation because we discussed it in the last hack. Let's focus on the code that embeds a Yahoo! Map and provides driving directions:

```
var map = null;
window.onload=function( ){
    createMap( );
    document.getElementById("submit").onclick=function( ){
        getDirections(document.forms[0]._street.value,
                document.forms[0]._city.value,
                document.forms[0]._state.value,
                document.forms[0]._dname.value,
                document.forms[0]._latitude.value,
                document.forms[0]._longitude.value);
    };
    document.getElementById("rem_bubbles").onclick=function( ){
        clearOverlays( );
    };

    document.getElementById("yah_maps").onclick=function( ){
        createYMap( );
    };
};
function createYMap( ){
    writeMap(document.forms[0]._latitude.value,
            document.forms[0]._longitude.value);
}
function createMap( ){
    map = new GMap(document.getElementById("map"));
    GEvent.addListener(map, 'click', function(overlay, point) {
        document.forms[0]._longitude.value=point.x;
        document.forms[0]._latitude.value=point.y;
        map.addOverlay(new GMarker(point));

    });
    map.addControl(new GLargeMapControl( ));
    map.addControl(new GMapTypeControl( ));
    //center on roughly middle of USA
    map.centerAndZoom(new GPoint(-97.20703, 40.580584), 14);
}
function clearOverlays( ){
    if(map != null){
```

HACK
#30

Use Ajax with a Google Maps and Yahoo! Maps Mash-up

```
            map.clearOverlays( );
        }
    }

    function getDirections(street,city,state,
            destName,lat,lng){

        var _str = encodeURIComponent(street);
        var _cit = encodeURIComponent(city);
        var url = "http://www.parkerriver.com/s/dd?"+_str+"&tlt="+
                lat+"&tln="+lng+"&csz="+
                _cit+"%2C"+state+"&country=us&tname="+destName;
        httpRequest("GET",url,true,handleResponse);
    }

    //event handler for XMLHttpRequest
    function handleResponse( ){
        try{
            if(request.readyState == 4){
                if(request.status == 200){
                    var _dirs = request.responseText;
                    var targDiv = document.getElementById("ymap_container");
                    targDiv.innerHTML=_dirs+
                    '<p><form><button type=\"button\" onclick=\
                    "window.print( )\">Print Directions</button></form></p>';
                } else {
                    //request.status is not 200; ommitted for brevity
                }
            }//end outer if
        } catch (err)   {
            //ommitted for brevity

        }
    }

    function writeMap(lat,lng){
        var _point = new YGeoPoint(parseInt(lat), parseInt(lng));
        var _map = new YMap(document.getElementById('ymap_container'));
        _map.drawZoomAndCenter(_point, 8);
        _map.addPanControl( );
        _map.addZoomLong( );
        document.getElementById('yah_maps').disabled=true;
    }
```

A good place to start explaining this program is with the writeMap( ) function. This code shows how easy it is to embed a Yahoo! Map. The code passes the latitude and longitude coordinates into the constructor for a YGeoPoint object (an object provided by Yahoo! Maps). The code then creates a YMap object, specifying the div element that will contain the Yahoo! Map. The next three method calls center the map on the specified coordinates at a certain zoom level (here, 8 in a range of 1 to 16), then add a couple of Yahoo! controls to the map.

Use Ajax with a Google Maps and Yahoo! Maps Mash-up

HACK
#30

The last bit of code disables the Yahoo! Map button, because one embedded map is enough; after loading the map, the user can manipulate it to show any other location.

Driving Directions

The code also contains a function for displaying driving directions:

```
function getDirections(street,city,state,
       destName,lat,lng){

    var _str = encodeURIComponent(street);
    var _cit = encodeURIComponent(city);
    var url = "http://www.parkerriver.com/s/dd?"+_str+"&tlt="+
              lat+"&tln="+lng+"&csz="+
              _cit+"%2C"+state+"&country=us&tname="+destName;
    httpRequest("GET",url,true);
}
```

This function is launched when the user clicks the Yahoo! Directions button. (See Figure 4-5 for a view of what this screen and button look like.) The function takes the street, city, and state where the user wants to start the trip, as well as the latitude, longitude, and (optionally) the preferred name for the destination, then sends this information to the server component that actually talks to the Yahoo! application.

The function uses the global JavaScript encodeURIComponent( ) function to make sure that the street and city, which may encompass more than one word (as in "New Orleans"), are properly encoded for an Internet address. In encoding phrases for URLs, New Orleans becomes New%20Orleans, for example.

How Do I Get to Latitude...?

I won't go into great detail about how the server component is programmed, except to say that the address of the component is a Java servlet at *http://www.parkerriver.com/s/dd/*. The servlet sends an HTTP request to the Yahoo! component, then sifts through the return value for the chunk of HTML representing driving directions. The servlet then sends these directions back to our Ajax application.

Developers can use their API of choice to harvest information from web pages. The servlet in this hack uses APIs from the Java software development kit (SDK), including javax. swing.text.html.parser.ParserDelegator and javax.swing. text.html.HTMLEditorKit.ParserCallback.

getDirections( ) appends a *querystring* to the end of the URL following a question mark (?). An example URL is:

http://www.parkerriver.com/s/dd?1%20Main%20St.&tlt=43.96119 0638920&tln=-70.13671875&csz=Smithtown%2CNE&country= us&tname=Main

In other words, the parameters in the querystring represent the origin address and the latitude/longitude of the destination. The server component attaches the Yahoo! application URL (*http://api.maps.yahoo.com/dd_ result?newaddr=*) to the querystring. The servlet then sends an HTTP request to this address, asking Yahoo! for driving directions. This is how the servlet obtains the driving directions for a particular address and map coordinate.

What's Next?

The request object enters the request/response cycle in the way described in "Use Your Own Library for XMLHttpRequest" **[Hack #3]**, using the simple XMLHttpRequest library *http_request.js* specifies.

The server component scrapes just the chunk of Yahoo!'s response that we plan to use—the driving directions that appear within a div element—and returns this to our JavaScript code. Here's the method that handles the response:

```
//event handler for XMLHttpRequest
function handleResponse( ){
    try{
        if(request.readyState == 4){
            if(request.status == 200){
                var _dirs = request.responseText;
                var targDiv = document.getElementById("ymap_container");
                targDiv.innerHTML=_dirs+
                    '<p><form><button type=\"button\" onclick=\
                    "window.print( )\">Print Directions</button></form></p>';
    //continued...
```

The request object returns the div element, itself containing a subset of HTML, in its responseText property. The code then adds this div dynamically to the right side of the browser screen, adding a little code at the end to allow the user to print out the directions.

That's all there is to it! The user can print out the directions by clicking the Print Directions button. The script in handleResponse( ) writes out the code for this button, which just calls window.print( ):

```
<button type=\"button\" onclick=\"window.print( )\">
```

In the spirit of mash-ups, this hack makes the case that two map APIs are better than one.

Display a Weather.com XML Data Feed

Display weather information on a web page and search a different location without a page submission.

This hack displays detailed weather information for a location, and allows the user to search another U.S. location for its temperature, humidity, and other weather-related data. The web page displays the new weather report without a complete page refresh. The information is derived from The Weather Channel Interactive, Inc. (*http://www.weather.com*).

Prepping

To use the Weather Channel's XML data feed in a hack, you have to sign up at Weather.com and download the software development kit. The SDK contains some logos and a couple of PDF guides explaining the requirements for usage of the data. If you want to implement this data feed, the signup begins at *http://www.weather.com/services/xmloap.html* (the URL is not a typo!).

This hack sends the name of a U.S. city and state to a Weather.com URL that implements a web service. As part of the usage requirements, a registered developer must send along a partner ID and license ID as parameters in the URL. Weather.com responds with an XML file containing detailed weather information for the specified location.

Figure 4-6 shows what the page looks like in Firefox 1.5.

Weather.com requires developers to display their logo and link back to their site.

When the browser loads the web page, the weather report for a default location is loaded into it. The user can then enter a city name, select a state, and then request the weather data for a new location. Here are highlights of the web page, which imports a couple of JavaScript libraries:

```
<!DOCTYPE html PUBLIC "-//W3C//DTD XHTML 1.0 Strict//EN"
        "http://www.w3.org/TR/2000/REC-xhtml1-20000126/DTD/xhtml1-strict.
dtd">
<html xmlns="http://www.w3.org/1999/xhtml" xml:lang="en" lang="en">
<head>
    <meta http-equiv="content-type" content="text/html; charset=utf-8" />
    <script type="text/javascript" src="js/http_request.js" />
    <script type="text/javascript" src="js/hacks_4_4.js" />
```

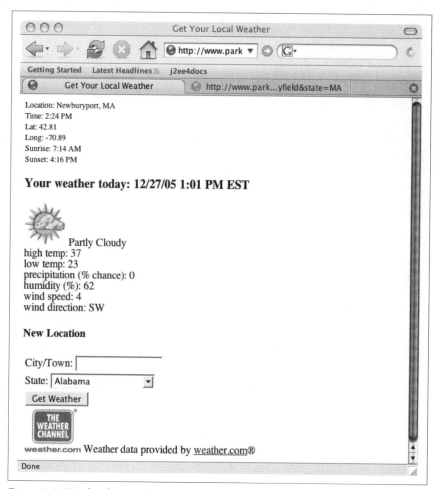

Figure 4-6. Weather for our default location

```
    <link rel="stylesheet" type="text/css" href="/css/hacks.css" />
    <title>Get Your Local Weather</title>
</head>
<body>
<div id="top_level">
    <span id="city_state" class="message"></span><br />
    <span id="time" class="message"></span><br />
    <span id="_lat" class="message"></span><br />
    <span id="_lng" class="message"></span><br />
    <span id="sunrise" class="message"></span><br />
    <span id="sunset" class="message"></span>
</div>

<h3>Your weather today: <span id="_date"></span></h3>
<div id="d_weather">
```

```
    <img id="w_icon" src="" width="64" height="64" align="left"/>
    <span id="_desc"></span><br />
    <span id="_high"></span><br />
    <span id="_low"></span><br />
    <span id="_precip"></span><br />
    <span id="_humid"></span><br />
    <span id="spd_wind"></span><br />
    <span id="dir_wind"></span>
</div>

<h4>New Location</h4>
<div id="_location">
    <form action="javascript:void%200" >
        <table border="0"><tr>
        <td>City/Town: <input type="text" name=
            "_city" size="15" maxlength="15" /></td></tr>
            <tr><td>State:  <select name="_state">
                <option value="al">Alabama</option>
                <option value="ak">Alaska</option>
                <option value="az">Arizona</option>
                <option value="ar">Arkansas</option>
                <option value="ca">California</option>
                <!-- SNIPPED -->
            </select></td></tr>
            <tr><td><button type="button" id="getWeather" name=
                "go" value="Go">Get Weather</button> </td></tr>
            <!—SNIPPED -->
</html>
```

Two div elements contain the weather data that you load in from an XML
file. The bottom of the page contains a form for entering in the new location
and requesting more weather info. The real guts of the application are represented by the JavaScript in *hacks_4_4.js*. *http_request.js* "Use Your Own
Library for XMLHttpRequest" [Hack #3] handles the XMLHttpRequest object.

Here's the code in *hacks_4_4.js*. A window.onload event handler gets things
going once the browser has finished loading the XHTML code:

```
var defaultLocationId="USMA0279";
var partId="101xxxxxxx";
var licId="67f74axxxxxxxxxx";
var _host="www.parkerriver.com"
//city and state of location user searched for
var _cit = "";
var _stat = "";
window.onload = function( ){
    document.getElementById("getWeather").onclick=function( ){
        getNewLocation( );
    }
    getWeather(defaultLocationId);
}
/* Get the weather XML data for a certain location */
```

```
function getWeather(locationId){
    if (locationId == null || locationId.length=="") { return; }

    var url = "http://"+_host+"/s/weathxml/weatherSearch?&locId="+
            locationId+"&cc=*&dayf=2&prod=xoap&par="+
            partId+"&key="+licId;
    httpRequest("GET",url,true,handleResponse);
}

function getNewLocation(){
    var val = document.forms[0]._city.value;
    if(val.length != 0){
        _cit = val;
    } else {
        //we need at least a city to do a search
        return;
    }
    var sval = document.forms[0]._state.value;
    if(sval.length != 0){
        _stat = sval;
        getLocation(_cit+","+_stat);
    } else {
        getLocation(_cit);      //We can do a search with only a city name
    }
}
/* The parameter can be a city alone or a city,state combo
as in Boston,MA */
function getLocation(_lcity){
    if (_lcity == null || _lcity.length=="") {alert("returning"); return; }
    //server component URL; the component connects with Weather.com
    var url = "http://"+_host+"/s/weathxml/addressSearch?city="+_lcity;
    httpRequest("GET",url,true,handleResponse);

}

//event handler for XMLHttpRequest
function handleResponse(){
    try{
        if(request.readyState == 4){
            if(request.status == 200){
                var _xml = request.responseXML;
                if(_xml != null){
                    var _root = _xml.documentElement;
                    switch(_root.tagName){
                        case "weather":
                            displayWeather(_root); break;
                        case  "search":
                            handleSearchResult(_root); break;
                        case "error" :
                            alert("Your weather or location search "+
                                "generated an error. "+
                                "Please try again."); break;
                        default: alert("Your search generated an "+
```

```
                                    "unspecified problem. "+
                                    "Please try again.");
                    }
                } else {
                    alert("The server returned a null value "+
                            "for the XML. Please try again in a few seconds.
");
                }

            } else {
                //See Hack #3...
            }
        }//end outer if
    } catch (err)   {
        //See Hack #3...


    }
}
/* Display the weather based on XML data derived from
the Weather.com API */
function displayWeather(rootElement){
    if(rootElement != null){
        var loc= rootElement.getElementsByTagName("loc")[0];
        setupToplevel(loc);
        var  dayf = rootElement.getElementsByTagName("dayf")[0];
        setupWeather(dayf);
    }
}

function handleSearchResult(rootEl){
    var locArray = rootEl.getElementsByTagName("loc");
    var elVal = null;
    for(var i = 0; i < locArray.length; i++){
        elVal = locArray[i].firstChild.nodeValue;
        //if a state was specified in the search, include in
        //the search here
        if(_stat.length != 0){
            if (elVal == _cit+", "+_stat.toUpperCase()) {
                getWeather(locArray[i].getAttribute("id")); }
        } else {
            alert("No state in search.");
            //just return the first result if no state is provided
            getWeather(locArray[i].getAttribute("id"));
            break;
        }
    }

}
/* Pull data from the XML and plug it into the proper span
tag in the XHTML */

function setupToplevel(_element){
    if(_element != null){
```

```
            setupElement( _element.getElementsByTagName("dnam")[0],
                    document.getElementById("city_state"),"Location");
            setupElement( _element.getElementsByTagName("tm")[0],
                    document.getElementById("time"),"Time");
            setupElement( _element.getElementsByTagName("lat")[0],
                    document.getElementById("lat"),"Lat");
            setupElement( _element.getElementsByTagName("lon")[0],
                    document.getElementById("lng"),"Long");
            setupElement( _element.getElementsByTagName("sunr")[0],
                    document.getElementById("sunrise"),"Sunrise");
            setupElement( _element.getElementsByTagName("suns")[0],
                    document.getElementById("sunset"),"Sunset");
        }
}

function setupElement(_node,_span,txtMsg)  {
    if(arguments.length == 3){
        _span.innerHTML= txtMsg+": "+_node.firstChild.nodeValue;
    } else {
        _span.innerHTML= _node.firstChild.nodeValue;
    }
}
//embed the weather image
function setupImgElement(_node,_imgElement)  {
    _imgElement.src="http://"+_host+"/ajaxhacks/img/"+
            _node.firstChild.nodeValue+".png";
}

function setupWeather(_element){
    if(_element != null){
        var parts = _element.getElementsByTagName("part");
        /* Contains sub-elements describing day/night weather */
        var dpart = null;
        setupElement( _element.getElementsByTagName("lsup")[0],
                document.getElementById("date"));
        setupElement( _element.getElementsByTagName("hi")[0],
                document.getElementById("high"),"high temp");
        setupElement( _element.getElementsByTagName("low")[0],
                document.getElementById("low"),"low temp");
        for(var i = 0; i < parts.length; i++)   {
            if(parts[i].getAttribute("p") == "d") { dpart=parts[i];}
        }
        setupImgElement( dpart.getElementsByTagName("icon")[0],
                document.getElementById("w_icon"));
        setupElement(dpart.getElementsByTagName("ppcp")[0],
                document.getElementById("precip"),"precipitation (%
chance)");
        setupElement( dpart.getElementsByTagName("hmid")[0],
                document.getElementById("humid"),"humidity (%)");
        setupElement(dpart.getElementsByTagName("t")[0],
                document.getElementById("desc"));
        var _wind = dpart.getElementsByTagName("wind")[0];
        setupElement( _wind.getElementsByTagName("s")[0],
```

```
            document.getElementById("spd_wind"),"wind speed");
        setupElement( _wind.getElementsByTagName("t")[0],
            document.getElementById("dir_wind"),"wind direction");
    }


}
```

Most of this code involves pulling the content out of the returned XML and displaying it on the web page. Two functions request weather data for a location and search for a "location ID" associated with a city/state combination, such as Oakland, CA. To access this weather XML feed, the requestor has to provide a location ID in the URL, representing a city or city/state combination. If the user provides a city and/or state for weather information, our application has to request the location ID first (we already know the location ID for our default location), then use this ID to fetch its weather data:

```
/* Get the weather XML data for a certain location */
function getWeather(locationId){
    if (locationId == null || locationId.length=="") { return; }

    var url = "http://"+_host+"/s/weathxml/weatherSearch?&locId="+
            locationId+"&cc=*&dayf=2&prod=xoap&par="+
            partId+"&key="+licId;
    httpRequest("GET",url,true,handleResponse);
}

function getNewLocation( ){
    var val = document.forms[0]._city.value;
    if(val.length != 0){
        _cit = val;
    } else {
        //we need at least a city to do a search
        return;
    }
    var sval = document.forms[0]._state.value;
    if(sval.length != 0){
        _stat = sval;
        getLocation(_cit+","+_stat);
    } else {
        getLocation(_cit);    //we can do a search with only a city name
    }
}
/* The parameter can be a city alone or a city,state combo
as in Boston,MA */
function getLocation(_lcity){
    if (_lcity == null || _lcity.length=="") {alert("returning"); return; }
    //server component URL; the component connects with Weather.com
    var url = "http://"+_host+"/s/weathxml/addressSearch?city="+_lcity;
    httpRequest("GET",url,true,handleResponse);

}
```

The URL points to a server component you use to connect with Weather.com's web service.

 Using XMLHttpRequest, you cannot connect directly to a web site that is different than the one from which you downloaded the Ajax application. Therefore, developers must use a server component or intermediary to connect with other services. This intermediary can be written in the language of your choice, such as Java Servlets, PHP, Ruby, or ASP.NET.

This hack uses a Java servlet that implements a different Weather.com request based on the path info of the request that the servlet receives. The *path info* comprises the characters in a URL following the path to the server component, but preceding the querystring, as in *addressSearch* in the following URL:

http://www.parkerriver.com/s/weathxml/addressSearch?city=Boston,MA

The servlet, if its handshake with Weather.com is successful, grabs and returns to our application a pretty big XML file representing the weather information. Here is an example of the XML returned from Weather.com:

```
<!-- top-level: time. lat-long,sunrise, sunset-->
<loc id="30066">
    <dnam>Marietta, GA (30066)</dnam>
    <tm>10:40 AM</tm>
    <lat>34.04</lat>
    <lon>-84.51</lon>
    <sunr>7:02 AM</sunr>
    <suns>6:37 PM</suns>   <zone>-5</zone>
</loc>
<!--  daily forecast: -->
<dayf>
    <lsup>3/5/03 9:50 AM EST</lsup>
    <day d="0" t="Wednesday" dt="Mar 5">
        <hi>64</hi>
        <low>54</low>
        <sunr>7:02 AM</sunr>
        <suns>6:37 PM</suns>
        <part p="d">
            <icon>26</icon>
            <t>Sprinkles</t>
            <wind>
                <s>10</s>
                <gust>N/A</gust>
                <d>0</d>
                <t>W</t>
            </wind>
            <ppcp>20</ppcp>
            <hmid>77</hmid>
```

Use Ajax with a Yahoo! Maps and GeoURL Mash-up

HACK
#32

```
        </part>
        <part p="n">
            <icon>47</icon>
            <t>Scattered T-Storms</t>
            <wind>
                <s>13</s>
                <d>0</d>
                <t>SW</t>
            </wind>
            <ppcp>60</ppcp>
            <hmid>77</hmid>
        </part>
    </day>
</dayf>
```

This is the type of XML content that the servlet returns to your application when you already know the location ID for a certain city and state. The XML even includes an `icon` element so that your page can display a Weather.com image representing the weather conditions.

HACK #32 Use Ajax with a Yahoo! Maps and GeoURL Mash-up

Display the location of a cluster of bloggers on a Yahoo! Map.

This hack describes the GeoURL Yahoo! mapping application. You can access this mash-up of the GeoURL service and Yahoo! Maps at *http://www.premshree.org/geourlmap.htm*. This application uses the Yahoo! Maps API and data from GeoURL (*http://geourl.org*). When given a weblog address (*http://jeremy.zawodny.com/blog/*, for example), this hack displays a map of the weblogger's neighbors—bloggers who are geographically close to the blogger associated with the URL. It asks for a URL, then uses the Ajax request object to connect with GeoURL and download some necessary XML data for sending along to the Yahoo! Maps site.

Registering sites with GeoURL involves adding tags to web pages that associate longitude/latitude coordinates with URLs. An example set of HTML tags for this purpose is:

```
<meta name="ICBM" content="XXX.XXXXX, XXX.XXXXX">
<meta name="DC.title" content="THE NAME OF YOUR
SITE">
```

Figure 4-7 shows what the GeoURL Yahoo! mapping application looks like in a browser.

When you enter a weblog address that is stored at GeoURL, the application displays a map with icons indicating the locations of nearby bloggers or mapped URLs. Figure 4-8 shows one of these maps.

HACK
#32

Use Ajax with a Yahoo! Maps and GeoURL Mash-up

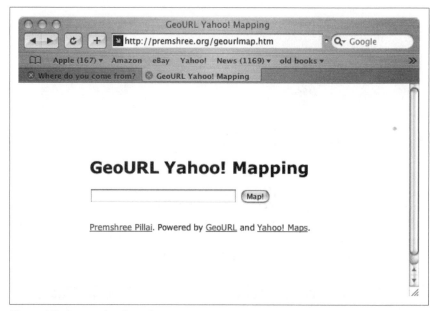

Figure 4-7. Geographical mash-up

How It Works

The GeoURL service maps weblog addresses, as well as other kinds of URLs, to geographical latitude/longitude locations. The service can also plot neighboring or clustered locations of URLs.

 Geographical locations can be plotted for any URLs with web page source code that contains tags indicating longitude/latitude coordinates.

The GeoURL service provides an RSS feed in XML format that can specify a weblogger's neighbors, and the Yahoo! Maps API accepts latitude/longitude values so that it can display markers in a map. Therefore, these two web services are all we need for this application.

To generate the map, we need to pass a chunk of XML data originating from GeoURL to the Yahoo! Maps API. A typical application for this purpose involves an HTTP request to a server-side script, which in turn makes HTTP requests to the GeoURL service, constructs the required XML, and then sends the XML in a request to the Yahoo! Maps web service.

Use Ajax with a Yahoo! Maps and GeoURL Mash-up

HACK
#32

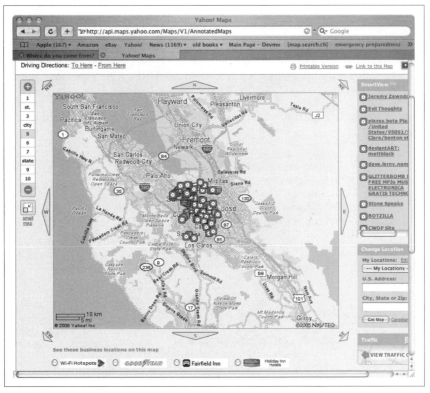

Figure 4-8. Finding adjacent geo-mapped locations

Mashed-up Requests

However, do we really need to make a traditional server-side call to construct the XML, and have the user experience a complete page rebuild? We can avoid a page refresh by using Ajax and the request object! To this end, simply add a DIV element to the web page (to give the user feedback about sending the requests and map loading). Here's a snapshot of the code for the web page:

```
<H1>GeoURL Yahoo! Mapping</H1>
<FORM METHOD="POST" ACTION=
"http://api.maps.yahoo.com/Maps/V1/AnnotatedMaps" onSubmit=
"loadMapData(); return false;">
<INPUT TYPE="TEXT" NAME="url" size="30" />
<INPUT TYPE="HIDDEN" NAME="appid" value="geourlmap" />
<INPUT TYPE="HIDDEN" NAME="xmlsrc" value="" />
<INPUT TYPE="SUBMIT" VALUE="Map!" />
<BR /><BR /><DIV ID="load" STYLE="display: none"></DIV>
</FORM>
```

HACK
#32

Use Ajax with a Yahoo! Maps and GeoURL Mash-up

When the user clicks the Map! button, the application calls the loadMapData( ) function, which sends the user's entered URL to a server component. The component fetches the GeoURL XML data and returns it to our application. The JavaScript in our application then receives the XML response and submits it to the Yahoo! Maps URL, *http://api.maps.yahoo.com/Maps/V1/AnnotatedMaps/*.

Here is the mash-up application's code, which the web page includes in a script tag:

```
<SCRIPT LANGUAGE="JavaScript">
    function getXmlHttpObject( ){
        if (window.XMLHttpRequest)
            return new XMLHttpRequest( );
        else if (window.ActiveXObject)
            return new ActiveXObject("Microsoft.XMLHTTP");
        else {
            alert("XMLHttpRequest not supported!");
            return null;
        }
    }

    function handleHttpResponse( ) {
        if (http.readyState == 4) {
            document.getElementById('load').
                innerHTML += ' [done]<br />Generating map...';
            results = http.responseText;
            if (!results.match('rss')) {
                document.getElementById('load').
                innerHTML = '[ERROR] This URL is probably '+
                    'not listed at GeoURL.';
            } else {
                document.forms[0].xmlsrc.value = results;
                document.forms[0].submit( );
            }
        }
    }

    function loadMapData( ) {
        resetLoadDiv( );
        showLoadDiv( );
        var url = document.forms[0].url.value;
        var post_url = '/cgi-bin/geourlmap.cgi'
            post_data = 'url=' + url;
        http.open("POST", post_url);
        http.setRequestHeader('Content-Type',
            'application/x-www-form-urlencoded; charset=UTF-8');
        http.send(post_data);
        http.onreadystatechange = handleHttpResponse;
        return false;
    }
```

```
function resetLoadDiv( ) {
    document.getElementById('load').
        innerHTML = 'Loading map data ...';
}

function showLoadDiv( ) {
    document.getElementById('load').
        style.display = 'block';
}

var http = getXmlHttpObject( );
</SCRIPT>
```

Anyone who wants their site included in a mash-up like this can add their URL to the GeoURL service. Simply go to *http://geourl.org/add.html* and follow the instructions!

—Premshree Pillai

HACK #33 Debug Ajax-Generated Tags in Firefox

Look at the new tags in a tree structure using Firefox's DOM Inspector.

View → Page Source has always been a popular (if primitive) programmer tool for inspecting a web page's code, but the HTML generated by this menu command will not show the newly generated widgets that your Ajax applications might produce. It shows only the original HTML source code. Firefox, however, includes a DOM Inspector tool that shows these newly generated tags in a detailed hierarchical tree-type widget. Let's look at the web page *http://www.parkerriver.com/ajaxhacks/ajax_hack2_5.html*.

The page, from "Submit Checkbox Values to the Server Without a Round Trip" [Hack #17], shows two sets of checkboxes representing team sports and individual sports. The application asks users to participate in a poll, choosing their favorite sports by checking the appropriate checkboxes. It then gets the latest results of the poll from a server program and displays them on the page. The checkboxes exist in the HTML source code; however, the text that eventually displays the poll results is dynamically generated on the page, without any visual submission or page refresh. To view the relevant code using Firefox, choose the menu command Tools → DOM Inspector. Figure 4-9 shows the Inspector window that pops up.

The left side of the window shows the entire hierarchical structure of the page's Document Object Model, with all the parent and child tags available for inspection—simply click the little triangle widget next to a tag's name, then select an element or Node. These are the DOM nodes for the entire web page.

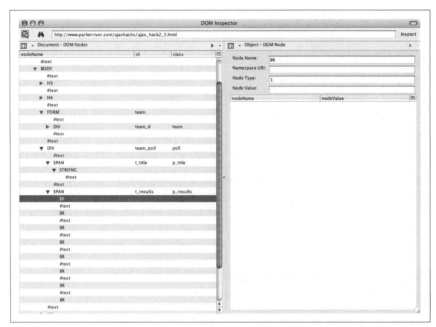

Figure 4-9. DOM Inspector view in Firefox

Viewing the HTML page as a tree structure beginning from the top-level or root element, html, the nodes are the tree branches. Nodes contain parent nodes and child nodes, such as the body element containing p or div elements. In the DOM, Node objects represent the web page nodes.

Click on an individual Node, such as the DIV tag in Figure 4-7, and the right side of the DOM Inspector shows all the Node object's properties and methods.

 The pop-up menu at the top-right of the Inspector window includes the view "Object - Javascript Object," which specifically indicates the properties and methods for the selected Node.

The provided information is highly valuable for programmers who write dynamic HTML (DHTML), which involves altering web pages on the fly. Despite all of this "DOM speak," believe me, this is heaven for a web developer who is working on a page with Ajax techniques!

Inspecting Dynamic Creations

What if your page does not display as expected, and you want to look at the underlying code to see what's going on? View → Page Source just shows the page's original HTML or XML. However, open up a new Inspector window, and you can look at the new structure that your DOM programming created, as shown in Figure 4-10.

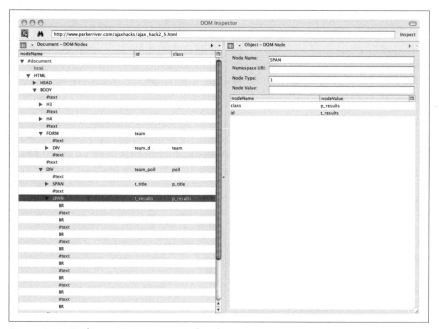

Figure 4-10. Voilà, JavaScript-generated nodes

 Choosing the Firefox menu command Tools → DOM Inspector will open up a new Inspector window alongside any existing ones.

Figure 4-10 shows that an existing span element has new content in the form of BR tags and text nodes. If you click on a text node in the Inspector, the right side of the Inspector window shows the value of the node. This information can be invaluable for DOM programmers who are encountering a lot of text nodes, for example, that are empty strings. These empty nodes sprinkled throughout a page often pose difficulties for any code that iterates through the document nodes looking for specific nodes or structures.

The DOM Inspector is a great tool for debugging Ajax applications, not to mention a handy way to examine the DOM structure of any web page and to learn about the available object properties and methods.

Fetch a Postal Code

#34 Type in a city and choose a state name; this hack quickly generates the U.S. postal code.

This hack asks the user for the name of a city and state, then generates the associated postal code in a text field (using a web service accessible at *http://www.webservicex.net/uszip.asmx?op=GetInfoByState*). Nothing else about the web page changes. Cool, and useful, too. How many people remember postal codes other than their own?

The hack gets the city and state values, then uses the request object to fetch the ZIP Code from a server-side component, which interacts with the web service. The server-side component pulls the ZIP Code out of an XML file it gets from the service and sends the code to our Ajax application.

We started out using the U.S. Postal Service's Web Tools API, which likely contains the most up-to-date ZIP Codes, as well as the four-digit codes that extend some of the five-digit codes. However, the USPS was very restrictive in terms of allowing us to write about the use of its web tools in our hacks—fairly *bureaucratic* and not very cooperative—so we were not able to use a full implementation of its ZIP Code service for this hack.

Figure 4-11 shows what the page looks like in the browser.

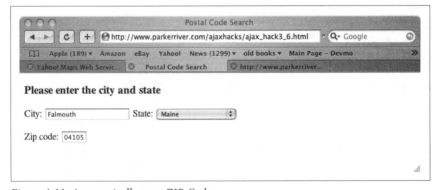

Figure 4-11. Automatically get a ZIP Code

When the user chooses a state from the pop-up list, the application code sends the city and state to the server component, but only if the city field contains content (the user could leave it empty by mistake). Here is what the web page's code looks like:

```
<!DOCTYPE html PUBLIC "-//W3C//DTD XHTML 1.0 Strict//EN"
        "http://www.w3.org/TR/2000/REC-xhtml1-20000126/DTD/xhtml1-strict.
dtd">
<html xmlns="http://www.w3.org/1999/xhtml" xml:lang="en" lang="en">
<head>
    <script type="text/javascript" src="js/http_request.js"></script>
    <script type="text/javascript" src="js/hacks3_6b.js"></script>
    <meta http-equiv="content-type" content="text/html; charset=utf-8" />
    <title>Postal Code Search</title>
</head>
<body>
<h3>Please enter the city and state</h3>
<form action="javascript:void%200" method="get">
<p>
City: <input type="text" id="city" size="20" maxlength="20" />
State: <select id="sts">
            <option value="al">Alabama</option>
            <option value="ak">Alaska</option>
            <option value="az">Arizona</option>
            <option value="ar">Arkansas</option>
            <option value="ca">California</option>
            <option value="co">Colorado</option>
            <!--etc. -->
        </select>
</p><p>
Zip code: <input type="text" id="zip5" size="5" maxlength="5" />
</p>
<div id="message"></div>
</form>
</body>
</html>
```

The web page imports two JavaScript files, *http_request.js* and *hacks3_6b.js*. *http_request.js* (see "Use Your Own Library for XMLHttpRequest" [Hack #3]) is responsible for setting up and using XMLHttpRequest. This file contains the httpRequest( ) function that *hacks3_6b.js* uses. The code in *hacks3_6b.js* handles the user's clicks on the pop-up list, sends a request with the city and state values, and then displays the returned ZIP Code in the zip5 text field. Here is the code in *hacks3_6b.js*:

```
window.onload=function( ){
    var sts = document.getElementById("sts");
    sts.onclick=function( ){
        var cit = document.getElementById("city");
        //Only make a request if the city text field
        //has a value
```

```
                if(cit.value) {getZipcode(cit.value,sts.value.toUpperCase( ));}

        };
    };

    function getZipcode(_ct,_st){
        if(_ct.length > 0 && _st.length > 0){
            httpRequest("GET","http://www.parkerriver.com/s/zip?city="+
                    encodeURIComponent(_ct)+"&state="+
                    encodeURIComponent(_st),
                    true,handleResponse);
        } else {
            document.getElementById("zip5").value="";
        }
    }

    function handleResponse( ){
        var xmlReturnVal;
        try{
            if(request.readyState == 4){
                if(request.status == 200){
                    xmlReturnVal=request.responseXML;
                    if(xmlReturnVal != null)  {
                        var zip5=xmlReturnVal.getElementsByTagName("zip")[0];
                        if(zip5 && zip5.childNodes.length > 0) {
                            document.getElementById("zip5").
                                value=zip5.childNodes[0].data;
                        }
                    }
                } else {
                    //request.status is 503
                    //if the application isn't available;
                    //500 if the application has a bug
                    alert(
                            "A problem occurred with communicating between"+
                            " the XMLHttpRequest object and the server program.
");
                }
            }//end outer if
        } catch (err)   {
            alert("It does not appear that the server "+
                "is available for this application. Please"+
                " try again very soon. \nError: "+err.message);

        }
    }
```

You've probably encountered this window.onload event handler in other hacks.
It's an "event handler that sets up another event handler." When the browser
completes loading the web page, window.onload specifies what happens when
the user makes a selection from the pop-up list displaying the U.S. states:

```
window.onload=function( ){
    var sts = document.getElementById("sts");
    sts.onclick=function( ){
        var cit = document.getElementById("city");
        //Only make a request if the city text field
        //has a value
        if(cit.value) {getZipcode(cit.value,sts.value.toUpperCase( ));}

    };
};
```

The code gets the value of the city text field and the U.S. states pop-up, then calls getZipCode( ). This function puts together the URL that will connects this application to the server component. The code then calls the httpRequest( ) function to fetch the ZIP Code:

```
httpRequest("GET","http://localhost:8080/parkerriver/s/zip?city="+
encodeURIComponent(_ct)+"&state="+
encodeURIComponent(_st),
true,handleResponse);
```

Again, httpRequest( ) is defined in *http_request.js*.

Server, Take Over

The server component has to connect with the web service, which sends back a large XML file containing all the ZIP Codes for a specific state. You have to use your own server intermediary because of the XMLHttpRequest restriction on connecting with a host that is different from the host from which the user downloaded the web page.

 This particular web service, which is generously made available to our code, does not have an operation that returns just a ZIP Code in response to a city and state name. Therefore, you have to take this extra step to glean the ZIP Code from the XML file.

The web service returns an XML file that looks like this:

```
<NewDataSet>
    <Table>
        <CITY>Abington</CITY>
        <STATE>MA</STATE>
        <ZIP>02351</ZIP>
        <AREA_CODE>781</AREA_CODE>
        <TIME_ZONE>E</TIME_ZONE>
    </Table>
    <Table>
        <CITY>Accord</CITY>
        <STATE>MA</STATE>
```

```
        <ZIP>02018</ZIP>
        <AREA_CODE>781</AREA_CODE>
        <TIME_ZONE>E</TIME_ZONE>
    </Table>
  ...
  </NewDataSet>
```

The server component uses the Simple API for XML (SAX) to parse this return value. When the Java component finds the city name the user provided, it pulls out the associated ZIP Code and sends it to our Ajax application in the form <zip>02351</zip>. The handleResponse( ) function then makes sure this value is placed in the ZIP Code–related text field. It all happens quite fast, considering the complexity involved!

Here is a snippet from handleResponse( ):

```
if(request.status == 200){
    xmlReturnVal=request.responseXML;
    if(xmlReturnVal != null)  {
        var zip5=xmlReturnVal.getElementsByTagName("zip")[0];
        if(zip5 && zip5.childNodes.length > 0) {
            document.getElementById("zip5").
                value=zip5.childNodes[0].data;
        }
    }
}
```

A property of the request object called responseXML stores the returned ZIP Code, which is encapsulated in a <zip> tag. The code xmlReturnVal. getElementsByTagName("zip")[0] returns the tag holding the ZIP Code. The last line of the code sample then stores the ZIP Code in the text field with id zip5.

The Servlet

As mentioned earlier, the application cannot connect directly with the web service using XMLHttpRequest because our web page has a different host than the web service's host. As a final step, let's look at the Java servlet that acts as the intermediary between the web service and the Ajax code. It sifts through all the ZIP Codes for a certain state and returns the first ZIP Code it finds that is associated with the specified city (this is a potential flaw in the application, as some cities can have multiple ZIP Codes):

```
package com.parkerriver;

import java.net.*;
import java.io.*;
import javax.servlet.*;
import javax.servlet.http.*;
import javax.xml.parsers.*;
import org.apache.log4j.*;
```

```
import org.xml.sax.helpers.DefaultHandler;
import org.xml.sax.*;

public class ZipServlet2 extends HttpServlet {
    private Logger log = null;
    private String zipCode = null;

    public String getZipCode() {
        return zipCode;
    }

    public void setZipCode(String zipCode) {
        this.zipCode = zipCode;
    }

    private static String wsUrl=
            "http://www.webservicex.net/uszip.asmx/GetInfoByState?USState=";

    public void init() throws ServletException {
        log = Logger.getLogger(ZipServlet2.class);
    }

    protected void doGet(HttpServletRequest httpServletRequest,
                        HttpServletResponse httpServletResponse) throws
                        ServletException, IOException {
        String stte = httpServletRequest.getParameter("state");
        String _city = httpServletRequest.getParameter("city");
        String resp = null;
        if(stte != null && _city != null){
            URL usps = new URL(wsUrl+stte);
            HttpURLConnection usp = (HttpURLConnection) usps.
                    openConnection();
            usp.setRequestMethod("GET");
            usp.setDoInput(true);
            usp.connect();

            BufferedReader in = new BufferedReader(
                    new InputStreamReader(
                            usp.getInputStream()));
            StringBuffer buf = new StringBuffer("");
            String inputLine;
            while ((inputLine = in.readLine()) != null) {
                buf.append(inputLine);    }
            in.close();
            resp = buf.toString();
            try {
                getZipSax(resp,_city);
                resp="<zip>"+this.getZipCode()+"</zip>";
            } catch (ParserConfigurationException e) {
                e.printStackTrace();
            }
        } else {
            resp="<error />";
```

```
        }
        httpServletResponse.setContentType("text/xml; charset=UTF-8");
        //Convey to the user agent or browser that it should
        //not cache the responses
        httpServletResponse.setHeader("Cache-Control", "no-cache");
        httpServletResponse.getWriter( ).write(resp);
    }

    protected void doPost(HttpServletRequest httpServletRequest,
                          HttpServletResponse httpServletResponse) throws
                          ServletException, IOException {
        doGet(httpServletRequest, httpServletResponse);
    }
/* Parse the XML file of zip codes using our own DefaultHandler. Give
the ContentHandler the name of the city the user provided. */
    private void getZipSax(String zipXML,String _city)
            throws ParserConfigurationException, IOException {
        try {
            SAXParser parser =  SAXParserFactory.
            newInstance( ).newSAXParser( );
            parser.parse(new InputSource(new StringReader(zipXML)),
                    new MyHandler(_city));
        } catch (SAXException sxe) {
            log.info("Caught SAXException: "+sxe.getMessage( ));
        }

    }
/* A SAX ContentHandler that parses an XML file; it sets the
parent class's zipCode property when it finds the correct zip
code in the XML, then throws a SAXException to halt the parsing. */
class MyHandler extends DefaultHandler{
    private String city;
    private boolean foundCityFlag,foundCityVal,foundZipFlag;
    public MyHandler( ) {
        super( );
    }
    public MyHandler(String _city) {
        this( );
        this.city=_city;
    }
    public void startElement(String string, String string1,
      String string2,
      Attributes attributes) throws SAXException {
      if(string2.equalsIgnoreCase("city")){
          foundCityFlag=true;
      }
      if(foundCityVal){
          if(string2.equalsIgnoreCase("zip")){
              foundZipFlag=true;
          }
      }
```

```
        }

        public void characters(char[] chars, int i,
        int i1) throws SAXException {

            if(foundCityFlag){
                if(new String(chars,i,i1).equalsIgnoreCase(city)){
                    foundCityVal=true;
                } else {
                    foundCityFlag=false;
                }
            }
            if(foundZipFlag){
                setZipCode(new String(chars,i,i1));
                throw new SAXException("We found the zip code.");
            }
        }

    }
}
```

The SAX technique uses a callback object—in this case, a class called MyHandler—to look for city tags that contain the user's specified city. The MyHandler object implements an interface that is part of the SAX API called ContentHandler. A ContentHandler lets the programmer decide what should happen as the parser sifts through the XML stream at different stages: when the handler finds the beginning of an XML element, the content of an element, the end of an element, and so on.

If the ContentHandler finds a city tag whose content matches the user's chosen city, it looks for an associated zip tag and grabs the value of that tag. It then throws a SAXException—the Java way of signaling that the XML parsing can stop—because the code has found the ZIP Code value.

 See *http://www.saxproject.org* for more information on SAX.

This is a nifty way to display ZIP Codes to the user because they generally appear in the text field very quickly, without the page refreshing or changing in any other way. The user just has to correctly spell the city, choose a state in the pop-up, and presto, there's the ZIP Code.

HACK   Create Large, Maintainable Bookmarklets
#35   Create easy-to-maintain bookmarklets of arbitrary size.

A bookmarklet is a special piece of JavaScript code that can be dragged into a user's Links toolbar and later clicked on to implement cross-site behavior. Bookmarklets have size limitations, which differ based on browser and platform, since they must fit into a certain number of characters. They can also be difficult to maintain for more sophisticated scripts, since every line of JavaScript code has to be jammed into one line.

This hack presents a mechanism to create arbitrarily sized bookmarklets, where most of the code resides outside of the bookmarklet link. It has been tested in IE 6 and Firefox.

Bookmarklet Code

Let's begin by viewing the full bookmarklet source code:

```
<p>Drag the following link to your toolbar to
install this bookmarklet:</p>
<a href=
"javascript:function loadScript(scriptURL) { var scriptElem =
document.createElement('SCRIPT'); scriptElem.setAttribute('language',
'JavaScript'); scriptElem.setAttribute(
'src', scriptURL); document.body.appendChild(scriptElem); }
loadScript('helloworld.js');">Say Hello World</a>
```

The essential idea in this code is that we dynamically insert a new script element into the DOM through our bookmarklet. Here is the code within the bookmarklet URL, formatted to be more readable:

```
function loadScript(scriptURL) {
    var scriptElem = document.createElement('SCRIPT');
    scriptElem.setAttribute('language', 'JavaScript');
    scriptElem.setAttribute('src', scriptURL);
    document.body.appendChild(scriptElem);
}
loadScript('http://216.203.40.101/projects/tutorials/'
        + 'creating_huge_bookmarklets/helloworld.js');
```

The previous code sample created a new script element and set it to the new URL. We then append the new script block to the document. The script we append, *helloworld.js*, is very simple:

```
alert("Hello World!");
```

When this script is loaded, the "Hello World!" message appears immediately.

The loadScript( ) function definition and function call are rolled into a single JavaScript URL to turn it into a bookmarklet.

You can enter the script yourself by dragging the link to your toolbar. Then navigate to another site and click the bookmarklet link. You will see the message "Hello World!" appear, loaded from an external script.

The external script loaded through the bookmarklet can come from a different domain than the web site itself, opening the door to sophisticated bookmarklets that aggregate data from different web sites. See *http://www. bookmarklets.com* for some of the interesting work people have done with bookmarklets.

—Brad Neuberg

H A C K
#36
Use Permanent Client-Side Storage for Ajax Applications

Use an open source framework that allows applications to store large amounts of data persistently on the client side.

This hack describes the Ajax Massive Storage System (AMASS). AMASS is an open source library that uses a hidden Flash applet to allow JavaScript Ajax applications to store an arbitrary amount of sophisticated information on the client side. This information is permanent and persistent; if the user closes the browser or navigates away from the web site, the information is still present and can be retrieved later by the web page. Information stored by web pages is private and locked to a single domain, so other web sites cannot access this information.

AMASS makes it possible to store an arbitrary amount of sophisticated data, past the 4K limit of cookies or the 64K limit of Internet Explorer's proprietary client-side storage system.

> See the site *http://codinginparadise.org/weblog/2005/08/ajax-internet-explorer-has-native.html* for details on Internet Explorer's 64K storage system.

An AMASS-enabled web site can store up to 100K of data without user permission. Above that limit, the web site must prompt users for permission to store the requested amount of information. The AMASS system informs the client-side application whether the storage request was allowed or denied. In tests, AMASS has been able to store up to 10 MB of user data with good performance.

AMASS works on Internet Explorer 6+ and Gecko-based browsers such as Firefox. Users must have Version 6+ of the Flash plug-in installed to use AMASS, but according to Macromedia's statistics (*http://www.macromedia. com/software/player_census/flashplayer/*), Flash 6+ is already installed on 95% of machines.

The latest release of AMASS can be found at *http://codinginparadise.org/ projects/storage/latest.zip*; at the time of publication the latest release of AMASS was Version 0.02 and was in alpha development. AMASS is under a BSD license.

Using AMASS

Working with AMASS is simple. The AMASS framework creates the abstraction of a permanent hash table that persists even after the user has left the page or closed the browser.

The first step in working with AMASS is to load the AMASS script:

```
<!-- Load the Permanent Storage framework -->
<script src="storage.js"></script>
```

In order to use AMASS, you must wait for its internal machinery to finish loading. To find out when this happens, add a listener:

```
storage.onLoad(initialize);
function initialize() {
}
```

Once AMASS is loaded, you can begin to work with it by using its hash table methods, such as put( ), get( ), and hasKey( ):

```
var keyName = "message";
var keyValue = new Object();
keyValue.message = "hello world";
keyValue.testArray = ["test1", "test2", "test3"];
keyValue.testObject = {someProperty: "someValue"};

if (storage.hasKey(keyName) == false) {
    storage.put(keyName, keyValue, statusHandler);
}
else {
    var results = storage.get(keyName);
}
```

The AMASS framework makes it possible to serialize entire JavaScript objects into the storage system, such as the keyValue object we serialized earlier. Note that DOM nodes and browser objects such as the XMLHttpRequest object will not be serialized.

As mentioned earlier, applications can store up to 100K of data without user permission. After this, a pop-up is generated by the underlying Flash system that prompts the user for permission. The AMASS framework knows when the pop-up appears, generating a div and bringing the Flash file to the forefront of the application. Figure 4-12 shows the application centering the pop-up on the screen.

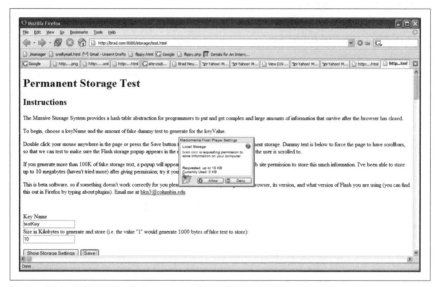

Figure 4-12. Asking permission to store large data amounts

Users can either approve or deny a storage request, so you must create your application so that it's ready if its storage request is denied. The put( ) method takes as its third argument a status handler that informs your code whether the storage request was successful or not. In the following code, statusHandler( ) is a callback function that receives the outcome of whether the request succeeded or failed:

```
function statusHandler(status) {
    if (status == Storage.SUCCESS) {
        var results = storage.get(keyName);
        alert("Results from statusHandler="+results);
    }
    else if (status == Storage.PENDING) {
        alert("Results pending approval of storage space from user");
    }
    else if (status == Storage.FAILED) {
        alert("Storage request denied");
    }
};
```

status can be one of three values: Storage.SUCCESS, Storage.PENDING, or Storage.FAILED. If the pop-up appears, you will get a callback of Storage.PENDING. Later, if the user approves the request, you will receive Storage.SUCCESS; if the request is denied, you will receive Storage.FAILED. Upon approving the request, users can also indicate whether they give permission to future requests to automatically store information without the application popping up the permission dialog again.

How AMASS Works Internally

Internally, AMASS uses a hidden Flash file and Flash's SharedObject functionality to permanently store the information. AMASS scripts the Flash applet using the Flash plug-in's ActiveX methods on Internet Explorer and its LiveConnect methods on Firefox. AMASS then uses the Flash SharedObject's callbacks to detect when the request storage dialog is on the screen and pass these back to the JavaScript application.

—Brad Neuberg

Control Browser History with iframes

H A C K
#37   Learn the black art of iframes and browser history.

An iframe is an internal frame that can point to and load an arbitrary URL within your HTML page. Here is an example small iframe showing Google:

```
<iframe src="http://www.google.com" style=
  "width: 320px; height: 300px;">
</iframe>
```

Your browser history is the list of pages you have visited. When you press the back and forward buttons in your browser, you are jumping through your browser history.

Sometimes, for various reasons, programmers want to control what is placed into the browser's history. Think of this as a primitive mechanism that can be used in more elaborate Ajax and DHTML hacks; it's a building block useful in all kinds of crazy Ajax kung-fu. It's good to know about tricks such as this one when you're confronted with Ajax design issues or when you stumble across very strange bugs that might be caused by the different kinds of iframe we will discuss here.

There are two kinds of iframe. The first kind are located right within your HTML and are loaded in the page:

```
<html>
<body>
<iframe id="testFrame"
```

```
    src="http://www.google.com">
</iframe>
</body>
</html>
```

Code can also create `iframes` dynamically, through the DOM and JavaScript, after the page is finished loading:

```
<html>
<head>
<script language="JavaScript">
function initialize( ) {
    var testFrame = document.createElement("IFRAME");
    testFrame.id = "testFrame";
    testFrame.src = "http://www.google.com";
    document.body.appendChild(testFrame);
}
</script>
</head>

<body onload="initialize( )">
</body>
</html>
```

Okay, so there are two kinds of `iframe`. Who cares? Well, it turns out these two kinds of `iframe` have completely different behaviors when it comes to history in different browsers!

Browser Lowdown

Here's the lowdown for each kind of browser:

- In Firefox, if the `iframe` is inside the HTML and was loaded in the page, any location changes to it are stored in the browser's history. If the `iframe` was written into the DOM through JavaScript after the page finished loading, no location changes are stored in the browser's history.

- In Internet Explorer, location changes are stored in the browser's history for both kinds of `iframe`.

- In Safari, location changes are not stored in the browser's history for either kind of `iframe`.

You can see this for yourself in the demos discussed in the next section.

Browser Demos

Two demos have been provided to illustrate how Firefox and Internet Explorer handle the different kinds of `iframe`. In both demos, we dynamically change the `iframe`'s location between four different web sites.

In the first demo, viewable at *http://codinginparadise.org/projects/tutorials/ tale_of_two_iframes/static_iframe.html*, we are dealing with an `iframe` that is in the HTML on page load. In this case, you will find that all of these sites are in the browser's history in both Firefox and IE. Press the back and forward buttons when the pop-up saying "Finished" appears, and you will see the `iframe`'s contents change between each site.

In the second demo, viewable at *http://codinginparadise.org/projects/tutorials/ tale_of_two_iframes/dynamic_iframe.html*, we are dealing with a dynamically created `iframe`. Here, you will find that only the initial page load is in the browser's history in Firefox, while all sites are in the history in IE.

One small footnote is that if you have a static `iframe` that is loaded in the HTML, and that `iframe` has a `src` value initially (as in `<iframe src="http:// www.google.com"></iframe>`, this initial value is not placed in the browser's history. In this case, only successive changes to that static `iframe` are placed in the history.

You can use the special behavior of these two kinds of `iframe` for some real trickery. First, make them invisible using CSS. You can then decide whether you want something to enter the history or not, choosing the appropriate kind of `iframe`. If you are working with a DHTML application that uses iframes for remote communication (detailed at *http://developer.apple.com/ internet/webcontent/iframe.html*) instead of `XMLHttpRequest`, for old browser compatibility, knowing the difference between these two kinds of `iframe` can be very useful, because you can choose whether remote `iframe` communication is placed in the browser's history or not.

> For a discussion of how you can use `iframes` to make the browser back button work normally with Ajax applications, check out "Fix the Browser Back Button in Ajax Applications" **[Hack #68]**.

—Brad Neuberg

HACK #38 Send Cookie Values to a Server Program

Create cookies within the web application and send cookie values to a server without refreshing the page.

A cookie is a small piece of data that a web application can store on a user's machine. A web site can set one or more cookies using a `Set-Cookie` header in the server response. The number of cookies that a server can set and their individual sizes are restricted based on the standards used by the first browser makers, such as Netscape.

A web server may set no more than 20 cookies for one
browser, and each cookie's size is limited to 4K. (Very few
cookies reach that size.) If you want to view the cookies in
your Firefox installation, go to Preferences → Privacy →
Cookies → View Cookies. Most browsers, including Firefox,
allow the user to remove cookies.

If Google or Yahoo!, for instance, has set a cookie on your machine, that
business's web applications will be able to read the cookie name and value
the next time you go to its site. For example, Google may set a unique ID on
your machine so that it can identify you and display your preferential news
headlines when you visit the Google News site. The upcoming sections will
explain how code sets the accessibility of the information the cookies store.

Bake Your Own Cookie

This hack allows a user to enter the name and value of a cookie. The application then uses this information to generate a new cookie. Figure 4-13
shows the interactions that take place in this hack between the browser and
the server.

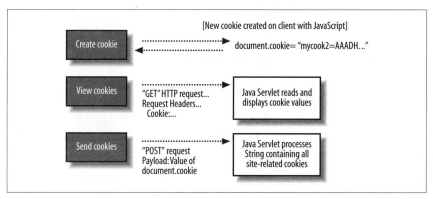

Figure 4-13. Creating, viewing, and posting cookie data

The simplest cookie comprises a name and value, as in
mycookie=uniqueADDAA. Most cookies are set by the server using a short string
of data that includes the web server path that is linked to the cookie, as well
as the date on which the cookie expires and can be deleted by the web
server:

```
mycookie=uniqueADDAA; expires=Thu, 01 Dec 2005 20:35:16 GMT;
path=/ajaxhacks; domain=parkerriver.com
```

In this hack, the user also has the option to view existing cookies by click-ing a button, as well as to send the existing cookie collection, including their own cookies, to a server component.

Figure 4-14 shows the web page for this application.

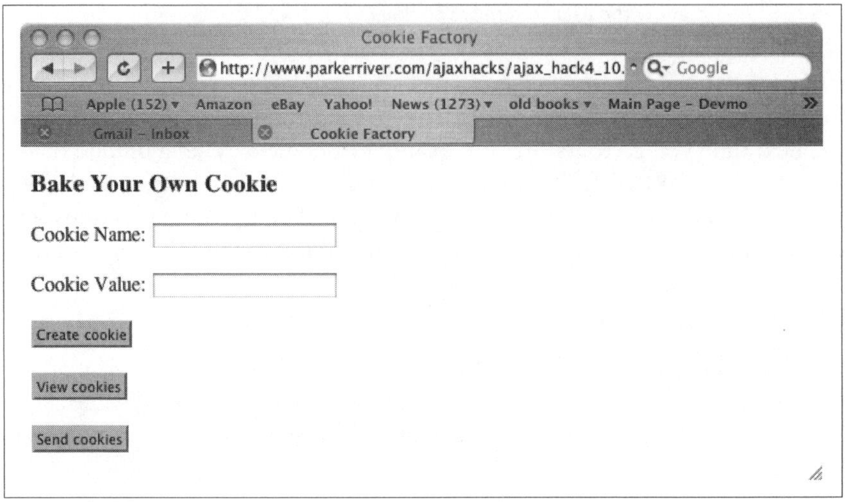

Figure 4-14. Fire up your own cookie

Here's what the underlying HTML looks like—nothing earth shattering here. The script tags import the JavaScript that does the application's work, including initializing and using XMLHttpRequest. The HTML includes a span element for displaying a user message after the application creates a cookie:

```
<!DOCTYPE html PUBLIC "-//W3C//DTD XHTML 1.0 Strict//EN"
        "http://www.w3.org/TR/2000/REC-xhtml1-20000126/DTD/xhtml1-strict.
dtd">
<html xmlns="http://www.w3.org/1999/xhtml" xml:lang="en" lang="en">
<head>
    <meta http-equiv="content-type" content="text/html; charset=utf-8" />
    <script type="text/javascript" src="js/hacks4_10.js"></script>
    <script type="text/javascript" src="js/http_request.js"></script>
    <link rel="stylesheet" type="text/css" href="/css/hacks.css" />
    <title>Cookie Factory</title>
</head>
<body>
<h3>Bake Your Own Cookie</h3>
<form action="javascript:void%200">
<p>
Cookie Name: <input type="text" id="ck_nm" name=
        "ck_name" size="20" maxlength="20" />
</p>
<p>
```

```
Cookie Value: <input type="text" id="ck_val" name=
        "ck_value" size="20" maxlength="20" />
</p>
<p>
<span id="msg" class="message" style="color:green"></span>
</p>
<p>
<button id="ckCreate" type="button">Create cookie</button>
</p>
<p>
<button id="ckView" type="button">View cookies</button>
</p>
<p>
<button id="ckSend" type="button">Send cookies</button>
</p>
</form>
</body>
</html>
```

When the user types a cookie name and value into the text fields and clicks the "Create cookie" button, the application generates a new cookie with a default path, domain, and expiration attribute (see the upcoming explanation). Figure 4-15 shows the browser after the user has created a new cookie.

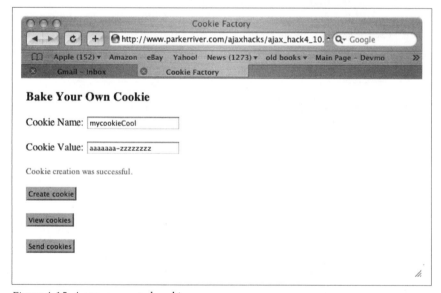

Figure 4-15. A user-generated cookie

Figure 4-16 shows the view resulting from clicking the "View cookies" button, which shows the cookies that are accessible from responses originating from a certain domain (e.g., *www.parkerriver.com*). You can see that the cookie added in Figure 4-15 was identified by this cookie-reading servlet.

Figure 4-16. Reading all cookies

JavaScript

By now you are probably interested in the *hacks4-10.js* code, which provides the Ajax-related functionality for this application. "Use Your Own Library for XMLHttpRequest" [Hack #3] describes *http_request.js*, which sets up and uses XMLHttpRequest. Here's the code from *hacks4-10.js*:

```
var _host="www.parkerriver.com";
var _fpath="";
var _path="/";
//Cookie object definition
function MyCookie(name,val,domain,path) {
    this.name=name;
    this.value=val;
    this.domain=domain;
    this.path=path;
    //The cookie lives for three days by default
    var dtsec=new Date();
    dtsec.setSeconds(dtsec.getSeconds()+(60*60*24*3));
    this.expires=dtsec.toGMTString();
    this.toString=function(){
        return this.name+"="+this.value+"; expires="+this.expires+
            "; path="+this.path+"; domain="+this.domain;
    }
}//End of Cookie object definition
//This event handler is called when the web page
//is first loaded.
window.onload=function(){
    var b1 = document.getElementById("ckCreate");
    var b2 = document.getElementById("ckView");
    var b3 = document.getElementById("ckSend");
    var _url="";
```

```
    if(b1 && b2 && b3){
        b1.onclick=function( ){
            //The new Cookie's name/value
            var nm = document.getElementById("ck_nm");
            var v=document.getElementById("ck_val");
            try{
                if(nm && nm.value && v && v.value){
                    var cook=new MyCookie(encodeURIComponent(nm.value),
                            v.value,_host,_path);
                    //Add the cookie to the current cookie collection
                    document.cookie=cook.toString( );
                    //Display a user message
                    showMsg(document.getElementById("msg"),
                            "Cookie creation was successful.");
                }
            } catch(errv) {
                alert("Sorry, but we failed to create a cookie because "+
                    "of this error: "+errv.message);
            }

        }
        //Display the cookies visible from a specific host
        b2.onclick=function( ){
            location.href="http://"+_host+_fpath+"/s/ckreader";
        }
        //POST all available cookies to a server component
        b3.onclick=function( ){
            _url="http://"+_host+_fpath+"/s/ckserv";
            httpRequest("POST",_url,true,function( ){},
                    "allCookies="+encodeURIComponent(document.cookie));
        }
    }
    //Create initial cookie when the application starts up
    _url="http://"+_host+_fpath+"/s/ckserv";
    httpRequest("GET",_url,true,handleInit);
}
function showMsg(_id,txt){
    if(_id && txt){_id.innerHTML=txt;}
}
//Response handler that XMLHttpRequest will use;
//see Hack #3
function handleInit( ){
    try{
        if(request.readyState == 4){
            if(request.status == 200){
                var resp =  request.responseXML;
                if(resp != null){
                    var outcome=resp.getElementsByTagName("outcome")[0];
                    var msg = document.getElementById("msg");
                    if(outcome != null){
                        if(outcome.childNodes[0].nodeValue != "success")  {
                        showMsg(msg,
```

```
                            "Initial Cookie creation was not successful.");
                        }
                    }
                }
            } else {
                //request.status is 503
                // if the application isn't available;
                //500 if the application has a bug
                alert(
                "A problem occurred with communicating between "+
                "the XMLHttpRequest object and the server program.");
            }
        }//end outer if
    } catch (err)   {
        alert("It does not appear that the server "+
            "is available for this application. Please"+
            " try again very soon. \nError: "+err.message);


    }
}
```

The Cookie Object

This code defines a MyCookie object, then uses that object to create the new
cookie for the user. This is a small example of object-oriented JavaScript.
The code declares a constructor function that sets the typical properties of a
cookie:

```
//Cookie object definition
function MyCookie(name,val,domain,path) {
    this.name=name;
    this.value=val;
    this.domain=domain;
    this.path=path;
    //The cookie lives for three days by default
    var dtsec=new Date();
    dtsec.setSeconds(dtsec.getSeconds()+(60*60*24*3));
    this.expires=dtsec.toGMTString();
    this.toString=function(){
        return this.name+"="+this.value+"; expires="+this.expires+
            "; path="+this.path+"; domain="+this.domain;
    }
}
```

These properties include:

- The cookie name
- The cookie value
- The domain connected to the cookie, as in *www.parkerriver.com*

Only subsequent requests that involve the same domain will include this cookie. In other words, the browser will include a Cookie request header that includes any cookie name/value pairs associated with this domain and path.

- The path, which further differentiates whether an HTTP request will include a particular cookie in its Cookie header
- The expires property, a date string in Greenwich mean time (GMT) format specifying when the cookie will expire and thereafter be unavailable on this browser

Here's the code can create the cookier:

```
var new_cookie = new MyCookie("mycookie","myvalue","www.parkerriver.com",
"/ajaxhacks")
```

The object generates a default expiry date of three days in the future, but code can change that later. For example:

```
var ndate=new Date();
//1 year from now
ndate.setSeconds(ndate.getSeconds()+(60*60*24*365));
new_cookie.expires= ndate.toGMTString();
document.cookie=new_cookie.toString();
```

The MyCookie object's toString() method conveniently generates a string that represents the cookie, and allows it to be set using client-side JavaScript. The previous code sample shows how this is done using the document.cookie property.

Oddly, setting document.cookie to a properly formatted cookie string has the effect of adding a new cookie to the browser's existing collection for that domain. If the code then displays the value of document.cookie, it shows not only the new cookie, but all other existing cookies as well, put together in one string.

Figure 4-17 shows an alert box displaying the value of the MyCookie object's toString() method.

Another task initiated by this application is to send the values of all current cookies in a POST HTTP request. As mentioned in the earlier note, the values of all the cookies are available lumped together in a string returned by the document.cookie property. This string can easily be POSTed to an application, which can do whatever it wants with these cookie values, using the following code:

Figure 4-17. A new cookie's string value

```
_url="http://www.parkerriver.com/s/ckserv";
httpRequest("POST",_url,true,function(){},
        "allcookies="+encodeURIComponent(document.cookie));
```

This call of `httpRequest( )` assumes that the application does not yet have any plans for a return value; consequently, it passes an empty function literal value to the function.

HACK #39   Use XMLHttpRequest to Scrape an Energy Price from a Web Page

Allow the user to choose an energy fuel type and generate the current price without refreshing the page.

The Web includes lots of different places for getting the latest energy prices, such as for a barrel of crude oil or the average cost of U.S. residential propane. These web sources usually involve loading into the browser a particular business-oriented page over and over again (such as from *cnnfn.com*) or visiting multiple web sites in search of various prices. This hack offers an alternative: it automatically grabs an energy price based on the user's choice in a select list element. The hack doesn't involve any page rebuilding, so the feature can be built into a broader application for handling energy prices.

Getting in a Scrape

The source of the energy price is a public-domain site managed by the U.S. Energy Information Agency (U.S. EIA). You can also use a commercial web service to access instantaneous energy prices, which avoids having to scrape or harvest the price from the HTML—a better solution from an application-design standpoint but not free of charge. The EIA site suits our purpose, however, because it illustrates how to the access multiple data pieces from third-party sources, then displays of the data value without rebuilding the entire page. The sequence for this hack's behavior goes like this:

1. The user chooses a fuel type in the select list.
2. This choice triggers the `select`'s onchange event handler.
3. The event handler uses `XMLHttpRequest` to send a request to a Java JSP page.
4. The JSP uses a predefined component to scrape the energy price from the U.S. EIA page, then sends the price as text back to the web page.
5. The web page shows a "Fetching energy price…" message, then displays the latest price in a colorful font.

Figure 4-18 shows the hack's web page.

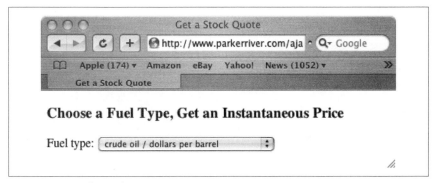

Figure 4-18. Fetching a live energy price

When the user makes a select-list choice, Figure 4-19 shows what the result looks like.

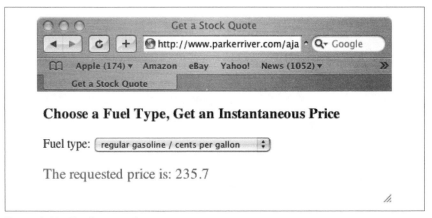

Figure 4-19. Checking out the price

The JavaScript code the page uses is rather simple:

```
window.onload=function(){
    var _url=
```

```
            "http://www.parkerriver.com/energy.jsp?priceTyp=";
            if($("fuelType")){
                $("fuelType").onchange=function(){
                    try{
                        showQuote($("msg"),
                         "Fetching energy price...");
                        httpRequest("GET",_url+$F("fuelType"),
                         true,handlePrice);
                    } catch(errv) {
                        alert("Sorry, but we failed to get the energy price "+
                             "because "+
                             "of this error: "+errv.message);
                    }

                };
            }


        }
        function showQuote(_id,txt){
            if(_id && txt){_id.innerHTML=txt;}
        }
        function handlePrice(){
            try{
                if(request.readyState == 4){
                    if(request.status == 200){
                        var resp =  request.responseText;
                        if(resp != null && resp.length > 0){
                            showQuote($("msg"),
                            "The requested price is: "+resp);
                        }  else {
                            showQuote($("msg"),
                            "The price is not available at this time.");
                        }
                    } else {
                        //request.status is 503 if the application
                        // isn't available;
                        //500 if the application has a bug
                        alert(
                        "A problem occurred with communicating between"+
                        " the XMLHttpRequest object and the server program.");
                    }
                }//end outer if
            } catch (err)   {
                alert("It does not appear that the server "+
                    "is available for this application. Please"+
                    " try again very soon. \nError: "+err.message);

            }
        }
```

window.onload sets up the onchange event handler for our lone select element containing the choices of fuel types. onchange points to a function that

the browser will call each time the user chooses a different option in the select list. The hack then takes the fuel choice and sends it to the JavaServer Pages component using the request object.

 See "Use Your Own Library for XMLHttpRequest" [Hack #3] for an explanation of the *http_request.js* library this hack uses for handling XMLHttpRequest.

The JavaScript uses a couple of handy shortcuts from the Prototype library (see Chapter 6). The select element's id value is "fuelType", as in <select id="fuelType"/>. $("fuelType") is the equivalent of document.getElementById("fuelType"), and $F("fuelType") provides the current value of the select element.

The hack finally inserts the return value, an energy price that the EIA refreshes about once per week, inside a span element on the web page. This final step occurs inside handlePrice(), which is the readystate handler for the request object.

```
var resp =  request.responseText;
if(resp != null && resp.length > 0){
   showQuote($("msg"),
   "The latest price is: "+resp);}
```

For Java Jocks

In case you're interested in the "scraping" code, here's the OilpriceCallback Java class that fetches a crude-oil price:

```java
package com.eeviewpoint;

import java.io.BufferedReader;
import java.io.IOException;
import java.io.InputStreamReader;
import java.net.URL;
import javax.swing.text.html.HTMLEditorKit.ParserCallback;
import javax.swing.text.MutableAttributeSet;
import javax.swing.text.html.parser.ParserDelegator;
import javax.swing.text.html.HTML;

public class OilpriceCallback extends ParserCallback
     implements Scraper{
   private boolean crudeOilCrumb=false;
   private boolean foundCurrPrice=false;
   private String urlSource=
   "http://tonto.eia.doe.gov/dnav/pet/pet_pri_fut_s1_d.htm";
   private String result = "";

   public String getUrlSource() {
```

```
        return urlSource;
    }

    public void setUrlSource(String urlSource) {
        this.urlSource = urlSource;
    }

    public String getResult() {
        return result;
    }

    public void setResult(String result) {
        this.result = result;
    }

    public void handleText(char[] chars, int i) {
        String str = new String(chars);
        if(str.indexOf("Crude Oil") != -1){
            crudeOilCrumb=true;
        }
        if(this.crudeOilCrumb && this.foundCurrPrice &&
                getResult().length() == 0){
            setResult(str.trim());
        }
    }

    public void handleStartTag(HTML.Tag tag,
        MutableAttributeSet mutableAttributeSet, int i) {
        if((crudeOilCrumb) && tag ==  javax.swing.
            text.html.HTML.Tag.TD){
            String val = (String) mutableAttributeSet.
            getAttribute(HTML.Attribute.CLASS);
            if(val != null && val.equalsIgnoreCase("Current")){
                foundCurrPrice=true;
            }
        }
    }

    public String toString() {
        return getResult();          .
    }
}
```

A class named EnergyHarvester contains a list (in an object called
scraperMap) of various callback classes (such as OilpriceCallback) that
scrape prices for the different fuel types. Here is the code from
EnergyHarvester for returning the requested price.

```
public String getNugget() throws ClassNotFoundException,
    IllegalAccessException, InstantiationException, IOException {
    String nm = ((String)scraperMap.get(priceType));
```

```
ParserCallback callback = (ParserCallback) Class.forName(nm).
newInstance();
URL eia = new URL(((Scraper) callback).getUrlSource());
BufferedReader webPagestream = new BufferedReader(
  new InputStreamReader(eia.
  openStream()));
super.parse(webPagestream,callback,true);
return callback.toString();
}
```

Here's the JSP component our web page calls. The code uses an instance of EnergyHarvester, which in turn uses different implementations of the HTML-parsing code to fetch the various energy prices.

```
<%@taglib uri="http://java.sun.com/jsp/jstl/core" prefix="c" %>
<% response.addHeader("Content-Type","text/plain");
    response.addHeader("Cache-Control","no-cache"); %>
<jsp:useBean id="parser" class="com.eeviewpoint.EnergyHarvester"/>
<jsp:setProperty name="parser" property=
    "priceType" value="${param.priceTyp}"/>
<c:out value="${parser.nugget}"/>
```

HACK #40 Send an Email with XMLHttpRequest

Allow the user to enter the email properties in text fields and then send an email without a page round trip.

This hack not only sends an email without a page round trip, but also validates the syntax of the entered email addresses and provides useful messages in the event of invalid entries. Figure 4-20 shows what the hack's web page looks like in the Safari browser.

It looks pretty basic, but a lot happens behind the scenes. A server component awaits a request to receive the data and send it as an email. The web page itself imports three JavaScript libraries:

```
<script type="text/javascript" src="js/email_lib.js"></script>
<script type="text/javascript" src="js/hacks4_12.js"></script>
<script type="text/javascript" src="js/http_request.js"></script>
```

email_lib.js contains a bit of object-oriented JavaScript that is designed to validate an email address [Hack #23] and provide a useful message in the event of any invalid syntax. *http_request.js* (see "Use Your Own Library for XMLHttpRequest" [Hack #3]) initializes XMLHttpRequest and uses it to send the email information. *hacks4_12.js* contains this Ajax application's code, which is reproduced in the next section.

Figure 4-21 shows a message that is dynamically generated when the user enters an address with improper syntax in either of the first two text fields.

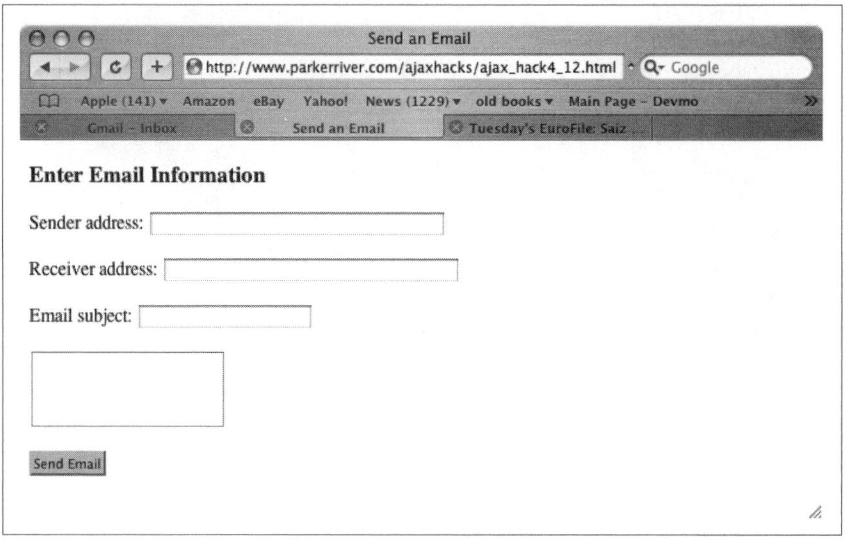

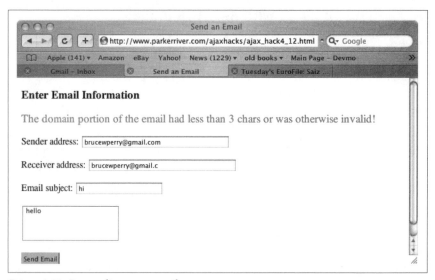

Figure 4-20. *An email application without round trips*

Figure 4-21. *Responding to an email typo*

In this case, the user left a couple of letters off of the email suffix (the domain) in the second field. Our email-syntax checker in *email_lib.js* ensures that, among other things, email addresses end with a period followed by two to three characters. (For more validation rules, check out [Hack #23].)

If the user's entries are valid, the Java servlet responds with an <outcome> true</outcome> message so that the application can notify the user that the email is on its way, as in Figure 4-22.

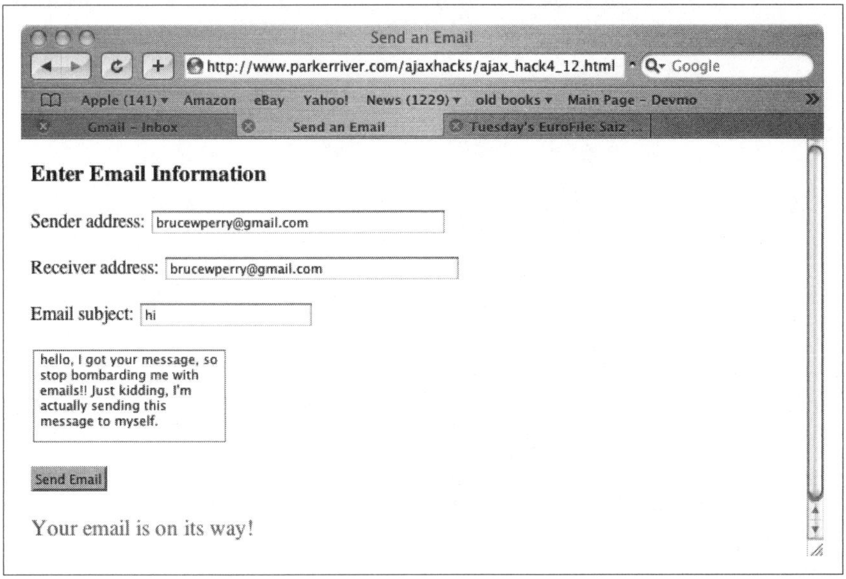

Figure 4-22. All systems go for emailing

How It Works

First we'll look at the code in *hacks4_12.js*, which uses elements of the other two imported libraries to check the email address syntax and then send the email, all without a page rebuild. Then we'll look at the Java servlet that receives the email data. Here is the page's underlying code:

```
var queryString="";
window.onload=function( ){
    var _url="http://www.parkerriver.com/s/em";
    var b1 = document.getElementById("b1");
    if(b1){
        b1.onclick=function( ){
            //clear any existing messages
            clearMsg(document.getElementById("err"),"");
            clearMsg(document.getElementById("msg"),"");
            var isValidEmail=validate(document.getElementById("sender").
                value,
                document.getElementById("receiver").value);
            if(isValidEmail){
                try{
                    showMsg(document.getElementById("msg"),
                    "Sending email...");
```

```
                    setQueryString( );
                    httpRequest("POST",_url,true,
                    handleResponse,queryString);
                } catch(errv) {
                    alert("Sorry, but we failed to send the email because "+
                        "of this error: "+errv.message);
                }
            }

        }; //end function
    }


}
//Validate however many email addresses have been
//passed in as arguments using the Arguments array.
//Break and return false if one of them is invalid
function validate(em1) {
    var bool = false;
    var eml = null;
    for(var i = 0; i < arguments.length; i++)  {
        eml = new Email(arguments[i]);
        eml.validate( );
        bool=eml.valid;
        if(! bool) {  showMsg(document.getElementById("err"),
                eml.message);break;}
    }
    return bool;
}
function showMsg(_id,txt){
    if(_id && txt){_id.innerHTML=txt;}
}
function clearMsg(_id){
    if(_id){_id.innerHTML="";}
}
function handleResponse( ){
    try{
        if(request.readyState == 4){
            if(request.status == 200){
                var resp =  request.responseXML;
                if(resp != null){
                    var outc=resp.getElementsByTagName("outcome")[0];
                    if(outc.childNodes[0].nodeValue == "true") {
                        showMsg(document.getElementById("msg"),
                                "Your email is on its way!");
                    } else {
                        showMsg(document.getElementById("msg"),
                        "The email could not be sent at this time.");
                    }
                } else {
                    showMsg(document.getElementById("msg"),
                            "The email could not be sent at this time.");
                }
            } else {
```

```
                //snipped...
            }
        }//end outer if
    } catch (err)   {
        alert("It does not appear that the server "+
            "is available for this application. Please"+
            " try again very soon. \nError: "+err.message);

    }
}
function setQueryString( ){
    queryString="";
    var frm = document.forms[0];
    var numberElements =  frm.elements.length;
    for(var i = 0; i < numberElements; i++)  {
        if(i < numberElements-1)  {
            queryString += frm.elements[i].name+"="+
                        encodeURIComponent(frm.elements[i].value)+"&";
        } else {
            queryString += frm.elements[i].name+"="+
                        encodeURIComponent(frm.elements[i].value);
        }

    }
}
```

When the browser loads the web page, it sets up the Send Email button's
onclick event handler.

> window.onload is triggered when the browser completes load-
> ing the web page. This is a good place in the code to set up
> the event-handling attributes, such as onclick, for the other
> tags on the page. window.onload is an alternative to using
> event handlers as tag attributes embedded in the HTML.

When the user clicks this button, the application validates the syntax of the
values entered into the email address text fields. If the values represent valid
email addresses, setQueryString( ) assembles a querystring of all the email
information suitable for sending in a POST request:

```
b1.onclick=function( ){
    //clear any existing messages
    clearMsg(document.getElementById("err"),"");
    clearMsg(document.getElementById("msg"),"");
    var isValidEmail=validate(document.getElementById("sender").
            value,
            document.getElementById("receiver").value);
    if(isValidEmail){
        try {
            showMsg(document.getElementById("msg"),"Sending email...");
            setQueryString( );
```

```
                    httpRequest("POST",_url,true,handleResponse,queryString);
                } catch(errv) {
                    alert("Sorry, but we failed to send the email because "+
                          "of this error: "+errv.message);
                }
            }

        }; //end function
```

Here is a sample of a querystring from this application encoded for trans-feral over the Web:

```
//encodeURIComponent( ) function converts '@' to '%40'
fromAddr=brucewperry%40gmail.com&toAddr=brucewperry%40gmail.com&subj=
hello&emessage=hello%20there!
```

Finally, httpRequest( ) sends the POST request to our server component, which ultimately sends the email. See "Use Your Own Library for XMLHttpRequest" [Hack #3] for an explanation of this method.

Server Snippet

What does our server component look like? Here is a snippet from the Java servlet class that sends the email:

```
package com.parkerriver;

import javax.servlet.*;
import javax.servlet.http.*;
import java.io.IOException;

public class NewEmailServlet extends HttpServlet{
    protected void doGet(HttpServletRequest httpServletRequest,
                         HttpServletResponse httpServletResponse) throws
                         ServletException, IOException {
        doPost(httpServletRequest,httpServletResponse);
    }

    protected void doPost(HttpServletRequest httpServletRequest,
                          HttpServletResponse httpServletResponse) throws
                          ServletException, IOException {
        String fromAddr = httpServletRequest.getParameter("fromAddr");
        String toAddr = httpServletRequest.getParameter("toAddr");
        String eMsg = httpServletRequest.getParameter("emessage");
        String subj = httpServletRequest.getParameter("subj");
        boolean outcome = false;
        if(check(fromAddr) && check(toAddr) && check(eMsg)){
            EmailBean bean = new  EmailBean( );
            bean.setFrom(fromAddr);
            bean.setTo(toAddr);
            bean.setSubject(subj);
            bean.setContent(eMsg);
            outcome = bean.sendMessage( );
```

```
        }
        AjaxUtil.sendXML(httpServletResponse,"<outcome>"+
            outcome+"</outcome>");

    }
    private boolean check(String content) {
        if(content != null && content.length( ) > 0) {return true;}
        return false;
    }
}
```

This servlet uses an EmailBean object with various setter or "mutater" meth-ods that build an email. EmailBean has a sendMessage( ) method that sends the email and returns true if everything goes okay (in Java terms, if the method call does not result in a thrown exception). The servlet returns this value to the Ajax application as a bit of XML in an outcome element.

The EmailBean class uses default values for the SMTP server address and authentication (username/password) attributes, which are almost always required when a server component automates email sending.

HACK #41 Find the Browser's Locale Information

Use XMLHttpRequest to find out more specific locale information about a user.

When a user requests a web page, the browser typically sends along some extra data as part of a request header that indicates the user's preferred lan-guage. This information is the value of the Accept-Language request header—for example, en_us for the English language as spoken in the United States, or ko_kr for Korean as spoken in South Korea.

In JavaScript, you can use the navigator.language (or, for Internet Explorer, navigator.userLanguage) property value to pick up this internationalization data. This hack grabs this information for display to the user, then gives the user the option of displaying a more specific translation of the [language code]_[country code] term, as in English_United States.

This hack uses the following sources: *http://www.unicode.org/ unicode/onlinedat/languages.html* for the language codes, and *http://www.iso.org/iso/en/prods-services/iso3166ma/02iso-3166-code-lists/index.html* for country codes.

Figure 4-23 shows the hack in the Safari browser.

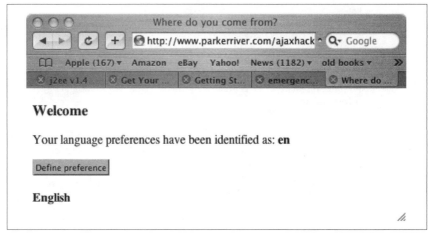

Figure 4-23. An English language preference

When a user loads the page into the browser, it displays the value of that user's language preference in the form [two-letter language code] or [two-letter language code]_[two-letter country code]. The user then clicks the "Define preference" button, and a translation of the code(s) appears, without a page refresh. XMLHttpRequest provides a country and/or language code to a server component, which checks the sources referenced in the previous note and returns a translation of the code or codes (e.g., Korean instead of ko).

 I found that changing my language preferences in the browser (from, say, en_us to es_es) did not cause the value of navigator.language or navigator.userLanguage to change. This property value appears to be a rather static value associated with the browser. To get around this, applications can use a server component that reads the Accept-Language request header directly. Accept-Language typically contains a list of any language codes that the user has set in the browser.

Here is a subset of the web page code for this hack:

```
<head>
    <meta http-equiv="content-type" content="text/html; charset=utf-8" />
    <script type="text/javascript" src="js/hacks4_13.js"></script>
    <script type="text/javascript" src="js/http_request.js"></script>
    <link rel="stylesheet" type="text/css" href="/css/hacks.css" />
    <title>Where do you come from?</title>
</head>
<body>
<h3>Welcome</h3>
<p>
```

```
        Your language preferences have been identified as:
        <span id="_country"></span>
</p>
<form action="javascript:void%200">
    <p>
        <button id="b1" type="button">Define preference</button>
    </p>
</form>
<p>
    <span id="msg"></span>
</p>
```

hacks4_13.js contains the JavaScript for this hack. The request object is powered by *http_request.js* (see "Use Your Own Library for XMLHttpRequest" [Hack #3]).

The Interpreter

Here is the code in *hacks4_13.js*. It reads the navigator.language/navigator. userLanguage value and, after parsing the value, sends it to a server component:

```
var lgn="";
window.onload=function( ){
    if(navigator.language) {
        lgn=navigator.language;
    } else if(navigator.userLanguage) {
        lgn=navigator.userLanguage;
    }
    if(lgn.length >= 2){
        displayLanguage(lgn);
    } else {
        showMsg(document.getElementById("msg"),
                "Sorry, no language information is available "+
                "from your browser.");
    }
    var b1 = document.getElementById("b1");
    if(b1) {
        //Extract the language and country codes
        //The value may be a language code only
        //as in "es" for Spanish
        b1.onclick=function( ){
            var lg = lgn.substring(0,2);
            var ct = lgn.length > 2 ? lgn.substring(3) : "";
            var _url="http://www.parkerriver.com/s/lang?lang="+
                    lg+"&country="+ct;
            httpRequest("GET",_url,true,handleResponse);
        }
    }
}
function showMsg(_id,txt){
    if(_id && txt){_id.innerHTML=txt;}
```

```
    }
    function clearMsg(_id){
        if(_id){_id.innerHTML="";}
    }
    function displayLanguage(_code){
        showMsg(document.getElementById("_country"),
            "<strong>"+_code+"</strong>");
    }
    function handleResponse( ){
        try{
            if(request.readyState == 4){
                if(request.status == 200){
                    var resp =  request.responseXML;
                    //Pull out the content of the country
                    //and language elements and display them
                    //to the user
                    if(resp != null){
                        var intl=resp.getElementsByTagName("intl")[0];
                        var c= intl.getElementsByTagName("country")[0];
                        var l= intl.getElementsByTagName("language")[0];
                        var lval="";
                        var cval="";

                        if(l.hasChildNodes( )){lval=l.childNodes[0].nodeValue;}
                        if(c.hasChildNodes( )){cval=c.childNodes[0].nodeValue;}

                        if(lval && cval) {
                            showMsg(document.getElementById("msg"),
                                    "<strong>"+lval+
                                    "_"+cval+"</strong>");
                        } else if (lval && ! cval) {
                            showMsg(document.getElementById("msg"),
                                    "<strong>"+lval+"</strong>");
                        } else if (! lval && cval){
                            showMsg(document.getElementById("msg"),
                                    "<strong>"+cval+"</strong>");
                        }
                    } else {
                        showMsg(document.
                         getElementById("msg"),
                         "The language info could not be accessed "+
                         "at this time.");
                    }
                } else {
                    //snipped...See Hack #3
    }
```

When the application uses the request object to connect with the server
component, the component sends back some XML. Here is a sample XML
return value:

```
<intl>
<country>KOREA, REPUBLIC OF</country>
```

```
<language>Korean</language>
</intl>
```

The handleResponse( ) function acquires the XML with var resp = request. responseXML. The function then parses the XML, displaying these values to the user.

Hacking the Hack

As mentioned earlier, a most likely improved iteration of this hack would use a server component to read the Accept-Language header directly, rather than depend on the navigator.language property in JavaScript. For example, you can use a JavaServer Pages (JSP) file that reads the Accept-Language header, then uses the embedded Ajax code to display the translation as done here.

HACK #42 Create an RSS Feed Reader

Grab and display XML-based RSS news feeds.

Really Simple Syndication (RSS) is an XML-based format for publishing news, blog entries, and other fast-changing information. Thousands of web sites now provide RSS news feeds as an alternative to visiting the actual sites in a browser. An RSS feed reader lets you subscribe to various feeds. The reader periodically (usually not more than once per half hour) grabs the latest RSS file from each subscribed site, then lets you view those feeds. Some RSS feed readers are built into browsers (Firefox), others are integrated into mail clients (Opera), and others are entirely web-based.

Because RSS feeds are simply XML files, they're easy for an Ajax application to digest. This hack will show you how to read an RSS feed from your server, parse the XML data, and format it for the browser.

Handling RSS feeds is not limited to standalone feed readers. You may want to incorporate RSS data into other applications, such as web portals. RSS feeds are now used for a variety of data beyond just news. For example, the U.S. National Weather Service has weather forecasts and warnings available as RSS feeds (go to *http://www.weather.gov/data/current_obs/* for a listing of available weather feeds).

The following abridged RSS file illustrates the basic structure of an RSS feed:

```
<?xml version='1.0' encoding='utf-8'?>

<rss version='2.0'
xmlns:dc='http://purl.org/dc/elements/1.1/'
xmlns:itunes='http://www.itunes.com/dtds/podcast-1.0.dtd'>
```

```
<channel>
<title>O'Reilly Media, Inc. New Books</title>
<link>http://www.oreilly.com/</link>
<description>O'Reilly's New Books</description>
<copyright>Copyright 2005, O'Reilly Media, Inc.</copyright>
<itunes:author>O'Reilly Media, Inc.</itunes:author>
<itunes:category text='Technology' />
<itunes:explicit>no</itunes:explicit>
<language>en-US</language>
<docs>http://blogs.law.harvard.edu/tech/rss</docs>

<item>
    <title>C in a Nutshell</title>
    <link>http://www.oreilly.com/catalog/cinanut</link>
    <description><![CDATA[Covering the C programming language and C
    runtime library, this book. . .]]>
    </description>
    <author>webmaster@oreillynet.com (Tony Crawford, Peter Prinz)</author>
    <dc:date>2005-12-16T22:51:09-08:00</dc:date>
</item>

<item>
    <title>Run Your Own Web Server Using Linux &amp; Apache</title>
    <link>http://www.oreilly.com/catalog/0975240226</link>
    <description><![CDATA[Learn to install Linux and Apache 2.0 on a
    home or office computer for testing and development, and . . .]]>
    </description>
    <author>webmaster@oreillynet.com (Tony Steidler-Dennison)</author>
    <dc:date>2005-12-15T22:52:17-08:00</dc:date>
</item>

</channel>
</rss>
```

Most RSS feeds contain a single channel element. In RSS files for news and blogs, the channel usually contains multiple items (one for each article).

The RSS files our Ajax application reads must reside on the same server, or within the same domain, as our application itself. For security reasons, most browsers don't let an application from one domain grab data from another domain. This makes browsing safer but limits functionality a bit.

A Simple RSS Reader

For our RSS reader, let's assume you've set up some mechanism to grab fresh RSS files periodically and store them on your server. This can be as simple as setting up a crontab entry on your Linux server:

```
0/30 * * * * wget -q -O /var/www/html/feeds/oreilly_new_titles.rss.xml \
            http://www.oreillynet.com/pub/feed/29?format=rss2
```

Figure 4-24 shows the simple user interface of our RSS reader: a pull-down list to select the RSS feed, and a checkbox to let users select more details for each article displayed.

Figure 4-24. A simple RSS feed reader

Select a news feed, and the matching RSS file is grabbed from the server. The RSS reader extracts information from the file and builds the HTML for the web page, as shown in Figure 4-25.

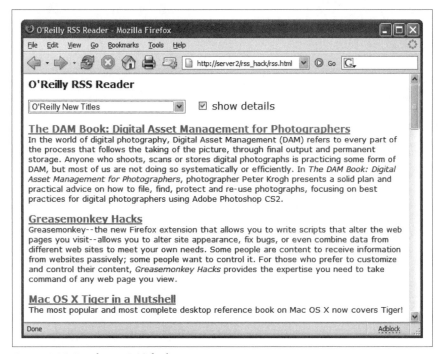

Figure 4-25. Displaying RSS feed content

Our RSS feed reader is contained in the files *rss.html* and *rss_parse.js* (and the ubiquitous JavaScript file *xhr.js*, which provides a browser-neutral XMLHttpRequest object). The first file, shown here, defines the web page itself:

```
<HTML>
<HEAD>
<TITLE>O'Reilly RSS Reader</TITLE>

<script language="javascript" src="xhr.js"></script>
<script language="javascript" src="rss_parse.js"></script>

</HEAD>

<BODY>
<b>O'Reilly RSS Reader</b><p>
<form id="frmRSSParse">

<select id="lbFeeds" onChange="get_rss_feed( );">
    <option value="">SELECT A FEED</option>
    <option value="oreilly_news_articles.rss.xml">
        O'Reilly News and Articles
    </option>
    <option value="oreilly_new_titles.rss.xml">
        O'Reilly New Titles
    </option>
    <option value="oreillynet_articles_blogs.rss.xml">
        O'Reilly Network Articles and Weblogs
    </option>
</select>

 
<input id="cbDetails"
        type=checkbox
        onClick='format_rss_data ("content", last_xml_response);'
>
show details
</form>

<div id="content">
 
</div>

</BODY>

</HTML>
```

The web page references *rss_parse.js*, which defines the three JavaScript functions needed to implement the RSS reader.

How It Works

A handler is attached to the listbox's onChange event. When the user selects an item from the list, the get_rss_feed( ) JavaScript function is called:

```
<select id="lbFeeds" onChange="get_rss_feed( );">
```

This function grabs the URL of the selected RSS file from the listbox and passes it to the get_xml_file( ) function. The second function does the work of retrieving the XML file from the server. This code shows these functions:

```
function get_xml_file (url) {
    var httpreq = getHTTPObject( );

    //Precondition: must have a URL
    if (url == "") return;

    httpreq.open("GET", url, true);

    httpreq.onreadystatechange = function ( ) {
        if (httpreq.readyState == 4) {
            var content = document.getElementById("content");
            content.innerHTML = "Parsing XML...<br>";

            last_xml_response = httpreq.responseXML;
            format_rss_data ("content", last_xml_response);
        }
    }

    var content = document.getElementById("content");
    content.innerHTML = "Retrieving XML...<br>";
    httpreq.send (null);
}

function get_rss_feed ( ) {

    //Get selected RSS feed
    var lbFeeds = document.getElementById("lbFeeds");
    if (lbFeeds.value != "") {
        get_xml_file (lbFeeds.value);
    }

}
```

 The Document object has its own methods for loading an XML file, using the createDocument and load methods. However, let's use XMLHttpRequest in our example because this is more "Ajaxy." Either technique works fine, and both can be made to work (with a little effort) in most of the popular browsers.

The retrieved XML file is stored as a Document object. We pass this object to our third and final function, format_rss_data( ). This is where the Document object is examined and we pull out the items we need. Each news snippet is enclosed in an item element. For our RSS reader, we want to extract three pieces of information from each item: the *title*, the *link* to the full article, and a brief *description* of the article. Here's how it works:

```
function format_rss_data (divname, response) {
    var html = "";
    var doc = response.documentElement;
    var items = doc.getElementsByTagName('item');

    for (var i=0; i < items.length; i++) {

        var title = items[i].getElementsByTagName('title')[0];
        var link = items[i].getElementsByTagName('link')[0];

        html += "<b><a href='"
            + link.firstChild.data
            + "'>"
            + title.firstChild.data
            + "</a></b><br>";

        var cbDetails = document.getElementById("cbDetails");
        if (cbDetails.checked) {
            var desc = items[i].getElementsByTagName('description')[0];
            html += "<font size='-1'>"
                    + desc.firstChild.data
                    + "</font><p>";
        }
    }

    var target_div = document.getElementById(divname);
    target_div.innerHTML = html;
}
```

The format_rss_data( ) function uses a for loop to iterate over each item element in the RSS Document object. Using the getElementsByTagName( ) method, extract the title, link, and description information, and build the HTML displayed on the web page.

Now save the most recent Document object in the last_xml_response variable. If the user checks (or unchecks) the "show details" checkbox, you can reformat the current RSS data with another call to format_rss_data( ), and *without* another request to the server. Figure 4-26 shows the page with "show details" unchecked. In this view, the descriptions are hidden, and the user is presented with a simple list of article links.

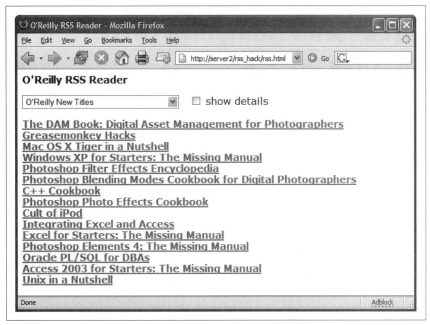

Figure 4-26. The RSS reader with descriptions hidden

Hacking the Hack

This hack doesn't display all the information for each article—author and date information is omitted, and no general channel information is displayed. If you want to use this hack as a generic way to include feed information in web pages, you need to expand format_rss_data( ) to (at least) display the channel title.

Having the RSS feeds hardcoded into the listbox isn't very flexible, either. You can maintain a list of RSS feeds on your server (as an XML file, perhaps), but even this may be unwieldy if you monitor hundreds of feeds. You might consider using a "categories" listbox that populates the "feeds" listbox instead.

—*Mark Pruett*

CHAPTER 5

Direct Web Remoting (DWR) for Java Jocks

Hacks 43–49

What if you want to work with Ajax without having to deal with programming the XMLHttpRequest object? An open source toolkit called Direct Web Remoting (DWR) provides a software layer built on top of this object, completely insulating web page developers from directly programming the request object. DWR also allows Java developers to create Java classes, then use the server-side Java objects from within JavaScript client code (thus the moniker "Web Remoting").

One advantage of DWR is that you can forget about the boilerplate code we have used in other hacks to get the XMLHTTP and XMLHttpRequest objects working. This framework also includes easy techniques for populating web page widgets with server data, while largely removing the required knowledge of Document Object Model programming. The one caveat to using DWR is that *you must use a Java-based server-side solution*, because DWR works with Java servlets and objects behind the scenes.

DWR provides a neat mapping between Java objects and JavaScript code. In other words, you can set up the logic for your application using Java objects on the server, then call those objects' methods with JavaScript code when need be. This is called *remoting* your objects, or making remote Java method calls with JavaScript objects that are bound to the Java objects on the server. This chapter's first hack explains the process for setting up DWR and integrating it into a web application.

 HACK #43 ### Integrate DWR into Your Java Web Application

Design your Ajax application around a JavaScript framework bound to Java objects on the server.

The Direct Web Remoting code comes in the form of an archived or zipped Java Archive (JAR) file, *dwr.jar*. The download address is *http://www.getahead.ltd.uk/dwr/download.html*.

The top-level web page for this open source software is *http://www.getahead.ltd.uk/dwr/*. Check out the license details for more information while you are visiting this page.

To get started with DWR, you must first set it up in your server-side web application. Place the *dwr.jar* file in the */WEB-INF/lib* directory of your Java web application *on the server*, then restart or reload the application.

For those not familiar with Java web applications, they all have a top-level directory named *WEB-INF*. Inside *WEB-INF* are XML configuration files, the main one being *web.xml*. *WEB-INF* also contains a directory named *lib*, which encloses code libraries or JAR files that the application depends on, such as database drivers and helper classes. The *dwr.jar* file goes in this *lib* directory.

Configuring the Application

To get DWR going with your JavaScript, you have to declare in *web.xml* a Java servlet that DWR uses. Here is the chunk of code that you have to add to *web.xml*. If *web.xml* already includes registered servlets, nest this newly declared servlet in with the existing ones (the same goes for the servlet-mapping element):

```
<servlet>
    <servlet-name>dwr-invoker</servlet-name>
    <servlet-class>uk.ltd.getahead.dwr.DWRServlet</servlet-class>
    <init-param>
        <param-name>debug</param-name>
        <param-value>true</param-value>
    </init-param>
</servlet>

<servlet-mapping>
    <servlet-name>dwr-invoker</servlet-name>
    <url-pattern>/dwr/*</url-pattern>
</servlet-mapping>
```

You may have to restart the Java web application for the servlet container to create a new instance of this DWR-related servlet.

You also have to create a simple XML file declaring the Java classes that you want to use from your client-side JavaScript code. Don't worry, I'll show you how to use the JavaScript objects that are bound to Java classes shortly! The file is named *dwr.xml*. Place this XML file in */WEB-INF/*:

```
<dwr>
    <allow>
        <create creator="new" javascript="JsDate">
            <param name="class" value="java.util.Date"/>
        </create>
        <create creator="new" javascript="JsBikeBean">
            <param name="class" value="com.parkerriver.BikeBean"/>
        </create>
    </allow>
</dwr>
```

This XML states that the client-side JavaScript can use two Java classes remotely. The JavaScript objects that bind the client-side code remotely to the Java classes are named JsDate and JsBikeBean. As part of the server-side preparations, you must have already developed the Java class com.parkerriver. BikeBean and installed it in your application. java.util.Date is part of the Java software development kit; it's not your own custom class. Date is already available as part of the Java virtual machine your server component is using.

> The BikeBean class file is typically stored in */WEB-INF/classes*, as in */WEB-INF/classes/com/parkerriver/BikeBean.class*.

This XML file binds the two JavaScript names to the Date and BikeBean objects, so that these objects are available to use in your client-side JavaScript. This means that JavaScript code can call all the public methods of these Java objects. But how is the JavaScript in the local web page connected to the remote Java instances running on the server? Figure 5-1 shows in general terms the path a JavaScript method call takes in DWR's form of web remoting.

The web page that will use DWR contains these script tags, which connect the JavaScript code via the DWR servlet to the server code:

```
<script type="text/javascript" src=
        "/[name of web app]/dwr/interface/JsBean.js">
</script>
<script type="text/javascript" src=
        "/[name of web app]/dwr/interface/JsDate.js">
</script>
<script type="text/javascript" src=
        "/[name of web app]/dwr/engine.js"></script>
<script type="text/javascript" src=
        "/[name of web app]/dwr/util.js"></script>
```

Think back to the simple XML file that we just added to the web application. The first two script tags reference the JavaScript names we bound to the Java classes that we want to remote: JsBikeBean and JsDate. The XML

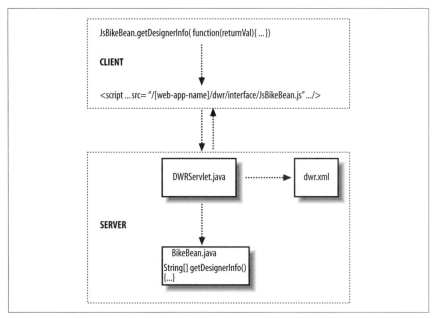

Figure 5-1. Calling a Java method remotely

file configured certain Java classes to be used with these names in JavaScript code. Remember the *dwr.jar* file that we installed in the web application? It contains two JavaScript libraries, *engine.js* and *util.js*. The first of these files is required to use DWR; the second is optional and contains a bunch of DWR functions that the client-side code can use.

The URL that the script tag uses, such as */parkerriver/dwr/interface/JsBean. js*, connects to the special DWR servlet that we enabled. The servlet in turn makes available to our code the public methods of the Java classes that we configured in XML. The next few hacks will use these classes and functions.

Use DWR to Populate a Selection List from a Java Array

HACK #44

Remotely get an array return value from a Java object and use the data to populate a selection list.

Sounds awesome, huh? You can take existing Java objects that have methods returning Java arrays, and use those return values to populate a select list on a web page. Figure 5-2 shows the web page that we will use in the next few hacks. The page lists some bike manufacturers in a pop-up widget, a few product codes associated with those companies, and then some date/ time values. This hack fills the first pop-up or select list with its values when the browser loads the page.

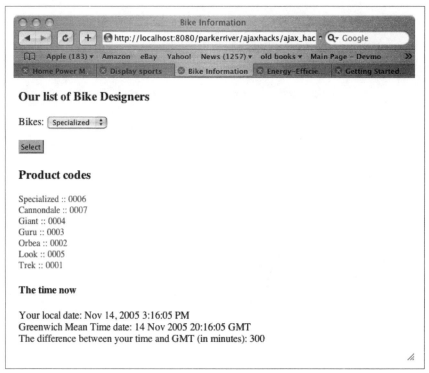

Figure 5-2. Dynamically fill a select list with server values

The page imports several JavaScript files using script tags. The first four files allow the application to use DWR; the last one contains the code for our application. Here is the underlying web page code:

```
<!DOCTYPE html PUBLIC "-//W3C//DTD XHTML 1.0 Strict//EN"
        "http://www.w3.org/TR/2000/REC-xhtml1-20000126/DTD/xhtml1-strict.
dtd">
<html xmlns="http://www.w3.org/1999/xhtml" xml:lang="en" lang="en">
<head>
    <meta http-equiv="content-type" content="text/html; charset=utf-8" />
    <script type="text/javascript" src=
            "/parkerriver/ajaxhacks/js/hacks5_1.js"></script>
    <script type="text/javascript" src=
            "/parkerriver/dwr/interface/JsBikeBean.js"></script>
    <script type="text/javascript" src=
            "/parkerriver/dwr/interface/JsDate.js"></script>
    <script type="text/javascript" src=
            "/parkerriver/dwr/engine.js"></script>
    <script type="text/javascript" src=
            "/parkerriver/dwr/util.js"></script>
    <title>Bike Information</title>
</head>
<body>
```

```
<h3>Our list of Bike Designers</h3>
<form action="javascript:void%200">
    <p>
        Bikes: <select id="bikes"></select>
    </p>
    <p>
        <button type="button" name="selection" value="Select">Select</
button>
    </p>
</form>
<h3>Product codes</h3>
<div id="prodCodes"></div>
<h4>The time now</h4>
<div id="showDates"></div>
</body>
</html>
```

To use one of these bound JavaScript objects in your code, you have to set up the server component in the way the previous hack described, then use a script tag with the following syntax:

```
<script type="text/javascript" src=
        "/[name-of-your-web-app]/dwr/interface/JsBikeBean.js"></script>
```

Substitute [name-of-your-web-app] with the name of your web application, or *context root* in Java web parlance.

In addition, every Ajax application using DWR has to import the *engine.js* library, using similar syntax:

```
<script type="text/javascript" src=
        "/[name-of-your-web-app]/dwr/engine.js"></script>
```

util.js is optional, but it contains a lot of useful JavaScript functions (a few of which the upcoming hacks use).

Getting an Array from the Server

This hack's code populates the select list using a Java array value it receives from a server component. The component is a Java servlet that this chapter's first hack installed, and the array source is an instance of a Java object we have running on the server. The array derives from the BikeBean class's getDesignerInfo( ) method. This method returns all the keys, such as "Trek" or "Cannondale," contained in a HashMap (a Java object that represents a hash table or associative array) named bikeInfo. Here is the code for the BikeBean class:

```
package com.parkerriver;

import java.util.Map;
import java.util.HashMap;
import java.util.Collections;
```

```java
public class BikeBean {
    private static Map BIKE_INFO;
    static {
        BIKE_INFO = Collections.synchronizedMap(new HashMap( ));
        BIKE_INFO.put("Trek","0001");
        BIKE_INFO.put("Orbea","0002");
        BIKE_INFO.put("Guru","0003");
        BIKE_INFO.put("Giant","0004");
        BIKE_INFO.put("Look","0005");
        BIKE_INFO.put("Specialized","0006");
        BIKE_INFO.put("Cannondale","0007");
    }
    public String[] getDesignerInfo( ){
        return (String[])BIKE_INFO.keySet( ).toArray(new String[]{});
    }

    public static Map getBikeInfo( ) {
        return BIKE_INFO;
    }
}
```

This BikeBean object is loaded into and stored in the server's memory (specifically, inside the Java Virtual Machine that the server is using). How does the JavaScript code running inside a distant user's browser get access to the Java object's methods? The XML configuration that this chapter's first hack explained bound a JavaScript name (JsBikeBean) to the BikeBean object. The DWR servlet and the *engine.js* file that the web page imports handle the intermediate magic that connects the browser code to the server code. Here is the JavaScript code in *hacks5_1.js* that gives the select list its values:

```javascript
window.onload=function( ){
    setupSelect( );
    setupMap( );
    setupDates( );};

function setupSelect( ){
    JsBikeBean.getDesignerInfo(populate);
}
function populate(list){
    DWRUtil.removeAllOptions("bikes");
    DWRUtil.addOptions("bikes", list);
}
/* CODE SNIPPED FOR:
setupMap( );
setupDates( );
*/
```

When the browser finishes loading the web page, the window.onload code calls three different functions. This hack deals with setupSelect( ); upcoming hacks feature the other two functions. setupSelect( ) remotely calls (via JsBikeBean) the getDesignerInfo( ) method. This method returns an array of strings that represent the names of some bike manufacturers. These names will end up as the labels for a select list (see Figure 5-2).

> The DWR servlet returns Java values in JSON format, so a HashMap in Java is returned as:
>
> ```
> { "Trek":"0001","Specialized":"0005",...}
> ```

DWR uses a '*callback design pattern* as one of the options for initiating its remote calls. When the code calls Java methods from JavaScript, an additional parameter representing a callback function is added at the end of the method's parameter list (or is the *only* parameter, for methods that are not defined in Java as having any parameters).

The only parameter to getDesignerInfo( ) is the name of a function that will handle the Java method's return value (an array). The callback function's name is populate( ), and its parameter is the returned array, here represented by the list variable. This code can also pass in a function literal instead of a function name to getDesignerInfo( ), as in:

```
JsBikeBean.getDesignerInfo(
    function(list){
        DWRUtil.removeAllOptions("bikes");
        DWRUtil.addOptions("bikes", list);
    }
);
```

The code is in essence saying, "I'm calling this Java method remotely, and here is the JavaScript function that will handle the return value."

> You can also call DWR remote methods using a different syntax involving options to specify a timeout period and an error handler:
>
> ```
> JsBikeBean.getDesignerInfo({
>     callback: function(list){
>         DWRUtil.removeAllOptions("bikes");
>         DWRUtil.addOptions("bikes", list);
>     },
>     timeout:5000,
>     errorHandler:myErrHandler
> });
> ```

Eccentric Utility

The rest of the code takes this array of bike-maker names and dynamically fills a select list with them, using a couple of DWR's utility functions. The web page made these functions available by importing *util.js* using a script tag, as this hack explained earlier.

`DWRUtil.removeAllOptions()` takes the `id` of a select list as a parameter, then removes all the options (a logical first step before you change the options in the list). The web page's select list looks like:

```
<select id="bikes"></select>
```

`DWRUtil.addOptions()`, on the other hand, takes the `id` of a select list as its first parameter and an `array` as its second parameter. The `array` members then become the options or labels in the `select` list. You might recall that the `list` variable contains the array returned by the Java method to which our JavaScript code is bound. Again, our code looks like:

```
DWRUtil.addOptions("bikes", list);
```

If you are a Java web developer, this is cool stuff. The next hack populates a select list from a Java `Map` type such as `java.util.HashMap`.

HACK #45   Use DWR to Create a Selection List from a Java Map

Create a selection list with the Map keys as option values and the Map values as the option content.

This hack creates a pop-up selection list on a web page from a Java `Map`. The list is made up of a `select` tag with one or more nested `option` tags. Each option can have a `value` attribute, which is what the web application sends to the server instead of the content of the `option`. For example, the application sends `uk` or `fr` in the following cases, not `United Kingdom` or `France`:

```
<select>
    <option value="uk">United Kingdom</option>
    <option value="fr">France</option>
</select>
```

This hack uses DWR to generate the pop-up from a Java `Map`, using `Map` keys as the values of the `option` value attributes. The hack uses the same web page as that depicted in Figure 5-2, but it generates the select element in a slightly different manner. Here are the important parts of the web page's underlying HTML code, including the `script` tags that import various JavaScript libraries and the select tag itself:

```
<head>
    <meta http-equiv="content-type" content="text/html; charset=utf-8" />
    <script type="text/javascript" src=
    "/parkerriver/ajaxhacks/js/hacks5_3.js"></script>
    <script type="text/javascript" src=
    "/parkerriver/dwr/interface/JsBikeBean.js"></script>
    <script type="text/javascript" src=
    "/parkerriver/dwr/engine.js"></script>
```

```
<script type="text/javascript" src="/parkerriver/dwr/util.js"></script>
    <title>Bike Information</title>
</head>
<!--snipped... -->
<p>
    Bikes: <select id="bikes"></select>
</p>
```

engine.js is a required JavaScript code library for web pages that use the DWR framework. *JsBikeBean.js* enables our code to make remote calls to *BikeBean.java*. Importing *util.js* is optional; I do it here because we're using one of its functions.

Code Ahead

Here is the code in *hacks5_3.js* for making a remote Java call and loading up the select list:

```
window.onload=function( ){ JsBikeBean.getBikeInfo(populate);};

function populate(map){
    DWRUtil.removeAllOptions("bikes");
    addOptionValues("bikes", map);
}
function addOptionValues(_id,_map){
    var sel = document.getElementById(_id);
    var opt = null;
    if(sel != null){
        for(var prop in _map) {
            opt=document.createElement("option");
            opt.setAttribute("value",_map[prop]);
            opt.appendChild(document.createTextNode(prop));
            sel.appendChild(opt);
        }
    }
}
```

Ponder window.onload, which points to the function that the browser's Java-Script runtime calls when the web page is finished loading. This code makes the remote Java method call, passing the return value to a function named populate( ):

```
JsBikeBean.getBikeInfo(populate);
```

populate( ) in turn removes any existing options from the select element and then creates new option elements by calling addOptionValues( ). The latter function uses Document Object Model programming to create new option elements and add them to the existing select element. The _map variable refers to the JavaScript object to which the server component's return value was converted.

In the for/in loop, prop represents the names of each of the original Map keys, and _map[prop] returns the values of these elements. In the code, _map is a JavaScript object, as in:

```
{"Trek":"0006"}
```

Using the syntax _map["Trek"] returns that property value, as in 0006.

The options that this code creates look like <option value="0006">Trek</option>. As described earlier in this hack, when the user makes a selection from the pop-up list, the browser sends the value of that option's value attribute (here, 0006) to the server.

This hack represents a handy technique for converting hash table values running as Java objects to select options. "Display the Keys/Values from a Java HashMap on a Web Page" [Hack #46] shows the keys and values from a Java Map type as text on a web page.

Display the Keys/Values from a Java HashMap on a Web Page

HACK #46

Connect to a Java object running on the server and use JavaScript to display a HashMap's contents on a web page.

This hack takes a java.util.HashMap containing the names of bike manufacturers keyed to their product codes and displays this information on a web page. The earlier hacks in this chapter introduced the reader to this web page, which Figure 5-2 shows.

> A java.util.HashMap in Java is a hash table structure that contains keys pointing to values. Its JavaScript representation could look like {firstname: "Bruce", lastname: "Perry"}.

The place on the web page where we want to display these values looks like this in the HTML code:

```
<h3>Product codes</h3>
<div id="prodCodes"></div>
```

This code represents a subheading and a div element with the id prodCodes. When the web page loads, the code asks the server component for the contents of a Java HashMap. The code displays the Map keys followed by "::" then the Map values, as in "Specialized :: 0006," with a little styling added to boot. The server component and web page are set up and configured just as in "Integrate DWR into Your Java Web Application" [Hack #43]. To refresh your memory, here are the script tags that the web page uses, so that the application can use DWR and *hacks5_1.js*, which contains our own JavaScript:

```
<script type="text/javascript"
       src="/parkerriver/ajaxhacks/js/hacks5_1.js"></script>
<script type="text/javascript" src="/parkerriver/dwr/interface/JsBikeBean.
js">
       </script>
<script type="text/javascript" src="/parkerriver/dwr/interface/JsDate.js"></
script>
<script type="text/javascript" src="/parkerriver/dwr/engine.js"></script>
<script type="text/javascript" src="/parkerriver/dwr/util.js"></script>
```

The code from *hacks5_1.js* calls a JsBikeBean method to display the converted HashMap's values inside the div element. Here is the Java code to which the bound JavaScript object JsBikeBean has access:

```
private static Map BIKE_INFO;
    static {
        BIKE_INFO = Collections.synchronizedMap(new HashMap( ));
        BIKE_INFO.put("Trek","0001");
        BIKE_INFO.put("Orbea","0002");
        BIKE_INFO.put("Guru","0003");
        BIKE_INFO.put("Giant","0004");
        BIKE_INFO.put("Look","0005");
        BIKE_INFO.put("Specialized","0006");
        BIKE_INFO.put("Cannondale","0007");
    }

    public static Map getBikeInfo( ) {
        return BIKE_INFO;
    }
```

The getBikeInfo( ) method simply returns the Map with all these values.

> A comprehensive real-world application might return a Map
> derived from an underlying database. Also, Map is the inter-
> face implemented by HashMap, so a HashMap is also a Map type
> in Java.

Traveling at the speed of light from the server to the browser code, here is the web page's underlying JavaScript:

```
//This method is called by the window.onload event handler
function setupMap( ){
    JsBikeBean.getBikeInfo(setProdCodes);
}
//"jsHashmap" is the JS object representation of a HashMap
function setProdCodes(jsHashmap){
    var div = document.getElementById("prodCodes");
    //remove old messages
    div.innerHTML="";
    div.style.color="purple";
    div.style.fontSize="0.9em";
    var tmpText;
```

```
for(var prop in jsHashmap) {
    tmpText = prop + " :: "+ jsHashmap[prop];
    div.appendChild(document.createTextNode(tmpText));
    div.appendChild(document.createElement("br"));
    }
}
```

getBikeInfo( ) returns the HashMap value and passes it as the parameter to the setProdCodes( ) function:

```
JsBean.getBikeInfo(setProdCodes);
...
function setProdCodes(jsHashmap){...}
```

setProdCodes( ) represents the callback mechanism that DWR uses to exchange data between the server's return values and the web page's code.

 The JavaScript code passes a callback function name as a parameter to the Java method. Make sure to leave out the parentheses when calling DWR-related methods in this manner. In other words, *don't* use:

```
JsBean.getBikeInfo(setProdCodes());
```

The HashMap values that originated on the server manifest as the callback function's parameter. The jsHashmap parameter in setProdCodes(jsHashmap) contains the bike-maker names as keys and the product codes as values. The code gets a reference to the div within which this information will be displayed, then specifies the font size and color of the text:

```
div.style.color="purple";
div.style.fontSize="0.9em";
```

The DWR framework does a lot of useful work for a script and an Ajax developer. The framework returns the hash table value in JSON format [Hack #7] as a JavaScript object.

 The DWR framework returns a Java HashMap, for example, as:

```
{"Trek":"0001","Specialized":"0005",...}
```

As a result, the code can easily display the keys and values of the object using a for/in loop:

```
for(var prop in jsHashmap) {
    tmpText = prop + " :: "+ jsHashmap[prop];
    div.appendChild(document.createTextNode(tmpText));
    div.appendChild(document.createElement("br"));
    }
```

The code writes the bike-maker names and product codes by displaying the key and value followed by a line break (br) tag:

```
/* i.e., jsHashmap["Trek"]returns "0001" */
tmpText = prop + " :: "+ jsHashmap[prop];
div.appendChild(document.createTextNode(tmpText));
div.appendChild(document.createElement("br"));
```

tmpText contains the line of text that the web page displays, as in "Trek :: 0001." During each iteration of the for/in loop, the code writes out a separate line representing a different bike company and product code.

"Use DWR to Populate an Ordered List from a Java Array" [Hack #47] dynamically generates an ordered or unordered list from Java values on the server.

Use DWR to Populate an Ordered List from a Java Array

Use a framework to dynamically populate a web page widget from values derived from a Java object.

This hack automatically (you might say automagically) generates an ordered or unordered list using server content, such as a list of high-end bike makers. A typical list on a web page is hardcoded into the web page's HTML code. It looks like a series of bullets or numbers, each accompanied by a label. These list types are fine for content that never (or hardly ever) changes. However, some lists must be dynamically generated from a server object, based on persistent information such as that contained in a database. For example, think of a bike shop that is constantly adding new products to its online store, and/or changing product attributes.

A dynamically generated list is necessary only for persistent information that is updated frequently.

The web page code in this hack derives its content by calling a Java method via Direct Web Remoting, which is designed to bind JavaScript objects to Java objects running on the server. "Integrate DWR into Your Java Web Application" [Hack #43] sets up and configures the Java application on the server end, which is the first step to running this hack.

This hack generates an ordered list on the same web page other hacks in this chapter have used. This is an ol element that contains a numbered list of bike makers. We include the option to generate an unordered list (a ul element) containing bullets to the left of the labels. When the web page loads, its underlying code automatically fetches an array of bike-maker names from a server and generates the list. Figure 5-3 shows what the web page looks like.

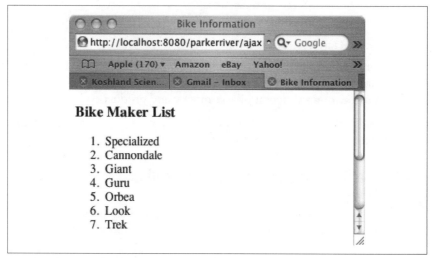

Figure 5-3. A list of bike makers

The web page imports all of the necessary JavaScript files with script tags, and includes the list within a div tag with id orlist:

```
<!DOCTYPE html PUBLIC "-//W3C//DTD XHTML 1.0 Strict//EN"
        "http://www.w3.org/TR/2000/REC-xhtml1-20000126/DTD/xhtml1-strict.
dtd">
<html xmlns="http://www.w3.org/1999/xhtml" xml:lang="en" lang="en">
<head>
    <meta http-equiv="content-type" content="text/html; charset=utf-8" />
    <script type="text/javascript" src=
        "/parkerriver/ajaxhacks/js/hacks5_1.js"></script>
    <script type="text/javascript" src=
        "/parkerriver/dwr/interface/JsBikeBean.js"></script>
    <script type="text/javascript" src=
        "/parkerriver/dwr/interface/JsDate.js"></script>
    <script type="text/javascript" src=
        "/parkerriver/dwr/engine.js"></script>
    <script type="text/javascript" src=
        "/parkerriver/dwr/util.js"></script>
    <title>Bike Information</title>
</head>
<body>
<!--SNIPPED -->
<p><input id="hid" type="hidden" value="ordered" /></p>
<!--SNIPPED -->
<div id="orlist"></div>
<!-- ... -->
</body>
```

```
</html>
```

hacks5_1.js includes our custom code, which I'll show in a moment. All the other imported JavaScript files are DWR-related. *engine.js* is required if your code is using the DWR framework; *util.js* is an optional library of utility functions, one of which is used in this hack. JsBikeBean is a JavaScript class that is bound to a Java object.

Here is the *hacks5_1.js* code:

```
window.onload=function( ){ callSetups( )};

function callSetups( ){
    setupSelect( );
    setupMap( );
    setupList(document.getElementById("hid").value);
    setupDates( );
}
function setupList(typ){
    JsBikeBean.getDesignerInfo(function(list) {
        var div = document.getElementById("orlist");
        var el = null;
        if(div != null){
            //remove any existing lists
            div.innerHTML="";
            if(typ.indexOf("un") == -1) {
                //create an ordered list
                el=document.createElement("ol");
            } else {
                //create an unordered list
                el=document.createElement("ul");
            }
            el.setAttribute("id","servlist");
            div.appendChild(el);
            //create li elements from server information
            DWRUtil.addOptions("servlist", list);
        }
    });
}
//Rest of code snipped...
```

One salient aspect is that the code does not require either XMLHttpRequest or our custom library for using the request object, *http_request.js* (see "Use Your Own Library for XMLHttpRequest" [Hack #3]). The DWR framework takes care of its remote binding between JavaScript and Java.

An event handler linked to window.onload calls a setupList( ) function. setupList( ) has a string specifying "ordered" or "unordered" as a parameter. The code gets this value from a hidden element on the web page, so that a web page designer or author can specify the type of list. Inside setupList( ), the code calls the Java method getDesignerInfo( ), via its client-side proxy JsBikeBean. This method returns an array of bike-maker names.

The way DWR works when remotely calling Java methods is that a parameter representing a function for handling the Java return value is added to the method call, as in:

```
JsBikeBean.callFoo(function(returnValue){//handle callFoo return value})
```

This approach, used in the web page code, handles the return value with a function literal. You can, alternatively, use JsBikeBean.callFoo(myFunc) and then define myFunc(returnVal) somewhere. In this case, the framework passes the Java method return value to this handler function as its parameter.

In our code, the function literal that handles the getDesignerInfo( ) return value looks like this:

```
function(list) {
    var div = document.getElementById("orlist");
    var el = null;
    if(div != null){
        //remove any existing lists
        div.innerHTML="";
        /* The function literal has access to the
        type parameter of the outer function; typ
        can be "ordered" or "unordered" */
        if(typ.indexOf("un") == -1) {
            //create an ordered list
            el=document.createElement("ol");
        } else {
            //create an unordered list
            el=document.createElement("ul");
        }
            el.setAttribute("id","servlist");
            div.appendChild(el);
            //create li elements from server information
            DWRUtil.addOptions("servlist", list);
    }
}
```

list is the array returned from the server, which looks like ["value1","value2"]. First the code determines whether to create an ordered or unordered list. The code then appends the new element with id servlist as a child within an existing div element. Finally, the function uses a DWR utility function to generate the new list:

```
DWRUtil.addOptions("servlist", list);
```

Figure 5-4 shows what the browser looks like after generating an unordered list.

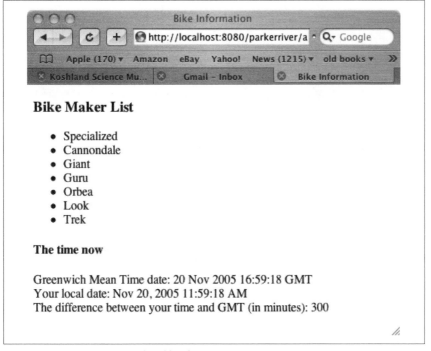

Figure 5-4. *Creating an unordered list from remote Java*

 The content at the bottom of Figure 5-4 relates to calling a built-in Java object using DWR. "Call a Built-in Java Object from JavaScript Using DWR" **[Hack #49]** covers this mechanism.

The addOptions() function takes the id of the list as the first argument, and the array of values as the second. If the code has to remove existing options from a list first, one option is to use DWRUtil.removeOptions("servlist").

Access a Custom Java Object with JavaScript

#48 Receive a serialized Java object via Ajax, then use that object with JavaScript.

The programming model for a number of Java applications involves generating JavaBeans that represent data. A JavaBean is an object representation of a concrete thing like a bicycle, with its wheels, pedals, seat, chain rings, and other components as object properties. The purpose of a JavaBean is to represent these concrete entities for a software program that accomplishes a set of practical tasks involving the entity data type, such as an e-commerce site that sells bikes. Therefore, it is natural that some Ajax applications will receive data from a server component in the form of JavaBeans.

This hack uses the DWR framework to access a JavaScript representation of a Java object from the server. The hack then displays the object on a web page.

The Big Set-up

To use DWR with Ajax, you have to set it up on the server first. "Integrate DWR into Your Java Web Application" **[Hack #43]** describes this process in detail, so I won't repeat it here, except to show this hack's XML configuration file. On the server end, this file must be stored in /WEB-INF/. The file gives DWR its instructions for creating an instance of the Java class that your application calls remotely from JavaScript:

```
<dwr>
    <allow>
        <create creator="new" javascript="JsBikeJavaBean">
            <param name="class" value="com.parkerriver.BikeJavaBean"/>
        </create>
    </allow>
</dwr>
```

As specified in this configuration file, the JavaScript name your code uses for the remote method call is JsBikeJavaBean. Figure 5-5 shows the web page when it's first requested. The underlying code requests a serialized version of the BikeJavaBean object when the web page is first loaded. It then displays this object as a string in an alert window.

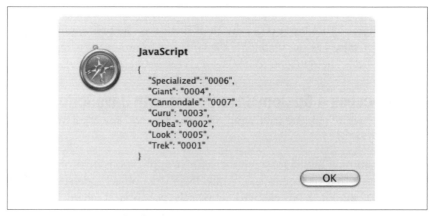

Figure 5-5. Voilà, a serialized Java object

Here is the code for the BikeJavaBean class, for which JsBikeJavaBean is remoted:

```java
package com.parkerriver;

import java.util.Map;
import java.util.HashMap;
import org.json.JSONObject;

public class BikeJavaBean {
    private Map bikeInfo;

    public BikeJavaBean(Map bikeInfo) {
        this.bikeInfo = bikeInfo;
    }

    public BikeJavaBean() {
        bikeInfo = Collections.synchronizedMap(new HashMap());
        bikeInfo.put("Trek","0001");
        bikeInfo.put("Orbea","0002");
        bikeInfo.put("Guru","0003");
        bikeInfo.put("Giant","0004");
        bikeInfo.put("Look","0005");
        bikeInfo.put("Specialized","0006");
        bikeInfo.put("Cannondale","0007");
    }

    public String[] getbikeMakers(){
        return (String[])bikeInfo.keySet().
                toArray(new String[]{});
    }

    public Map getBikeInfo() {
        return bikeInfo;
    }

    public String toJSON(){
        /* There are different ways to serialize a Java object
        using a JSONObject constructor; here we are constructing
        a JSONObject using the Java object's HashMap */
        JSONObject jo = new JSONObject(getBikeInfo());
        return jo.toString(4);
    }
}
```

This is an object that contains a hash table structure involving the names of bike makers keyed to some imaginary product codes. Our JavaScript object named JsBikeJavaBean (check out the earlier configuration) is bound to this Java object. Pay special attention to the toJSON() method. This is the method that our Ajax code will call to access a serialized version of the JavaBean.

The code uses a JSONObject type, which derives from the Java API for JavaScript Object Notation. The Java API for JSON offers Java classes that make it easier to return JSON-formatted values to Ajax applications [Hack #7]. We have bundled this API and related classes in with the rest of our server-side Java classes.

The purpose of returning JSON-formatted values to Ajax is that they can easily be converted to JavaScript objects, which often makes it easier for Ajax to work with the data (see *http:////www.json.org*).

The bean's code creates a JSONObject by passing into the JSONObject's constructor the bean's HashMap of bike-maker data. This code essentially wraps the bean's data inside this special object:

```
JSONObject jo = new JSONObject(getBikeInfo());
return jo.toString(4);
```

The code then calls the JSONObject's toString( ) method, which returns the string version of the bike-maker names and product codes that show up in the browser alert window.

> In the programming world, representing an instance of an object in a different format while preserving its internal state or property values is sometimes called *marshalling*. So, in this case, we're marshalling a Java object into JSON format. Going the other way—say, from XML back into a Java object—is called *unmarshalling*.

Here is the HTML code for the web page. As usual, the key parts of this page are the script tags that import the necessary JavaScript libraries:

```
<!DOCTYPE html PUBLIC "-//W3C//DTD XHTML 1.0 Strict//EN"
        "http://www.w3.org/TR/2000/REC-xhtml1-20000126/DTD/xhtml1-strict.
dtd">
<html xmlns="http://www.w3.org/1999/xhtml" xml:lang="en" lang="en">
<head>
    <meta http-equiv="content-type" content="text/html; charset=utf-8" />
    <script type="text/javascript" src=
            "/parkerriver/ajaxhacks/js/hacks5_5.js"></script>
    <script type="text/javascript" src=
            "/parkerriver/dwr/interface/JsBikeJavaBean.js"></script>
    <script type="text/javascript" src=
            "/parkerriver/dwr/engine.js"></script>
    <script type="text/javascript" src=
            "/parkerriver/dwr/util.js"></script>
    <title>Bike Information</title>
</head>
<body>
<h3>Our list of Bike Designers</h3>
<div id="bean"></div>
```

```
    </body>
    </html>
```

The two highlighted script tags import the JavaScript libraries that are required to use DWR: *JsBikeJavaBean.js*, which in our case binds a JavaScript object of that name to the JavaBean running on the server; and *engine.js*, which is the framework code. *hacks5_5.js* represents the code for this hack, and *util.js* is an optional library that contains several useful functions.

When the user dismisses the alert window, the web page's code uses the returned JavaBean object (in JSON format) to display the object's data on the page. Figure 5-6 shows this page.

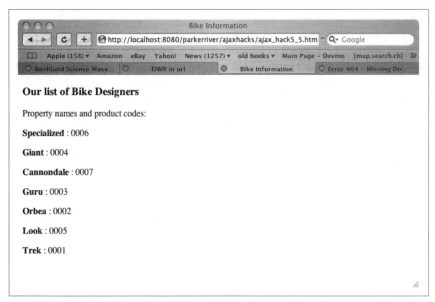

Figure 5-6. Displaying a serialized JavaBean

You are probably curious by now what the code in *hacks5_5.js* does. How does the web page code display the JavaBean information that the server component returns? How does the web page make the request in the first place? Let's take a look:

```
window.onload=function( ){
    JsBikeJavaBean.toJSON(function(javaStr){
        alert(javaStr);
        var div = document.getElementById("bean");
        //remove old content
        div.innerHTML="";
        //convert the return value to a Java object
        var javaObj = new Function("return "+javaStr)( );
        var innerHt="<p>Property names and product codes:</p>";
```

```
        for(var propName in javaObj) {
            innerHt += "<p>";
            innerHt += "<strong>";
            innerHt += propName;
            innerHt += "</strong> : ";
            innerHt += javaObj[propName];
            innerHt += "</p>";
        }
        div.innerHTML=innerHt;
    });
};
```

The framework takes care of making the HTTP request, so the code does
not contain any references to XMLHttpRequest or the httpRequest( ) function
you have seen in other hacks. The JsBikeJavaBean.toJSON( ) function is a
remote method call that returns the serialized (or JSONized) JavaBean.
DWR uses the callback mechanism, in which the argument to the remote
method is a function that handles the server's return value. That function, in
turn, has the return value as its lone argument. Our code uses a *function literal*, in which the entire function definition is passed in to the remote
method call.

First, an alert window shows the returned string. The code then converts
the JSON-formatted string into a JavaScript object using a special
technique.

> "Receive Data in JSON Format" **[Hack #7]** describes this tech-
> nique, a line of code that makes JavaScript interpret the
> JSON-formatted string as an object.

In the code, the variable javaObj now represents a plain old JavaScript object
that the code easily explores with a for/in loop. This loop builds a string,
which displays the object's values inside a div element:

```
for(var propName in javaObj) {
    innerHt += "<p>";
    innerHt += "<strong>";
    innerHt += propName;
    innerHt += "</strong> : ";
    innerHt += javaObj[propName];
    innerHt += "</p>";
}
div.innerHTML=innerHt;
```

Hacks like this can easily integrate existing JavaBeans that various server
components might use. Using the Java API for JSON is just a matter of
downloading and compiling the source code for objects such as JSONObject
and JSONArray, which you can find at *http://www.crockford.com/JSON/java/*.

Call a Built-in Java Object from JavaScript Using DWR

Extend your code's reach by calling built-in Java objects remotely.

What if you had to read a file like a log on a server from a JavaScript object on the client browser? You might want to use the java.io.FileReader class on the server. (This class is part of the Java 2 Standard Edition—a fancy way of saying that FileReader is built into Java but not JavaScript.) The DWR framework allows you to easily call standard Java methods from your JavaScript. This hack displays some date information on a web page. The data derives from remote method calls using the java.util.Date object.

> JavaScript has a robust Date object and several associated methods, which you would use in most real-world applications that display dates on a web page. It's still nice to know, from at least a hack writer's perspective, that a great variety of standard Java objects and their methods are available from JavaScript. At the very least, you can adapt these techniques to several other similar situations.

The code in this hack displays the current date and time, and compares this data to the Greenwich mean time (GMT) date and time. Figure 5-4 in "Use DWR to Populate an Ordered List from a Java Array" [Hack #47] shows what the Date information looks like on a web page.

Setting up this code involves a little server configuration, as this chapter's first hack explained. (If you're still setting up DWR on the server, check back to "Integrate DWR into Your Java Web Application" [Hack #43] for a summary of the required steps.) Here is the configuration file to place on the server:

```
<dwr>
    <allow>
        <create creator="new" javascript="JsDate">
            <param name="class" value="java.util.Date"/>
        </create>
    </allow>
</dwr>
```

This XML file binds the JavaScript name JsDate to a corresponding Java Date object. In a Java web application, this XML file belongs in /WEB-INF. Make sure dwr.jar is also in /WEB-INF/lib.

The next step on the client side is to import all of the necessary JavaScript libraries into the web page that is calling the Java object remotely:

```
<head>
    <script type="text/javascript" src=
```

```
                        "/parkerriver/ajaxhacks/js/hacks5_1.js"></script>
        <script type="text/javascript" src=
                "/parkerriver/dwr/interface/JsDate.js"></script>
        <script type="text/javascript" src=
                "/parkerriver/dwr/engine.js"></script>
        <script type="text/javascript" src=
                "/parkerriver/dwr/util.js"></script>
        <title>Bike Information</title>
    </head>
```

The first imported script, *hacks5_1.js*, includes the code for our application. The second (highlighted) script tag involves the JsDate object, which DWR binds to the java.util.Date object. We can use this JavaScript object to call *public* methods on the Java Date object. The next two imported libraries, *engine.js* and *util.js*, represent a required library for using DWR and an optional utilities library, respectively.

The hack's web page includes an h3 subheading tag and a div for containing the Date information:

```
<h4>The time now</h4>
<div id="showDates"></div>
```

Here is the code for remotely calling the Date object:

```
window.onload=function(){setupDates();};

function setupDates(){
    var div = document.getElementById("showDates");
    //remove old messages
    div.innerHTML="";
    //define callback function for displaying a local date
    JsDate.toLocaleString(function(dateString){
        div.appendChild(document.createTextNode(
                "Your local date: "+dateString));
        div.appendChild(document.createElement("br"));
    });
    //define callback function for displaying
    //Greenwich Mean Time
    JsDate.toGMTString(
            function(dateString){
        div.appendChild(document.createTextNode(
                "Greenwich Mean Time date: "+
                dateString));
        div.appendChild(document.createElement("br"));});

    JsDate.getTimezoneOffset(
            function(dateString){
        div.appendChild(document.createTextNode(
                "The difference between your time and GMT (in minutes): "+
                dateString));
    });
}
```

This code displays the date information as part of the window.onload event handler, which the browser's JavaScript implementation calls when the browser finishes loading the web page. setupDates( ) then displays different elements of the current time by calling three Java Date methods remotely:

- toLocaleString( ) generates a current time and date string, as in Nov 21, 2005 7:58:16 AM.
- toGMTString( ) displays the same kind of string, but in Greenwich mean time.
- getTimezoneOffset( ) displays the number, in minutes, representing the difference between the user's current local time and GMT. For example, my local time in Massachusetts is 300 minutes, or 5 hours, behind GMT.

The code uses the JsDate object to remotely call these Java methods. As part of the DWR mechanism, the lone parameter for these method calls is a function that handles the Java return values (in these cases, various date/time strings). For example, here is the function that handles the toLocaleString( ) return value:

```
function(dateString){
    div.appendChild(document.createTextNode(
        "Your local date: "+dateString));
    div.appendChild(document.createElement("br"));
}
```

The dateString parameter represents the actual string returned by remotely calling java.util.Date.toLocaleString( ). The div tag our page uses for displaying this information creates a new text node representing this string followed by a line break (br) tag.

> For information on all the different options for making Java remote method calls from JavaScript, see the DWR page at *http://www.getahead.ltd.uk/dwr/browser/intro/*.

After initially loading the web page, the user can refresh the page, and the date/time strings will change to reflect the current time (local and GMT).

> You could hack the hack by including a Refresh button with an onclick event handler that updates the date information without refreshing the entire page.

Hack Ajax with the Prototype and Rico Libraries

Hacks 50–54

Prototype is a well-known open source library of JavaScript extensions that gives developers power tools to use with their Ajax applications. The library provides an alternative to developing and testing your own XMLHttpRequest library [Hack #3].

The upcoming hacks show how to use major Prototype objects and extensions, such as Ajax.Request, Ajax.Updater, Class.create( ), Object.extend( ), PeriodicalExecuter, and a number of extensions that (at the very least) help reduce typing for JavaScript developers. Prototype includes a lot more functionality than can be shown in this chapter (such as a powerful Enumeration object and a number of extensions to JavaScript's string methods); therefore, I recommend that you download the library and explore its various tools.

Rico is an open source JavaScript library that builds on Prototype. Rico includes built-in Ajax capabilities and objects that allow developers to add cool special effects and drag-and-drop capabilities to their applications. Rico "originated as work done in Sabre Airline Solutions to create a suite of rich Internet components, behaviors, and effects," according to its web site (*http://www.openrico.org*).

Prototype is distributed under an MIT-style license, and Rico uses an Apache 2.0 license.

Use Prototype's Ajax Tools with Your Application

#50 Use an open source software library to handle XMLHttpRequest.

This hack uses the Prototype library's Ajax.Request object to communicate with a backend server, rather than our own. The first step in implementing this hack is to download Prototype from *http://prototype.conio.net*. (This step may not be necessary; certain frameworks, such as Ruby on Rails, come bundled with the Prototype library.)

Now import the library via a script tag in the web page:

```
<script src="js/prototype.js" type="text/javascript"></script>
<script src="js/mylib.js" type="text/javascript"></script>
```

The second imported file, *mylib.js*, contains some custom code the hack will use. Let's put both files in an application directory called *js*.

This hack requests that the user enter some information in a text field. Then, when the user clicks outside the field or presses Tab, the application connects with a server component using Prototype's Ajax.Request object. The hack then displays the server response in the textarea beneath the entry field as soon as the server returns the call. Figure 6-1 shows what the web page looks like in the Safari browser.

Figure 6-1. Responding to user interaction with Prototype

Figure 6-2 shows what it looks like when the user enters a name in the text field, then clicks somewhere else on the page. The textarea beneath the text field shows the server name, the posted data, the version of Prototype we are using, and the value of the X-Requested-With request header.

> Prototype includes this header with Ajax requests, which is a
> nice feature for when the server component checks whether
> a request originates from XMLHttpRequest **[Hack #59]**.
> Beware, though, because a determined hacker can easily
> include an X-Requested-With header in order to impersonate
> this type of request.

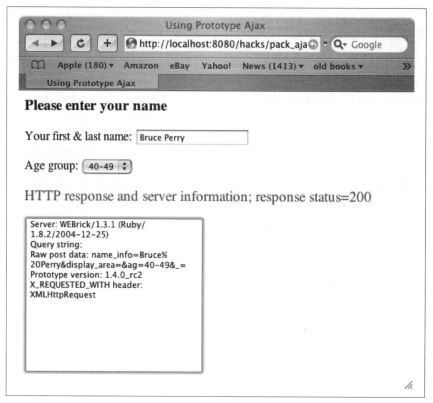

Figure 6-2. Connecting to the server using Ajax.Request

Here is the code in *mylib.js*. It uses various Prototype extensions, including
the Ajax.Request object:

```
window.onload=function( ){
    if($("name_info")) {
        $("name_info").onblur=function( ){
            if($F("name_info")){
                _url="http://localhost:8080/hacks/proto";
                showInfo(_url);
            }
        }
    }
```

```
    }
};
function showInfo(go_url){
    if($("display_area") && go_url){
        var xmlHttp= new Ajax.Request(go_url, {method: "post",
                parameters: Form.serialize(document.forms[0]),
                onComplete:function( ){
            if(xmlHttp.responseIsFailure( )) {
                var sts = xmlHttp.transport.status ? xmlHttp.
                transport.status : "undefined";
                $("display_area").value=
                "XMlHttpRequest returned response status "+sts;
                document.getElementById("msg").innerHTML=
                "HTTP response and server information; "+
                "response status="+
                xmlHttp.transport.status;
            } else {
                $("display_area").value=xmlHttp.transport.responseText;
                document.getElementById("msg").innerHTML=
                "HTTP response and server information; "+
                "response status="+
                xmlHttp.transport.status;
            }
        }});
    }
}
```

The code uses window.onload to set up the web page's interactive behavior. The text field's onblur event handler executes when the keyboard focus enters and then exits the field (when the user presses Tab or clicks somewhere else on the page).

> $("name_info") is a handy Prototype shortcut for document.
> getElementById('name_info'). $F("name_info") is another
> shortcut for accessing a text field's or another kind of ele-
> ment's value. Its parameter is either the element's id or an
> existing element reference, as in:
>
> ```
> var n = $("name_info");
> //displays the value of the 'name_info' text field
> alert($F(n) );
> ```

The code then uses a Prototype shortcut to determine if the text field has a value. If it does, the code calls show_info( ). $F("name_info") returns the value of the text field, whose id attribute is name_info.

The URL that the code passes show_info( ) is the address of our server component. The return value from this component ends up in the textarea. But how is the URL sent in the first place? We'll look at that next.

Request Object to Go

Prototype contains an object called Ajax.Request. The code creates this object with the new JavaScript keyword, then considers the job almost finished. You do not have to deal with the XMLHttpRequest nuances, except for creating a callback to handle the server response:

```
var xmlHttp = new Ajax.Request(go_url, {method: "post",
            parameters: Form.serialize(document.forms[0]),
            onComplete:function( ){
    if(xmlHttp.responseIsFailure( )) {
        var sts = xmlHttp.transport.status ? xmlHttp.
                transport.status : "undefined";
        $("display_area").value=
                "XMlHttpRequest returned response status "+sts;
        document.getElementById("msg").innerHTML=
                "HTTP response and server information; response status="+
                xmlHttp.transport.status;
    } else {
        $("display_area").value=xmlHttp.transport.responseText;
        document.getElementById("msg").innerHTML=
                "HTTP response and server information; response status="+
                xmlHttp.transport.status;
    }
}});
```

You can also use the syntax function(request){...} (notice that request is the first callback parameter). For example:

```
onComplete:function(request){
        $("display_area").value=request.responseText;
```

The first parameter, go_url, is a variable pointing to the server component location. This seems to work best with a relative URL format, as in */hacks/ pack_ajax*, without the protocol and host information. The method: "post" part is a reminder to hack writers and readers of what kind of HTTP request the code sends; POST is the default, and this explicit parameter is not actually necessary if the code is not using GET.

The hack passes the parameters to the POST request using a Prototype method. The following line:

```
parameters: Form.serialize(document.forms[0])
```

generates a chunk of data formatted for posting to a server, based on the form elements' current values (as in name_info=Bruce%20Perry&display_ area=&ag=20-29).

The onComplete callback parameters place the response text into the textarea with the code:

```
onComplete:function(){
    $("display_area").value=xmlHttp.transport.responseText;
```

The transport property of Ajax.Request returns the underlying XMLHttpRequest object, from which the code derives the server response in a textual format.

> You can get the HTTP status code of the response with xmlHttp.transport.status.

The code also calls an Ajax.Request method called responseIsFailure() to determine if the request resulted in a response error. This bit of *prototype.js* code illustrates what the method is doing:

```
responseIsSuccess: function() {
    return this.transport.status == undefined
        || this.transport.status == 0
        || (this.transport.status >= 200 && this.transport.status < 300);
},

responseIsFailure: function() {
    return !this.responseIsSuccess();
}
```

H A C K #51 Update an HTML Element's Content from the Server

Use Prototype's Ajax.Updater object to easily update web page content with server information.

Prototype comes with its own object that uses a few lines of code to update a subset of a web page with server data. This hack presents the user with the web page that Figure 6-1 shows, plus a new Go Updater! button. It is similar to "Use Prototype's Ajax Tools with Your Application" [Hack #50], except that it uses a different type of Prototype Ajax object to update an HTML element's content in the web page.

When the user clicks the Go Updater! button, the code uses the Ajax. Updater object to specify that the textarea should be updated with the text from the server response. Figure 6-3 shows what the web page looks like after the user clicks the button.

The first order of business for this hack is to make sure that the web page imports the *prototype.js* library, which you can download from *http://*

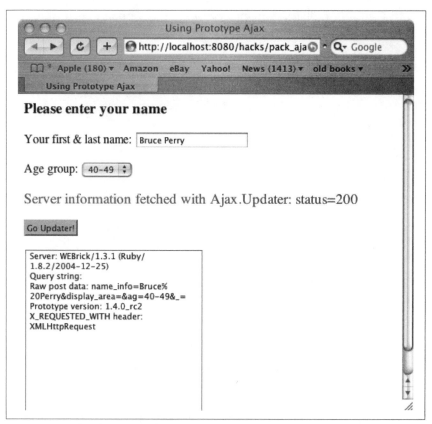

Figure 6-3. Updated content with little programming

prototype.conio.net. Place this file in a common directory for JavaScript, then use a `script` tag to import the file into the web page:

```
<script src="/javascripts/prototype.js" type="text/javascript"></script>
<script src="/javascripts/mylib.js" type="text/javascript"></script>
```

The second imported library, *mylib.js*, is where the hack uses the objects and extensions from the Prototype package.

Here's the web page code that shows the various user interface controls that this hack depends on, including the Go Updater! button and the `textarea` that receives server data:

```
<html>
<head>
    <meta http-equiv="content-type" content="text/html; charset=utf-8" />
    <script src="/javascripts/prototype.js" type="text/javascript"></script>
    <script src="/javascripts/mylib.js" type="text/javascript"></script>
    <title>Using Prototype Ajax</title>
</head>
```

```
<body>
<h3>Please enter your name</h3>
<form action="javascript:void%200" method="get">
<p>
Your first & last name: <input type="text" name="name_info" id=
"name_info" size="20" maxlength="25" value="anonymous user">
</p>
<p>
Age group: <select name="ag" id="ag">
<!--options part snipped...-->
</select>
</p>
<p>
<span id="msg" style="font-size:1.2em; color: green"></span>
</p>
<button type="button" id="but1" name="but1">Go Updater!</button>
<p>
<textarea name="display_area" id="display_area" rows="30" cols="30">
</textarea>
</p>
</form>
</body>
</html>
```

The purpose of the hack is to automatically fill the textarea with backend data at the user's urging, using just a handful of code lines:

```
window.onload=function( ){
    if($("but1")) {
        $("but1").onclick=function( ){
            if($F("name_info")){
                _url="http://localhost:8080/hacks/proto";
                showUpInfo(_url);
            }
        }
    }
};
function showUpInfo(go_url){
    if($("display_area") && go_url){
        var xmlHttp= new Ajax.Updater("display_area",go_url, {
            parameters:Form.serialize(document.forms[0]),
                onComplete:function(request){
                if(xmlHttp.responseIsFailure( )) {
                    var sts =  xmlHttp.transport.status ? xmlHttp.
                    transport.status : "undefined";
                    $("display_area").value=
                    "XMlHttpRequest returned response status "+sts;
                    document.getElementById("msg").innerHTML=
                    "HTTP response and server information; "+
                    "response status="+
                    request.status;
                } else {
                    $("display_area").value=request.responseText;
```

```
                        document.getElementById("msg").innerHTML=
                        "Server information fetched with Ajax.Updater:"+
                        "status="+request.status;
                    }
                }
            });
        }
    }
```

When the browser loads the web page (window.onload), the button's onclick event handler points to the showUpInfo( ) function. This is the techie way of explaining that when the web page loads, the JavaScript will define the button's behavior. This behavior includes checking whether the button with id but1 actually exists (a web page designer could have mistakenly left it out).

> The code uses two Prototype extensions: $("but1") is a shortcut for document.getElementById("but1"), and $F("name_info") returns the value of a form element with the specified id.

On the Server Side

showUpInfo( ) creates a new Ajax.Updater object, passes some information into its constructor, and that's it: the request is on its way. The code didn't have to fuss with XMlHttpRequest because this object was wrapped and tucked away in the *prototype.js* file. The Ajax.Updater object is different from Ajax.Request, which the previous hack deals with, because its first parameter is the id of the page element that is updated with server data. In this case, the code passes in the id of the textarea.

Now let's look at what's happening at the server end. This application is running on Ruby on Rails. The URL *http://localhost:8080/hacks/proto* (the second parameter inside of Ajax.Updater) posts the web page's data to an action called proto.

> Chapter 7 summarizes Ruby on Rails and describes what an action is.

Here is how the action is defined in Ruby code:

```
def proto
    if @request.xml_http_request?( )
        #en is a hash type in Ruby
        #en["SERVER_SOFTWARE"]returns the vlaue of the
        #SERVER_SOFTWARE environment variable
        en=@request.env( )
```

```
        str="Server: "
        str+=en["SERVER_SOFTWARE"].to_s+"\n"
        str+="Query string: "+en["QUERY_STRING"].to_s+"\n"
        str+="Raw post data: "+en["RAW_POST_DATA"].to_s+"\n"
        str+="Prototype version: "+en["HTTP_X_PROTOTYPE_VERSION"].to_s+"\n"
        str+="X_REQUESTED_WITH header: "+
        en["HTTP_X_REQUESTED_WITH"].to_s +"\n\n"
        render :text => str
    end
end
```

This is a method that gathers environment variable information related to the request, then sends it back to the requester. An action in Ruby on Rails assumes the same role as a servlet or JSP in Java (see "Dynamically View Request Information for XMLHttpRequest" **[Hack #62]**). The proto action is designed to send this information only if the request originates from XMLHttpRequest, as discussed in "Find Out Whether Ajax Is Calling in the Request" **[Hack #59]**. It does not make sense to make this action available to a typical browser request because its return value is meant only for fine-grained web page updates.

> Prototype requests using Ajax include a request header, X_Requested_With, with the value XMLHttpRequest.

Checking for Errors

The code displays an error message if the HTTP response involves status codes such as 404 (Not Found), 500 (Server Error), or 503 (Service Unavailable):

```
onComplete:function(request){
    if(xmlHttp.responseIsFailure()) {
        var sts = xmlHttp.transport.status ? xmlHttp.
            transport.status : "undefined";
        $("display_area").value=
            "XMlHttpRequest returned response status "+sts;
        document.getElementById("msg").innerHTML=
            "HTTP response and server information; response status="+
            request.status;
    } else {//...continued
```

Create Observers for Web Page Fields
Launch code that monitors changes in a web page field.

This hack sets up a textarea to receive a steady supply of timestamps from a server. The web page displays these dates one after another, every 10 seconds. Nothing else changes on the web page as the responses come in, because a Prototype object makes the requests in the background without disrupting the user's view of the page.

Another piece of code monitors that textarea at a slightly longer interval. If the code detects a change in the textarea's value, it displays a message that acts as a kind of log on the screen. To stop the monitoring—a good idea before getting up from the computer and embarking on a world tour—the user can press the Pause Monitor button. Figure 6-4 shows what this hack's web page looks like in Firefox 1.5.

The hack automates the entire sequence of updating a field's value from a server and using an object to monitor and report on a field, without any page refreshes. However, it does not really matter how the field's value is changing; it could be a scientist periodically entering the readings from her instruments. The nice aspect is that we have a continuous monitor that can report changing information on a live basis without refreshing or resubmitting the whole web page.

How It Works

Here is the web page code, which is a view template within Ruby on Rails (see Chapter 7):

```html
<html>
<head>
    <meta http-equiv="content-type" content="text/html; charset=utf-8" />
    <script src="/javascripts/prototype.js" type="text/javascript"></script>
    <script src="/javascripts/mylib.js" type="text/javascript"></script>
    <title>Observe a text field</title>
</head>
<body>
<h3>Trackable and observable data</h3>
<form action="javascript:void%200">
<p>
<span style="vertical-align: top"><strong>Updated Time from server: </strong>
</span> <textarea style="border: thin solid black;" name="time_info" id=
"time_info" rows="15" cols="25">
</textarea>
</p>
<p>
<span id="msg" style="font-size:1.2em; color: green"></span>
</p>
<h4>Data Log</h4>
<p><button id="pause">Pause Monitor</button></p>
<p>
<textarea name="display_area" id="display_area" style=
"border: thin solid black;" rows="15" cols="25">
</textarea>
</p>
```

Figure 6-4. Observing Ajax responses from code

```
    </form>
    </body>
    </html>
```

The code imports the *prototype.js* file, in order to use its Ajax capabilities, and *mylib.js*, which contains the custom code for our hack. When the browser loads the web page, this action creates a Prototype object that then makes backend requests to a server and displaying the return value in the time_info textarea. Every 10 seconds, another object observes this textarea for any changes to its value. If it detects a change, the observer displays a message in the display_area textarea.

Here is the hack's *mylib.js* code:

```
window.onload=function( ){
    if($("pause")){
        $("pause").onclick=function( ){
            if(executer){
                executer.currentlyExecuting=true;
            }
        };
    }
    var _uurl='/hacks/increment';
    var executer;
    var counter=0;
    if($("time_info") && $("display_area")) {
        executer=new PeriodicalExecuter(function( ) {
        new Ajax.Updater('time_info',_uurl,
        {insertion: function(obj,txt){$("time_info").
            value+= txt + "\n"},
    onComplete: function(request){$("msg").style.
    color="green"; counter++;
    $("msg").innerHTML="Update #"+
    counter+"; request status="+
    request.status}})}, 10);
    new Form.Element.Observer("time_info",15,function( ){
    $("display_area").
    value+=("Change detected on: "+new Date( ) + "\n\n");
    });
    }

};
```

First, the code defines the onclick event handler for the Pause Monitor button. The button interacts with the Prototype Form.Element.Observer object to induce it to stop observing.

> The Form.Element.Observer object has a currentlyExecuting
> property, a boolean. If you set this property to true, the
> Observer stops monitoring.

What's a Prototype Object?

Prototype objects are objects that Prototype defines in *prototype.js*. This hack uses a PeriodicalExecuter, which, as its name suggests, repeatedly executes the function or code that you pass into its constructor. The hack specifies the interval in seconds as the second parameter.

The new Ajax.Updater part represents the code that the hack periodically executes. Recall that the Ajax.Updater object was introduced in the previous hack. This object removes the necessity for developers to explicitly program XMLHttpRequest when they want to send Ajax-style requests to a backend server. The Ajax.Updater object updates an HTML element with id time_info with data from the relative URL /hacks/increment. It automatically takes the server response and updates the specified field by inserting the new content before any existing content.

When the request processing has reached a stage called "complete" (onComplete), a callback function updates a text message with the sequential number of the request and the response status code.

> The $("msg") syntax represents a Prototype shortcut for document.getElementById('msg'). The $("msg").style part dynamically changes the visual style of an element (see "Generate a Styled User Message on the Fly" [Hack #11]).

Passive Observer

The Observer object uses Prototype's Form.Element.Observer. The object parameters represent the id of the form field that the object observes, the interval in seconds, and a callback function that executes if the field's value has changed. Here, the code adds a date string to a textarea:

```
new Form.Element.Observer("time_info",15,function(){
    $("display_area").value+=("Change detected on: "+new Date( ) + "\n\n");
});
```

"Use Prototype's Ajax Tools with Your Application" [Hack #50] shows an example of the code that handles any request errors involving the Ajax. Updater object. As with the other objects this chapter discusses, the *prototype.js* library makes it very easy to add advanced JavaScript code such as Observer objects to your Ajax applications.

HACK #53 Use Rico to Update Several Elements with One Ajax Response

Use the Rico library to automatically update several weather-related web page elements with one Ajax request.

This hack uses Rico to make a single Ajax request that can update several weather-related page elements at once without refreshing the page. It grabs the weather information for four U.S. cities from the Weather.com web service.

Using Rico requires the hack to import the *rico.js* and *prototype.js* libraries upon which Rico is built (see "Use Prototype's Ajax Tools with Your Application" [Hack #50]). The custom code for the hack resides in *multiple.js*. Here are the script tags for the HTML page:

```
<script src="js/prototype.js" type="text/javascript"></script>
<script src="js/rico.js" type="text/javascript"></script>
<script src="js/multiple.js" type="text/javascript"></script>
```

The hack shows the weather information in several regions of the page.

> The weather icons derive from the Weather.com SDK [Hack #31].

When the user clicks the Update Weather! button, the code makes an Ajax connection using the Rico.AjaxEngine object, which is included in the Rico library. Figure 6-5 shows what the page looks like in Firefox 1.5.

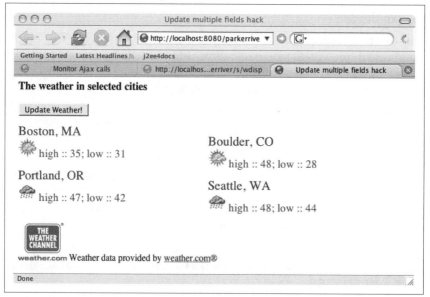

Figure 6-5. Updating weather information

Our own JavaScript in *multiple.js* uses only a few lines of AjaxEngine code to implement an XMLHttpRequest object and update the content of four elements on the page. You *do* have to craft the format of the server's response to Rico, but we'll get to that code in a moment.

The code that sets up the Update Weather! button's behavior is found in our JavaScript file for this page:

```
window.onload=function( ){
    if($("w_update")){
        $("w_update").onclick=function( ){
            updateWeather( );
        }
    }
};

function updateWeather( ){
    ajaxEngine.registerRequest("multiple", "/parkerriver/s/wdisp");
    ajaxEngine.registerAjaxElement("boston");
    ajaxEngine.registerAjaxElement("boulder");
    ajaxEngine.registerAjaxElement("portland");
    ajaxEngine.registerAjaxElement("seattle");
    ajaxEngine.sendRequest("multiple","");
}
```

ajaxEngine is a variable that refers to the Rico.AjaxEngine object. This variable is automatically available from *rico.js* and does not have to be instantiated by the hack's code. The Rico.AjaxEngine object is the object that does all the request-related work for the hack and uses XMLHttpRequest beneath the surface. To implement the multiple-update task of this hack, the code must call this object's registerRequest( ) method, specifying the name you are giving the URL to the server component (here, "multiple"), as well as the actual URL.

Specifying the relative URL (i.e., without a protocol or host) seems to work fine for this method.

The engine also has to know about the page elements or nodes that it will update. Thus, the code calls registerAjaxElement( ) with the id of each span element that is updated from the server. Finally, the code calls sendRequest( ) with the registered name of the URL and any parameters (this code does not include any parameters). Here is the part of the web page that this request updates:

```
<div id="east" style="float: left">
<span class="cityhead">Boston, MA</span><br />
<span id="boston">
</span>
<br /><br />
<span class="cityhead" >Portland, OR</span><br />
<span id="portland">
</span>
</div>
```

```
<div style="float: left">    </div>
<div id="west" style="float: left">
<span class="cityhead">Boulder, CO</span><br />
<span id="boulder">
</span>
<br /><br />
<span class="cityhead">Seattle, WA</span><br />
<span  id="seattle">
</span>
</div>
```

The `Rico.AjaxEngine` object then updates the entire contents of each of the highlighted spans.

Ajax Convention

Rico uses a response convention to implement this task. With this hack, a typical response (formatted for printing in this book) looks like:

```
<?xml version="1.0" encoding="UTF-8"?>
<ajax-response>
<response type="element" id="seattle">
<img src="/parkerriver/ajaxhacks/img/11.png"/>
<span id="rng_seattle" class="therm">high :: 48; low :: 44</span>
<span id="dt0" style="visibility: hidden">1/4/06 6:08 AM PST</span>
</response>
<response type="element" id="portland">
<img src="/parkerriver/ajaxhacks/img/11.png"/>
<span id="rng_portland" class="therm">high :: 48; low :: 42</span>
<span id="dt1" style="visibility: hidden">1/4/06 5:04 AM PST</span>
</response>
<response type="element" id="boston">
<img src="/parkerriver/ajaxhacks/img/28.png"/>
<span id="rng_boston" class="therm">high :: 34; low :: 31</span>
<span id="dt2" style="visibility: hidden">1/4/06 9:06 AM EST</span>
</response>
<response type="element" id="boulder">
<img src="/parkerriver/ajaxhacks/img/30.png"/>
<span id="rng_boulder" class="therm">high :: 50; low :: 28</span>
<span id="dt3" style="visibility: hidden">1/4/06 7:08 AM MST</span>
</response>
</ajax-response>
```

The response is in XML format. It must have a root element of ajax-response, which itself can have any number of response child elements. This is how Rico manages to do multiple updates and more with one request.

Make sure that the response has a Content-Type of application/xml or text/xml.

The response element looks like:

```
<response type="element" id="seattle">
```

The id references the id that we "registered" with the Rico.AjaxEngine object. This is how Rico knows where all the returned HTML goes. Pretty straightforward, eh?

On the Server End

This hack has to initiate a certain amount of heavy lifting on the server end, in terms of fetching the weather data from Weather.com and then sending the formatted XML back to our Ajax application. Because XMLHttpRequest cannot connect with a different host from the host from which the user downloads the web page, the hack uses a server intermediary to talk to Weather.com and send the XML back to the web page. We use a Java servlet called *WeatherManager.java* and the JDOM API (see *http://www.jdom.org*) to make an HTTP connection with Weather.com. Weather.com returns weather data for the four cities specified in the response elements in XML format (see "Display a Weather.com XML Data Feed" **[Hack #31]**).

A Java servlet called *WeatherDisplay.java* then accesses an array of four HashMap objects from *WeatherManager*, each containing the latest available high and low temperatures, a date/time string, as well as associated image icons for the U.S. cities. With this information in hand, the servlet builds the required ajax-response element using a buffer of character data. The servlet then sends the response using a Content-Type of text/xml. Here's the servlet code; AjaxUtil is our own utility class:

```
public class WeatherDisplay extends HttpServlet {
    protected void doGet(HttpServletRequest httpServletRequest,
                        HttpServletResponse httpServletResponse) throws
                        ServletException, IOException {
        StringBuffer buf = new StringBuffer("<ajax-response>");
        try {
            Map[] map = WeatherManager.getAllWeather( );
            for(int i = 0; i < map.length; i++) {
                buf.append(getRicoResponse(map[i],i));
            }
        } catch (JDOMException e) {
            throw new ServletException(e);
        }
        buf.append("</ajax-response>");
        AjaxUtil.sendXML(httpServletResponse,buf.toString( ));
    }

    protected void doPost(HttpServletRequest httpServletRequest,
                        HttpServletResponse httpServletResponse) throws
                        ServletException, IOException {
```

```
        doGet(httpServletRequest, httpServletResponse);
    }

    private String getRicoResponse(Map map,int counter) {
        StringBuffer buf = new StringBuffer(
                "<response type=\"element\" id=\"");
        buf.append((String)map.get("id")).append("\">\n");
        buf.append("<img src=\"/parkerriver/ajaxhacks/img/").
                append((String)map.get("img"));
        buf.append(".png\"/>");
        buf.append(" <span id=\"rng_").append((String)map.get("id")).
                append("\" class=\"therm\">high :: ");
        buf.append((String)map.get("hi")).append("; low :: ").
                append((String)map.get("low"));
        buf.append("</span>\n");
        buf.append("<span id=\"dt").append(counter).
                append("\" style=\"visibility: hidden\">").
                append((String)map.get("date"));
        buf.append("</span>\n</response>");
        return buf.toString();
    }
}
```

Hacking the Hack

The response XML also includes the date and time associated with the weather data:

```
<span id="dt2" style="visibility: hidden">1/4/06 9:06 AM EST</span>
```

This data can be used in another iteration of the application to display more information to the user or to reduce server hits by updating the weather only if the current data display is a specified number of hours old.

HACK #54 Create a Drag-and-Drop Bookstore

Set up a book shelf from which users can drag books into a basket, with their choices logged on a server.

This hack allows the user to drag an image of a book from one area of the page into another region of the view called the "basket." The book is then processed as though it was being purchased, and a small message appears from the server. The application sends the book information as an Ajax-style request, and the rest of the view does not change as this transaction takes place. The hack uses the Rico library's drag-and-drop functionality. This open source JavaScript library makes it fairly easy to designate some regions of the page as "drop zones" and other page elements as "draggable." Rico takes care of the underlying graphical programming, which is a real win for the developer.

Figure 6-6 shows what the hack looks like in the Mac OS X version of Firefox 1.5.

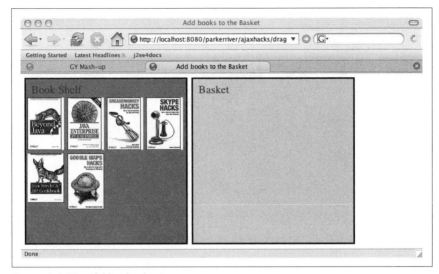

Figure 6-6. Tasteful book selection

When the user selects a book from the book shelf and drags it into the basket, the page sends the book information to the server, and a reply message appears. Figure 6-7 shows what happens when you drag the *Google Maps Hacks* book into the basket.

Here's the code for the web page:

```html
<html>
<head>
    <meta http-equiv="content-type" content="text/html; charset=utf-8" />
    <script src="js/prototype.js" type="text/javascript"></script>
    <script src="js/rico.js" type="text/javascript"></script>
    <script src="js/mydraggable.js" type="text/javascript"></script>
    <script src="js/talkdrop.js" type="text/javascript"></script>
    <style type="text/css">
        @import "/parkerriver/stylesheets/hacks.css";
    </style>
    <title>Add books to the Basket</title>
</head>
<body>
<div id="shelf"  class="shelf" style="background-color: #6198C4">
<div id="title" class="title">Book Shelf</div>
<div id="b1" class="book_con"><img src=
    "img/books/0596100949_xs.gif" id="Beyond Java" alt="Beyond Java"/></div>
<div id="b2" class="book_con"><img src=
    "img/books/0596101422_xs.gif" id="Java Enterprise" alt="Java Enterprise"/>
</div>
```

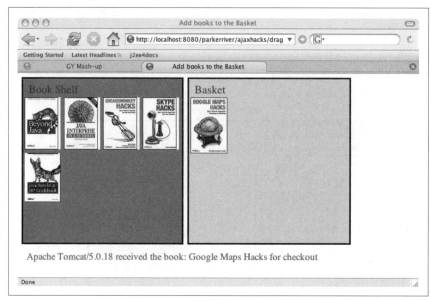

Figure 6-7. The checkout commences on Google Maps Hacks

```
<div id="b3" class="book_con"><img src=
  "img/books/0596101651_xs.gif" id="Greasemonkey Hacks" alt="Greasemonkey
Hacks"/>
</div>
<div id="b4" class="book_con"><img src=
  "img/books/0596101899_xs.gif"  id="Skype Hacks" alt="Skype Hacks"/></div>
<div id="b5" class="book_con"><img src=
  "img/books/jsvltjspckbk.s.gif" id="Java JSP Cookbook" alt=
  "Java JSP Cookbook"/></div>
<div id="b6" class="book_con"><img src=
  "img/books/googlemapshks.s.gif" id="Google Maps Hacks" alt=
  "Google Maps Hacks"/></div>
</div>
<div style="float: left;">  </div>
<div id="basket" class="basket" style="background-color: #ffD800">
<div id="shelftitle" class="title">Basket</div>
</div>
<div style="clear: both;"> </div>
<div id="outcome" class="msg" style=
  "clear: both; font-size: 1.2em; color: green "></div>
</body>
</html>
```

The page imports four JavaScript files, beginning with *prototype.js* and *rico.*
js. The Rico library depends on Prototype, as discussed in "Use Prototype's
Ajax Tools with Your Application" [Hack #50]. The third imported file,
mydraggable.js, is a JavaScript file that encapsulates an object definition.
This object defines a page control or widget that can be dragged. I'll show

and explain that one in a moment. Finally, *talkdrop.js* contains the JavaScript that uses the object defined in *mydraggable.js*.

The regions of the page comprising the book shelf and basket are div elements that are styled using a stylesheet in */parkerriver/stylesheets/hacks.css*. Here is the key part of this stylesheet:

```
msg {font-size: 0.8em;
        margin-bottom: 0.5em;
        margin-left: 0.5em;}
div.title { font-family: Times, Verdana,Arial;
            font-size: 1.4em; color: purple;
            vertical-align: top;
            margin-top: 0.5em;
            margin-left: 0.5em;}
div.shelf { width: 320px;
            height: 320px;
            border: solid medium;
            float: left;}
div.basket { width: 320px;
             height: 320px;
             border: solid medium;
             float: left;}
div.book_con { float: left;
               padding: 0.2em 0.2em;}
```

Draggables and Drop Zones

Now it's time to look at the code for this hack. When the web page is loaded, the code designates the div elements that contain books as draggable and the div elements that represent the shelf and basket as drop zones. The new MyDraggable sections refer to objects defined in *mydraggable.js*:

```
window.onload=function( ){
    dndMgr.registerDraggable( new MyDraggable('b1','firstbook') );
    dndMgr.registerDraggable( new MyDraggable('b2','book2') );
    dndMgr.registerDraggable( new MyDraggable('b3','book3') );
    dndMgr.registerDraggable( new MyDraggable('b4','book4') );
    dndMgr.registerDraggable( new MyDraggable('b5','book5') );
    dndMgr.registerDraggable( new MyDraggable('b6','book6') );
    dndMgr.registerDropZone( new Rico.Dropzone('basket') );
    dndMgr.registerDropZone( new Rico.Dropzone('shelf') );
};
```

The emphasized code is all that is necessary to designate an element as a drop zone. Of course, the objects themselves have to be registered as draggable, or there will be nothing to drop into these hot zones. If you just want to get started with basic drag-and-drop functionality, this code will suffice:

```
dndMgr.registerDraggable( new Rico.Draggable('firstbook','b1') );
```

The dndMgr object doing the registering in this design pattern has already been instantiated for you by the Rico package. The first parameter to the Rico.Draggable constructor is a name that the code gives the object; the second is the element's id attribute value on the web page.

> The parameters are switched in the MyDraggable constructor; the id of the div is first, and the name is second:
>
> ```
> new MyDraggable('b6','book6');
> ```

Our hack, however, is designed to do a little bit more than just allow users to drag objects on the page to new locations. The hack wants to identify the objects only when they are dropped into the "basket" drop zone, then make an Ajax connection to communicate the identities of these objects to the server. Therefore, this hack extends Rico.Draggable so that the object can implement these other tasks.

> This object is derived from instructions and code explained on the demo page found at *http://www.openrico.org/rico/ demos.page?demo=rico_drag_and_drop_custom_draggable.*

To extend the Rico object, the code uses a popular function of the Prototype library called Class.create(). If the code creates a JavaScript object using this method, the new object has an initialize() method that gets called when the object is created (this feature is not built into JavaScript itself). Prototype also includes an oft-used extension called Object.extend() that, in this case, adds the newly declared functions to Rico.Draggable's existing methods:

```
var MyDraggable = Class.create();
MyDraggable.prototype = (new Rico.Draggable()).extend( {

    initialize: function( htmlElement, name ) {
        this.type        = 'MyDraggable';
        this.htmlElement = $(htmlElement);
        this.originZone   = "not defined";
    },
    //return the parentNode id, or an alternative if
    //the parentNode does not have a valid id
    getContainer: function() {
        var el = this.htmlElement;
        if(el.parentNode) {
            if(el.parentNode.id){
                return   el.parentNode.id;
            } else {
```

```
                    return "no_id_"+el.parentNode.nodeName;
            }
        } else {
            return this.name+"_no_supported_parentNode";
        }
    },
    //store the origin of the drag as in "shelf"
    //We'll only make an Ajax request if the origin
    //is "shelf"
    startDrag: function() {
        this.originZone=this.getContainer();
    },
    //We'll only make an Ajax request if the origin
    //is "shelf" and the drop zone is "basket"
    endDrag: function() {
        if(this.originZone == "shelf" &&
                this.getContainer() == "basket"){
            var bk=this.htmlElement.childNodes[0].id;
            new Ajax.Request("/parkerriver/s/checkout", {method: "get",
                    parameters: "book="+bk,
                    onComplete:function(request){
                $("outcome").innerHTML=request.responseText;}});

        }
    }

} );
```

The methods are callback functions; in other words, the Rico library calls
these methods at different stages of the object's drag behavior. The request
trigger is when an object is dragged from the shelf to the basket and then
dropped there. Watch what happens when you drag a book to the basket
but do not drop it: an animation occurs (the zone darkens and shifts a bit),
but the code does not send a request.

 This application does not work in the Safari browser.
According to its web page, Rico does not yet fully support
Safari.

The code uses Prototype's Ajax.Request object, which makes it very easy to
put together an Ajax-style request (see "Use Prototype's Ajax Tools with
Your Application" [Hack #50]). Ajax.Request makes an asynchronous request
by default.

Grabbing the Book Titles

How does the code get the book title to pass along to the server? The draggable objects are div tags containing the book's image. This code gets the book's title:

```
var bk=this.htmlElement.childNodes[0].id;
//we could also use this, if it is supported in the
//major browsers
var bk=this.htmlElement.childNodes[0].alt;
```

this.htmlElement refers to the div element; its first (and only) child node is the image. The code then gets the value of the image's id, such as Google Maps Hacks.

Hacking Draggables

There's room to enrich the behavior of this hack. Just because the user drags a book into the basket does not mean that the user wants to check out right away. We could have other drop zones, such as "Wish List" or "Final Checkout," each doing something unique when the book is dropped into it. Obviously, if this code went beyond a fun hack, the server component would do a lot more than send simple response messages.

Work with Ajax and Ruby on Rails

Hacks 55–62

If you haven't yet worked with Ruby on Rails (RoR), you're in for a great treat. Ruby on Rails is a web development framework that makes it very easy to create database-driven web applications. (A *framework* is a software structure that provides developers with scripts, packages, and objects with which they can build their own applications.) Ruby on Rails uses the programming language Ruby, including an embedded version of Ruby for HTML or XML templates that is similar to JavaServer Pages (JSP) or PHP. *Rails* is the name of the framework (or set of packages, such as the `ActionController` class) that programmers use to develop web applications with this toolkit.

 The first edition of a Ruby programming book can be found here: *http://www.ruby-doc.org/docs/ProgrammingRuby/*. You can find another Ruby tutorial at *http://www.math.umd.edu/~dcarrera/ruby/0.3/*.

Ruby on Rails can run on the Apache web server and another open source server called *lighttpd*; it also has a handy built-in web server, WEBrick, which we will use in this chapter. Ruby on Rails only found its way into the general development community in the summer of 2004. However, its ease of use, elegant design, and numerous built-in features—such as Ajax and virtually automated object-relational mapping (ORM) with many popular databases—have impressed the software developer crowd. Prototyping a functional database-driven web application using RoR is faster and more efficient than using other frameworks or doing it from scratch.

Sensible MVC

Except to make a point about Ruby's high-level design as a Model-View-Controller (MVC) architecture, it's impossible to do this framework justice in a short introduction.

MVC is a design pattern that separates the three components of an application into different software modules or units of code. The purpose of this division is to allow the components to evolve independently, to decouple software objects that have different roles, and to ensure that changes to one module do not inadvertently affect other modules. The *model* represents the application's data or state, such as database information; the *view* is what the user sees, as in a web page or user interface (UI); and the *controller* is the part of the application that responds to the user's interaction (for example, handling keyboard events and deciding which view to display).

RoR explicitly uses MVC in the design of its runtime code and directory structure. This is reflected in its subframeworks: Active Record, which handles the model, and Action Pack, which comprises the Action Controller and Action View pieces. (According to the RoR documentation, these two are bundled together because of their "heavy interdependence.")

The hacks in this chapter attempt to summarize the pertinent aspects of RoR's tools and structure. However, RoR is a complex beast. The best thing to do is to install it on a development or prototype machine and give it a ride.

HACK #55   Install Ruby on Rails

Install a cool web application framework that wraps the creation and use of XMLHttpRequest.

This hack installs Ruby on Rails on Windows; it includes information and pointers for installing RoR on Mac OS X and Linux.

> You can install Ruby on Rails on Mac OS X Tiger (10.4.x) by following this detailed tutorial: *http://www.maczealots.com/tutorials/ruby-on-rails/*. In addition, you can install an all-in-one bundle for Mac OS X, including the lighttpd web server, the SQLite database, and RubyGems ("a packaging system for Ruby that makes it simple to deploy gems, or small applications," according to the aforementioned tutorial), from *http://locomotive.sourceforge.net*. The Ruby programming language itself comes built into Tiger; you can find out the version of Ruby on your system by opening up a Terminal window and typing ruby -v. For information on installing Ruby on Rails on the Linux flavor called Fedora, see *http://www.digitalmediaminute.com/howto/fc4rails/*.

To develop a beginning Rails web application, install the following software:

- Ruby (1.8.2 is the required minimum version for using RoR)
- The Rails framework
- Your database of choice, such as SQLite3 or MySQL

Step 1: Installing Ruby

Installing Ruby couldn't be any simpler:

1. Download the latest One-Click Ruby Installer for Windows from *http:// rubyforge.org/projects/rubyinstaller*. As of this writing, the latest version is *ruby182-15.exe*.

2. Double-click on the downloaded executable, and follow the installation instructions. Unless you have some special needs, just press Enter to accept all the defaults.

 Another one-stop solution for installing Ruby on Rails on Windows is Instant Rails, available at *http://instantrails. rubyforge.org/wiki/wiki.pl?Instant_Rails*. It includes Ruby, Rails, Apache, and MySQL, "all preconfigured and ready to run." This is designed for Windows, but there are plans to create packages for Linux, Mac OS X, and BSD.

Step 2: Installing Rails

Now you can use the RubyGems package manager to download and install Rails 0.9.4 (the version covered by this hack):

1. Open a command window and run the command:

    ```
    gem install rails --remote.
    ```

2. RubyGems will also install all of the other libraries that Rails depends on. You'll be asked if you want to install each dependency. Answer "y" (yes) to each question.

Figure 7-1 shows what the installation procedure looks like in the command window.

Finally, you'll need to install a database server, if you haven't already. Rails supports many different databases, including PostgreSQL, SQL Server, DB2, and Oracle. MySQL is a popular database used with Ruby on Rails, and it can easily be installed on Windows, Mac OS X, and Linux systems.

Figure 7-1. Installing Rails through RubyGems

> You can download installers for MySQL 5.0 Community
> Edition for Windows, Mac OS X, and Linux from this site:
> *http://dev.mysql.com/downloads/mysql/5.0.html*.

Creating an Empty Rails Web Application

Rails is both a runtime web-application framework and a set of helper
scripts that automate many of the things you do when developing a web
application. In this hack, we will use one such helper script to create the
entire directory structure and the initial set of files to start a "cookbook"
application:

1. Open a command window and navigate to where you want to create
   this cookbook web application. I used *c:\rails*.

2. Run the command `rails cookbook`.

This creates a *cookbook* subdirectory containing a complete directory tree of
folders and files for an empty Rails application.

Testing the Empty Web Application

A Rails web application can run under virtually any web server, but the most convenient way to develop a Rails web application is to use the built-in WEBrick web server. Let's start this web server and then browse to our cookbook application. In your open command window, move into the *cookbook* directory. Run the command `ruby script/server` to start the server. You should see something like Figure 7-2.

```
C:\WINDOWS\system32\cmd.exe - ruby script/server

C:\rails>cd cookbook

C:\rails\cookbook>ruby script/server
=> Rails application started on http://127.0.0.1:3000
[2005-01-02 22:18:06] INFO  WEBrick 1.3.1
[2005-01-02 22:18:06] INFO  ruby 1.8.2 (2004-12-25) [i386-mswin32]
[2005-01-02 22:18:06] INFO  WEBrick::HTTPServer#start: pid=4528 port=3000
```

Figure 7-2. Starting the WEBrick server

Leave the command window open and the web server running; we'll use them as we proceed. Now open your browser, and browse to *http://127.0.0.1:3000/* or *http://localhost:3000/*. You should see the page shown in Figure 7-3.

> Unless you're following along by installing Rails, these links probably won't work for you. Don't panic—127.0.0.1 is a special address reserved for the local machine.

A Rails Application Directory Structure

RoR tries very hard to minimize the number of decisions you have to make and to eliminate unnecessary work. When you used the RoR helper script to create your empty application, it created the entire directory structure for the application (see Figure 7-4). Rails knows where to find things it needs within this structure, so you don't have to tell it. Remember, no configuration files!

Here's a quick rundown of how to use these directories:

- The *controllers* subdirectory is where Rails looks to find controller classes. A controller handles a web request from the user.

- The *views* subdirectory holds the display templates to fill in with data from our application, convert to HTML, and return to the user's browser.

- The *models* subdirectory holds the classes that model and wrap the data stored in our application's database. In most frameworks, this part of

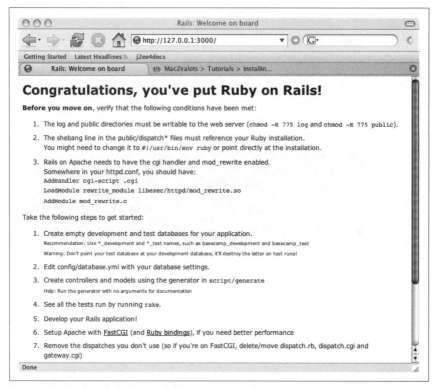

Figure 7-3. Forthwith, Ruby on Rails

the application can grow pretty messy, tedious, verbose, and error-prone. Rails makes it dead simple!

- The *helpers* subdirectory holds any helper classes that assist the model, view, and controller classes. This helps to keep the model, view, and controller code small, focused, and uncluttered.

Here's a typical configuration file (# characters comment out lines) for MySQL used with RoR is:

```
#MySQL (default setup). Versions 4.1 and 5.0 are recommended.
#
#Get the fast C bindings:
#  gem install mysql
#  (on OS X: gem install mysql -- --include=/usr/local/lib)
#And be sure to use new-style password hashing:
#  http://dev.mysql.com/doc/refman/5.0/en/old-client.html
development:
    adapter: mysql
    database: Energy
    username: root
```

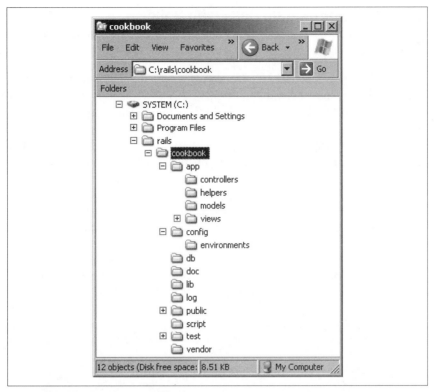

Figure 7-4. Where Rails puts stuff

```
password:
#socket: /path/to/your/mysql.sock

#Connect on a TCP socket. If omitted, the adapter will connect on the
#domain socket given by the socket instead.
host: localhost
port: 3306
```

Here are two other commonly used RoR commands you can use to automate the generation of application files. The first:

```
ruby script/generate model cookbook
```

generates the application's model objects for database table interaction (if the database table was named cookbook). The second:

```
ruby script/generate controller hacks
```

generates a controller object for the web application path named hacks.

—Curt Hibbs

HACK #56   Monitor Remote Calls with Rails

Display the status of your XMLHttpRequest remote calls in a Ruby on Rails application.

When debugging applications, it is handy to see the status of your remote request as the response handling unfolds. This hack displays the request status in a Ruby on Rails view before it displays the return value. The user sees the status message without a page refresh or rebuild. Developers do not have to explicitly deal with XMLHttpRequest at all, because the hack uses a method that is part of the RoR framework to implement the remote calls.

> See the "XMLHttpRequest" section at the beginning of Chapter 1 for an explanation of the various stages of an XMLHttpRequest request: uninitialized, loading, loaded, interactive, and completed.

Like the other hacks in this chapter, this one runs within a Ruby on Rails application. Figure 7-5 shows what the hack looks like in the Safari browser.

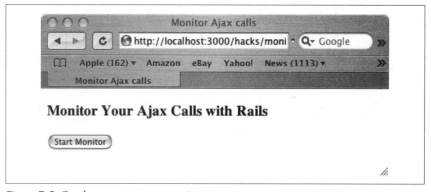

Figure 7-5. Gentlemen, start your monitors

When the user clicks the Start Monitor button, the application sends a request to a server component, called an *action* in Rails parlance. This action returns some content to update a div in the web page, without refreshing the page itself. As Figure 7-6 depicts, the page shows the request status at each of its stages, in real time as it's happening.

The code for the Rails template associated with this action is shown below. It's very similar to the code for an HTML page, but the template has an . *rhtml* suffix, as in *monitor.rhtml*. This view name is mapped to the URL the user enters in the browser: *http://localhost:3000/hacks/monitor*.

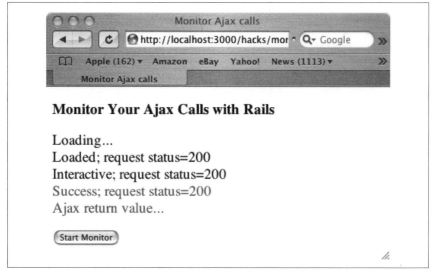

Figure 7-6. Display the request's status in real time

When you start up Ruby on Rails (using the ruby script/
server command), WEBrick binds to port 3000 by default.
You can change the port number via the command line. For
example:

```
ruby script/server -p 8000
```

Here's the template code:

```
<!DOCTYPE html PUBLIC "-//W3C//DTD XHTML 1.0 Strict//EN"
        "http://www.w3.org/TR/2000/REC-xhtml1-20000126/DTD/xhtml1-strict.
dtd">
<html xmlns="http://www.w3.org/1999/xhtml" xml:lang="en" lang="en">
<head>
    <meta http-equiv="content-type" content="text/html; charset=utf-8" />
    <%= javascript_include_tag :defaults %>
    <title>Monitor Ajax calls</title>
</head>
<body>
<%= form_remote_tag(:update => "complete",:url => { :action => :zero_update
},
:position => "top", :success => "$('success').innerHTML='Success; request
status='+request.status",
:loading => "$('loading').innerHTML='Loading...'",
:loaded => "$('loaded').innerHTML='Loaded; request status='+request.status",
:interactive => "$('inter').innerHTML='Interactive; request status=
'+request.status", :failure => "$('failure').innerHTML='Failure; request
status='+request.status") %>
<h3>Monitor Your Ajax Calls with Rails</h3>
<div id="loading" style="font-size: 1.2em"></div>
```

```
<div id="loaded" style="font-size: 1.2em"></div>
<div id="inter" style="font-size: 1.2em"></div>
<div id="success" style="font-size: 1.2em; color: green"></div>
<div id="failure" style="font-size: 1.2em; color: red"></div>
<div id="complete" style="font-size: 1.2em; color: green" ></div>
<p>
<%= submit_tag "Start Monitor" %>
</p>
<%= end_form_tag %>
</body>
</html>
```

The RoR views use embedded Ruby script tags (<%...%>), similar to the tags used in JSP or PHP applications. One of these tags contains a Rails method, form_remote_tag( ). This method takes care of all the XMLHttpRequest initializing and sending for you, so you can focus on the behavior you want your applications to initiate.

The parameters for form_remote_tag( ) are fairly dense, but they accomplish an awful lot beneath the surface. First, the :update parameter specifies the id of the page element (a div, in this case) that the action will update with the request's return value. Next, the :url parameter points to the name of the action that will handle the request (here, zero_update):

```
:url => { :action => :zero_update }
```

 In Rails method calls, the code has to use the syntax :url as opposed to url. That's easy to forget, but if you do, the method will not be successfully called. Ruby refers to these types of references, which represent variable names rather than evaluating to variable values, as Symbol objects. See *http://www.ruby-doc.org/docs/ProgrammingRuby/*.

This is similar to other mapping mechanisms used by web development APIs such as Java Servlets (see the further explanation below). The rest of the method parameters specify the JavaScript code that the application should execute at each stage of the request's processing:

```
:success => "$('success').innerHTML='Success; request status='+request.
status",
:loading => "$('loading').innerHTML='Loading...'",
:loaded => "$('loaded').innerHTML='Loaded; request status='+request.status",
:interactive=>"$('inter').innerHTML='Interactive; request status='+request.
status",
:failure => "$('failure').innerHTML='Failure; request status='+request.
status"
```

For example, when the request object's readystate property equals loaded (it's actually a numerical value of 2; see Chapter 1), this part of our parameter specifies what will happen with the application:

```
:loaded => "$('loaded').innerHTML='Loaded; request status='+request.status"
```

The code will get a reference to an HTML element with an id of loaded. The code does so using a shortcut included in the *prototype.js* package, which this page imports: $('loaded'). This JavaScript code is the equivalent of document.getElementById('loaded'), but it sure is easier to type! With the reference to that Element object, the code sets its innerHTML property to Loaded; request status= plus the status code returned by the HTTP response.

If All Else Fails

What if the request fails? Figure 7-7 shows what the displayed message looks like when you add code to the server component to raise a response error.

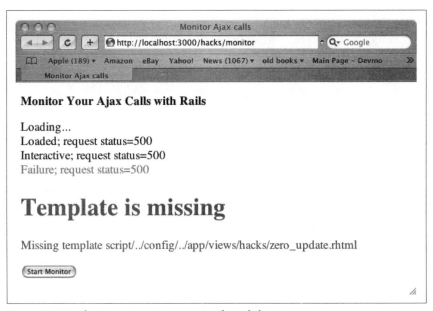

Figure 7-7. Displaying a response status signifying failure

The return value is a bit of HTML announcing a problem, along with an HTTP response status code of 500.

The XMLHttpRequest object connects with a server component, or action, named zero_update. As described in "Install Ruby on Rails" **[Hack #55]**, Rails explicitly uses a MVC architecture in the way that it sets up the directories for your web application. If your RoR URL is *http://localhost:3000/hacks/monitor*, the controller component is in the *controllers* directory at the following path: *<app-root>/hacks/controllers/hacks_controller.rb*. Let's take a look inside *hacks_controller.rb* for the definition of the zero_update action.

Controller objects are written in Ruby code. To generate an action, all you have to do is define a method inside the controller class (literally, a class that extends ActionController, which is part of the Rails API) with the action's name:

```
class HacksController < ApplicationController
    def index
    #defined in index.rhtml
    end

    def zero_update
        render :text => "Ajax return value..."
    end
#rest of class...
end
```

Complicated, huh? All the zero_update action does is return the specified text in the HTTP response using the Rails method render( ).

> The code can also use the syntax render(:text => "Ajax return value...") to call this method, which takes a hash Ruby type as a parameter.

The request object handles the response behind the scenes, placing its content within the div with id complete. However, all the developer is responsible for is calling the method: you do not have to touch the request object or its response handlers. It's useful to have a look at the source code that Rails returns when the user requests the *monitor.rhtml* template:

```
<!DOCTYPE html PUBLIC "-//W3C//DTD XHTML 1.0 Strict//EN"
        "http://www.w3.org/TR/2000/REC-xhtml1-20000126/DTD/xhtml1-strict.
dtd">
<html xmlns="http://www.w3.org/1999/xhtml" xml:lang="en" lang="en">
<head>
    <meta http-equiv="content-type" content="text/html; charset=utf-8" />
    <script src="/javascripts/prototype.js" type="text/javascript"></script>
    <script src="/javascripts/effects.js" type="text/javascript"></script>
    <script src="/javascripts/dragdrop.js" type="text/javascript"></script>
    <script src="/javascripts/controls.js" type="text/javascript"></script>
    <script src="/javascripts/application.js" type="text/javascript"></
script>
    <title>Monitor Ajax calls</title>
</head>
```

```
<body>
<form action="/hacks/zero_update" method="post"
onsubmit="new Ajax.Updater('complete', '/hacks/zero_update',
{asynchronous:true, evalScripts:true, insertion:Insertion.Top,
onFailure:function(request){$('failure').innerHTML='Failure; request
status='+request.status},
onInteractive:function(request){$('inter').innerHTML='Interactive;
request status='+request.status},
onLoaded:function(request){$('loaded').innerHTML='Loaded; request
status='+request.status},
onLoading:function(request){$('loading').innerHTML='Loading...'},
onSuccess:function(request){$('success').innerHTML='Success; request
status='+request.status}, parameters:Form.serialize(this)}); return false;">
<h3>Monitor Your Ajax Calls with Rails</h3>
<div id="loading" style="font-size: 1.2em"></div>
<div id="loaded" style="font-size: 1.2em"></div>
<div id="inter" style="font-size: 1.2em"></div>
<div id="success" style="font-size: 1.2em; color: green"></div>
<div id="failure" style="font-size: 1.2em; color: red"></div>
<div id="complete" style="font-size: 1.2em; color: green"
onclick="clearIt($('complete'))"></div>
<p>
<input name="commit" type="submit" value="Start Monitor" />
</p>
</form>
</body>
</html>
```

Notice all the script tags embedded in the HTML source. This was made
possible by the <%= javascript_include_tag :defaults %> embedded
method (see "Make Your JavaScript Available to Rails Applications" [Hack #57]
for details on that one).

> The server has to issue a separate GET request for each of
> these JavaScript files, so if you only need the *prototype.js* file,
> for instance, use <%= javascript_include_tag "prototype.
> js" %> instead of <%= javascript_include_tag :defaults %>.
> The *effects.js*, *dragdrop.js*, and *controls.js* files derive from the
> *script.aculo.us* library (see Chapter 8).

The imported JavaScript files include *prototype.js*, and the Prototype library
just happens to include the Ajax.Updater JavaScript object that wraps the
initializing and use of XMLHttpRequest. (See Chapter 6 for more details on
this package.) So there you have it—the form_remote_tag( ) method represents a wrapper enclosing another wrapper, which handles the request
object automatically.

_{HACK} **Make Your JavaScript Available to Rails**
#57 Applications

Call custom JavaScript functions in Rails templates without including long
script tags.

Even though Ruby on Rails takes care of a lot of the JavaScript-related functionality in Ajax applications with its own methods, you still may want to
have access to your own JavaScript functions. This is particularly true if you
come to Ruby on Rails with a JavaScript background. This hack uses the
RoR setup to call a JavaScript function that does not come with Ruby on
Rails or its included packages. Here's the drill.

Figure 7-8 shows a typical Rails web directory setup, with the contents of
the *public* directory revealed. This directory includes a subdirectory named
javascripts, which in turn contains a file called *application.js*, into which you
can write or cut and paste your function. RoR creates the *application.js* file
for you when it auto-generates the core directories and files for a web
application.

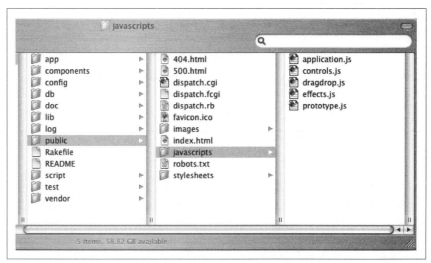

Figure 7-8. application.js in the javascripts directory

Now, back up a bit to a template you are using. The *monitor.rhtml* template
referred to in the last hack includes this embedded method call:

```
<%= javascript_include_tag :defaults %>
```

The code includes the `defaults` parameter with `javascript_include_tag()`,
which automatically generates the `script` tag importing *application.js*, along
with a bunch of other Prototype- and *script.aculo.us*-related imports (see

Chapters 6 and 8, respectively, for discussions of the Prototype and *script. aculo.us* libraries). As a result, the JavaScript in *application.js* is available for code in the template to call. For example, *monitor.rhtml* includes this code:

```
<div id="complete" style=
"font-size: 1.2em; color: green" onclick="clearIt($('complete'))"></div>
```

clearIt( ) is defined in *application.js*. It sets the innerHTML property of the element referenced by its parameter to the empty string "":

```
function clearIt(elId){
    if(elId != null){
        elId.innerHTML="";
    }
}
```

Using javascript_include_tag( ) involves a single step for importing *application.js* and any other necessary packages (such as Prototype), but you are certainly free to place your own JavaScript file in the *javascripts* directory and then include a script tag to import it in the Rails template:

```
<script src="/javascripts/myfunctions.js" type="text/javascript"></script>
```

You can use javascript_include_tag( ) with different parameters to import individual JavaScript files, as in these two examples:

```
javascript_include_tag "/javascripts/myfunctions.js","/scripts/morefuncs.js"
#As long as the scripts directory is located in
#the Rails <web-app-root>/public directory
```

HACK #58 Dynamically Generate a Selection List in a Rails Template

Generate a selection list from server-side data using Ajax and Ruby on Rails.

This hack creates a select element from server-side data using a Ruby on Rails application. Unlike the typical manner in which a web widget is generated in a web page, the user chooses the content for the pop-up, and then the pop-up appears out of the blue, without anything else on the page changing. The selections that the user sees in the pop-up derive from a server-side component; they are not just hard-coded JavaScript or HTML that is part of the web page.

This hack has the same behavior as some of our earlier hacks, but the path our code takes to produce its effects is quite different. A Rails application wraps all of the XMLHttpRequest mechanics behind its own methods. Figure 7-9 shows what the web page looks like. The user reaches this page by typing *http://localhost:3000/hacks/* into a web browser's location field.

We're using the WEBrick server that comes with Ruby on Rails.

Figure 7-9. Cop your own pop-up

The user chooses either Team or Individual from the pop-up and clicks the Show Sports button, and another select list (whose values are determined by the user's choice in the first list) appears just above the button.

In a Rails application, a *controller* component takes charge of the views that the web user sees. The controller component is located inside the *<web-app-root>/app/controllers* directory. Using *http://localhost:3000/hacks/* as an example, the framework looks in *<web-app-root>/app/controllers/hacks_controller.rb* for an action or method named index that generates the response. Actions start out as Ruby methods within a controller object (a *class*, in object-oriented terms) defined in this file.

The entire path on my Mac OS X machine is *~/Rails/Energy/app/controllers/hacks_controller.rb. Energy* is the top-level directory of the web application.

Let's take a look at *hacks_controller.rb* for the index( ) method:

```
class HacksController < ApplicationController
    def index
    end
#rest of class definition...
end
```

Nothing happening there; it's an empty method definition. In this case, Rails looks for a template named *index.rhtml* in the *app/views/hacks* directory.

One of the intuitive aspects of the Rails framework is that the framework maps URL path information, such as the *hacks* part of *http://localhost:3000/hacks*, to directories of the same name in sensible locations, such as *views*.

index.rhtml provides the template for our hack:

```
<html>
<head>
    <meta http-equiv="content-type" content="text/html; charset=utf-8" />
    <%= javascript_include_tag :defaults %>
    <title>Ajax Rails &amp; Select lists</title>
</head>
<body>
<%= form_remote_tag(:update => "sel_con",:url => { :action => :create_select
},
:position => "top",:success => "$('sel_con').innerHTML='''" ) %>
<p>
Please select a sports category:
</p>
<p>
<%= select_tag "categories",
"<option>Team</option><option>Individual</option>" %>
</p>
<div id="sel_con"></div>
<p>
<%= submit_tag "Show Sports" %>
</p>
<%= end_form_tag %>
</body>
</html>
```

This template calls the form_remote_tag( ) method to update the div positioned beneath the form tag. This method wraps all of the Ajax- and request object–related functionality, updating the div with server data and positioning any more information on top of or before any existing div content (as specified by the :position => "top" parameter). In other words, when the user clicks the Show Sports button, an XMLHttpRequest object is created, and its send( ) method sends a request to a Rails action named create_select. This action is defined as a Ruby method in the *hacks_controller.rb* file we peeked at before.

The create_select action renders the HTTP response, which specifies the tags and content of a new pop-up or select list. Figure 7-10 shows the result of clicking the Show Sports button.

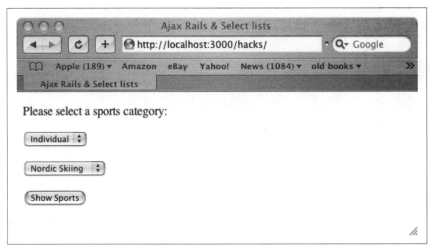

Figure 7-10. Voilà, up pops a select list

How is that response rendered, anyway? Let's look at that part of the controller object:

```ruby
class HacksController < ApplicationController
    def index
    end

    def create_select

        indArr=["Nordic Skiing", "Inline Skating","Tennis",
        "Triathlon","Road Racing","Figure Skating","Weight Lifting",
        "Speed Skating","Snowboarding"];
        teamArr=["Soccer","Basketball","Football","Hockey",
        "Baseball","Lacrosse"];
        str="";

        if params[:categories].index('Team') != nil
            render :partial => "options",
                    :locals => { :sports => teamArr,:sptype => "team"}
        elsif params[:categories].index('Individual') != nil
            render :partial => "options",
                    :locals => { :sports => indArr, :sptype => "individual" }
        else
            str="<select id='individual' name='individual'>
                    <option>unknown</option></select>";
            render :text => str;
        end

        #end method
    end
    #end class definition
end
```

This controller object stores two Ruby arrays in the variables indArr and teamArr (these values could alternatively be generated from a database). Remember the web page's existing select list that gives the user a choice of Team or Individual? This is a select element with the name categories. The browser submits this value as a form parameter to the Rails action. The code uses the syntax params[:categories] to get this parameter's value. Then things get interesting, in a Rails kind of way. The server still has to provide an HTTP response to the Ajax request object.

The action uses the RoR render( ) method to send the HTML for a select list back to our application, with the array values as the select list contents:

```
render :partial => "options",
:locals => { :sports => teamArr,:sptype => "team"}
```

render( ) specifies in its first parameter a partial named options. In Rails lingo, a partial is just a template that contains a chunk of content that can be used over and over again—for example, one or a few HTML tags. Using the Rails naming convention, the partial (really a text file) is placed in the *app/views/hacks* directory with its name preceded by an underscore, as in *_options.rhtml*. So, in plain English, the method call declares, "Render the response as the *_options* partial content, and hand the partial two local variables, :sports and :sptype."

 Don't forget the : before the variable names!

A Little Partial Pizzazz

The partial needs the array values to build the select list; these are stored in the teamArr variable. Rails uses its built-in naming convention for partials (the underscore requirement) to find the correct content and render it as the response. Let's look at the partial *_options.rhtml* file:

```
<select id="<%= sptype %>" name="<%= sptype %>">
<% sports.each do |sport| %>
<option><%= sport %></option>
<% end %>
</select>
```

A little embedded Ruby code gives the select element its id and name. The embedded code then iterates through the array (passed into the partial by the render( ) method) and creates an option element for each array member, as in <option>hockey</option>. Although a little server-side Ruby code was involved, the code did not have to touch the request object or deal with fetching or massaging the return value.

Cleanup Code

The only bit of trickery involved is making sure that the application does not append one new select list after another inside the div as the user clicks the button. We want all the existing selects in that div to be replaced by any new ones. Therefore, we include a little cleanup code that empties the div before it's updated with a new select list:

```
<%= form_remote_tag(:update => "sel_con",:url => { :action => :create_select
},
:position => "top",success => "$('sel_con').innerHTML=''" ) %>
```

success sequentially precedes the complete stage, so this code sets the div's content to the empty string before the new select list appears.

> To handle any request failures, such as a downed web server, add this code from a prior hack as a form_remote_tag( ) parameter:
>
> ```
> #$('failure') is Prototype's shortcut for
> #document.getElementById('failure')
> :failure => "$('failure').innerHTML='Failure;
> request status='+request.status"
> ```

Find Out Whether Ajax Is Calling in the Request
HACK #59

Discover whether XMLHttpRequest or a URL in a browser is requesting an action.

One of the issues with defining simple actions in Ruby on Rails is that once an action that responds with a fine-grained value (such as a string or small HTML chunk) is defined, users can make direct requests for that little value in their browsers. But chances are, those values were designed only for XMLHttpRequest objects.

For example, "Periodically Make a Remote Call" **[Hack #61]** uses the request object to periodically get a string representing the current date. It calls an action named increment, which looks like this in the controller object:

```
def increment
    tz=TimeZone.create("TZ",-60*60*5)
        render :text => tz.now( ).to_s
    end
end
```

You don't want the users to be able to call this action directly in their browsers, as in *http://localhost:3000/hacks/increment*, because it is designed only for calling by Ajax behind the scenes.

Are You XMLHttpRequest?

Thankfully, the Rails API has a method that can detect whether a request involves XMLHttpRequest or not. Here's how we can change our action in the controller:

```
def increment
    tz=TimeZone.create("TZ",-60*60*5)
    if @request.xml_http_request?( )
    render :text => tz.now( ).to_s
    end
end
```

This action renders the specified text only if the request originates from XMLHttpRequest. @request is an instance variable that is available inside the ActionController class. Its xml_http_request?( ) method returns true if the request includes an X-Requested-With header containing the value XMLHttpRequest.

> The Prototype package will include this header with those types of requests.

If the if condition returns false in the code sample, the controller object displays a view with the action name increment. In other words, it looks *for* <*web-app-root>/views/hacks/increment.rhtml*. If this view is not available, Rails raises an exception along the lines of "template increment.rhtml missing."

If you use Ajax a lot with Rails, you will find that a number of actions are defined solely for Ajax-related requests. This technique is a handy way to ensure that requests that don't originate from the request object are rejected.

HACK #60 Dynamically Generate a Selection List Using Database Data

Create a select element using database data in a Rails web application.

This hack generates a select element with options that have values and content derived from live database data. The cool twist is that the user initiates the creation of the element, and the select list appears loaded with database data without any page refreshes or rebuilds. This hack is a snap to build with Ruby on Rails, which automatically provides the developer with objects that are directly mapped to database tables.

This hack assumes that the user is interacting with a web server that uses RoR components. It uses the built-in WEBrick server to handle the HTTP requests and responses.

Tracking Energy Use

This hack is an energy-monitoring tool that allows the user to track the kilowatts usage of a system. It generates a web page that asks the user to choose a year, and then pulls monthly kilowatts-usage data from a database and displays the month options in a new select element. The select list appears on the page without any perceptible page rebuild in the browser.

When the user chooses a month, the page immediately displays the kilowatts used that month in a text field beneath the newly created select list. Figure 7-11 shows the web page before the user clicks the Show Months button.

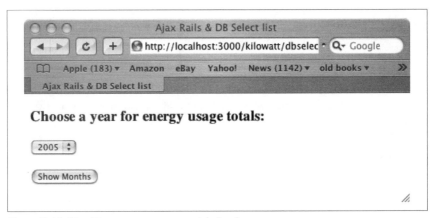

Figure 7-11. Use Ajax to generate tags with database content

When the user clicks the Show Months button, the application sends a request to the RoR server, which responds with content for updating the web page. The content is a new select element containing MySQL database data and a text field, as Figure 7-12 shows.

When the user selects a month from the select list, the data for that month appears in the text field.

Let's see how the code is put together. Here is the view that RoR uses to output the page, located at *<web-app-root>/app/views/kilowatt/dbselect.rhtml*:

```
<html>
<head>
    <meta http-equiv="content-type" content="text/html; charset=utf-8" />
    <%= javascript_include_tag "prototype.js" %>
```

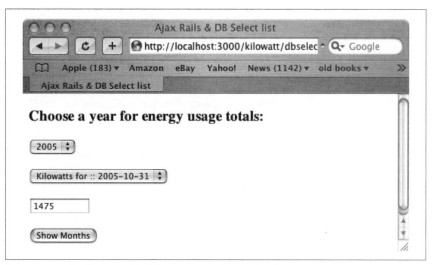

Figure 7-12. Display monthly kilowatt usage from a database

```
    <title>Ajax Rails &amp; DB Select list</title>
</head>
<body>
<%= form_remote_tag(:update => "db_div",:url => { :action => :db_element },
:position => "top",:success => "$('db_div').innerHTML=''" ) %>
<h3>Choose a year for energy usage totals:</h3>
<p>
<%= select_tag "year","<option>2005</option><option>2006</option>
<option>2007</option>" %>
</p>
<div id="db_div"></div>
<p>
<%= submit_tag "Show Months" %>
</p>
<%= end_form_tag %>
</body>
</html>
```

The page requires the Prototype JavaScript package to initiate its dynamic Ajax-driven update. See   for an explanation of *prototype.js*. javascript_ include_tag( ) is an RoR API method you can use in embedded scripts to make it easier to output script tags. form_remote_tag( ) creates a form element that uses XMLHttpRequest to update an HTML element on the page. The form submits its request to a server-side component (in Rails parlance, an action) called db_element. Let's take a look at db_element.

```
class KilowattController < ApplicationController
    scaffold :kilowatt

    def db_element
```

```
            @kwatts = Kilowatt.find_all
            render :partial => "options"
      end

  end
```

`db_element` is just a method defined in Ruby. In the Rails framework, controller objects, well, *control* the processing of requests. `KilowattController` is a class that handles requests involving *<web-app-root>/kilowatt*-type URLs. All the related actions are defined in this controller object. First, the method creates an instance variable, `@kwatts`, which contains the data for all the rows of a database table. The `Kilowatt.find_all` part is a model object that calls a `find_all( )` method, which queries the database table `kilowatts` for its rows.

> Ruby on Rails uses an object-relational mapping mechanism that allows application code written in Ruby to create, update, and delete database data. Ruby on Rails is already well known for automating much of this development process.

Next, `db_element` calls render( ), which renders the response (the `select` element and text field) using a chunk of a template called a `partial`. The partial's name is options, and it is located at *<web-app-root>app/views/kilowatt/_options.rhtml* (Ruby on Rails knows where to find it). The partial has access to the `@kwatts` variable mentioned above. Here it is:

```
<select id="dbselect" name="dbselect" onchange=
"$('monthly_total').value=this.value">
<% @kwatts.each do |kilowatt| %>
<option value="<%=kilowatt.kwatts%>">Kilowatts for :: <%=kilowatt.kdate%>
</option>
<% end %>
</select>
<p>
<input type="text" id="monthly_total" size="10" maxlength="10">
</p>
```

The template generates an `option` element for each database table row. The values for two of the table columns are used: `kilowatt.kwatts` is a number reflecting the kilowatts used, and `kilowatt.kdate` is a date `string`. Here's an example option in the output:

```
<option value="2200">Kilowatts for :: 11-07-2005</option>
```

The server sends the output of this `partial` as the HTTP response.

Good Form

The form element looks like this in the web page's underlying source code:

```
<form action="/kilowatt/db_element" method="post"
onsubmit="new Ajax.Updater('db_div', '/kilowatt/db_element',
{asynchronous:true, evalScripts:true, insertion:Insertion.Top,
onSuccess:function(request){$('db_div').innerHTML=''},
parameters:Form.serialize(this)});
return false;">
```

Like "Periodically Make a Remote Call" **[Hack #61]**, this code uses the Ajax.
Updater object from the *prototype.js* package (see Chapter 6). While this
object is interesting, the RoR developer deals only with the form_remote_
tag( ) method. The framework does a lot of the work for you.

Periodically Make a Remote Call
#61
Make an HTTP request at a specified interval and update the web page with
the response.

This hack updates a web page with new data every five seconds, without
ever refreshing or rebuilding the page. The behavior is automatic and does
not involve the user taking any action. The conventional way of initiating
this behavior is to use a "client pull" page involving a Refresh response
header set to a specified interval, but even this strategy involves requesting
and rebuilding the entire page each time the refresh takes place.

> See Chapter 18 of Bruce Perry's *Java Servlet and JSP Cook-
> book* (O'Reilly) for an example.

From the users' perspective, it may also be a little weird for the browser to
suddenly "go on automatic" without them touching the keyboard, with the
page going blank temporarily and the delays involved in the redisplaying of
images and other embedded items. This hack updates only the content in a
single div, with nothing else changing on the page and no page rebuild.

No Fooling Around

As this is a Ruby on Rails application, all of the handling of the request
object and its return values is taken care of for the developer. Figure 7-13
shows what the application's view looks like in the Safari browser. The user
requests the URL *http://localhost:3000/hacks/interval*. In a Rails application,
this causes the calling of an action named interval, or a view template
located at *<web-app-root>/app/views/hacks/interval.rhtml*.

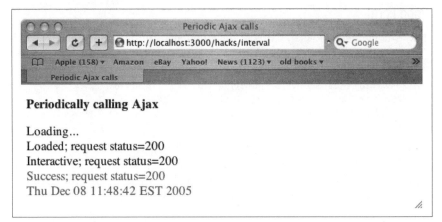

Figure 7-13. Display new data periodically

This page monitors the Ajax request the same way as "Monitor Remote Calls with Rails" [Hack #56], but the displayed date is refreshed every five seconds in a very subtle manner. All this was accomplished by calling one built-in Rails method in the view, as well as four lines of server-side code. You don't have to fool around with initializing the request object and writing functions to handle its return values!

Here is the code for the view *interval.rhtml*, which shows the method the application uses, periodically_call_remote( ):

```
<!DOCTYPE html PUBLIC "-//W3C//DTD XHTML 1.0 Strict//EN"
        "http://www.w3.org/TR/2000/REC-xhtml1-20000126/DTD/xhtml1-strict.
dtd">
<html xmlns="http://www.w3.org/1999/xhtml" xml:lang="en" lang="en">
<head>
    <meta http-equiv="content-type" content="text/html; charset=utf-8" />
    <%= javascript_include_tag :defaults %>
    <title>Periodic Ajax calls</title>
</head>
<body>
<%= periodically_call_remote(:update => "complete",:frequency => 5,
:url => { :action => :increment },
:position => "top",
:success => "$('complete').innerHTML='';$('success').innerHTML='Success;
request status='+request.status",
:loading => "$('loading').innerHTML='Loading...'",
:loaded => "$('loaded').innerHTML='Loaded; request status='+request.status",
:interactive => "$('inter').innerHTML=
  'Interactive; request status='+request.status",
:failure => "$('failure').innerHTML='Failure; request status='+request.
status") %>
<h3>Periodically calling Ajax</h3>
<div id="loading" style="font-size: 1.2em"></div>
<div id="loaded" style="font-size: 1.2em"></div>
```

```
<div id="inter" style="font-size: 1.2em"></div>
<div id="success" style="font-size: 1.2em; color: green"></div>
<div id="failure" style="font-size: 1.2em; color: red"></div>
<div id="complete" style="font-size: 1.2em; color: green"></div>
</body>
</html>
```

The `<%= javascript_include_tag :defaults %>` part ensures that the view imports the script tags that the application requires to use the JavaScript-based Ajax mechanism (see "Make Your JavaScript Available to Rails Applications" [Hack #57]). You'll see these tags a little later.

Here are the first few parameters to `periodically_call_remote( )`:

```
periodically_call_remote(:update => "complete",:frequency => 5,
:url => { :action => :increment }
```

These parameters:

- Specify the `id` of the HTML element (or `div` with `id` `complete`, in this case) that the request object will update.

- Specify the frequency or interval in seconds for sending requests (five seconds).

- Point to a Ruby on Rails action (`increment`) that will generate the response.

> The entire parameter to `periodically_call_remote( )` is a Ruby hash type, which is a lot like a JavaScript object literal. You can also call this method in the following manner:
>
> ```
> <% _hash = {:update => "complete",:frequency => 5, :
> url => { :action => :increment },
> :position => "top",
> :success => "$('complete').
> innerHTML='';$('success').innerHTML='Success;
> request status='+request.status",
> :loading => "$('loading').innerHTML='Loading...'",
> :loaded => "$('loaded').innerHTML='Loaded; request
> status='+request.status",
> :interactive => "$('inter').innerHTML='Interactive;
> request status='+request.status",
> :failure => "$('failure').innerHTML='Failure;
> request status='+request.status"} %>
>
> <%= periodically_call_remote(_hash) %>
> ```

Where's All the Action?

The `increment` action is the server-side component or code that provides the HTTP response to these periodic requests. In Rails, an action can be created as a Ruby method inside of the controller object. The method name is the name of the action. Our action, defined here, simply updates the current date:

```
class HacksController < ApplicationController

    def increment
        tz=TimeZone.create("TZ",-60*60*5)
        render :text => tz.now( ).to_s
    end
#rest of Controller code
end
```

The increment( ) method creates a TimeZone object, which is included in the RoR API. This TimeZone is set for a five-hour negative offset from Greenwich mean time, which lines it up with Eastern standard time (EST). The object's now( ) method returns the current time in a formatted string, as Figure 7-13 shows. The code then uses RoR's render( ) method, which sends the date string as an HTTP response. The Ajax application calls this bit of code every five seconds, so the date string represents a date and time five seconds later than the previous one.

> That's a lot of requests to hit the server with from one client! The requests will stop once another web page replaces this one in the browser, or the browser tab containing this page is closed. You can also provide a button or internal behavior to stop the periodical execution, as discussed in "Create Observers for Web Page Fields" [Hack #52].

Shrink-Wrapped

If you ventured through some of the earlier hacks in this chapter, you've probably already encountered the discussion about how these Ajax methods wrap objects that are made available by the Prototype package. Using View → View Source from the Safari browser menu, you can see what the generated code for this page looks like. Here are the tags that import the JavaScript files:

```
<script src="/javascripts/prototype.js" type="text/javascript"></script>
<script src="/javascripts/effects.js" type="text/javascript"></script>
<script src="/javascripts/dragdrop.js" type="text/javascript"></script>
<script src="/javascripts/controls.js" type="text/javascript"></script>
<script src="/javascripts/application.js" type="text/javascript"></script>
```

Rails views are templates; the embedded method calls are replaced by the generated HTML code, which the web server sends back to the browser in response to a request for an RoR view.

Make sure that you import only the JavaScript files the page needs, because a separate GET request is required for each one.

The Rails application replaces the periodically_call_remote( ) code with the following:

```
<script type="text/javascript">
//<![CDATA[
new PeriodicalExecuter(function( ) {new Ajax.Updater('complete',
'/hacks/increment', {asynchronous:true, evalScripts:true,
insertion:Insertion.Top,
onFailure:function(request){$('failure').innerHTML='Failure; request
status='+request.status},
onInteractive:function(request){$('inter').innerHTML='Interactive;
request status='+request.status},
onLoaded:function(request){$('loaded').innerHTML='Loaded; request
status='+request.status},
onLoading:function(request){$('loading').innerHTML='Loading...'},
onSuccess:function(request){$('complete').innerHTML='';$('success').
innerHTML=
'Success; request status='+request.status}})}, 5)
//]]>
</script>
```

This is a script tag that encloses some JavaScript. The script creates a PeriodicalExecuter and an Ajax.Updater object from the Prototype package (see). The PeriodicalExecuter takes as parameters to its constructor a call-back function and the number of seconds to lapse before it executes again. The Ajax.Updater takes care of the Ajax- and request object–related work for us. Depending on how the developer likes to code, the Ajax magic is virtually shrink-wrapped!

HACK #62 Dynamically View Request Information for XMLHttpRequest

Display the values of environment variables when you make an Ajax request.

It can be useful to know what environment variables are available along with requests made with XMLHttpRequest. In this context, environment variables contain information about the server environment that is associated with a request involving XMLHttpRequest, such as the server name, the querystring, the raw POST data, and the values of various HTTP request headers. (For more on environment variables, see *http://en.wikipedia.org/wiki/Environment_variable*.) Even if you don't need all this information, it's still cool that you can get a look at it, and Ruby on Rails makes this easy.

This hack displays a textarea on a web page. When the web page launches XMLHttpRequest in response to a button click, the textarea immediately fills up with the environment variable information, without a page rebuild. Figure 7-14 shows the page after the user has clicked the Go Ajax! button. The textarea shows a bunch of useful information, including an HTTP_X_REQUESTED_WITH variable indicating that this was an Ajax-related request.

Figure 7-14. Environment variables accompanying XMLHttpRequest

How Does It Work?

The page, or view, is simple enough. It's just a Rails template that includes some embedded Ruby code:

```
<html>
<head>
<meta http-equiv="content-type" content="text/html; charset=utf-8" />
    <%= javascript_include_tag "prototype.js" %>
    <title>Have a look at request headers</title>
</head>
```

```
<body>
<p>
[ Lots of cool UI stuff in the body of the application...]
</p>
<form action="javascript:void%200">
<p>
<%= submit_to_remote("submit","Go Ajax!",:update => "env",
:url => { :action => :show_env},:position => "top",
:failure => "$('env').innerHTML='XML request failed...'")%>
</p>
<h3>Request Environment Information</h3>
<p>
<%= text_area_tag "env", nil, :size => "40x20" %>
</p>
</form>
</body>
</html>
```

The view imports the Prototype JavaScript package in *prototype.js*, which is required to use the Ajax-related Rails methods. The submit_to_remote( ) method is part of the RoR API. It creates a submit button that makes a remote request using XMLHttpRequest. When the user clicks the button, this mechanism submits the request to an action called show_env. Then, when the HTTP response arrives from the action, the application updates the element (the textarea with an id of env.)

Here is how the action generates the environment variable data for the textarea. Remember that a Rails action can be defined as a simple Ruby method inside the controller class:

```
class HacksController < ApplicationController
    def index
    end

    def show_env
        if @request.xml_http_request?( )
            @headers["Content-Type"] = "text/plain; charset=UTF-8"
            str="";
            @request.env( ).each do |key,value|
                str+=key.to_s + "==" + value.to_s+"\n\n"
            end
            render :text => str
        end
    end
end #end class
```

First, show_env checks whether the request actually involves XMLHttpRequest (see "Find Out Whether Ajax Is Calling in the Request" [Hack #59]). The action then uses the instance variable @request.env( ) method to iterate through each of the environment variables and store their values. The code then renders this string as the response.

The response text ends up plunked inside the textarea. An important ease-of-use factor with this hack is that you never had to set up or deal at all with the innards of XMLHttpRequest; the Rails method submit_to_remote( ) takes care of that. Sweet!

Hacking the Hack

If the user clicks the Go Ajax! button more than once, the textarea's chunk of data is submitted in the request and ends up as a giant lump inside the RAW_POST_DATA environment variable. To avoid this problem, you can use code to clear the textarea's contents first each time the button is clicked:

```
$('the_textarea').innerHTML="";
```

Savor the script.aculo.us JavaScript Library

Hacks 63–67

Your web-application development efforts can substantially benefit from open source JavaScript libraries, if only because they save you time that would otherwise be spent reinventing the wheel. Chapter 6 used the Ajax tools of the powerful Prototype library. The hacks in this chapter use practical controls such as Mac OS X–style login boxes and auto-complete email fields deriving from *script.aculo.us*, an open source JavaScript library that Thomas Fuchs, a software architect in Vienna, Austria, has made available under an MIT-style license (see *http://script.aculo.us*). The library includes an impressive variety of special effects such as shakes, fades, and pulsations, as well as custom controls such as draggables, droppables, and auto-completing input fields.

script.aculo.us is built upon Prototype's Ajax objects. Version 1.5 of *script. aculo.us*, for example, depends on Prototype v1.4. Thus, to use *script.aculo.us*'s collection of widget controls and special effects, you must import *prototype.js* along with *scriptaculous.js*. Simply use `script` tags in your web pages to include these two files; *scriptaculous.js* itself then loads its associated dependent code files, such as *controls.js* and *effects.js*.

script.aculo.us includes dozens of effects and tools. The following hacks will help you get started with this versatile library.

Integrate script.aculo.us Visual Effects with an Ajax Application

#63

Include an impressive array of special effects with your Ajax application.

script.aculo.us includes a variety of special effects and custom controls developers can use to enliven their Ajax applications or just to give them the advanced capabilities users have come to expect from desktop applications. It also has some built-in Ajax features that use Prototype, the library that *must* accompany *script.aculo.us* in order to use its widget controls and special effects.

Setting Up

The first step in using *script.aculo.us* is to download the library from *http://script.aculo.us/downloads*. This site makes the library available as an archive (currently *scriptaculous-js-1.5.1.tar.gz*), which contains various JavaScript files that you have to add to whichever web application directory you have designated for JavaScripts. The files are: *builder.js*, *controls.js*, *dragdrop.js*, *effects.js*, *scriptaculous.js*, and *slider.js*. (A file called *unittest.js*, useful if you want to run unit tests on your code, is also included.) The main JavaScript directory for this hack, which is built on the Tomcat web container, is */parkerriver/ajaxhacks/js*, so that's where I put all of these files. *script.aculo.us* depends on *prototype.js*, so make sure this library is included in the directory as well (see "Use Prototype's Ajax Tools with Your Application" **[Hack #50]**).

Next, you must make sure that the *script.aculo.us* library is properly loaded. A simple hack like this one will also work when the web page is loaded into the browser from the filesystem.

While your designated directory for JavaScript files has to contain the various *script.aculo.us*-dependent files, your web page only has to include *prototype.js* and *scriptaculous.js* (which loads all of its dependencies itself). This hack's web page also imports *efflib_2.js*, which is the JavaScript file that contains our application code. Here's what the head section of the web page should look like:

```html
<html lang="en">
<head>
    <meta http-equiv="content-type" content="text/html; charset=utf-8" />
    <script src="js/prototype.js" type="text/javascript"></script>
    <script src="js/scriptaculous.js" type="text/javascript"></script>
    <script src="js/efflib_2.js" type="text/javascript"></script>
    <style type="text/css">
        @import "/stylesheets/hacks.css";
    </style>
    <title>Toggle a control</title>
</head>
```

With the setup complete, let's take a look at how easy it is to include a useful control or effect with your Ajax application.

Toggling and Switching

Some applications need to be able to show or hide a control or page region, depending on what the user wants to do with the application. For example, this hack contains a textarea that shows instant messages, similar to an emailer that auto-fetches emails. The application enables users to show or hide the textarea (in other words, to get it out of the way when they are not examining their messages).

The hack uses the toggle effect of Prototype and the SwitchOff effect of *script.aculo.us*.

Figure 8-1 shows the section of the web page that contains a viewport for instant messages.

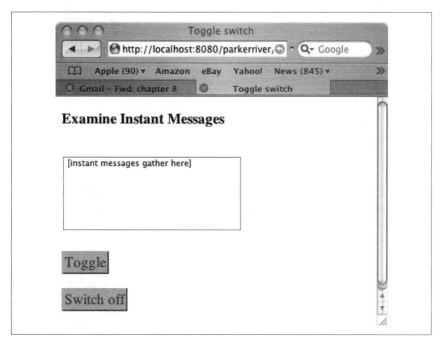

Figure 8-1. Embed script.aculo.us controls in a view

When the user clicks the Toggle button, the textarea or view port disappears, and the two buttons move up the page to take its place. Clicking the "Switch off" button elicits a more interesting animation—that of a TV screen of the older cathode-ray tube vintage switching off—as the textarea disappears. Again, the two buttons move up to inhabit the region where the view port used to be. Clicking the Toggle button again restores the viewport.

So, how does this work? Here's all the code that's necessary:

```
window.onload=function( ){
    if($("msg_screen") && $("toggle") && $("switchoff")){
        $("toggle").onclick=function( ){
            Element.toggle($("msg_screen"));
```

```
        };
         $("switchoff").onclick=function( ){
          Effect.SwitchOff("msg_screen"));
          };
      }
    };
```

The onclick event handlers of each button are set to call Element.toggle( ) and Effect.SwitchOff( ). toggle( ) takes the toggled element as a parameter; the code uses the Prototype shortcut $("msg_screen"). Effect.SwitchOff takes the switched-off element's id as a parameter.

> The code also checks that each of these elements, including the textarea, exists on the web page before it assigns behaviors.

Hacking the Hack

You can make the code feed the message screen with new server messages using Prototype's Ajax.Updater object, perhaps in conjunction with the PeriodicalExecuter (see "Create Observers for Web Page Fields" [Hack #52]).

H A C K
#64   Create a Login Box That Shrugs Off Invalid Logins
Use script.aculo.us to create a login control that shakes like a Mac OS X control if the login is invalid.

This hack sets up *script.aculo.us* with a web page, as explained in "Integrate script.aculo.us Visual Effects with an Ajax Application" [Hack #63], and then implements a text entry box that shakes if the user types in an invalid entry. If you've ever tried to log into Mac OS X with an incorrect username, you'll recognize this behavior. If the user enters a valid value in the text box, the hack makes an Ajax request, submitting the value to a server. The server's response to the request is displayed beneath the login button; this message automatically fades away in 10 seconds.

> Whenever you implement a login-type widget, make sure that the application is designed to prevent any outsiders from mining your systems for valid usernames.

Here is the web page code for the hack, with script tags that import the required JavaScript files:

```
<html>
<head>
    <meta http-equiv="content-type" content="text/html; charset=utf-8" />
    <script src="/javascripts/prototype.js" type="text/javascript"></script>
```

```
<script src="/javascripts/scriptaculous.js" type=
"text/javascript"></script>
<script src="/javascripts/efflib.js" type="text/javascript"></script>
<style type="text/css">
    @import "/stylesheets/hacks.css";
</style>
<title>Use script.aculo.us</title>
</head>
<body>
<div id="entry_box" class="box">
<span class="instruct">Enter your login name: </span>
<form action="javascript:void%200" method="get">
<input id="login_nm" type="text" size="25" maxlength="30" class=
"txtbox"><br />
 <button class="ajbut" id="gobut">login</button>
 <div id="answer" class="answer" style="display:none;"></div>
</form>
</div>
</body>
</html>
```

Figure 8-2 shows what this web application looks like in Firefox 1.5.

Figure 8-2. Don't get shaken down

Users are invited to type their login names in the text field, and then click the "login" button to submit them. If the name entered is less than six characters long or contains any numbers, the box "shakes" or moves back and forth quickly, like a Mac OS X login field when a user enters an invalid name. If the login name passes muster, the application sends an Ajax request with the login name to a server, which returns the server name and the login name it received. This message is displayed beneath the login button, as Figure 8-3 shows.

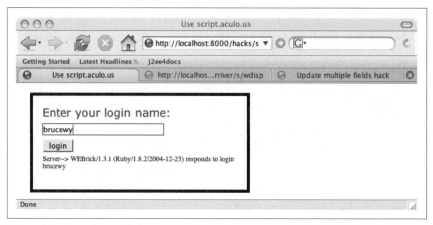

Figure 8-3. A good name fades away

This message remains for 10 seconds, then elegantly fades away. Now let's see how we did that. Here's the *efflib.js* code:

```
window.onload=function( ){
    if($("login_nm") && $("gobut")){
        $("gobut").onclick=function( ){
            if((! $F("login_nm")) || ($F("login_nm").length < 6) ||
                $F("login_nm").match(/\d+/g) ){
                $("login_nm").value="";
                Effect.Shake('entry_box');
            } else {
                $var xmlHttp= new Ajax.Request("/hacks/shake_resp",
                {method: "get",
                    parameters: "login_nm="+$F("login_nm"),
                    onComplete:function(request){
                        $("answer").innerHTML=request.responseText;
                        Effect.Appear("answer");
                        var vrl=window.setInterval(function( ){
                            Effect.Fade("answer");
                            window.clearInterval(vrl);
                        },10*1000);
                    }});

            }
        }
    }
};
```

Whole Lotta Shakin'

When the user clicks the login button, the code validates the text field, using a Prototype shortcut for getting the value of a form element (`$F("login_nm")`).

To use this shortcut, pass the id of the HTML element (nm_ info, in the following example) to $F( ):

```
<input type="text" id="nm_info" size="25" />
```

If the validation fails, the code implements the shake behavior in this way:

```
Effect.Shake('entry_box');
```

The parameter to the Shake method is the id of the div that does the shakin' and bakin'.

If the validation succeeds, the code initiates an Ajax-style request with Prototype's Ajax.Request object. This request sets the stage for a couple of additional *script.aculo.us* effects:

```
Effect.Appear("answer");
var vrl=window.setInterval(function( ){
Effect.Fade("answer");
window.clearInterval(vrl);
},10*1000);
```

Effect.Appear( ) makes an element visible if the code initially sets its display CSS property to none:

```
<div id="answer" class="answer" style="display:none;"></div>
```

Just pass in the id of the element you want to reveal as a parameter. One sort of hackish way to make the visible element fade away again on a timer is illustrated in the prior code snippet. I used the window.setInterval( ) method to wait 10 seconds and then call Effect.Fade("answer"). The code then clears that interval immediately, so it calls Effect.Fade( ) only once. This generates the effect where the server message appears beneath the login button for 10 seconds, then fades away.

Serve It Up

The server-side code is fairly trivial in the Ruby on Rails (RoR) framework:

```
class HacksController < ApplicationController

    def shake_resp
      if @request.xml_http_request?( )
        render :text => "Server--> "+
        @request.env( )["SERVER_SOFTWARE"].to_s+
        " responds to login "+params[:login_nm].to_s
      end
    end
```

This code checks if the request originates from XMLHttpRequest, then it sends back some text specifying the name of the server software and the request parameter value (see "Find Out Whether Ajax Is Calling in the Request" [Hack #59]).

You can find more information on the Effect.Shake API at *http://wiki.script.aculo.us/scriptaculous/show/Effect.Shake.*

HACK #65   Create an Auto-Complete Field with script.aculo. us

Implement your own auto-complete field using script.aculo.us effects.

An increasingly common control for Ajax applications is a text field that "senses" the user typing. When the user types one or more letters, the application immediately checks the field value with a cached or server database. If there are any matches, these are displayed in a drop-down box beneath the text field. This behavior is usually referred to as *auto-completion*.

This hack requests the user to start typing in an email address. The typed characters are compared behind the scenes to a server-side data store, and if any matches are found, a drop-down box populated with those values appears (as in Google's Gmail). Figure 8-4 shows this effect, which is simple to implement using *script.aculo.us*.

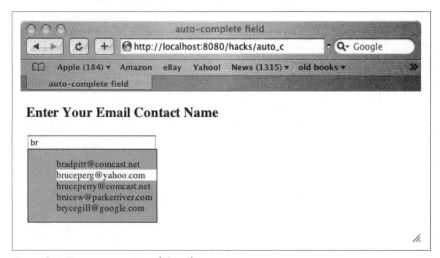

Figure 8-4. Your own version of Gmail

script.aculo.us uses the `Ajax.Request` object of the Prototype library. See "Integrate script.aculo.us Visual Effects with an Ajax Application" **[Hack #63]** for a description of Prototype and this object.

When the user selects one of these displayed email addresses, it becomes the value of the text field.

To implement this hack, the developer must import the *prototype.js* and *scriptaculous.js* libraries, as in the following web page code:

```
<!DOCTYPE html PUBLIC "-//W3C//DTD XHTML 1.0 Transitional//EN"
        "http://www.w3.org/TR/2000/REC-xhtml1-20000126/DTD/xhtml1-
transitional.dtd">
<html xmlns="http://www.w3.org/1999/xhtml" xml:lang="en" lang="en">
<head>
    <meta http-equiv="content-type" content="text/html; charset=utf-8" />
    <script src="/javascripts/prototype.js" type="text/javascript"></script>
    <script src="/javascripts/scriptaculous.js" type="text/javascript"></
script>
    <script src="/javascripts/auto_com.js" type="text/javascript"></script>
    <style type="text/css">
        @import "http://localhost:8080/stylesheets/hacks.css";
    </style>
    <title>auto-complete field</title>
</head>
<body>
<h3>Enter Your Email Contact Name</h3>
<div><form action="javascript:void%200">
<input type="text" id="ac" size="25" />
<div id="ac_choices" style=
        "background-color: #9EB5F2; font-size: 0.8em; border: solid thin;">
p</div>
</form></div>
</body>
</html>
```

The imported *auto_com.js* file contains this hack's custom code, which uses a *script.aculo.us* object to implement the fancy control. Here is the code for that file:

```
window.onload=function( ){
    new Ajax.Autocompleter("ac", "ac_choices",
            "/hacks/a_complete", {paramName: "chars", minChars: 2});
}
```

This code creates an `Ajax.Autocompleter` object when the browser finishes loading the web page. `Ajax.Autocompleter` is a built-in *script.aculo.us* object defined in *controls.js*. (Recall from "Integrate script.aculo.us Visual Effects with an Ajax Application" **[Hack #63]** that as long as your web page imports the

JavaScript library *scriptaculous.js*, it loads its various dependencies, such as *effects.js* and *controls.js*, itself.

The Ajax.Autocompleter parameters are:

- The id of the text field that implements auto-completion (this can also be implemented as a textarea; see the upcoming API information)
- The id of the div element, for instance, that will contain the drop-down list of matching text
- The URL of the server component that receives this control's Ajax request
- A set of optional parameters in JavaScript object literal format

The code's parameters specify that the name of the variable containing what the user has typed so far is chars. An Ajax request is sent when the user has typed a minimum of two characters. In other words, once the user has typed two characters in the text field, the auto-completer sends those characters to the server component in a request parameter named chars.

> There are several other parameters that developers can use with the Ajax.Autocompleter object. For details, see the API description at *http://wiki.script.aculo.us/scriptaculous/show/Ajax.Autocompleter*.

On the Server Side

The server component has to check the value of the sent parameter and then send the auto-completer some data in the response. The response has to be in the format of an HTML unordered list. First, here is the server-side code that receives the request at the URI */hacks/a_complete*. This component or action is implemented with Ruby on Rails (discussed in Chapter 7):

```
def a_complete
    #This data typically derives from a database
    #Call a method returning an array of email contacts
    #associated with a particular user
    @emails = ["boston@city.com","bruceperg@yahoo.com",
    "brucew@parkerriver.com",
    "bradpitt@comcast.net","brycegill@google.com",
    "billythorton@ycomcast.net",   "bruceperry@comcast.net",
    "christophe@comcast.net"]
    #The chars request parameter holds the
    #characters that the user has typed in so far
    chars = params[:chars].to_s
    #Regular expression matching a string beginning with
    #the characters the user typed in, followed by
    #zero or more characters
```

```
re = /^#{chars}.*$/
@mtch = []
for email in @emails
    if re.match(email) != nil
        @mtch.push(email)
    end
end
@mtch = @mtch.sort
#Pass the array of matched emails on to the template
render :partial => "auto_ul"
end
```

The comments (preceded by #) describe what's going on in the Ruby method a_complete( ). We skipped the step of pulling dozens of email addresses out of a database for a user, and began with an array of email addresses that would be the typical return value of the database interaction. The code uses a regular expression to match the beginning of each email address with the characters that the user has entered. The code then stores the matching addresses in an array, and passes this array to a template that forms the basis of the server's return value.

The render :partial => "auto_ul" part is the RoR method that processes the template with the matched email addresses. (Recall that in Rails parlance, the template file is called a partial.) Here is what it looks like:

```
<ul class="people">
<% @mtch.each do |_word| %>
<li class="person"><%=_word%></li>
<% end %>
</ul>
```

The @mtch variable contains all the matched addresses. This Ruby code is designed to build and return an unordered list, which the Ajax.AutoCompleter object expects as a return value. This value is a ul tag with nested li tags, each specifying an email address. The drop-down that appears when the user types is styled in a way that removes the bullets from the ul/li tags (list-style-type: none) and highlights the selected email address in white against a blue background:

```
<!--div holding the drop-down filled with email addresses -->
<div id="ac_choices" style=
        "background-color: #9EB5F2; font-size: 0.8em; border: solid thin;">
```

Here are the relevant rules in the *hacks.css* stylesheet that determines the display of the drop-down box:

```
ul.people li.selected { background-color: #ffffff; }
li.person { list-style-type: none; }
```

"Create an Auto-Complete Field" **[Hack #78]** discusses an
alternate usage and implementation of auto-complete fields.

 ## HACK #66 Create an In-Place Editor Field

Allow users to edit text right in the web application, without experiencing any
page refreshes or rebuilds.

You might have used a wiki before—it's a web page whose users can edit its
content. *script.aculo.us*'s Ajax.InPlaceEditor is an object that makes it very
easy to specify any text on a web page as editable; it uses Ajax requests to
handle any changed values. This hack's web page displays a quote from the
old patriot Thomas Paine, but it allows the devilish user to edit the word
"souls." Using the Ajax.InPlaceEditor object, the server component can
look at the new value and decide whether to keep it. The user interacts with
a text control; the code handles the server-related activity as Ajax requests in
the background.

Figure 8-5 shows what the web application looks like.

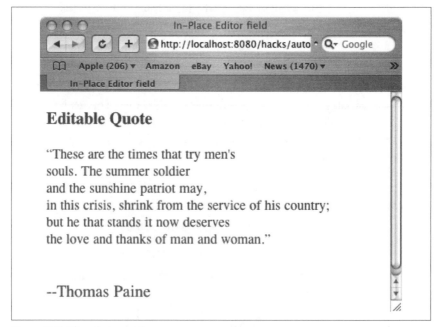

Figure 8-5. Alter that quote!

It may be deemed blasphemous, but the user can now edit the word "souls."
The application quietly submits the new word using XMLHttpRequest.

Only the quote as displayed in the user's browser is changed,
not the backend page (unless this is part of the server-side
process).

When the user passes the mouse pointer over the word "souls," this word is
highlighted in yellow. If the user clicks on it, it turns into a text control, as
Figure 8-6 shows. We have changed the word to "wrists."

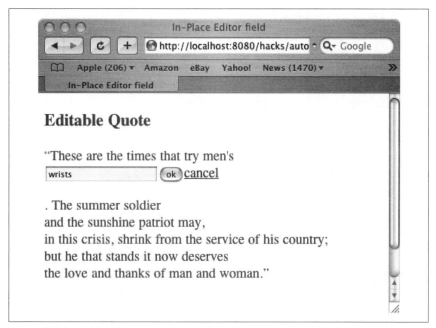

Figure 8-6. Rewriting history

When the user clicks the "ok" button, an Ajax request sends the field's value
to the server automatically. If the user clicks "cancel," the control vanishes
and the code does not send a request. Figure 8-7 shows the final result after
entering "wrists" and clicking "ok." Our server component just returns the
changed value as is, but obviously it could do a lot more (for example, check
for and reject offensive terms).

Now let's look at the rather pithy web page code and JavaScript. Here is the
view that the web page loads. I made sure to include the *prototype.js* and
scriptaculous.js files in script tags:

```
<!DOCTYPE html PUBLIC "-//W3C//DTD XHTML 1.0 Transitional//EN"
        "http://www.w3.org/TR/2000/REC-xhtml1-20000126/DTD/xhtml1-
transitional.dtd">
<html xmlns="http://www.w3.org/1999/xhtml" xml:lang="en" lang="en">
```

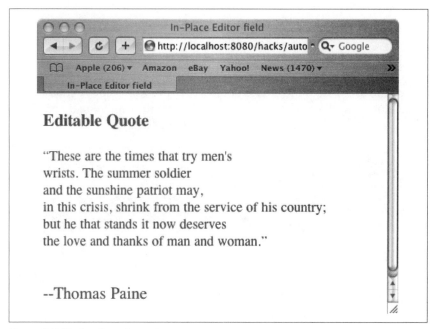

Figure 8-7. Trying times for typists

```
<head>
    <meta http-equiv="content-type" content="text/html; charset=utf-8" />
    <script src="/javascripts/prototype.js" type="text/javascript"></script>
    <script src="/javascripts/scriptaculous.js" type="text/javascript"></
script>
    <script src="/javascripts/auto_inp.js" type="text/javascript"></script>
    <style type="text/css">
        @import "http://localhost:8000/stylesheets/hacks.css";
    </style>
    <title>In-Place Editor field</title>
</head>
<body>
<h3 class="quoter">Editable Quote</h3>
    <pre class="quoter">
        &#8220;These are the times that try men's
        <span id="ed">souls</span>. The summer soldier
        and the sunshine patriot may,
        in this crisis, shrink from the service of his country;
        but he that stands it now deserves
        the love and thanks of man and woman.&#8221;
    </pre>
<p id="author" class="quoter">
    --Thomas Paine
```

```
</p>
</body>
</html>
```

Our code initially encountered a JavaScript error that necessitated upgrading from *scriptaculous.js* Version 1.5_rc5 to 1.5.0. This solved the problem. *scriptaculous.js* v1.5.0 requires Prototype v1.4 or greater.

The code surrounds the editable text with a span tag and gives the tag an id. Here's the code from the imported *auto_inp.js* file, which creates the Ajax.InPlaceEditor object:

```
window.onload=function( ){
    var inp = new Ajax.InPlaceEditor("ed", "/hacks/in_place",
            {formId: "value"});
}
```

This code specifies the id of the editable element (ed), the relative URL for the server component where the Ajax request will be sent, and a formId option specifying the name of the variable containing the editing result. In other words, the querystring for the Ajax request when the user clicks "ok" could be value=wrists.

There are many other options that the code can use. See the API description at *http://wiki.script.aculo.us/scriptaculous/show/Ajax.InPlaceEditor*.

In addition, when the user clicks "ok" to change the edited value, by default the word "saving…" appears temporarily in the editable space during the server interaction. You can style the appearance of this word by including the following class name in your CSS file:

```
.inplaceeditor-saving{font-family: Times,Verdana;font-size: 0.8em; color:
black; }
```

The .inplaceeditor-saving CSS class is the default name for the class that *script.aculo.us* will use to style the saving-related word. You can use a different word by including this option in the constructor (here, it's been replaced it with "waiting"):

```
var inp = new Ajax.InPlaceEditor("ed", "/hacks/in_place",
        {formId: "value", savingText: "waiting"});
```

HACK #67   Create a Web Form That Disappears When Submitted

Create a web form whose fields pulsate if the user has not filled them out;
the form then scrams when the user submits it.

This hack creates a form that displays special effects. If a field is left blank
when the user submits the form values, the field pulsates or flashes six times
and displays a message. Once the user submits the completed form, the
form pauses ever so briefly and then flees the page, leaving the server return
value behind.

We'll look at the code that generates the effects in a moment, but first,
here's the relevant part of the HTML for the page:

```
<head>
    <meta http-equiv="content-type" content="text/html; charset=utf-8" />
    <script src="/javascripts/prototype.js" type="text/javascript"></script>
    <script src="/javascripts/scriptaculous.js" type=
    "text/javascript"></script>
    <script src="/javascripts/disform.js" type="text/javascript"></script>
    <title>form effects</title>
</head>
<body>
<h3>Please Fill out the Form</h3>
<div id="allform">
<form action="javascript:void%200">
<p>
<label for="tfield">Please enter your full name:</label>
    <input id="tfield" type="text" name="fname" size="25" maxlength="25" />
</p>
<p>
<label for="email">Email address:</label>
    <input id="email" type="text" name="email" size="25" maxlength="25" />
</p>
<p>
<button id="but1">Submit</button>
</p>
</form>
</div>
```

The text fields labeled tfield and email are the potentially throbbing form
elements. The div with id allform is the space containing the content that
disappears when the code sends an Ajax request. Here is the code in *disform.
js*, which uses a couple of *script.aculo.us* and Prototype objects:

```
window.onload=function( ){
    if($("tfield") && $("but1")){
        $("but1").onclick=function( ){
            var _inputs = document.getElementsByTagName("input");
            var bool=true;
```

```
        for(var i = 0; i < _inputs.length;i++) {
            if (_inputs[i].type && _inputs[i].
                    type.toLowerCase( ) == "text" &&
                    ! _inputs[i].value)  {
                Effect.Pulsate(_inputs[i].id);
                _inputs[i].value="[Please enter a value]";
                bool=false;
            }
        }

        if(bool){
            Effect.Puff("allform");
            new Ajax.Updater("msg","/hacks/proto",
                    {insertion:Insertion.Top,
                    parameters: Form.serialize(document.forms[0]),
                    onComplete: function(request){
                if ((! request.status) ||
                (request.status > 400)) {
                    $("msg").innerHTML="The server may be unavailable "+
                    "for a moment; please try again soon.";
                }
            }});
        }
    };
    }//end outer if
};
```

When the user clicks the button on the form, the code iterates through each
text field, determining whether the user has left any of them blank. If so, the
code uses the *script.aculo.us* method Effect.Pulsate( ), passing in the id of
the offending text field and making it flash. If everything is okay, Effect.
Puff( ) causes the div and its child elements to vanish, leaving the server
message in its place. The Puff effect is similar to the way the Roadrunner
leaves Wile E. Coyote in its wake in the old cartoon.

> The code uses the Ajax.Updater object from the Prototype
> library (see Chapter 6).

You have to make sure to import both the *prototype.js* and *scriptaculous.js*
files into your web page to use these effects.

> For more details on the Effect.Pulsate API, see *http://wiki.
> script.aculo.us/scriptaculous/show/Effect.Pulsate.*

CHAPTER 9

Options and Efficiencies
Hacks 68–80

Chapter 4's discussion about Ajax's effect on the browser back button may seem like ancient history to you Ajax mavens. To refresh your memory, a single-page Ajax application has a self-contained navigation model; everything takes place in one web page, with client/server connections occurring using XMLHttpRequest. A user who clicks the browser's back button when the Ajax view changes in order to return to the previous Ajax view is instead returned to the page that preceded the Ajax application in that tab or window. This is a confusing outcome for fans of the browser forward and back buttons. The first two hacks in this chapter provide, well, hackish solutions to that conundrum.

In this chapter, you'll also find several hacks that use optional or alternative models to get their jobs done. These include a hack that uses declarative markup in XForms format instead of JavaScript to implement its tasks, another that sets up a search engine inside the browser, and a third that uses client-side JavaScript to cache the user's data. The common theme in these hacks is design simplification and the reduction of server hits whenever possible.

This chapter includes some practical applications that are almost "too pragmatic to be hacks." One hack includes techniques for reducing the size of and obfuscating* JavaScript code. Another uses strings and arrays in script code to dynamically generate content. Still another uses Apache server configuration to deal with Ajax's restrictions on cross-domain requests.

---

* This term refers to reformatting the code so that the JavaScript is very difficult to read for anyone who tries to reverse-engineer it, but the running program is not affected.

HACK
#68 **Fix the Browser Back Button in Ajax Applications**
Make the browser back button work the way web users expect it to in Ajax applications.

Some Ajax applications change the behavior of the browser back button in a way that is unacceptable to users who are big fans of the back and forward buttons. For example, if you use the back button while reading your Google mail messages, you might be greeted by a blank white page that displays the text "Loading..." without anything else happening (Gmail solves this problem by providing its own "Back to Inbox" navigation control within the Gmail application).

What is the usual role of a browser back button? The back button jumps you back through your browser's page history. In typical web applications, when the user clicks on a hyperlink, the data is updated by building a whole new page. A new page represents a new browser history entry.

When the user hits the back button, the browser typically either returns the cached version of the previous page or, if HTTP response headers have marked the page as not cacheable, requests a new version.

But Ajax applications don't create new pages. Rather, they update content within an existing page. And therein lies the problem: when users press the back button they jump back to the previously loaded page—and often out of the Ajax application.

How can you tell the browser to add a new entry to the browser history in an Ajax application? It depends on the browser.

The DOM `window` object has a property, `location`, that lets you set the URL to display on the user's screen. However, this normally means the user jumps to a new page, which doesn't help us. Is there any way to change the location URL without causing a page reload? It turns out there is.

You've seen URLs that look like this: *http://www.example.xyz/frobnitz#xyz*. The hash mark (#) is called a *fragment identifier* (or, more commonly, an anchor hash). The characters that appear after the hash point to a marker inside the current document. (You'd see the target of the above link written as `<a name="xyz">`.)

In the Firefox and Opera browsers, if you change the fragment identifier (hash) of `window.location` in JavaScript, a new history entry is created. When you hit the back button, the history pulls the previous page from the browser cache. This works in Internet Explorer, too—almost. Internet

Explorer adds a history entry but doesn't cache the page data, so when the user presses the back button the data on the page doesn't change. So, scratch `window.location`.

What else updates the browser's history? Changing the contents of an `iframe` adds a history entry, and it works across the major browsers (this hack, however, doesn't work with Safari 2.0). That's the approach we'll use in this hack.

 "Control Browser History with iframes" **[Hack #37]** revealed that there are two kinds of `iframe`: those that are located within the page's HTML and loaded with the page, and those that are loaded dynamically (via the DOM or JavaScript) after the page is finished loading. This hack deals with the former.

This hack is contained in a single JavaScript file, *bbfix.js*, so it's easy to plug into existing projects. Ideally, you should be able to drop this file into an existing Ajax application and, with minimal fuss, get a working back button.

 Macromedia Flash programmers use variations of this `iframe` hack to overcome similar back button problems with Flash.

Before looking inside this hack, let's look at how it's used within a program.

A Very Simple Ajax Program

This simple Ajax program, *uptime.html*, includes a form holding a single button. Press the button, and a JavaScript function fires off an `XMLHttpRequest` request for the web server's uptime value. The value is displayed on the page. Press the button again, and the uptime value is updated.

 On a Linux server, the uptime value is stored as a floating-point value. It represents the number of seconds the server has been up and running.

Here's the web page code:

```
<HEAD>
<TITLE>Ajax Back Button Hack</TITLE>

<script language="javascript" src="/bbfix/xhr.js"></script>
<script language="javascript" src="/bbfix/bbfix.js"></script>
<script language="javascript" type="text/javascript">
```

```
function onClick_btnGetUptime () {

    var httpreq = getHTTPObject();
    httpreq.open("POST", "/cgi-bin/bbfix/uptime.cgi", true);

    httpreq.onreadystatechange = function () {
        if (httpreq.readyState == 4) {
            //Update the uptime results.
            var content = document.getElementById("divUptime");
            content.innerHTML = httpreq.responseText;

            //Store the new contents in the cache.
            bb_save_state ();
        }
    }

    //Opera needs "", not null, as a send()
    //parameter, else it fails.

    httpreq.send ("");
}

</script>

</HEAD>

<BODY onload="bb_init('divBody', true);">

<div id="divBody">

<b>Ajax Back Button Hack</b>
<div id="divUptime">
</div>

<form id="frm1">
<input
  type="button"
  id="btnGetUptime"
  value="Get Uptime"
  onClick="onClick_btnGetUptime();"
>
</form>

</div>

<!-- Invisible IFRAME required by bb_fix module: -->
<iframe
  name="bbFrame1"
  id="bbFrame1"
  width="0" height="0"
  style="visibility: hidden; inline: none;"
>
</iframe>
```

```
<!-- bbfix.js inserts debugging info here, if enabled: -->
<div id="divBBDebug">
</div>
</BODY>
</HTML>
```

Using *bbfix.js* requires just five steps:

1. Include the *bbfix.js* code in your web page, using a `script` tag.
2. Call the `bb_init( )` function in the page's `onLoad` event handler.
3. Specify a `div` tag encompassing the section of the page that will change when the back button is pressed.
4. Specify an `iframe` tag called `bbFrame1`, used by the *bbfix.js* module.
5. Include the `bb_save_state( )` function in your code where needed.

> An optional sixth step, adding a `div` tag called `divBBDebug`, can be included. This `div` tag displays useful information about the inner workings of *bbfix.js*.

Inside the Hack

This hack works by detecting when the back button is pressed, and then rolling back the web page to a previous state. Within your Ajax app, you determine these "rollback" points by calling `bb_save_state( )`.

Figure 9-1 shows what the web page looks like after the user clicks the Get Uptime button three times. Each button press gets a new uptime value from the server. The number always increases (such is the nature of time).

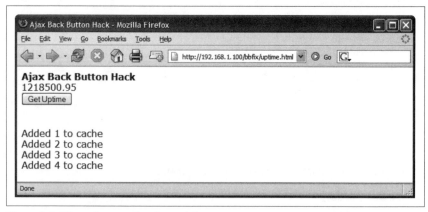

Figure 9-1. The web page after three updates

The bb_save_state( ) function stores a portion of the current web page into a JavaScript array. A global variable keeps track of the current index into that array. After saving the current state, the function then updates the contents of the hidden iframe bbFrame1. Updating the iframe is the hackish code piece that later lets us know when the back button has been pressed. The hidden iframe is updated by calling a very simple server-side script called *count.cgi*.* The sole function of this server script is to store the current array index. For array index 4, it will place this into the iframe:

```
<HTML>
<HEAD>
</HEAD>
<BODY onload='parent.bb_done_loading( );'>
<div id="divFrameCount">4</div>
</BODY>
</HTML>
```

The debugging information at the bottom of the page in Figure 9-1 shows that the cache has been updated via bb_save_state( ) four times (the initial state of the page is stored in the first cache entry).

The code calls the bb_init( ) function once, when the Ajax page is first loaded. Its most important job is to start up an interval timer. This timer fires off once a second, calling the function bb_check_state( ). This function detects if the back button has been pressed.

When the back button is pressed, the browser automatically rolls back the contents of the iframe to its previous state. The browser caches this state in its browser history. (If all browser versions consistently stored the rest of the page as well, there'd be no need for this hack.) When the interval timer fires, bb_check_state( ) looks at the index value stored in the iframe's tag. If it's changed, you know the back button has been pressed. You can use the contents of our own cache array to update the Ajax page.

Figure 9-2 shows *uptime.html* after the back button was pressed. Notice that the time is earlier than in Figure 9-1, proof that this data came from our cache, not the server. The debugging information at the bottom of the page bears this out. An iframe change was detected by bb_check_state( ), and the divBody tag was updated with the cached content.

---

* Using hidden iframes is a technique that predates the existence of XMLHttpRequest. A hidden iframe can be used to retrieve data from a server without a page refresh. Though not as elegant a solution as using XMLHttpRequest, in this application it has a big advantage: in all the major browsers (Safari 2.0 cannot run this hack correctly, however), changes to the iframe contents cause changes to the browser history.

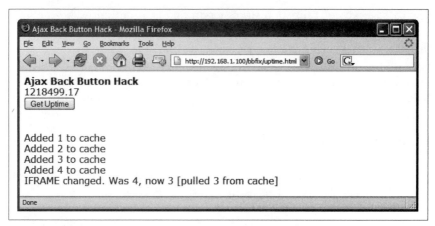

Figure 9-2. The page after the user has pressed the back button

Here is the code from *bbfix.js* that makes this work:

```
var bb_count = 0;
var bb_curr_idx = "";
var bb_cache = new Array;
var bb_debug = false;
var bb_iframe_script = "/cgi-bin/bbfix/count.cgi";
var bb_iframe_loaded = false;
var bb_target_div = "";

//If debug is enabled via bb_init(), then
//we append some data to the divTrail
//element.

function bb_debug_update (str) {
    if (bb_debug) {
        var divBBDebug = document.getElementById("divBBDebug");
        divBBDebug.innerHTML = divBBDebug.innerHTML + "<br>" + str;
    }
}

//Run from the interval timer (once a second),
//this function reads a cache index value
//stored in the DIV element of the child IFRAME.
//
//If this extracted cache index differs from the
//current cache index, then the back button was
//pressed. In this case, we pull the corresponding
//data from the cache and update the page.

function bb_check_state () {

    if (bb_iframe_loaded == false) {
        return;
```

```
    }

    var doc =  window.frames['bbFrame1'].document;
    var new_idx = doc.getElementById('divFrameCount').innerHTML;

    if (new_idx != bb_curr_idx) {

        var debug_msg = "IFRAME changed. Was "
                        + bb_curr_idx
                        + ", now "
                        + new_idx;

        //Pull a previous state from the cache (if it exists).

        if (bb_cache[new_idx]) {
            var divBody = document.getElementById("divBody");
            divBody.innerHTML = bb_cache[new_idx];

            debug_msg += " [pulled "
                        + new_idx
                        + " from cache]";
        }
        bb_curr_idx = new_idx;

        bb_debug_update (debug_msg);
    }
}

//Called by child IFRAME.

function bb_done_loading () {
    bb_iframe_loaded = true;
}

//Update the hidden IFRAME.

function bb_loadframe () {
    var bbFrame1 = document.getElementById("bbFrame1");
    bb_iframe_loaded = false;
    bbFrame1.src = bb_iframe_script + "?" + bb_count;
}

//When requested, save the current state
//in a cache.

function bb_save_state () {
    //Store the new contents in the cache.
    var div_to_cache = document.getElementById(bb_target_div);
    bb_count++;
    bb_cache[bb_count] = div_to_cache.innerHTML;

    bb_debug_update ("Added " + bb_count + " to cache");
```

```
    //Load the new page into the IFRAME.
    bb_loadframe ();

    bb_curr_idx = bb_count;
}

//Load the hidden IFRAME and start an interval timer.

function bb_init (div_name, debug_val) {
    bb_target_div = div_name;
    bb_debug = debug_val;

    bb_loadframe ();
    window.setInterval ('bb_check_state()', 1000);
    bb_save_state ();
}
```

Hacking the Hack

Using a server-side script to update the contents of the hidden iframe may seem kludgy. We can read and write values into the iframe with JavaScript and thereby avoid the need for the *count.cgi* script, but unfortunately, some versions of Firefox (through at least 1.0.7) set the domain of the iframe to null after the back button is pressed, and then refuse to let the parent page access the iframe contents.

As one kludge often leads to another, you may have also noticed that the server script calls a function in its onLoad event handler:

```
<BODY onload='parent.bb_done_loading();'>
```

While *count.cgi* is very simple, it does take some small amount of time to run. If the iframe hasn't yet updated when the next bb_check_state() timer is called, the function may become confused. You can avoid this by having the iframe let its parent know explicitly when loading is completed.

Hidden iframes are not the only approach to fixing the back button. As noted earlier, changing window.location works for some browsers, and for those browsers it's a simpler solution. You might even find a way to make it work with Internet Explorer as well.

—*Mark Pruett*

HACK
#69

Handle Bookmarks and Back Buttons with RSH

Use an open source JavaScript library that brings bookmarking and back button support to Ajax applications.

This hack introduces the Really Simple History (RSH) library, an open source framework that provides bookmarking and back-button solutions for

Ajax, and shows several working examples. It uses a hidden HTML form to initiate a large transient session cache of client-side information; this cache is robust against navigation to and away from the page. Second, a combination of hyperlink anchors and hidden iframes [Hack #68] can intercept and record browser history events, tying into the back and forward buttons. Both techniques are wrapped with a simple JavaScript library to ease development.

The Problem

Bookmarks and the back button work great for traditional multipage web applications. As users surf web sites, their browsers' location bars update with new URLs that can be pasted into emails or bookmarked for later use. The back and forward buttons also function correctly and shuffle users between the pages they have visited.

Ajax applications are unusual, however, in that they are sophisticated programs that live within a single web page. Browsers were not built for such beasts: they are trapped in the past, when web applications involved pulling in completely fresh pages on every mouse click.

In Ajax applications such as Gmail, the URL in the browser's location bar stays exactly the same as users select functions and change the application's state. Creating bookmarks for specific application views is impossible. Further, if users press their back buttons to "undo" previous actions, they will find to their surprise that the web pages they were looking at disappear, to be replaced with the last-visited (and completely different) pages.

The Solution

The Really Simple History framework solves these issues, bringing bookmarking and control over the back and forward buttons to Ajax applications. RSH is currently in beta and works with Firefox 1.0+, Netscape 7+, and Internet Explorer 6+; Safari is not currently supported (for an explanation, see the weblog entry "Coding in Paradise: Safari: No DHTML History Possible" at the following: *http://codinginparadise.org/weblog/2005/09/safari-no-dhtml-history-possible.html*).

Several Ajax frameworks currently exist to help with bookmarking and history issues; all of these frameworks, however, suffer from several important bugs due to their implementations (see "Coding in Paradise: Ajax History Libraries" *http://codinginparadise.org/weblog/2005/09/ajax-history-libraries.html* for details). Further, many Ajax history frameworks are monolithically bundled into larger libraries, such as Backbase (*http://www.backbase.com*) and the Dojo Toolkit (*http://www.dojotoolkit.org*). These frameworks introduce significantly different programming models for Ajax applications, forcing developers to adopt entirely new approaches to gain history functionality.

In contrast, RSH is a simple module that can be bundled with existing Ajax systems. Further, the Really Simple History library uses techniques to avoid the bugs that affect other history frameworks.

History Abstraction

The RSH framework consists of two JavaScript classes, named DhtmlHistory and HistoryStorage.

The DhtmlHistory class provides a history abstraction for Ajax applications. Ajax pages add( ) history events to the browser, specifying new locations and associated history data. The DhtmlHistory class updates the browser's current URL using an anchor hash, such as *#new-location*, and associates history data with this new URL. Ajax applications register themselves as history listeners, and as the user navigates with the back and forward buttons, history events are fired that provide the browser's new location and any history data that was persisted with an add( ) call.

The second class, named HistoryStorage, allows developers to store an arbitrary amount of saved history data. In normal pages, when a user navigates to a new web site the browser unloads and clears out all application and JavaScript state on the web page; if the user returns using the back button, all data is lost. The HistoryStorage class solves this problem through an API containing simple hash table methods such as put( ), get( ), and hasKey( ). These methods allow developers to store an arbitrary amount of data after the user has left a web page; when the user returns using the back button, the data can be accessed through the HistoryStorage class. You internally achieve this using a hidden form field, taking advantage of the fact that browsers auto-save the values in form fields even after a user has left the web page.

Example 1: Basic History

Let's jump right in with a simple example.

First, any page that wishes to use the Really Simple History framework must include the *dhtmlHistory.js* script:

```
<!-- Load the Really Simple History framework -->
<script type="text/javascript"
        src="../../framework/dhtmlHistory.js">
</script>
```

DHTML History applications must also include a special file named *blank. html* in the same directory as the Ajax web page; this file is bundled with the RSH framework, available at *http://codinginparadise.org/projects/dhtml_ history/latest.zip*, and is needed by IE. As a side note, RSH uses a hidden `iframe` to track and add history changes in Internet Explorer. This `iframe` requires that you point to a real location for the functionality to work correctly; hence *blank.html*.

The RSH framework creates a global object named `dhtmlHistory` that is the entry point for manipulating the browser's history. The first step in working with `dhtmlHistory` is to initialize the object after the page has finished loading:

```
window.onload = initialize;
function initialize() {
    //initialize the DHTML History
    //framework
    dhtmlHistory.initialize();
```

 dhtmlHistory is the global variable name; DhtmlHistory is the object name.

Next, you can use the `dhtmlHistory.addListener()` method to subscribe to history change events:

```
window.onload = initialize;
function initialize() {
    //initialize the DHTML History
    //framework
    dhtmlHistory.initialize();

    //subscribe to DHTML history change
    //events
    dhtmlHistory.addListener(historyChange);
```

This method takes a single JavaScript callback function that receives two arguments when a DHTML history change event occurs: the new location of the page and any optional history data that might be associated with this event.

The `historyChange()` method is straightforward. It consists of a function that receives the `newLocation` after a user has navigated to a new location, as well as any optional `historyData` that was associated with the event:

```
/* Our callback to receive history change
events. */
function historyChange(newLocation,
                       historyData) {
```

```
debug("A history change has occurred: "
    + "newLocation="+newLocation
    + ", historyData="+historyData,
    true);
}
```

The debug( ) method used above is a utility function defined in the example's source file, which is bundled with the full example download for this hack at the following: *http://www.onjava.com/onjava/2005/10/26/examples/downloads/examples.zip*. debug( ) simply prints a message into the web page; the second Boolean argument, true in the code above, controls whether all pre-existing messages are cleared before the new debug message is printed.

As described earlier, you can add history events using the add( ) method. Adding a history event involves specifying a new location for the history change, such as *edit:SomePage*, as well as providing an optional historyData value that is stored with this event.

Browsers allow JavaScript to change the URL in the location bar only by appending an anchor to the end of the current location; for example, if I was at *http://codinginparadise.org/test.html*, the JavaScript could append *#someAnchor* to the end of the URL in the location bar, resulting in *http://codinginparadise.org/test.html#someAnchor*. We use this capability in the RSH library to save bookmarkable state; the *edit:SomePage* location above is what is added to the end of the URL: *http://codinginparadise.org/test.html#edit:SomePage*.

Here's the code:

```
window.onload = initialize;
function initialize( ) {
    //initialize the DHTML History
    //framework
    dhtmlHistory.initialize( );

    //subscribe to DHTML history change
    //events
    dhtmlHistory.addListener(historyChange);

    //if this is the first time we have
    //loaded the page...
    if (dhtmlHistory.isFirstLoad( )) {
        debug("Adding values to browser "
                + "history", false);
        //start adding history
        dhtmlHistory.add("helloworld",
                        "Hello World Data");
        dhtmlHistory.add("foobar", 33);
        dhtmlHistory.add("boobah", true);
```

```
var complexObject = new Object( );
complexObject.value1 =
        "This is the first value";
complexObject.value2 =
        "This is the second data";
complexObject.value3 = new Array( );
complexObject.value3[0] = "array 1";
complexObject.value3[1] = "array 2";

dhtmlHistory.add("complexObject",
                  complexObject);
```

Immediately after add( ) is called, the new location is shown to the user in the browser's location bar as an anchor value. For example, after calling dhtmlHistory.add("helloworld", "Hello World Data") for an Ajax web page that lives at *http://codinginparadise.org/my_ajax_app*, the user sees the following in the browser's location bar: *http://codinginparadise.org/my_ajax_app#helloworld*.

The user can then bookmark this page; if the bookmark is used later, your Ajax application can read the *#helloworld* value and use it to initialize the web page, based on the meaning the application attributes to the hash-marked value. Location values after the hash are URL encoded and decoded transparently by the RSH framework.

historyData is useful for saving more complicated state with an Ajax location change than what can easily fit on the end of a URL. It is an optional value that can be any JavaScript type, such as a number, string, or object. One example use of historyData is to save all of the text in a rich text editor, for example, if the user navigates away from the page. When the user navigates back to this location, the browser returns the object to the history change listener.

Developers can provide a full JavaScript object for historyData, with nested objects and arrays representing complex state; whatever JavaScript Object Notation allows is allowed in the history data, including simple data types and the null type. References to DOM objects and scriptable browser objects such as XMLHttpRequest, however, are not saved. Note that historyData is not persisted with bookmarks and disappears if the browser is closed, if the browser's cache is cleared, or if the user erases the browser's history.

The last step in working with dhtmlHistory is using the isFirstLoad( ) method. In some browsers, if you navigate to a web page, jump to a different page, and then press the back button to return to the initial site, the first page completely reloads and fires an onload event. This can create havoc with code that wants to initialize the page in a certain way the first time it loads, but not on subsequent reloads. The isFirstLoad( ) method makes it possible to differentiate between the very first time a web page is loaded versus a false load event fired if the user navigates back to a saved web page in the browser's history.

In the following example code, we want to add history events only the first time a page loads. If the user presses the back button to return to the page after browsing to a different site, we do not want to re-add all the history events:

```
window.onload = initialize;

function initialize( ) {
    //initialize the DHTML History
    //framework
    dhtmlHistory.initialize( );

    //subscribe to DHTML history change
    //events
    dhtmlHistory.addListener(historyChange);

    //if this is the first time we have
    //loaded the page...
    if (dhtmlHistory.isFirstLoad( )) {
        debug("Adding values to browser "
            + "history", false);
        //start adding history
        dhtmlHistory.add("helloworld",
                        "Hello World Data");
        dhtmlHistory.add("foobar", 33);
        dhtmlHistory.add("boobah", true);

        var complexObject = new Object( );
        complexObject.value1 =
                "This is the first value";
        complexObject.value2 =
                "This is the second data";
        complexObject.value3 = new Array( );
        complexObject.value3[0] = "array 1";
        complexObject.value3[1] = "array 2";

        dhtmlHistory.add("complexObject",
                        complexObject);
```

Let's move on to using the historyStorage class. Like dhtmlHistory, historyStorage exposes its functionality through a single global object named historyStorage. This object has several methods that simulate a hash table, such as put(keyName, keyValue), get(keyName), and hasKey(keyName). Key names must be strings, while key values can be sophisticated JavaScript objects or even strings filled with XML. In our example source code, we put( ) simple XML into historyStorage the first time the page is loaded:

```
window.onload = initialize;

function initialize( ) {
    //initialize the DHTML History
    //framework
    dhtmlHistory.initialize( );

    //subscribe to DHTML history change
    //events
    dhtmlHistory.addListener(historyChange);

    //if this is the first time we have
    //loaded the page...
    if (dhtmlHistory.isFirstLoad( )) {
        debug("Adding values to browser "
            + "history", false);
        //start adding history
        dhtmlHistory.add("helloworld",
                        "Hello World Data");
        dhtmlHistory.add("foobar", 33);
        dhtmlHistory.add("boobah", true);

        var complexObject = new Object( );
        complexObject.value1 =
                "This is the first value";
        complexObject.value2 =
                "This is the second data";
        complexObject.value3 = new Array( );
        complexObject.value3[0] = "array 1";
        complexObject.value3[1] = "array 2";

        dhtmlHistory.add("complexObject",
                        complexObject);

        //cache some values in the history
        //storage
        debug("Storing key 'fakeXML' into "
            + "history storage", false);
        var fakeXML =
                '<?xml version="1.0" '
            +       'encoding="ISO-8859-1"?>'
            +       '<foobar>'
            +           '<foo-entry/>'
            +       '</foobar>';
        historyStorage.put("fakeXML", fakeXML);
    }
```

Afterwards, if the user navigates away from the page and then returns via the back button, we can extract our stored value using the get( ) method or check for its existence using hasKey( ):

```
window.onload = initialize;

function initialize( ) {
    //initialize the DHTML History
    //framework
    dhtmlHistory.initialize( );

    //subscribe to DHTML history change
    //events
    dhtmlHistory.addListener(historyChange);

    //if this is the first time we have
    //loaded the page...
    if (dhtmlHistory.isFirstLoad( )) {
        debug("Adding values to browser "
              + "history", false);
        //start adding history
        dhtmlHistory.add("helloworld",
                        "Hello World Data");
        dhtmlHistory.add("foobar", 33);
        dhtmlHistory.add("boobah", true);

        var complexObject = new Object( );
        complexObject.value1 =
              "This is the first value";
        complexObject.value2 =
              "This is the second data";
        complexObject.value3 = new Array( );
        complexObject.value3[0] = "array 1";
        complexObject.value3[1] = "array 2";

        dhtmlHistory.add("complexObject",
                        complexObject);

        //cache some values in the history
        //storage
        debug("Storing key 'fakeXML' into "
              + "history storage", false);
        var fakeXML =
              '<?xml version="1.0" '
            +     'encoding="ISO-8859-1"?>'
            +     '<foobar>'
            +     '<foo-entry/>'
            +     '</foobar>';
        historyStorage.put("fakeXML", fakeXML);
    }

    //retrieve our values from the history
```

```
        //storage
        var savedXML =
                historyStorage.get("fakeXML");
        savedXML = prettyPrintXml(savedXML);
        var hasKey =
                historyStorage.hasKey("fakeXML");
        var message =
                "historyStorage.hasKey('fakeXML')="
                + hasKey + "<br>"
                + "historyStorage.get('fakeXML')=<br>"
                + savedXML;
        debug(message, false);
    }
```

prettyPrintXml( ) is a utility method defined in the full example source code, available at *http://www.onjava.com/onjava/2005/10/26/examples/downloads/ examples.zip*; this function prepares the simple XML to be displayed to the web page for debugging.

Note that data is persisted only in terms of this page's history; if the browser is closed, or if the user opens a new window and types in the Ajax application's address again, this history data is not available to the new web page. History data is persisted only in terms of the back and forward buttons and disappears when the user closes the browser or clears the cache.

Example 2: O'Reilly Mail

Our second example is a simple fake Ajax email application named O'Reilly Mail, similar to Gmail. O'Reilly Mail illustrates how to control the browser's history using the dhtmlHistory class and how to cache history data using the historyStorage object.

The O'Reilly Mail user interface has two pieces. On the left side of the page is a menu with different email folders and options, such as Inbox, Drafts, and so on. When a user selects a menu item, such as Inbox, we update the right side of the page is updated with this menu item's contents. In a real application, we would remotely fetch and display the selected mailbox's contents; in O'Reilly Mail, however, we simply display the option that was selected.

O'Reilly Mail uses the Really Simple History framework to add menu changes to the browser's history and update the location bar, allowing users to bookmark different views in the application and to jump to previous menu changes using the browser's back and forward buttons.

We'll add one special menu option, Address Book, to illustrate how historyStorage might be used. The address book is a JavaScript array of contact names and email addresses. In a real application, we would fetch this data from a remote server. In O'Reilly Mail, however, we create this array locally, add a few names and email addresses, and then store it into the historyStorage object. If the user leaves the web page and then returns, the O'Reilly Mail application retrieves the address book from the cache rather than having to contact the remote server again.

The address book is stored and retrieved in our initialize( ) method:

```
/* Our function that initializes when the page
is finished loading. */
function initialize( ) {
    //initialize the DHTML History framework
    dhtmlHistory.initialize( );

    //add ourselves as a DHTML History listener
    dhtmlHistory.addListener(handleHistoryChange);

    //if we haven't retrieved the address book
    //yet, grab it and then cache it into our
    //history storage
    if (window.addressBook == undefined) {
        //Store the address book as a global
        //object.
        //In a real application we would remotely
        //fetch this from a server in the
        //background.
        window.addressBook =
                ["Brad Neuberg 'bkn3@columbia.edu'",
                 "John Doe 'johndoe@example.com'",
                 "Deanna Neuberg 'mom@mom.com'"];

        //cache the address book so it exists
        //even if the user leaves the page and
        //then returns with the back button
        historyStorage.put("addressBook",
                            addressBook);
    } else {
        //fetch the cached address book from
        //the history storage
        window.addressBook =
                historyStorage.get("addressBook");
    }
```

The code to handle history changes is also straightforward. The following source calls handleHistoryChange( ) when the user presses the back or forward button. We take the newLocation and use it to update our user interface to the correct state, using a utility method O'Reilly Mail defines named displayLocation:

```
/* Handles history change events. */
function handleHistoryChange(newLocation,
                             historyData) {
```

```
//if there is no location then display
//the default, which is the inbox
if (newLocation == "") {
    newLocation = "section:inbox";
}

//extract the section to display from
//the location change; newLocation will
//begin with the word "section:"
newLocation =
        newLocation.replace(/section\:/, "");

//update the browser to respond to this
//DHTML history change
displayLocation(newLocation, historyData);
}

/* Displays the given location in the
right-hand-side content area. */
function displayLocation(newLocation,
                         sectionData) {
    //get the menu element that was selected
    var selectedElement =
            document.getElementById(newLocation);

    //clear out the old selected menu item
    var menu = document.getElementById("menu");
    for (var i = 0; i < menu.childNodes.length;
            i++) {
        var currentElement = menu.childNodes[i];
        //see if this is a DOM Element node
        if (currentElement.nodeType == 1) {
            //clear any class name
            currentElement.className = "";
        }
    }

    //cause the new selected menu item to
    //appear differently in the UI
    selectedElement.className = "selected";

    //display the new section in the right-hand
    //side of the screen; determine what
    //our sectionData is

    //display the address book differently by
    //using our local address data we cached
    //earlier
    if (newLocation == "addressbook") {
        //format and display the address book
        sectionData = "<p>Your addressbook:</p>";
        sectionData += "<ul>";
```

```
        //fetch the address book from the cache
        //if we don't have it yet
        if (window.addressBook == undefined) {
            window.addressBook =
                    historyStorage.get("addressBook");
        }

        //format the address book for display
        for (var i = 0;
                i < window.addressBook.length;
                i++) {
            sectionData += "<li>"
                        + window.addressBook[i]
                        + "</li>";
        }

        sectionData += "</ul>";
    }

    //If there is no sectionData, then
    //remotely retrieve it; in this example
    //we use fake data for everything but the
    //address book
    if (sectionData == null) {
        //in a real application we would remotely
        //fetch this section's content
        sectionData = "<p>This is section: "
                    + selectedElement.innerHTML + "</p>";
    }

    //update the content's title and main text
    var contentTitle =
            document.getElementById("content-title");
    var contentValue =
            document.getElementById("content-value");
    contentTitle.innerHTML =
            selectedElement.innerHTML;
    contentValue.innerHTML = sectionData;
}
```

Resources

You can download all the sample code for this hack from *http://www.onjava.
com/onjava/2005/10/26/examples/downloads/examples.zip,* and you can download the RSH framework from *http://codinginparadise.org/projects/dhtml_
history/latest.zip.*

Also, you can follow new developments in the RSH library at the framework author's web site, *http://codinginparadise.org.*

—*Brad Neuberg*

Set a Time Limit for the HTTP Request

HACK #70 Display a helpful message after a specified period of time if the XMLHttpRequest request has not succeeded.

The XMLHttpRequest object opens up a whole new bevy of exceptions that JavaScript programs can raise, having to do with the failure to connect successfully with the server. Why might this occur? Network latency might be the problem, or there might be something wrong with the server. You have no idea how fast your users' connections are, and the server-side program itself may be bogged down handling numerous simultaneous requests, or broken altogether. At any rate, as a developer, you want some control over how long your users wait for your application to respond. As we all know, chances are they won't be willing to wait very long—a delay of much more than a few seconds is often considered unacceptable.

This hack waits 10 seconds for the server to respond before it displays a friendly message to the user.

Make it 5 seconds or less if you prefer, or 60. The maximum tolerable wait depends on the nature of your application, the results of your user testing, and other factors. For example, a customer from the general public might expect a more peppy application and be less willing to wait than an intranet user who is highly dependent on and invested in the application.

The hack uses the JavaScript method of the top-level window object named setTimeout( ).

Thanks to Joshua Gitlin and his article at *http://www.xml.com/ pub/a/2005/05/11/ajax-error.html* for hints on this technique.

You can use window object methods without qualifying them with the window object. In other words, using setTimeout( ) alone works as well as using window.setTimeout( ).

setTimeout( ) takes a function name or literal as the first argument, then the number of milliseconds (1,000 per second) to wait before calling the method. It returns a numerical value that can be used to cancel the function call. I'll show you that in a moment; in the meantime, here is the code for *http_request.js*, which encapsulates the initialization and use of XMLHttpRequest. (See "Use Your Own Library for XMLHttpRequest" [Hack #3] for a comprehensive explanation.) Here is the the code, retrofitted to include setTimeout( ) and a new function, timesUp( ):

```
var request = null;
var timeoutId;
/* Wrapper function for constructing a request object.
 Parameters:
  reqType: The HTTP request type, such as GET or POST.
  url: The URL of the server program.
  asynch: Whether to send the request asynchronously or not.
  respHandle: The name of the function that will handle the response.
  Any fifth parameters represented as arguments[4] are the data a
  POST request is designed to send. */
function httpRequest(reqType,url,asynch,respHandle){
    //Mozilla-based browsers
    if(window.XMLHttpRequest){
        request = new XMLHttpRequest( );
    } else if (window.ActiveXObject){
        request=new ActiveXObject("Msxml2.XMLHTTP");
        if (! request){
            request=new ActiveXObject("Microsoft.XMLHTTP");
        }
    }
    //We test for a null request
    //if neither ActiveXObject was initialized
    if(request) {
        //If the reqType parameter is POST, then the
        //5th argument to the function is the POSTed data
        if(reqType.toLowerCase( ) != "post") {
            initReq(reqType,url,asynch,respHandle);
        } else {
            //the POSTed data
            var args = arguments[4];
            if(args != null && args.length > 0){
                initReq(reqType,url,asynch,respHandle,args);
            }
        }
    } else {
        alert("Your browser does not permit the use of all "+
            "of this application's features!");
    }
}
/* Initialize a request object that is already constructed */
function initReq(reqType,url,bool,respHandle){
    try{
        /* Specify the function that will handle the HTTP response */
        request.onreadystatechange=respHandle;
        request.open(reqType,url,bool);
        timeoutId = setTimeout(timesUp,10000);
        //If the reqType parameter is POST, then the
        //5th argument to the function is the POSTed data
        if(reqType.toLowerCase( ) == "post") {
            request.setRequestHeader("Content-Type",
```

```
                    "application/x-www-form-urlencoded; charset=UTF-8");
            request.send(arguments[4]);
        } else {
            request.send(null);
        }

    } catch (errv) {
        alert(
                "The application cannot contact "+
                "the server at the moment. "+
                "Please try again in a few seconds.\n"+
                "Error detail: "+errv.message);
    }
}
function timesUp(){
//see below...
```

The request.open() method prepares the XMLHttpRequest object for making an HTTP connection. Then the code calls setTimeout() just before the request is sent. Here's the rest of the code:

```
/* Event handler for XMLHttpRequest; this function
is not a part of http_request.js, but would be defined
in another code file that is using http_request.js, as in
httpRequest("GET",url,true,handleReq);  */
function handleReq(){
    if(request.readyState == 4){
        //timeoutId is declared in http_request.js
        //but can be referenced as a global var here
        clearTimeout(timeoutId);
            if(request.status == 200){
                //do cool stuff...
            }
    }//end outer if
}
function timesUp(){
    request.abort();
    alert("A problem occurred with communicating with "+
        "the server program. Please make sure you are connected "+
        "to the Internet and try again in a few moments.");
}
```

Recall that setTimeout() calls the timesUp() function in 10 seconds. If 10 seconds pass without request.readyState == 4 returning true (meaning that the HTTP request is complete), which clears the timeout, timesUp() aborts the request and displays an alert window to the user. This action stops the request; the user will have to restart the interaction with the application to launch another request.

If you want to make the timeout three seconds instead, for example, the setup code looks like:

```
timeoutId = setTimeout(timesUp,3000);
```

If the HTTP request completes its network journey without a hitch, the code calls `clearTimeout( )` with the aforementioned `timeoutId` as its parameter. This action cancels the call to `timesUp( )` just in time, allowing the application to go on its merry way doing its intended job.

HACK #71 Improve Maintainability, Performance, and Reliability for Large JavaScript Applications

Discover options for improving the maintainability, performance, and reliability of Ajax applications that have a large amount of JavaScript code.

Most Ajax applications contain far more JavaScript than typical web pages. The total amount of JavaScript in an Ajax app can easily exceed three or four hundred kilobytes, segmented across many separate files. Making sure these files are easy to maintain while also ensuring that they download quickly is very important. In addition, some browsers have bugs that manifest when new releases of JavaScript files are pushed out, hindering the reliability of large-scale JavaScript applications.

This hack presents techniques for compressing JavaScript files without sacrificing readable, maintainable code; improving page load times when dealing with many JavaScript files; and increasing the reliability of pushing out new versions of your JavaScript applications to web browsers.

It explains three techniques:

- Merging all JavaScript files into a single file
- Running your JavaScript through a compression tool
- Solving JavaScript caching issues

bash shell commands are used to implement these techniques. These bash shell commands are meant to be run as part of a large-scale JavaScript application's build process, before pushing the code to a production or development server. In your own application, you could choose to use other build tools to implement these techniques, such as Ant, Make, or Rake.

If you are on Windows and wish to use the bash shell commands in this hack, download the free, open source Cygwin package from *http://www. cygwin.com*. Having Cygwin installed on Windows is an absolute must for serious Ajax and web development.

Merging All JavaScript Files into a Single File

A typical, large-scale Ajax application incorporates many separate JavaScript files. Some files will be third-party frameworks and libraries that ease development, while others will be portions of the application that have been segmented into different files to ease development and maintenance. Due to network latency, in many Ajax applications a significant amount of time can be required for the browser to fetch all of these JavaScript files.

One way to minimize page load times is to simply concatenate all of the individual JavaScript files into a single JavaScript file before pushing your application to production. This has been found to have a drastic effect on the startup performance of many Ajax applications.

To merge a series of JavaScript files into a single file named *all.js*, for example, you can run the following bash shell commands:

```
cat script1.js \
    script2.js \
    script3.js \
    > all.js
```

 cat is a shell command for creating, viewing, and concatenating files.

You should typically not use a wildcard when merging your JavaScript files because the ordering of the merged files will be unknown. Most JavaScript files have dependencies and must usually be loaded in a certain order. For example, if your application is using the Prototype or Dojo Toolkit frameworks, you should merge those together first:

```
cat dojo.js \
    prototype.js \
    myScript.js
all.js
```

Once you have merged the files, in your main application's HTML page, simply load the *all.js* file:

```
<!-- Our merged JavaScript -->
<script src="all.js"></script>
```

If you keep a commented-out code block that loads each individual file separately, you can simply uncomment this while commenting out the *all.js* script load to ease debugging if errors arise:

```
<!-- Our merged JavaScript -->
<!-- <script src="all.js"></script> -->
```

```
<!-- Individual JavaScript files; useful for debugging. -->
<script src="dojo.js"></script>
<script src="prototype.js"></script>
<script src="myScript.js"></script>
```

When you are finished debugging, uncomment the *all.js* script load and recomment the loading of the individual files:

```
<!-- Our merged JavaScript -->
<script src="all.js"></script>

<!-- Individual JavaScript files; useful for debugging. -->
<!--
<script src="dojo.js"></script>
<script src="prototype.js"></script>
<script src="myScript.js"></script>
-->
```

> Make sure that the last line of each file has an extra carriage
> return, or the merged JavaScript files may overlap in ways
> that can cause errors.

Running Your JavaScript Through a Compression Tool

Traditionally, programmers have been faced with two options when designing JavaScript-heavy DHTML applications: they can either write extremely terse code with no comments, in order to minimize the size of their files; or they can choose to segment their JavaScript across several files, with descriptive method names and ample source comments.

In the past, programmers had to make a decision between small JavaScript file sizes and improved ease of maintenance and readability of the code. Most programmers chose smaller file sizes, leading to nightmare code that was unreadable and difficult to scale to larger applications.

This hack removes the need to compromise: you can write your application with descriptive source comments and fully object-oriented methods, and an open source JavaScript compression tool from the Dojo Toolkit (*http://www. dojotoolkit.org*) will strip out all comments and fully compress your code.

The Dojo Toolkit has created a full open source JavaScript compression tool based on the Mozilla Foundation's Rhino JavaScript parser. Commercial companies can use this compression tool freely. Full documentation on the Dojo compressor is available at *http://www.dojotoolkit.org/docs/compressor_system.html*.

To use the Dojo compressor in your own system, first download and install the Java JDK 1.4+ on the machine you will use for compression (if necessary). Next, download the compression tool from *http://www.dojotoolkit.*

org/svn/dojo/trunk/buildscripts/lib/custom_rhino.jar, and save it to your hard disk. Once you have merged your JavaScript files, as described earlier in the section "Merging All JavaScript Files into a Single File," run the following command:

```
java -jar custom_rhino.jar -c all.js > all_compress.js 2>&1
mv all_compress.js all.js
```

If you look at the *all.js* file, you will see that the file size has been considerably reduced.

The Dojo Toolkit and the JavaScript compressor are currently in beta, and the generated compressed code can cause an error in some rare cases, such as when using JavaScript closures combined with certain styles of object-oriented JavaScript programming. If you find that you are getting JavaScript errors after compressing your JavaScript, go into the original premerged, precompressed source code and slightly rewrite the line of code on which you received the error. This usually fixes the problem.

Solving JavaScript Caching Issues

The final major technique for improving large-scale JavaScript applications concerns caching. Internet Explorer currently has a serious bug in which cached versions of JavaScript files are used even if the server has newer versions. If the HTML page references JavaScript functions that are not included in the older files in the cache, users will see Internet Explorer's script error dialog and experience a broken application.

In the past, this bug was often encountered when rapid iterations of an Ajax application were pushed out, forcing users to know either how to manually clear the browser cache or to press Ctrl and click the Refresh icon to force the browser to grab the file from the server. Neither method is user-friendly or reliable enough.

The secret to solving the caching bug in Internet Explorer is to trick the browser into encoding a version into the filename:

```
<script src="all.js?version=1"></script>
```

Internet Explorer will "see" the filename of this JavaScript file as *all.js?version=1*. If you then created a new version of *all.js*, you could simply increment the version number:

```
<script src="all.js?version=2"></script>
```

To Internet Explorer, these are two different JavaScript files. The version parameter doesn't affect the JavaScript file's execution, but it tricks the caching system into correctly loading any newer versions of affected JavaScript files.

Hand-editing these values can get tedious quickly. One possible workaround is to introduce a token into your HTML (or JSP, PHP, etc.) files that holds the current version. In the following code, the token version= is used, starting with an initial version of 1:

```
<script language="JavaScript" src="./scripts/all.js?version=1"></script>

<!-- Uncomment when debugging -->
<!--
<script language="JavaScript" src="./scripts/script1.js?version=1"></script>
<script language="JavaScript" src="./scripts/script2.js?version=1"></script>
-->
```

You then create a bash shell script that can load our HTML, JSP, and other files, grab the current value after version= and increment its value, and then rewrite it into the files:

```
export HTML_FILE=$SRC/sample.html
# Any file that wishes to use this must have the following magic
# token, version=######, that we read in, increment,
# and then write back out. Internet Explorer incorrectly
# caches JavaScript files even if they have changed,
# causing versioning issues when new ones are pushed out;
# this solves this problem.

# read in the current version
oldVersion=`grep -o \version=[0-9]* $HTML_FILE | tail -n 1 |
sed "s/version=//"`

# increment the value
newVersion=$(( oldVersion + 1))

# write the new version back out into the file
sed "s/version=$oldVersion/version=$newVersion/" $HTML_FILE >
$HTML_FILE.new

mv $HTML_FILE.new $HTML_FILE
```

Your files will now always increment when you push out a new version of the JavaScript file, solving the caching issues in Internet Explorer.

> This technique can be implemented in other ways, such as using an application-scope JavaServer Pages variable that is dynamically written into your JSPs, rather than using bash shell scripts.

All Together

These three techniques are normally used together during the build phase of a project, so putting them into a single shell script makes sense. The following bash shell script can achieve all three together:

```bash
#!/bin/bash

# Performance booster for page load time; we bring all of the JavaScripts into
# one file, which prevents having to fetch each JavaScript file individually,
# which can be the number one impact on page load performance for Ajax apps.
# Then, we compress the final JavaScript file to reduce its size.
# We also use a technique to solve Internet Explorer's JavaScript cache bugs.
#
# @author, Brad Neuberg, bkn3@columbia.edu
# This script is under a BSD license and is freely usable

export SRC=./demo/compress
export SCRIPTS=$SRC/scripts
export HTML_FILE=$SRC/sample.html

rm -fr dist
mkdir dist

# Any file that wishes to use this must have the following magic
# token, version=######, that we read in, increment, and then
# write back out. Internet Explorer incorrectly caches JavaScript
# files even if they have changed, causing versioning issues when
# new ones are pushed out; this solves this problem.

# read in the current version
oldVersion=`grep -o \version=[0-9]* $HTML_FILE | tail -n 1 | sed "s/version=//"`

# increment the value
newVersion=$(( oldVersion + 1))

# write the new version back out into the file
sed "s/version=$oldVersion/version=$newVersion/" $HTML_FILE > $HTML_FILE.new

mv $HTML_FILE.new $HTML_FILE

# concatenate all code into one file
cat $SCRIPTS/script1.js \
    $SCRIPTS/script2.js \
    > dist/all.js

# now compress it
java -jar bin/compress.jar -c dist/all.js > dist/all_compress.js 2>&1
```

```
# install it
cp dist/all_compress.js $SCRIPTS/all.js

# clean up
rm -fr dist
```

You have to tailor this script for your own application. Change the SRC variable to point to the directory where you keep all of your application's source files, change SCRIPTS to point to the directory in SRC in which you hold your JavaScript, and change HTML_FILE to point to the HTML file that loads your JavaScript. You must also edit the section that merges the JavaScript files so that your JavaScript files are loaded in the correct order.

—Brad Neuberg

HACK #72 Obfuscate JavaScript and Ajax Code

Use a free application to obfuscate or hide Ajax source code.

Some companies or developers do not want to expose their JavaScript source code for anyone to cut, paste, and reuse. They want to make the code more difficult, if not exactly impossible, to reverse engineer. As we all know, it is very easy to look at the JavaScript source code for a web page by choosing the View → View Source (in Safari) or View → Page Source (in Firefox) command from the browser menu, or by requesting the URL for any *.js* file that the page imports.

However, development teams generally do not want to give away code that represents a big investment or a cool new proprietary technology. To this end, free-of-charge and commercial software is available to make the source code very difficult to read, but still work for your application in the browser. These programs are called *code obfuscators*.

> Software is also available for altering the code to make its download footprint smaller. This hack focuses on obfuscation, which effectively reduces the byte-size of the downloaded code as well. Many code obfuscators provide this feature.

Go to a search engine such as Google, and type in "JavaScript obfuscators," and you'll get a load of links for this kind of software. The software used in this hack, JavaScript Chaos Edition (JCE), is available from a company in Stockholm, Sweden named Syntropy Development. This hack uses a free version of Syntropy's commercial product, which is a Java program distributed as a Java Archive (JAR) file. You can download it from *http://www.syntropy.se/?ct=downloads*.

JCE is very easy to use. Simply launch the JAR file by typing `java -jar jce.jar` at a command-line prompt. This command generates a GUI application, which Figure 9-3 shows.

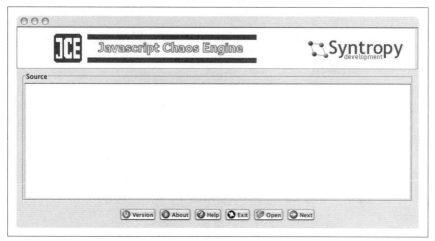

Figure 9-3. The JCE obfuscator GUI

Take the JavaScript or HTML that you want to obfuscate (this hack obfuscates only the JavaScript), and paste it into the main window. Then click the Next button to display another screen that lets you choose which functions and variables to obfuscate. Figure 9-4 shows this screen.

"Obfuscation" in this program means that the functions will be given truncated, nonsensical names, such as vH. You can choose to obfuscate all the functions and variables, to remove comments and/or linefeeds, and to use short identifiers. You then paste the altered code into a new file for your HTML to import.

> If any HTML element attributes contain JavaScript function calls (as in `onsubmit="myfunc(obj)"`, you have to ensure that the attributes use the new obfuscated function names. You'll have to make these changes in the HTML source code by hand, if you are just using this tool to obfuscate the imported JavaScript file.

The result is meaningless function and variable names mushed together into one giant line. The altered code by no means represents a heavy-duty security measure like encryption; it just generates code that is somewhat *harder* to crack and analyze for its functionality. At the very least, a large, nontrivial JavaScript program that has been obfuscated poses a major headache to pick apart.

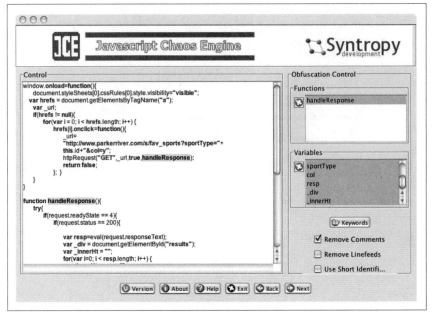

Figure 9-4. Scrambled code and home fries

Another problem that can arise from obfuscation is that sometimes the obfuscator changes the name of an object property inside your JavaScript code, such as the XMLHttpRequest object's onreadystatechange event handler. In this case, you have to hunt through the altered code to make the change back to the correct name, or the XMLHttpRequest object will not function properly.

Another *limitation* (rather than a problem) with obfuscation is that you cannot alter the URLs that are targeted by the XMLHttpRequest object. You have to rely on server-side security strategies to protect these URLs from unauthorized use.

Here is some JavaScript code for dynamic message generation. The actual code function does not matter here; we're just showing the before and after effects of obfuscation. Here's the "before" code:

```
var request,timeoutId;
function eMsg(msg,sColor){
    var div = document.getElementById("message");
    div.style.color=sColor;
    div.style.fontSize="0.9em";
    //remove old messages
    div.innerHTML="";
```

```
        div.appendChild(document.createTextNode(msg));

}
function checkIt(val){

    if (val.length < 3) {eMsg(
            "Please enter a valid value for the user name","red")
    }
    else{
        url="http://10.0.1.2:8080/parkerriver/s/checker?email=
                "+encodeURIComponent(val);
        httpRequest("GET",url);
    }
}
function httpRequest(reqType,url){
    //Mozilla-based browsers
    if(window.XMLHttpRequest){
        request = new XMLHttpRequest();
        request.onreadystatechange=handleCheck;
        request.open(reqType,url,true);
        timeoutId = setTimeout(timesUp,10000);
        request.send(null);

    }
    //for Internet Explorer
    else if (window.ActiveXObject){
        request=new ActiveXObject("Microsoft.XMLHTTP");
        if(request){
            request.onreadystatechange=handleCheck;
            request.open(reqType,url,true);
            timeoutId = setTimeout(timesUp,10000);
            request.send(null);
        }
    }
}
//event handler for XMLHttpRequest
function handleCheck(){
    var usedTag,msg, answer,xmlReturnVal;
    if(request.readyState == 4){
        clearTimeout(timeoutId);
        if(request.status == 200){
            //Implement Document object in DOM
            //last 15-20 code lines snipped for brevity...
```

And here's the code after scrambling it with the obfuscator:

```
<!-- This script has been obfuscated with Syntropy's JCE - Javascript
Chaos Engine which can be downloaded at http://www.syntropy.se. JCE is
free to use if this comment is not removed. -->

var dk,DS;function pv(Sg,IF){var Ug =
document.getElementById("message");Ug.style.color=IF;Ug.style.fontSize=
"0.9em";Ug.innerHTML="";Ug.appendChild(document.createTextNode(Sg));}
```

```
function jA(vX){if (vX.length < 3) {pv(;"Please enter a valid value
for the user name","red")}else{hp="http:;"+encodeURIComponent(vX);
eo("GET",hp);}}function eo(vh,hp){if(window.XMLHttpRequest){dk =
new XMLHttpRequest();dk.lg=PS;dk.open(vh,hp,true);DS = setTimeout(eR,10000);
dk.send(null);}else if (window.ActiveXObject){dk=new ActiveXObject
("Microsoft.XMLHTTP");if(dk){dk.lg=PS;dk.open(vh,hp,true);DS =
setTimeout(eR,10000);dk.send(null);}}}function PS(){var Yj,Sg,
wL,oY;if(dk.readyState == 4){clearTimeout(DS);if(dk.status == 200){oY =
dk.responseXML;Yj = oY.getElementsByTagName(;"is_used")[0];wL=
Yj.childNodes[0].data;if(wL==true){ pv(;"The user name you have chosen
is not available. "+"Kindly try again. ","red");  }else { pv("Your new user
name has been saved.","blue"); }} else {alert("A problem occurred with
communicating between "+"the XMLHttpRequest object and the server
program.");}}}function eR(){dk.abort();alert("A problem occurred with
communicating with "+"the server program.");}
```

As you can see, the resulting code is not eye-friendly and has no comments. Figuring out what a small program like this one is doing certainly won't be impossible, but the effort involved may put off less determined viewers. If the client-side JavaScript is much larger than this example and has dependencies on several files of obfuscated code, the reverse-engineering strain is much greater.

> The resulting code, without line breaks and comments and with shorter function names, is smaller (in this short example's case, by about 600 bytes), so it will also be faster to download.

Try out more than one obfuscator (even a commercial one) by Googling, for instance, and see which one works best for you.

HACK #73   Use a Dynamic script Tag to Make Web Services Requests

Use a dynamic script tag and a special JSON-related JavaScript class for easy, XML-less web services.

Making requests to third-party web services from an Ajax application is a pain, but new web services that offer the option of returning results in JSON format [Hack #7] instead of XML can provide significant relief. In fact, if you make web services requests using the dynamic script tag approach—and the web service lets you specify a JavaScript callback function—you can have unfettered access to the web service in a seamless, cross-domain, cross-browser fashion.

Here is what you need to try out this dynamic script tag request:

- My JSONscriptRequest class
- Access to a web service that returns JSON-formatted results and lets you specify a callback function

To create the JSONscriptRequest class, I distilled a lot of existing information, and then adapted it to the second requirement above. Until recently, finding a web service that met that requirement was, well, darn near impossible, unless you wrote one yourself. Fortunately, Yahoo! has recently begun to offer the option on many of its REST-ish web services. Notably, Yahoo!'s many search-related web services, as well as its geocoding, map image, and traffic web services, now can return JSON values wrapped in a callback function.

Using the Geocoding Web Service

Compared to using the XMLHttpRequest object and a proxy, this stuff is easy. The JSONscriptRequest class does the messy work of creating the script tag; this tag dynamically makes the actual web service request. For a quick example, I'll do some geocoding, turning a zip code—in this case, 94107—into a latitude/longitude pair, using Yahoo!'s Geocoding web service:

```html
<html>
<body>
//Include the JSONscriptRequest class
<script type="text/javascript" src="jsr_class.js"></script>
<script type="text/javascript">

//Define the callback function
function getGeo(jsonData) {
    alert('Latitude = ' + jsonData.ResultSet.Result[0].Latitude +
          ' Longitude = ' + jsonData.ResultSet.Result[0].Longitude);
    bObj.removeScriptTag();
}

//The web service call
var req = 'http://api.local.yahoo.com/MapsService/V1/geocode?appid=YahooDemo
          &output=json&callback=getGeo&location=94107';
//Create a new request object
bObj = new JSONscriptRequest(req);
//Build the dynamic script tag
bObj.buildScriptTag();
//Add the script tag to the page
bObj.addScriptTag();
</script>

</body>
</html>
```

Running this application makes a request to Yahoo!'s Geocoding web service and yields the alert box shown in Figure 9-5. The alert box displays the latitude and longitude of the zip code 94107.

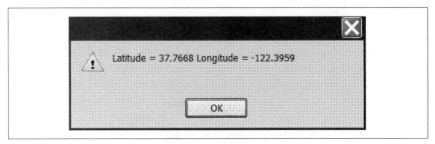

Latitude = 37.7668 Longitude = -122.3959

OK

Figure 9-5. A coordinate from Yahoo's Geocoding web service

The web service request—the req variable in the previous script—specifies that the web service should return JSON-encoded data (output=json) and that the data should be wrapped in a callback function named getGeo( ) (callback=getGeo). You can cut and paste the URL in the code into your browser to see the output of the web service. The output looks like this:

```
getGeo({"ResultSet":{"Result":[{"precision":"zip","Latitude":"37.7668"
,"Longitude":"-122.3959","Address":"","City":"SAN
FRANCISCO","State":"CA","Zip":"94107","Country":"US"}]}});
```

That is a valid JavaScript statement, so it can be the target of a script tag that returns JavaScript (raw JSON data, without the callback function, is not a valid JavaScript statement, so it will fail to load if it is the target of a script tag). For comparison, look at the XML version of the output of this call (formatted for the book):

```
<?xml version="1.0" encoding="UTF-8"?>
<ResultSet xmlns:xsi="http://www.w3.org/2001/XMLSchema-instance" xmlns=
"urn:yahoo:maps" xsi:schemaLocation=
"urn:yahoo:maps http://api.local.yahoo.com/MapsService/V1/GeocodeResponse.
xsd">
<Result precision="zip"><Latitude>37.7668</Latitude>
<Longitude>-122.3959</Longitude><Address></Address>
<City>SAN FRANCISCO</City><State>CA</State><Zip>94107</Zip>
<Country>US</Country></Result>
</ResultSet>
```

The buildScriptTag method of the JSONscriptRequest object builds a script tag that looks like this:

```
<script src="getGeo({"ResultSet":{"Result":[{"precision":"zip",
"Latitude":"37.7668","Longitude":"-122.3959","Address":"","City":"SAN
FRANCISCO","State":"CA","Zip":"94107","Country":"US"}]}});"
 type="text/javascript">
```

To actually execute the web service request, the script tag has to be added to the page. The addScriptTag method attaches the script tag to the HTML page that is already loaded in your browser window. That action causes the getGeo( ) function to be called and the JSON-encoded data to be passed to that function. Now comes the magic part of the script; it's a side effect of using JSON-encoded data instead of XML. When a string of JSON-encoded data is used as an argument to a JavaScript function, the JavaScript interpreter automatically turns the JSON return value into a JavaScript object. Essentially, the parsing step is done automatically, and you can reference the data immediately:

```
alert('Latitude = ' + jsonData.ResultSet.Result[0].Latitude +
      ' Longitude = ' + jsonData.ResultSet.Result[0].Longitude);
```

Pros and Cons

The HTML script tag is the last frontier of unfettered access for browser-based applications. Depending on your viewpoint, it is either a gaping security hole, or a tool to make rich clients even richer. Its most common use, though, is by Internet advertisers who use it to pull their colorful ads into your web pages.

For the average Ajax or Ajaj (Asynchronous JavaScript and JSON) developer, the dynamic script tag approach can make life easier in certain scenarios. The XMLHttpRequest object, however, is still a more reliable, flexible, and secure request mechanism (see Table 9-1).

Table 9-1. XMLHttpRequest compared to the dynamic script tag

	XmlHttpRequest	Dynamic script tag
Cross-browser compatible?	No	Yes
Cross-domain browser security enforced?	Yes	No
Can receive HTTP status codes?	Yes	No (fails on any HTTP status other than 200)
Supports HTTP GET and POST?	Yes	No (GET only)
Can send/receive HTTP headers?	Yes	No
Can receive XML?	Yes	Yes (but only embedded in a JavaScript statement)
Can receive JSON?	Yes	Yes (but only embedded in a JavaScript statement)
Offers synchronous and asynchronous calls?	Yes	No (asynchronous only)

The script tag's main advantages are that it is not bound by the web browser's cross-domain security restrictions and that it runs identically on more web browsers than XMLHttpRequest. Further, if your web service happens to offer JSON output and a callback function, you can nimbly access web services from within your JavaScript applications without having to parse the returned data.

XMLHttpRequest is available in all the latest browsers, but IE's implementation is somewhat different from that of the other major browsers and requires a compatibility layer (such as Sarissa) to make it work across all browsers. XMLHttpRequest can receive raw JSON data as well as XML, plain text, and HTML—in fact, it handles any non-binary data easily. It also can send and receive individual HTTP headers, can do both HTTP GETs and POSTs, and supports both synchronous and asynchronous calls. In short, if there's a problem with your web services request, such as invalid XML or a server error, XMLHttpRequest gives programmers tools to handle the situation.

In contrast, the script tag offers few of XMLHttpRequest's capabilities. The most notable downside is that it cannot handle errors gracefully. If the web service returns an invalid JavaScript statement to the script tag, a JavaScript error is generated. If the web service returns invalid JSON data wrapped inside a callback function, a JavaScript error is returned when the invalid JSON data is passed to the callback function. Also, if your web service returns an HTTP return code other than 200 (successful), the script tag will silently fail.

To be fair, script tag requests don't actually work exactly the same way across all browsers. The event handling—how you wait for the tag to load—is a bit different. Technically, dynamically generated script tags load asynchronously, but there is no reliable, cross-platform way to wait for a script tag to load. Microsoft's IE uses one method described here, while the HTML 4.0 specification suggests the onload event handler (although it doesn't seem to work across all browsers).

The security issues surrounding the script tag cannot be ignored, either. Malicious scripts downloaded into your browser run with the same authority as other scripts in your page, so a villainous script can steal your cookies or misuse any authorization that you may have with a server. These villainous scripts can more easily send and receive stolen data using the script tag. For this reason, applications using the dynamic script tag approach need to be carefully vetted.

With all of these drawbacks, it is unlikely that programmers will flock to implement or reimplement web services requests using script tags. Still, it's a useful technique for scripting applications where noncritical data needs to be retrieved from third-party sources easily.

Resources

The JSONscriptRequest class: *http://www.xml.com/2005/12/21/examples/ jsr_class.zip*; Yahoo! Web Services; Geocoding API: *http://developer.yahoo. net/maps/rest/V1/geocode.html*.

—Jason Levitt

Configure Apache to Deal with Cross-Domain Issues
#74

Configure the Apache web server so that an Apache module provides a solution to the Ajax domain restriction.

As you probably know by now, `XMLHttpRequest` does not work automatically across domains. For example, when you download a web page, you cannot make a request using the request object to a domain that is different from that web page's domain. Fortunately, there's a simple solution to this restriction—the Apache web server's `mod_rewrite`. "This module uses a rule-based rewriting engine (based on a regular-expression parser) to rewrite requested URLs on the fly," according to online Apache documentation (see *http://httpd.apache.org/docs/1.3/mod/mod_rewrite.html*).

Cross-Domain Blockade

Before we get into a description of this solution, let's examine an example set of functions that would typically form your `XMLHttpRequest` workhorse:

```
function getXmlHttpObject(){
    if (window.XMLHttpRequest)
        return new XMLHttpRequest();
    else if (window.ActiveXObject)
        return new ActiveXObject("Microsoft.XMLHTTP");
    else {
        alert("XMLHttpRequest not supported!");
        return null;
    }
}

function handleHttpResponse() {
    if (http.readyState == 4) {
        results = http.responseText;
        alert(results);
    }
}

function doSomeStuff() {
    var post_arg1 = document.my_form.post_arg1.value;
    var post_arg2 = document.my_form.post_arg2.value;
```

```
        var post_url = 'http://yahoo.com/form_do'
            post_data = 'post_arg1=' + post_arg1 + '&post_arg2=' + post_arg2;
        http.open("POST", post_url);
        http.setRequestHeader('Content-Type',
                'application/x-www-form-urlencoded; charset=UTF-8');
        http.send(post_data);
        http.onreadystatechange = handleHttpResponse;
        return false;
    }

    var http = getXmlHttpObject();
```

The last of the three functions that you see is the one that would be called on to perform the HTTP request.

Now, assume that this script is within an HTML file whose URL is, say, *http://premshree.org/form*. Some event handler (onBlur, onClick, onSubmit, etc.) in the form triggers doSomeStuff(), which in turn makes an XMLHttpRequest request to form_do, that resides on another domain (*yahoo.com*).

Notice the mismatch between the domains of the HTML file containing the form and the JavaScript and the file that does the action (*http://yahoo.com/form_do*). That domain mismatch is the source of the problem.

Cross-Domain XMLHttpRequest Works… Kinda

IE and the Mozilla-based browsers handle cross-domain requests differently. You can do cross-domain requests in IE; however, this involves changing the browser's default security settings, or adding certain hosts to your "trusted hosts" list. From *http://msdn.microsoft.com/msdnmag/issues/02/06/web/*:

> Since there is no way to specify which pages trust other pages to access their data, Internet Explorer simply says that if two pages are not in the same domain, they cannot communicate. More precisely, Zone Manager (found on the security tab in Internet Settings) does allow the user to say that a page may access another page, but as you point out, most people leave it set on prompt. You can suggest users add the page to the trusted site zone, or merely say Yes to the dialog box...

Mozilla, on the other hand, has the concept of signed scripts (see *http://www.mozilla.org/projects/security/components/signed-scripts.html*). In a Mozilla-based browser, you need to enable one or more of the UniversalBrowser privileges, depending on the different domains involved in the cross-domain request. For example, if you're accessing a remote host from your local filesystem—that is, accessing *http://* files from *file://*—you need to enable the UniversalBrowserRead privilege.

The reality of the situation is that cross-domain XMLHttpRequest requests don't work as well as you would want them to in the browsers you deeply care about (unless, of course, you're insane enough to compel unsuspecting, naive users to deal with things like signed scripts and trusted hosts).

Is There a Solution?

Yes, thanks to some `mod_rewrite` magic. All you need is the `RewriteRule` directive.

The configuration changes need to be made to the Apache configuration file (typically *httpd.conf*). Here are the steps involved:

1. Configure Apache with proxy enabled:

   ```
   ./configure --enable-proxy
   ```

2. Make sure `RewriteEngine` is enabled:

   ```
   RewriteEngine on
   ```

3. Add the following rule:

   ```
   RewriteRule ^/form_do$ http://yahoo.com/form_do [P]
   ```

   The `P` flag that you see there indicates a pass-through proxy.

> See *http://www.google.com/search?q=pass-through+proxying*.

Now, instead of requesting *http://yahoo.com/form_do*, use the URL */form_do* in the JavaScript code. The request code looks like this:

```
var post_url = '/form_do';
```

That's it—you're done! Many thanks to Gopal and *http://t3.dotgnu.info* for a lot of the information described in this hack.

—Premshree Pillai

Run a Search Engine Inside Your Browser

HACK
#75

Use many of the techniques of web search engines inside your browser.

In many cases, adopting Ajax techniques means tying a web application more tightly to the server; however, as this hack shows, that's not always the case. Using data stored in JSON format [Hack #7], it's possible to include all the required data through an ordinary `script` tag. Once the initial page is loaded, no further network access is required.

In fact, some purists might argue that since no special server interaction takes place, the techniques shown here shouldn't be considered part of Ajax. Nevertheless, a self-contained web application has many potential uses, from CD-ROM documentation to situations where the user might go offline at times.

The application we'll look at here demonstrates web search capabilities, using many of the same techniques employed by major search engines, but on a smaller scale. The material searched is my 2003 O'Reilly book, *XForms Essentials*, which was ideal because the amount of data needed by the searcher is small enough to easily fit into browser memory, and the text is available under an open content license favorable for the purposes of an online demo.

As with many different kinds of searches, the key is an appropriately constructed index.

Indexing 101

An inverted index, in its most basic form, is a simple data structure that maps terms to specific locations. For example, at the end of this book, you'll find an index containing a list of common terms used in the book, and for each term you'll find a list of page numbers where discussion of that topic occurs. The terms themselves are in alphabetical order, so readers can quickly find the terms they seek and go to the appropriate pages. (If you wanted to find, say, information in this book on the topic of JSON, you could either methodically page through the entire book, or turn to the index for a list of pages where it's discussed.)

In this hack, the index maps from individual words to a list of up to some 200 small documents in which those words occur, based on the version of the text at *http://www.xformsinstitute.com/essentials/browse/*. It turns out that an ordinary JavaScript object, acting as an associative array, is the perfect data structure for a simple index; it is designed to perform rapid lookups based on a given key.

Prior to a new page appearing in the search results, online search engines devote a significant amount of their resources to retrieving web pages and creating a suitable index. Similarly, this hack performs preprocessing to create the necessary index. For the heavy lifting of generating such an index, I used an excellent resource: David Mertz's public-domain Gnosis Utilities for Python, found at *http://www.gnosis.cx/download/* and described in the article at *http://www-128.ibm.com/developerworks/library/l-pyind.html*. Once the library code has constructed the index, a small fragment of Python writes out the data structure as a pair of object literals, a fragment of which is as follows (line breaks added for readability):

```
var jswords={'NFORMS':[18,45],'LATEX':[18,7],
'MODIFICATIONS':[10,11,18,6,7], 'EVERYONE':[18,78,5,6],
'OCCURRENCE':[18,26],'SUPPOSED':[18,50,21], LENGTHS':[40,72,18,21],
'APPEARANCE':[69,7,45,49,18,21,23,24,26,60,29,63]
...
```

```
var jsfiles=['unused','apa.php','apas02.php','apas03.php','apas04.php',
...
```

A few things of note in this code:

- All the words are normalized to uppercase, indicating a case-insensitive search mode.

- Instead of spelling out the full name of each result file over and over, file references are given as an offset into a separate array of filenames.

Further, to keep index size down, common stopwords such as "and," "the," and "a" are omitted from the index.

From this short fragment, it's obvious that "NForms" appears twice (in the 18th and 45th files), "LaTeX" appears twice (in the 18th and 7th files), and so on.

Putting It Together

Given the JavaScript index in a file named *xfi.js*, a small bit of additional script is needed to implement the query engine. Instead of a submit button, the code sets a timer of 250 milliseconds. When the time expires, it checks whether the value in the query control has changed and, if so, provides an immediate update:

```
<html>
<head>
    <title>Full-text search of XForms Essentials (beta)</title>

    <script type="text/javascript" src="xfi.js"></script>
    <script type="text/javascript">
        var lastq = "";
        var delay = 250;

        function requery() {
            if (!jswords || !jsfiles) return;  //still loading
            var currentq = document.query.q.value;
            if (currentq == lastq)
                    return;

            var results = localfind(currentq.split(" "))
            lastq = currentq;
            updateResults(results);
        }

        //This function is adapted from David Mertz's public domain
        //Gnosis Utils for Python with some extra gymnastics since
        //jsfiles uses the more compact js array instead of object/dicts
        function localfind(wordlist) {
            var entries = {};
            var hits = {}
```

```
            for (var idx=0; idx < jsfiles.length; idx++) {
                hits[idx] = jsfiles[idx];    //copy of the fileids index
            }
            for (var idx in wordlist) {
                var word = wordlist[idx]
                word = word.toUpperCase( )
                if (!jswords[word]) return {}   //nothing for this one word
                 (fail)
                var entry = {}
                //For each word, get index
                //of matching files
                for (var idx=0; idx < jswords[word].length; idx++) {
                    entry[jswords[word][idx]] = "hit";
                }

                //eliminate hits for every non-match
                for (var fileid in hits) {
                    if (!entry[fileid]) {
                        delete hits[fileid];
                    }
                }
            }
            return hits;
        }

        function updateResults(results) {
            var upd_loc = document.getElementById("results");
            var url_base = "http://xformsinstitute.com/essentials/browse/";
            //remove previous results, if any
            while (upd_loc.hasChildNodes( )) {
                upd_loc.removeChild(upd_loc.childNodes[0]);
            }
            var newh1 = document.createElement("h1");
            newh1.appendChild(document.createTextNode("results:"));
            upd_loc.appendChild(newh1);
            for (var fileid in results) {
                var hit = jsfiles[fileid];
                var newp = document.createElement("p");
                newp.appendChild( makeHyperlink( url_base + hit, hit ));
                upd_loc.appendChild(newp);
            }
        }

        function makeHyperlink( url, text, title ) {
            var aelem = document.createElement("a");
            if (title) aelem.setAttribute( "title", title );
            if (url) aelem.setAttribute( "href", url );
            aelem.appendChild(document.createTextNode(text))
            return aelem;
        }

    setInterval(requery, delay);</script>
    </head>
```

```
<body>
<p>Just type here, and watch the results magically appear. (JavaScript
required, but other than initially loading the document, no network access
is required)</p> <p>Currently, only whole-word matching is implemented.
Multiple words are ANDed together.</p>
<form name="query" action="no_submit" method="POST"> <input type="text"
name="q" autocomplete="off"/> </form> <div id="results"> </div>
<p><a href="http://dubinko.info/blog/2004/12.html#perm2004-12-
26_localindex">technical details</a></p> </body>
</html>
```

The function localfind( ) does the actual lookup, taking into account one
additional wrinkle: the query might contain more than one keyword. In that
case, the list of hits for each keyword needs to be combined. The code treats
this as a Boolean AND, so only documents containing all the keywords get
returned—that is, the intersection of the lists gets computed.

The functions updateResults( ) and makeHyperlilnk( ) use standard DOM
manipulation to show the results directly, as simple unstyled hyperlinks,
sidestepping the round trip normally associated with a search engine
request.

To operate the search engine, just open the document, found online at *http://
www.xformsinstitute.com/essentials/xfi.html*, in a browser, and enter some
terms in the text control. The results appear immediately in the page, providing hyperlinks to full-text sections of the book. Despite all the work going on
behind the scenes, the queries return results nearly instantly.

Hacking the Hack

In modifying the code for your own purposes, you might want to experi-
ment with different values for the timer—the delay variable in the
JavaScript—that periodically checks whether to rerun the query. Also take
note of the url_base variable, which sets the common part of the URL for
each result.

The search engine could be enhanced in a number of ways. Perhaps the
most obvious would be to include the ability to search for exact phrases,
typically indicated via quotation marks in web search engine queries. To do
so would require a more sophisticated index structure that keeps track of
not only what document each word occurs in, but also where in the document it occurs.

Another enhancement would be to add stemming, so, for instance, a search
for "appear" would find pages containing "appear," "appears," "appearance," and "appearing." Doing so also would involve using a slightly more
sophisticated data structure for the index.

Finally, since not every browser supports JavaScript or has it enabled, this hack could be modified to include a submit button to perform a normal, server-based query. When JavaScript is enabled, the button can be hidden, performing instant lookups as described above.

Resources

You can find more information on inverted indexes at *http://en.wikipedia.org/wiki/Inverted_index*.

For additional discussion of the Gnosis Utilities from David Mertz's *Text Processing in Python* (Addison-Wesley), check out *http://www.gnosis.cx/TPiP/*.

—*Micah Dubinko*

HACK #76 Use Declarative Markup Instead of Script via XForms

When scripting gets too burdensome, capture a web application's intent in markup.

JavaScript code tends to get complex in deployed Ajax applications. The essential problem is that encoding the intent of a web application requires a large amount of procedural script, often with branches for different levels of browser support. For example, if your intent is to dynamically add a section to the page to capture additional user input, the script gets bogged down in low-level details of Document Object Model manipulation and the like. A cleaner approach uses higher-level markup to capture the intent, leaving the interpretation of that intent to the client.

The World Wide Web Consortium (W3C)—the same folks who brought us HTML and XML—considered the things most commonly done by script, and agreed upon declarative ways to accomplish the same things. The result, called XForms, quite simply provides a vocabulary for authors to specify what they want to happen, instead of the usual approach of spelling out every tiny detail. Such a higher-level approach has additional benefits:

- Nonbrowser devices—such as phones and Interactive Voice Response systems—can easily work off the same design.
- Web search engines have an easier time processing markup than interpreting script.
- It's possible to interpret the markup on a server, allowing deployment across many different browsers.
- XForms is especially adept at handling XML data.

Consuming and Producing XML

The last bullet above bears further discussion. In many situations that call for Ajax, the most convenient format for data is XML. (Other times, it's not—see "Receive Data in JSON Format" [Hack #7] for a discussion of JSON, an alternate format.) XForms is designed to work from a piece of XML *instance data*, which provides initial data values from the outside world, keeps track of any user changes, and can submit the data back out. Instance data makes for a convenient "scratch pad" within which to store temporary client-side state.

Here's an example that maintains a syndication feed for a podcast. I recently asked a podcaster to show me how he updates his feed, and he proceeded to use a copy of Windows Notepad and FTP. Manual editing, however, is error-prone, due to the intricacies of how the RSS format, iTunes extensions, and XML namespaces all combine (to the chagrin of podcasters everywhere).

See *http://en.wikipedia.org/wiki/RSS_%28file_format%29* for more details on RSS.

An automatic fill-in-the-blanks solution, which opens the RSS, allows changes, and then writes the changes back, provides a better experience for both the content producer and the consumers.

For this hack, I'm using an XForms engine called FormFaces, implemented entirely in JavaScript. In accord with good design principles, it uses an HTTP GET to obtain the initial XML and an HTTP PUT to write it back. Because many servers don't yet work well with PUT, I included a simple PHP script to process the request:

```php
<?php
/* put.php */

/* PUT data comes in on the stdin stream */
$putdata = fopen("php://stdin", "r");

$fp = fopen("results.xml", "w");

while ($data = fread($putdata, 1024))
        fwrite($fp, $data);

fclose($fp);
fclose($putdata);
?>
```

The prior PHP script captures the PUT data and writes it to a file named *results.xml* in the same directory. For actual deployment, more sophisticated security arrangements is desirable.

Normally, this hack would modify an existing RSS file, but what about for someone just starting out? The usual approach in this situation is to produce a skeleton XML file that contains all the structure of the desired output format, populated with dummy values. Here's an example of that for podcast XML:

```
<!-- rss.xml -->
<rss xmlns:itunes="http://www.itunes.com/DTDs/Podcast-1.0.dtd" version="2.
0">
<channel>
<title>Podcast title here</title>
<link>http://</link>
<description>Description here</description>
<language>en-us</language>
<copyright>Copyright notice here</copyright>
<itunes:image>http://</itunes:image>
<itunes:link rel="image" type="image/jpeg" href="http://">Description
</itunes:link>
<itunes:owner>
<itunes:name>Name here</itunes:name>    </itunes:owner>
<itunes:author>Name here</itunes:author>
<managingEditor>Contact info here</managingEditor>
<generator>Powered by XForms</generator>    <category>Audio Blog</category>
<image>    <url>http://</url>    <title>Image Title here</title>
  <link>http://</link>    <width>300</width>    <height>300</height> </image>
<itunes:explicit>clean</itunes:explicit>
<itunes:subtitle>Show Subtitle here</itunes:subtitle>
<itunes:summary>Show Summary here</itunes:summary>
<itunes:category text="Audio Blogs" />
<lastBuildDate>Sun, 1 Jan 2006 10:00:00 PST</lastBuildDate>
<pubDate>Sun, 1 Jan 2006 10:00:00 PST</pubDate>
<item>    <title>Item Title here</title>
<description>Item Description here</description>
<pubDate>Sun, 1 Jan 2006 10:00:00 PST</pubDate>
<enclosure url="http://" length="1" type="audio/mpeg" />
<itunes:duration>1:00</itunes:duration>
<itunes:author>Author here</itunes:author>    </item>
</channel>
</rss>
```

Given XML structured like that in the prior code sample, XForms markup can then create a complete environment in which to view and edit the file. A few aspects about the structure, though, need to be accounted for. For one, data repetition is rampant in the format, especially in the case where a single person is running the entire podcast. Our solution should not make us enter identical data over and over again. Secondly, note that the item block toward the end will repeat as many times as there are syndicated shows. As the number of shows grows, both the user interface and the resulting RSS need to grow.

The next code sample shows the complete HTML file, which should be placed in the same directory as the files listed earlier. It also includes a reference to the FormFaces script, available from *http://www.formfaces.com.* Other than the implementation script, no JavaScript is needed for this example. In more complicated situations, some script might need to be combined with XForms, but even so, the result will generally be shorter and more straightforward than with other approaches. Here's the HTML:

```
<!-- editrss.html -->
<html xmlns="http://www.w3.org/1999/xhtml" xml:lang="en"
      xmlns:xf="http://www.w3.org/2002/xforms"
      xmlns:ev="http://www.w3.org/2001/xml-events"
      xmlns:itunes="http://www.itunes.com/DTDs/Podcast-1.0.dtd">
<head>
    <title>Edit iTunes RSS</title>
    <link rel="stylesheet" type="text/css" href="xforms.css" />
    <script type="text/javascript" src="formfaces.js"></script>
<xf:model>
    <xf:instance src="rss.xml"/>
    <xf:submission id="s1" action="put.php" method="put" replace="none"/>
</xf:model>
</head>
<body>
<h2>Overall Info</h2>
<xf:group ref="channel">
    <xf:input ref="title"><xf:label>Title</xf:label></xf:input>
    <xf:input ref="description"><xf:label>Description</xf:label></xf:input>
    <xf:input ref="itunes:subtitle"><xf:label>Subtitle</xf:label></xf:input>
<br/>
    <xf:input ref="itunes:author"><xf:label>Author</xf:label></xf:input>
    <xf:input ref="copyright"><xf:label>Copyright</xf:label></xf:input>
    <xf:input ref="managingEditor"><xf:label>Contact</xf:label></xf:input>
</xf:group> <br/>
<xf:trigger> <xf:label>Submit</xf:label>
    <xf:send submission="s1" ev:event="DOMActivate"/>
</xf:trigger>
<hr/> <h2>Shows</h2>
<xf:trigger> <xf:label>Add Show</xf:label>
    <xf:action ev:event="DOMActivate">
        <xf:insert nodeset="channel/item" at="1" position="before"/>
        <xf:setvalue ref="channel/item[1]/itunes:author" value=
            "../../itunes:author"/>
    </xf:action>
</xf:trigger>
```

```
<xf:trigger> <xf:label>Remove Highlighted Show</xf:label>
    <xf:delete ev:event="DOMActivate" nodeset="channel/item" at=
        "index('items')"/>
</xf:trigger> <br/>
<xf:repeat nodeset="channel/item" id="items">
<xf:input ref="title">
    <xf:label>Title</xf:label>
</xf:input>
    <xf:input ref="description"><xf:label>Description</xf:label></xf:input>
    <xf:input ref="pubDate"><xf:label>Date</xf:label></xf:input> <br/>
    <xf:input ref="enclosure/@url"><xf:label>MP3 URL</xf:label></xf:input>
    <xf:input ref="enclosure/@length"><xf:label>Length</xf:label></xf:input>
    <xf:input ref="itunes:duration"><xf:label>Duration</xf:label></xf:input>
<hr/> </xf:repeat>
</body>
</html>
```

Figure 9-6 shows a screenshot of this application in action. After loading the page and editing the data, clicking the submit button PUTs the data back on the server.

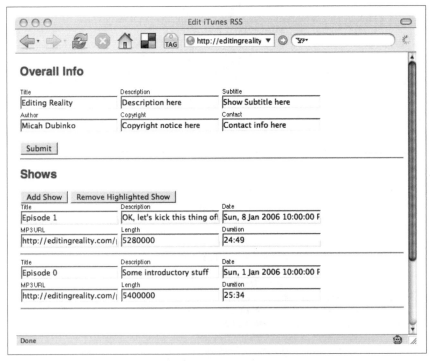

Figure 9-6. Updating RSS content with XForms

Some things to note about the code:

- XForms markup here appears in a different XML namespace, to ensure that the elements are uniquely distinguishable.

- The short xf:model section provides the URL for both incoming and outgoing XML.

- The ref attributes on the group and input elements are simple locators into the instance data. Full XPath syntax is available, as expressions like enclosure/@url show.

- The xf:repeat element provides the needed repeating structure.

- The value for itunes:author inside item is copied from the place where that piece of information is already specified. XForms includes a full spreadsheet-like system for resolving interdependencies on data relationships like these.

- Note the elements named xf:trigger, which appear as buttons in most browsers. Even down to the names of controls, XForms enforces a high-level view of an application that is not based on a particular user-interface design.

- Unlike conventional forms, XForms does not force a page churn during submission. This allows data to smoothly flow into the page, without worrying about details of XMLHttpRequest scripting.

As this example shows, XForms markup was not designed for terseness, but rather for comprehension. Even folks with no prior XForms experience should be able to look at an example like this and figure out what's going on. Of course, beyond what this short example shows, XForms has many more capabilities and conveniences. You can find out more about XForms in my book *XForms Essentials*, published by O'Reilly and available online under an open content license at *http://www.xformsinstitute.com*.

Hacking the Hack

This simple example edits only a few of the needed parts of a fully functioning syndication feed. Following the format established here, filling in the rest of the details is straightforward.

Besides FormFaces, other XForms engines have been written in JavaScript, not to mention Flash, Java, C++, and other languages. A good starting point for further XForms research is the article "Top 10 XForms Engines" at *http://www.xml.com/pub/a/2005/02/09/xforms.html*.

—*Micah Dubinko*

Build a Client-Side Cache

#77   Cut server traffic and improve performance by saving previously retrieved
       data.

Browsers know how to cache entire web pages. Often, when requesting a
web page that you've recently visited, your browser saves time by grabbing
the page from a local cache stored either in memory or on your hard drive.

However, Ajax applications often change only parts of a web page. The
browser doesn't cache this data, but your Ajax application can.

A good client-side cache needs to make it easy to store new data, and simple to find and retrieve it later. An associative array is the simplest JavaS-
cript structure to provide both easy storage and retrieval.

An associative array (often called a hash or hash table) is like a normal array,
with one important difference: a normal array is indexed by integers,
whereas an associative array can be indexed by arbitrary text strings. These
text indexes are called *hash keys*.

For example, a normal array may have an assignment like this:

```
Arr[5] = "some text";
```

while an associative array can have assignments like this:

```
Arr["Charles Dickens"] = "Tale of Two Cities";
```

Luckily for you, JavaScript allows you to index arrays in either form.

When you talk to a server with XMLHttpRequest, you provide two pieces of
information: the URL of the server script, and any parameters the script
needs. Combining these makes an excellent array index. Whenever you
retrieve data from the server for your Ajax application, you can save that
data in an associative array using the URL and parameters as a key. The next
time the user makes a request for the same URL, with the same parameters,
you check for a matching entry in your array. If it's there, use the data you
already have, rather than bothering the server again.

In the onreadystatechange function, you can save the data like this:

```
cache[url + parameters] = httpreq.responseText;
```

Later, before making another request to the server, check if a hash key is
already defined in the cache array:

```
if (cache[url + parameters]) {
    response = cache[url + parameters];
else {
    //Not cached, so call server
    ...
}
```

Building a Better Cache

There's one problem with this approach. While the Ajax program is running in the browser, each new, distinct request gets another entry in the cache array. For some applications, the JavaScript array can get quite large, eating up memory on the client machine.

The solution is to modify the hack to limit the size of the array. You can just start deleting elements in the array once it's reached some arbitrary size, but how do you decide which elements to delete? One approach is to use a Least Recently Used (LRU) algorithm. We'll keep our cache in an ordered list (see Figure 9-7), where the top of the list contains the oldest element (the one used least recently), and the bottom of the list contains our freshest, newest data.

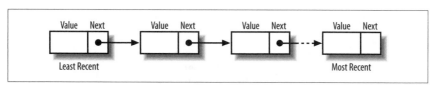

Figure 9-7. The LRU algorithm as a linked list

We'll still use an associative array, but we'll add some code to make it act like a linked list (also called a "queue"). A *linked list* is a set of data objects in which each element contains not just its data but also a pointer to the next data object in the list.

To show the LRU-based cache in action, let's look at the HTML code for the web page for a simple Ajax application that displays facts about planets in the solar system:

```
<HTML>

<HEAD>
<TITLE>Client-side Cache Test</TITLE>

<style>
    body,table,select { font-size: 12px; }
</style>

<script language="javascript" src="/cache_hack/xhr.js"></script>
<script language="javascript" src="/cache_hack/limited_cache.js"></script>
<script language="javascript" type="text/javascript">

function get_data () {

    var lbPlanets = document.getElementById("lbPlanets");

    async_cmd ("/cgi-bin/cache/planets.cgi?",
```

```
                        "p=" + lbPlanets.value,
                        "divAnswer");

    }

    </script>

    </HEAD>

    <BODY>
    <center>
    <b>Client-side Content Caching</b><p>

    <table style="border: 1px solid gray;" cellpadding="5" cellspacing="0"
    width="95%">

    <tr>
        <td width="35%" bgcolor="#f0f0f0" valign="top">
            <form id="frmMain">
                Select a planet:
                <select id="lbPlanets" onChange="get_data();">
                    <option value="mercury">Mercury</option>
                    <option value="venus">Venus</option>
                    <option value="earth">Earth</option>
                    <option value="mars">Mars</option>
                    <option value="jupiter">Jupiter</option>
                    <option value="saturn">Saturn</option>
                    <option value="uranus">Uranus</option>
                    <option value="neptune">Neptune</option>
                    <option value="pluto">Pluto</option>
                </select>
            </form>

            <div id="divAnswer">
             
            </div>
        </td>

        <td width="65%" bgcolor="#c0c0c0" valign="top">
            Cache Contents (oldest first):<p>
            <div id="divCacheContents">
                <b>Cache is empty</b>
            </div>
        </td>
    </tr>

    </table>

    </center>
    </BODY>

    </HTML>
```

This creates the initial web page shown in Figure 9-8.

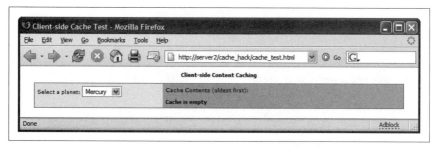

Figure 9-8. A client-side cache example

When a planet is selected from the pull-down select box, the JavaScript function get_data( ) is triggered. This function calls the function async_cmd( ), defined in the JavaScript file *limited_cache.js*, shown here:

```
var cache = new Array;

var top_key = null;
var prev_key = null;
var curr_cache_size = 0;

var MAX_CACHE_SIZE = 5;

//-----------------------------------------------------------
// Display the contents of the client-side cache in a
// DIV tag
//-----------------------------------------------------------
function show_cache_info (answer_from) {
    var divCache = document.getElementById("divCacheContents");
    divCache.innerHTML = "";
    var curr_key = top_key;
    while (curr_key != null) {
        divCache.innerHTML = divCache.innerHTML
                + "KEY: <b>" + curr_key
                + "</b> VALUE: <b>" + cache[curr_key].value
                + "</b><br>";
        curr_key = cache[curr_key].next;
    }

    divCache.innerHTML = divCache.innerHTML
            + "<p>Last answer retrieved from: <b>"
            + answer_from + "</b>";
}

//-----------------------------------------------------------
// Asynchronous (non-blocking) server query
//-----------------------------------------------------------
function async_cmd (url, parms, divname) {
```

```
    var httpreq = getHTTPObject( );

    var divAnswer = document.getElementById(divname);

    //Precondition: must have a URL
    if (url == "") return;

    var cache_key = url + parms;

    //If this is a cacheable request, then first
    //check if a response already exists for it

    if (cache[cache_key]) {
        divAnswer.innerHTML = "Answer: <b>" +
         cache[cache_key].value + "</b>";

        //Linked-list maintenance
        if (cache_key != prev_key) {
            var curr_key = top_key;

            if (cache_key != top_key) {
                //Find linked-list node preceding the
                //cache[cache_key] node
                while (cache[curr_key].next != cache_key) {
                    curr_key = cache[curr_key].next;
                }
            }
            else {
                top_key = cache[top_key].next;
            }
            //Point preceding node to point to which
            //cache[cache_key] currently points
            cache[curr_key].next = cache[cache_key].next;

            //Move cache[cache_key] to the end of our
            //linked list
            cache[prev_key].next = cache_key;
            cache[cache_key].next = null;
            prev_key = cache_key;
        }
        show_cache_info ("client-side cache");
    }
    else {
        //Send request to server
        httpreq.open("POST", url, true);

        //----------------------------------------------------
        // Response function
        //----------------------------------------------------
        httpreq.onreadystatechange = function ( ) {
            if (httpreq.readyState == 4) {
                var response = httpreq.responseText;
```

```
            if (curr_cache_size >= MAX_CACHE_SIZE) {
                //Remove oldest item from cache
                var oldest = top_key;
                top_key = cache[oldest].next;
                delete cache[oldest];

            }
            else {
                curr_cache_size++;
            }

            //Linked-list maintenance
            if (top_key == null) {
                top_key = cache_key;
            }
            if (prev_key != null) {
                cache[prev_key].next = cache_key;
            }

            //Add answer we just retrieved into cache
            cache[cache_key] = { value:response, next:null };
            prev_key = cache_key;

            //Display answer in DIV tag
            divAnswer.innerHTML = "Answer: <b>" + response + "</b>";

            show_cache_info ("server");
        }
    }
    httpreq.send (parms);
    }
}
```

The async_cmd( ) function expects three parameters. The first two, url and parm, are the URL and parameters that make the XMLHttpRequest call. As the function name implies, the server call is asynchronous. When the server reply is received, the reponseText is copied into the HTML div tag specified by the third parameter, divname.

The async_cmd( ) function also contains all the code for storing and retrieving data from the client-side cache. You don't need to know anything about how the cache works (or even that it exists) to use the function.

The Cache in Action

In the example program, a user selects a planet from the pull-down list, triggering the JavaScript function get_data( ), which in turn calls the function aync_cmd( ). The job of this function is to request information from the server and use it to update a div tag. But before it bothers the server, it first builds a cache key—an index into the cache array—by combining the URL and parameters. The program then checks the cache for a matching entry:

```
var cache_key = url + parms;

if (cache[cache_key]) {
    divAnswer.innerHTML = "Answer: <b>" + cache[cache_key].value + "</b>";
```

If a match is found, you use the data from the cache to update the page.

> The cache value in the previous code is referenced as cache[cache_key].value. To turn the cache array into a linked list, you have to give each array element two properties. The first, value, holds the cached data. The second, called next, is a pointer to the index of the next item in the linked list.

When no match is found, we have to contact the server as usual, but after the data's been retrieved, we need to insert it into our cache. We're using our array to simulate a linked list, and we must also be careful to keep the list in LRU order and to make sure the list doesn't grow too big. The size of the cache is controlled by the variable MAX_CACHE_SIZE, which in our example is set to 5. In practice, the size of the cache depends on the needs of the application.

Our example program includes a function, show_cache_info( ), that displays the contents of the cache on the right side of the web page. This display is refreshed every time a new planet is selected. Figure 9-9 shows the application after the five outermost planets have been selected (starting with Pluto and moving inward).

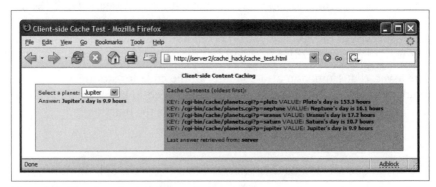

Figure 9-9. After five selections, the cache is now full

The oldest (least recent) item in our cache is Pluto, and the newest item is Jupiter. Because five items have been selected, there's no more room in the cache. When the next planet, Mars, is selected, our aync_cmd( ) function needs to do some cache rearranging. The results are shown in Figure 9-10; Pluto, the oldest entry in the cache, is deleted to make room for Mars.

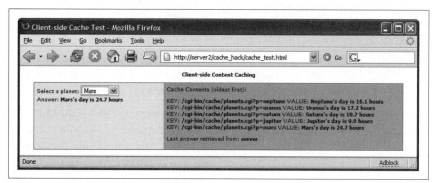

Figure 9-10. Pluto gets deleted to make room for Mars

Up to now, we've only rearranged the contents of the cache. Now let's see what happens when we select Saturn, an item inside the cache. The results are shown in Figure 9-11.

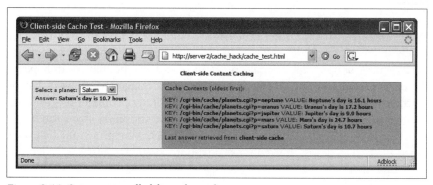

Figure 9-11. Saturn gets pulled from the cache

Saturn has moved from third position in the cache to the bottom, maintaining the list in Least Recently Used order. Using the cache also saves a trip to the server, which makes our application more responsive.

Hacking the Hack

If you want a cache size larger than five (and who doesn't?), you might consider adding a function to set the initial cache size. You can call it from your Ajax page's onLoad event handler.

In the async_cmd( ) function, when we're pulling a value from our cache, we need to find the list element that precedes our target one. We're moving the target element to the end of the list, and we need to splice the list back together. Our code to find the preceding element looks like this:

```
while (cache[curr_key].next != cache_key) {
    curr_key = cache[curr_key].next;
}
```

The code is simple, but it's woefully inefficient. Performance may suffer if the cache is very large. To remedy this problem, consider rewriting the cache as a doubly linked list. In a doubly linked list, each element points not just to the next element, but to the previous one as well.

There are cases in which you don't want to cache server data on the client. If you're receiving data that changes over time (for example, the current temperature in Denver), you'll always want to get this data from the server. Consider adding a parameter to async_cmd( ) to disable caching in these special cases.

—*Mark Pruett*

HACK #78   Create an Auto-Complete Field

Give the user helpful suggestions by changing the contents of a text box as they type.

Web surfers can always use a little help. Google took advantage of this fact when it created Google Suggest (*http://www.google.com/webhp?complete= 1&hl=en*), a simple Ajax variation on its massively popular search page. When the user types in a search term, Google Suggest displays a list of search suggestions beneath the text box. What many people don't notice is that the text in the text box is also altered—the top entry from the list is automatically entered. Figure 9-12 shows this behavior in action: I've only typed the letters "javas" into the text box, but Google Suggest has added the end of the word, "cript," for me.

This hack will show how to modify text in a text box as the user types, using suggestions received from the web server.

Of course, the list of possible suggestions depends entirely on the needs of your application. "Create an Auto-Complete Field with script.aculo.us" **[Hack #65]** discussed how to implement an auto-completion field for email addresses (using *script.aculo.us* effects). For this hack, I wrote a tiny server script that scans a list of dictionary words on the server and returns the first match.

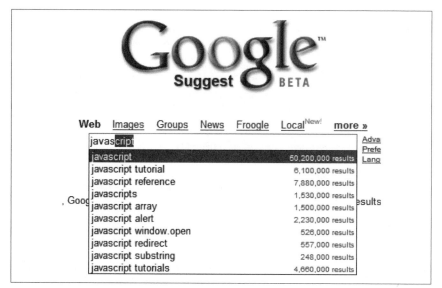

Figure 9-12. Google makes suggestions

 Many Linux and Unix servers have a text file called *words* that contains a list of words (one per line) used by spelling and password checkers. It's usually located at */usr/dict/words* or */usr/share/dict/words*.

My little server receives a single parameter, var. This contains the letters the user has typed thus far. The server finds a match and sends back the remaining portion of the word. So, like in the previous Google example, if I type in "javas" and the server matches on the word "javascript," it sends back the remaining part of the word: "cript."

To make things easy on the client side, we'll have a single function, autocomplete( ), that's hooked into a text box's onKeyup event. It gets called every time the user presses a key:

```
<input type="text"
       id="txtAuto" name="txtAuto"
       onkeyup="autocomplete (this,event);"
/>
```

The autocomplete( ) function, shown in the upcoming code sample, first checks that the most recent keystroke is an alphanumeric character. It thensends the current value of the text box to the server. The server responds with the remaining portion of the matching word:

```
var url = "/cgi-bin/autocomplete/suggest.cgi?";

function autocomplete (sender, ev) {
```

```
//Only process alphanumeric keystrokes
if (( ev.keyCode >= 48 && ev.keyCode <= 57 )
        || ( ev.keyCode >= 65 && ev.keyCode <= 90 )) {

    //Prepare a server request
    var httpreq = getHTTPObject( );
    var parms = "val=" + sender.value;
    httpreq.open("GET", url + parms, true);

    //Response function
    httpreq.onreadystatechange = function ( ) {
        if (httpreq.readyState == 4) {
            var suggestion = httpreq.responseText;
            var txtAuto = document.getElementById ('txtAuto');

            if ((suggestion) && (txtAuto.value == original_text)) {
                //Firefox and Opera
                if (document.getSelection) {
                    var initial_len = txtAuto.value.length;
                    txtAuto.value += suggestion;
                    txtAuto.selectionStart = initial_len;
                    txtAuto.selectionEnd = txtAuto.value.length;
                }
                //Internet Explorer
                else if (document.selection) {
                    var sel = document.selection.createRange ( );
                    sel.text = suggestion;
                    sel.move ("character", -suggestion.length);
                    sel.findText (suggestion);
                    sel.select ( );
                }
            }
        }
    }
    httpreq.send (null);
}
}
```

At this point, we need to work around the quirks of different browsers. Microsoft's Internet Explorer uses different methods for handling text selected in a listbox than browsers such as Firefox and Opera. The goal is the same in all browsers: we need to graft the end of the word (grabbed from the server) onto the beginning of the word (that the user typed). But we also must *select* that new text.

Why? A user who is typing and not paying close attention to what's on the screen may not notice that we just added several characters to the text. That's bad, especially if our suggestion is wrong. By selecting (highlighting) the text we've added, we allow the user to obliterate our suggestion on the next keystroke. For example, say the user wants to type "intense." After the user has entered the first three letters, the program suggests the word "intact" in Figure 9-13.

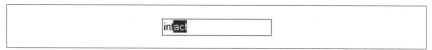

Figure 9-13. A not quite intact word

But the last half of the word, "act" is selected, so when the user enters the next letter, "e," that letter replaces the selected text. The server now sends back a match for the first four letters, "inte," as shown in Figure 9-14.

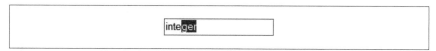

Figure 9-14. Auto-selection in action

If this still isn't quite what the user wants, she can continue to type without worrying that the program will capriciously alter the entered text.

Hacking the Hack

This hack works best if the server can keep up with the user's typing. Make sure your server script is as fast as possible. You may get better performance by sending several potential matches to the server and caching the ones you don't yet need. When the user enters "a," for example, you can retrieve all the words that start with "a" and store them in a JavaScript array. Then, when the user types the next letter, you'll already have those matches ready.

—Mark Pruett

HACK
#79 Dynamically Display More Information About a Topic
Use a simple technique to let users manage their own screen real estate.

You've got too much information to display, and not enough room on the screen. What do you do? You can cram it all on the page and let the user scroll down through your content. You can make two pages and force the user to navigate between them. Or you can let the user dynamically choose which sections of your page to display.

Figure 9-15 shows a simple web page with two content sections: Quote of the Day and Weather Forecast. By themselves, they don't take up much room, but add another dozen sections to the page and you're on the road to information overload.

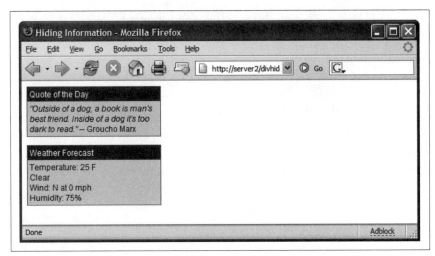

Figure 9-15. Two content sections, eating up page real estate

The two page sections are built with HTML tables. The following code sample shows the Quote of the Day table. The Weather Forecast table has an identical structure:

```html
<table border=0 width="35%" cellpadding="3">
<tr>
    <td bgcolor="404080" onclick="toggle_visible('divQOTD');">
        <font color="#FFFFFF">
        Quote of the Day
        </font>
    </td>
</tr>
<tr>
    <td bgcolor="#E0E0E0">
        <div id="divQOTD">
            <em>"Outside of a dog, a book is man's best friend.
            Inside of a dog it's too dark to read."</em>
            -- Groucho Marx<br>
        </div>
    </td>
</tr>
</table>
```

The table has two rows: the top row displays the title, and the bottom row contains the quotation. The quote is surrounded by a div tag named divQOTD. You'll also notice that we've hooked a callback to the top row's onClick event. When the user clicks the mouse on the Quote of the Day title, the toggle_visible() function makes the content within the div tag disappear, as in Figure 9-16. If the content is already hidden, clicking the title makes it reappear.

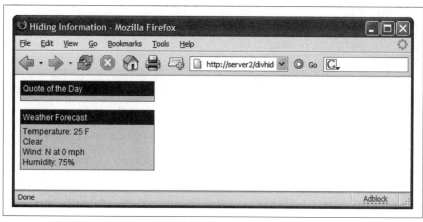

Figure 9-16. Hiding the Quote of the Day

The `toggle_visible()` function simply modifies a couple of the style attributes of any Document object element. You pass the element as a parameter, and `toggle_visible()` checks to see if it's currently visible. If it is, the element is rendered invisible. If the element is already invisible, it reappears:

```
function toggle_visible (elName) {

    var el = document.getElementById (elName);
    var isVisible = (el.style.visibility == "hidden") ? true : false;

    el.style.visibility = isVisible ? "visible" : "hidden";
    el.style.display = isVisible ? "inline" : "none";
}
```

Figure 9-17 shows the page with both content boxes invisible. You can use the function to make any page element disappear. You can even attach it to the body tag's onClick event and make the entire page disappear, if so inspired.

Figure 9-17. Both content boxes rendered invisible

The only bit of trickery in the function is when you set the el.style.display attribute. You might think that setting the el.style.visibility attribute would be sufficient to render the element invisible, but alas, no. Setting visibility to hidden makes the text disappear, but the browser still reserves space for it. Setting the display attribute to none (instead of the normal inline) lets the browser take back the space it occupied and adjust other page elements accordingly.

Hacking the Hack

The toggle_visible( ) function isn't limited to tiny sections of the page. You can use it to make large sections appear or disappear, too. A variation of this function might receive a Boolean parameter that sets the visibility. This technique can allow the user to toggle between radically different views of your page without a page refresh or a trip back to the server.

—Mark Pruett

 HACK #80 Use Strings and Arrays to Dynamically Generate HTML

Speed up the dynamic writing of HTML tables and CSS styles.

DOM programming in the latest versions of modern browsers, despite their compatibility differences, is a powerful technique for generating new content in the client. However, the large client-side programs that dynamically write HTML tables, for instance, from persistently stored data, can gain performance benefits by using core or "raw" JavaScript objects instead of the DOM. This hack uses JavaScript strings and arrays to dynamically generate an HTML table for a browser view; it shows a code sample for this approach and the DOM-based technique as a basis for comparison.

The hack also describes a technique for dynamically setting Cascading Style Sheet (CSS) styles that helps increase the performance of JavaScript code that alters the appearance of an HTML element.

Writing a Table

In many situations, such as dynamically writing an HTML table, minimizing your code's use of the web page's DOM objects can increase your program's performance. Following are two different examples of building an HTML table. The first one emphasizes DOM scripting, and the second uses JavaScript arrays and strings. The first approach looks like this:

```
function buildTable(nRows, nCols) {
    var idx = 0, idx2 = 0;
```

```
        var oTable = document.createElement("TABLE");
        var oTBody = document.createElement("TBODY");
        var oTRow = null;
        var oTCol = null;

        for (idx; idx < nRows; idx++) {
            oTRow = document.createElement("TR");
            for (idx2 = 0; idx2 < nCols; idx2++) {
                oTCol = document.createElement("TD");
                oTCol.innerText = nRow + ", " + nCol;
                oTCol.style.fontSize = "12px";
                oTCol.style.fontWeight = 700;
                oTCol.style.fontFamily = "tahoma";
                oTRow.appendChild(oTCol);
            };
            oTBody.appendChild(oTRow);
        };
        oTable.appendChild(oTBody);
        document.body.appendChild(oTable);
    };
```

And here's the second approach:

```
function buildTable(nRows, nCols) {
    var idx = 0, idx2 = 0;
    var bufferHTML = new Array( );
    var bufferCount = 0;
    bufferHTML[bufferCount++] = "<table><tbody>";

    for (idx; idx < nRows; idx++) {
        bufferHTML[bufferCount++] = "<tr>";
        for (idx2 = 0; idx2 < nCols; idx2++) {
            bufferHTML[bufferCount++] =
                    "<td style='font-size:12px;font-family:"+
                    "tahoma;font-weight:700'>";
            bufferHTML[bufferCount++] = nRow;
            bufferHTML[bufferCount++] = ", ";
            bufferHTML[bufferCount++] = nCol;
            bufferHTML[bufferCount++] = "</td>";
        };

        bufferHTML[bufferCount++] = "</tr>";
    };

    bufferHTML[bufferCount++] = "</tbody></table>";
    document.body.innerHTML += bufferHTML.join("");
};
```

Using arrays and strings to write HTML dynamically into the page is, relatively, faster than using the DOM APIs.

Running a test program that times the two code pieces indicates that the DOM table-writing example took roughly twice as many milliseconds to run as the second code sample (about 1000 ms, compared with 500).

Performance Matters

In the second code sample, the code accesses the DOM with one code line, rather than with several method calls as in the first example:

```
document.body.innerHTML += bufferHTML.join("");
```

In addition, the code uses an `Array` object to store all the various pieces of the HTML string. This strategy avoids using unnecessary CPU cycles to continually concatenate new pieces of text to the `string` (similar to a `java.lang.StringBuffer` object in the Java language).

There are times when using only `strings` to build HTML is not an option; the code has to make a DOM call to create or change the content of a particular element. The following code samples illustrate two more examples of how this can be done.

Here is one example that changes a web page element dynamically. The function changes the appearance of an element by accessing the element's style property, thus altering its visual aspects (such as the size and color of the font):

```
function changeElementContents(sID) {
    var oEl = document.getElementById(sID);
    oEl.style.fontWeight = 700;
    oEl.style.fontFace = "Arial";
    oEl.style.fontSize = "20px";
    oEl.style.backgroundColor = "red";
    oEl.style.color = "white";
    oEl.innerHTML = "Hello World, Contents Changed";
    oEl.noWrap = true;
};
```

The second version of this task minimizes the number of times the code accesses DOM APIs by reducing the number of `.style` references:

```
function changeElementContents(sID) {
    var oEl = document.getElementById(sID);

    with (oEl) {
        style.cssText=
                "font-weight:700;font-face:Arial;font-size:20px;"+
                "background-color:red;color:white;";
        innerHTML = "Hello World, Contents Changed";
        noWrap = true;
```

```
    };
};
```

In addition, the `style.cssText` property allows the code to change all CSS style properties in one shot, rather than altering them piece by piece. Similar optimization strategies may improve the performance of large programs that include a lot of DOM scripting.

 Even though a number of tutorials and blogs do not recommend using `with`, the `with` statement can provide a small increase in performance if used correctly. However, developers should be wary about putting any other code inside a `with` block unless it strictly deals with setting the values of existing object properties.

—Sean Snider

Index

Symbols

We'd like to hear your suggestions for improving our indexes. Send email to *index@oreilly.com*.

Colophon

The image on the cover of *Ajax Hacks* is ping pong paddles. Ping pong originated in Victorian England, played in the homes of the upper class, who would use everyday household objects to create an indoor tennis "court." A row of books, for instance, would serve as a net, the top of a champagne cork as a ball, and cigar box tops as paddles. Looking to capitalize on the popularity of this "table tennis" game, manufacturers began selling small paddles constructed of wooden frames and parchment paper. The sound that this early equipment made gave table tennis the name ping pong, which was first trademarked in 1901. More innovations came in the early 1900s, when players began using the modern equipment of celluloid balls and wooden paddles covered in stippled rubber. Around the same time, organized tournaments began to spring up around England, and soon after that, the game spread throughout the world.

Ping pong was introduced as an Olympic game in 1988. The incredible speed and accuracy of modern players made the game difficult to follow on television. In an effort to make the game more watchable, in 2000, the International Table Tennis Association slowed down ping pong by introducing larger balls and shortened the length of the games by decreasing the winning score from 21 to 11.

The cover image is taken from *http://www.gettyimages.com*. The cover font is Adobe ITC Garamond. The text font is Linotype Birka; the heading font is Adobe Helvetica Neue Condensed; and the code font is LucasFont's TheSans Mono Condensed.

Better than e-books

Buy *Ajax Hacks* and access the digital
edition FREE on Safari for 45 days.

Go to www.oreilly.com/go/safarienabled
and type in coupon code T9HI-RUWI-1V1T-6VIL-REM4

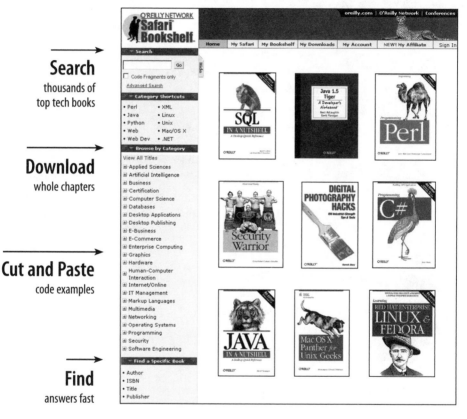

Search
thousands of
top tech books

Download
whole chapters

Cut and Paste
code examples

Find
answers fast

Search Safari! The premier electronic reference
library for programmers and IT professionals.

Related Titles from O'Reilly

Web Programming

ActionScript Cookbook

ActionScript for Flash MX: The
Definitive Guide, *2nd Edition*

Ajax Hacks

Dynamic HTML: The Definitive
Reference, *2nd Edition*

Flash Hacks

Essential PHP Security

Google Advertising Tools

Google Hacks, *2nd Edition*

Google Map Hacks

Google Pocket Guide

Google: The Missing Manual,
2nd Edition

HTTP: The Definitive Guide

JavaScript & DHTML
Cookbook

JavaScript Pocket Reference,
2nd Edition

JavaScript: The Definitive
Guide, *4th Edition*

Learning PHP 5

PHP Cookbook

PHP Hacks

PHP in a Nutshell

PHP Pocket Reference,
2nd Edition

PHPUnit Pocket Guide

Programming ColdFusion MX,
2nd Edition

Programming PHP

Upgrading to PHP 5

Web Database Applications
with PHP and MySQL,
2nd Edition

Web Site Cookbook

Webmaster in a Nutshell,
3rd Edition

Web Administration

Apache Cookbook

Apache Pocket Reference

Apache: The Definitive Guide,
3rd Edition

Perl for Web Site Management

Squid: The Definitive Guide

Web Performance Tuning,
2nd Edition

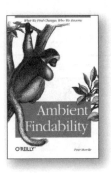